Jodie McQuade

HAIR DESIGN

A DESIGNER'S APPROACH®

© 2009, 2013 Pivot Point International, Inc.

ISBN 978-1-937964-30-6

3rd Edition
1st Printing, June 2013
Printed in Hong Kong

Pivot Point International, Inc.
World Headquarters
1560 Sherman Avenue, Suite 700
Evanston, IL 60201 USA

847-866-0500
pivot-point.com

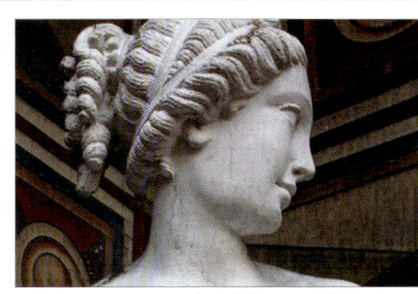

Jack Hollingsworth/Getty Images

SEE AND THINK AS A DESIGNER

CREATE AS A DESIGNER

SEE AND THINK AS A DESIGNER

CREATE AS A DESIGNER

CHANGING A HAIR DESIGN

During your career you will have many different opportunities to work with many clients to change and enhance their hair designs. These opportunities may be wet and thermal hair design or in long hair design. You may be creating directional movement and texture or you may be straightening curly hair. You may even be creating a long hair design for a special occasion. The hair design transformations that you create will allow your clients to achieve the looks they are going for. Hair design and long hair design services create temporary results, so the opportunities are vast.

The *Hair Design, A Designer's Approach®* program has been specially developed to help you build your skill, proficiency and confidence in wet and thermal hair design and long hair design techniques and prepare you for success in the salon. The foundation provided by the Pivot Point educational library you are using is built upon the individual designer's approach to learning new material and performing new skills. Understanding this approach will put you at the top tier of entry-level professionals when you complete your cosmetology training.

A DESIGNER'S APPROACH®

COSMETOLOGY FUNDAMENTALS	SCULPTURE	HAIR DESIGN	COLOR	TEXTURE	SALON SUCCESS

A Designer's Approach® consists of 6 core disciplines: *Cosmetology Fundamentals, Sculpture, Hair Design, Color, Texture* and *Salon Success*, which are color-coded for easy recognition. The entire library is designed to deliver licensure-based education as well as salon-relevant training, while promoting mindful learning and future success in the salon. *A Designer's Approach* focuses on visualizing and creating hair designs that are as unique as each individual client. It includes:

- Theory that gives you the thought process you'll need to guide your design decisions
- Procedures and techniques that will help you produce predictable results
- Language that allows you to think and communicate clearly with your clients and other designers

The goal is to give you confidence that comes with knowing that the final look you produce will be functional, aesthetic and correspond with the design you had envisioned for your client. Being able to align your final results with your design vision is the true benefit of using *A Designer's Approach.*

A DESIGNER'S APPROACH
REVOLVES AROUND FOUR CORNERSTONES

 SEE    **THINK**    **CREATE**    **ADAPT**

In hair design to **SEE** as a designer means that you have the ability to observe forms, directions and movements all around you—in fashion, nature and art as well as in hair—then connect these different expressions of design to one another and to the design elements and principles. Observing various expressions of design and making connections will give you the inspiration to see the range of possibilities that exist for transforming your clients' hair with hair design services.

To **THINK** as a designer means that you know how to *analyze* your client's hair, features and lifestyle, *visualize* a final design, and *organize* a plan for achieving that design.

Hair design transformation is all about subtly or dramatically changing the texture of the hair, changing direction and adding or diminishing volume within a design. Long hair design can create stunning transformations by completely rearranging the hair from the way it is normally worn—generally moving the hair upward, hence the common term, "up-do." As you think about the design, you'll be analyzing which of the client's features you want to emphasize, or balance. You will visualize the types of lines you'll use, where you'll place or diminish volume and which hair design or long hair design techniques you will use to achieve your desired results.

To **CREATE** as a designer means dedicating yourself to *practice* all aspects of wet and thermal hair design and long hair design to build your expertise and to *perform* them with focus and precision. Creating as a designer means that you are able to perform the basic wet-setting, air-forming, thermal and long hair design techniques and combine them as necessary to give clients a professional salon result.

To **ADAPT** is the highest level of design proficiency. Adapting as a designer means that you are able to *compose* innovative and artistic hair designs by drawing upon your knowledge, skill and vision. Then you can *personalize* an overall design that complements your client's individual characteristics and needs.

With *A Designer's Approach* as your guiding principle, you have a framework for success that will last your entire career. You will see this guiding principle revealed throughout this hair design program.

LEARNING STRATEGIES WITHIN *HAIR DESIGN*

This program has been specifically designed using state-of-the-art educational methods to make your learning process engaging as well as systematic and effective. To help you make the most of your time with your coursebook, a brief description of these learning strategies is provided here so you can become familiar with them before diving into the chapters.

First, take a look at the icons to the left. These icons will appear throughout your coursebook to help guide you through this program and help you make the most out of *Artist Access*, your online resource for all the coursebooks, video segments and other activities and learning resources.

This icon indicates that there are additional learning resources for the topic the icon is positioned with on *Artist Access*. These resources can be found by logging in to artist-access.com and navigating to the particular program and topic. These resources can range from answer keys for Brainworks activities, to supplemental workshop exercises and deeper content on some concepts presented in your coursebook.

Some exercises offer a left-handed view available exclusively on *Artist Access*. This icon invites left-handed learners to log in and navigate to the specific topic and exercise to view the technical workshop, performed by a left-handed designer.

01

UNDERSTANDING THE
WIDE RANGE
OF TRANSFORMATIONS
POSSIBLE IN HAIR
DESIGN INSPIRES
YOUR CREATIVITY

1.1 HAIR DESIGN: UP CLOSE AND PERSONAL
HAIR DESIGN TRANSFORMATION
BRINGING HAIR DESIGN INTO FOCUS

1.2 WET AND THERMAL HAIR DESIGN: THE BIGGER PICTURE
WET AND THERMAL HAIR DESIGN DECISIONS
CHANGE THE WET AND THERMAL HAIR DESIGN, CHANGE THE EFFECT

1.3 LONG HAIR DESIGN: THE BIGGER PICTURE
LONG HAIR DESIGN DECISIONS
CHANGE THE LONG HAIR DESIGN, CHANGE THE EFFECT

FOLLOWING THIS LESSON
YOU WILL BE ABLE TO:

Identify the types of hair design transformations possible in the areas of wet, thermal and long hair design

Explain the elements of form, texture and direction and how they relate to hair design

Summarize a series of design decisions that will lead to the desired wet and thermal hair design result

Compare the changes in volume and expansion that occur when creating different wet and thermal designs

Summarize a series of design decisions that will lead to the desired long hair design result

Compare the changes in placement of volume and directional emphasis that occur when creating different long hair designs

---

The chapter overview is located on the first two opening pages of the chapter and provides a preview of the chapter in a concise, easy-to-read format. It contains four elements that will orient you to the chapter so you are prepared and keyed-in to the important learning concepts.

CHAPTER TITLE (1)
This is the overriding theme of the chapter.

ADVANCE ORGANIZER (2)
A "mini-outline" of the chapter headings and subheadings that identifies the main content points and provides an overall view of the chapter in its entirety.

CENTRAL MESSAGE (3)
A statement that highlights the critical value of the chapter.

LEARNING GOALS (4)
Learning outcomes that pinpoint exactly what you will learn as a result of working with the material in the chapter and preview how you will be evaluated.

SIGNATURE COLOR (5)
Each title in the *Designer's Approach* library is easily identifiable by its signature color. Shades of green you see on the pages as graphic treatments and titles, help identify *Hair Design*.

Immediately following the chapter overview is an **INTROVIEW (1)**, which is an introduction to the chapter that not only previews the content, but also relates the content to you in a personal way. The introview answers questions such as, "Why is this important to me?" "Why should I care about this?" and "How will I be better off in the future as a result of understanding this subject?"

Material contained in **SIDEBARS (2)** provides examples and additional information that make the content clearer and/or more relevant to real-life salon settings.

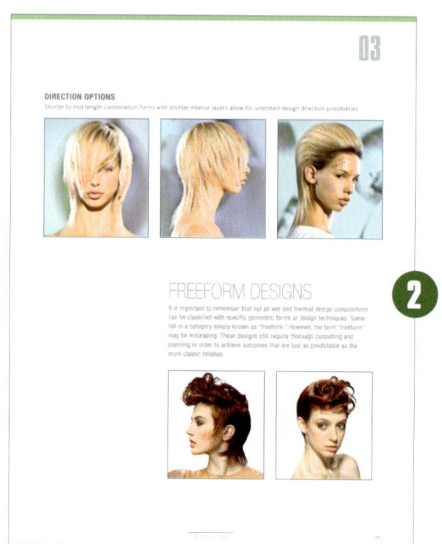

Following each full exercise is a **DESIGN DECISIONS CHART (3)** to guide you in planning the finished design before it is executed. By filling in each of the blank sections of the chart, you will be better able to visualize the finished design composition before you even begin.

At the very end of each full exercise, **RUBRICS (4)** appear. Rubrics are self-assessment tools that help gauge your level of performance. These are designed to compare your skill and technique to industry standards.

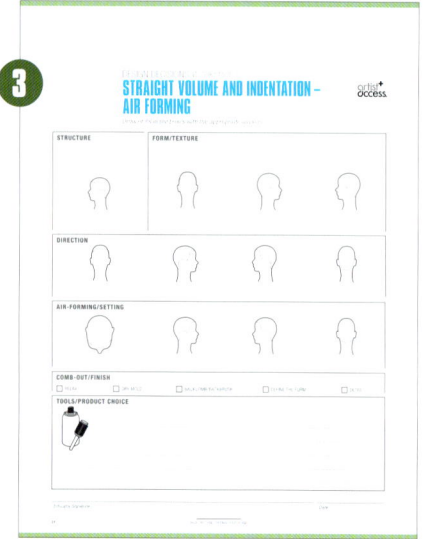

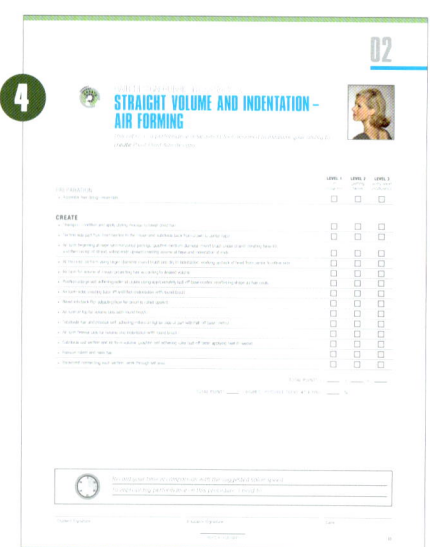

VOICES OF SUCCESS (5) speak to you from four different and important points of view: the salon owner, the educator, the designer and the client. By capturing these industry voices, you have the advantage of discovering what is important to those people in a position to have a huge influence in your career. This creates a credible and personal bridge between your training and your career.

The primary assessment tool in each chapter is called the **LEARNING CHALLENGE (6)**. This challenge allows you to test your recall and understanding of the most important material in the chapter.

IN OTHER WORDS (7) summarizes the content with a brief statement at the end of every chapter.

LESSONS LEARNED (8) provides a list of statements that recaps the chapter's critical messages and learning objectives. These are "words of wisdom" that you can take with you throughout your career.

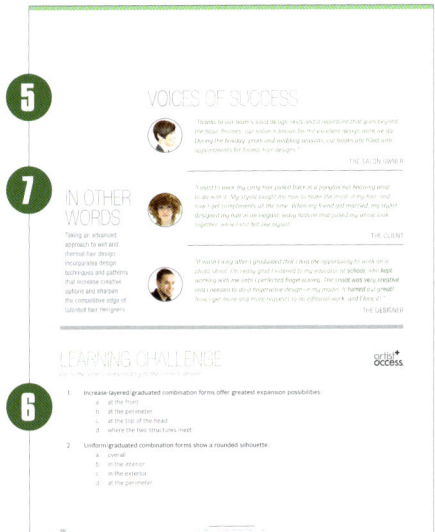

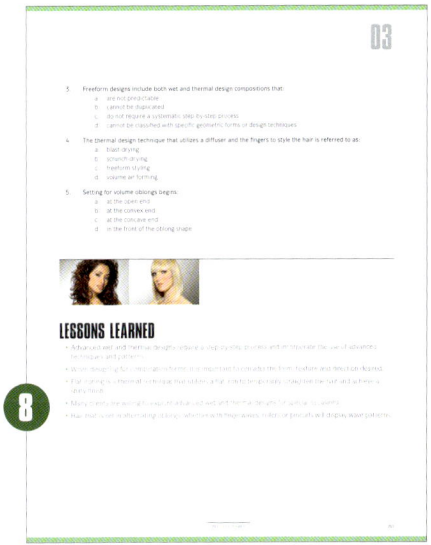

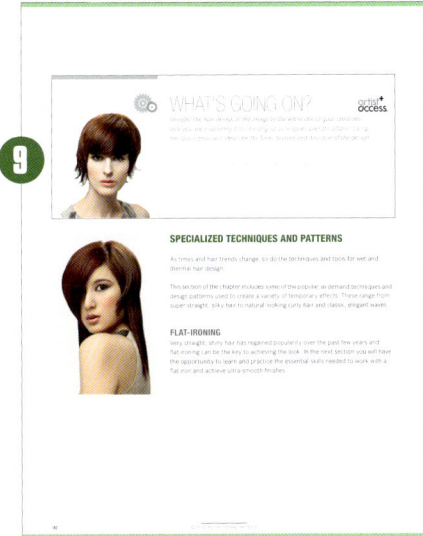

BRAINWORKS (9) are exercises that follow major learning topics and are designed to reinforce and build meaning. By working with exercises that reflect interesting or real-world situations, Brainworks allow you to relate personally to the topic and construct new meanings to affirm your understanding of the material. These exercises give you opportunities to engage in thinking about the ideas presented in the book and explore your ideas with other students.

DIVING INTO *HAIR DESIGN*

Hair Design, A Designer's Approach consists of two main areas of study: See and Think as a Designer and Create as a Designer. Each chapter within these two areas presents a discussion of key concepts, new insights on familiar topics, and practical examples. These themes build on one another from chapter to chapter. Immerse yourself in each chapter, take your time with the material, and enjoy the learning process.

SEE AND THINK AS A DESIGNER

Jack Hollingsworth/Getty Images

In the first chapter, you will learn about many different aspects of wet and thermal hair design and long hair design that are taken into consideration when performing these services. Your professional knowledge and personal connection with your clients will assist you in making design decisions that will allow you to create the result you envision.

CREATE AS A DESIGNER

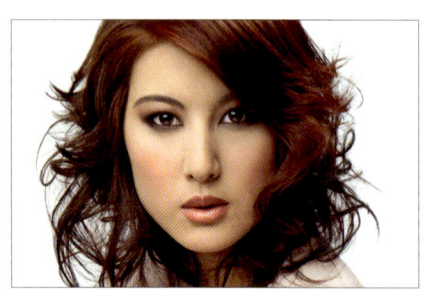

The second chapter of *Hair Design, A Designer's Approach* deals with essential skills for creating successful hair designs using the appropriate basic wet or thermal hair design techniques. These techniques are performed on the four basic forms.

The third chapter moves from basic into advanced wet and thermal hair design techniques. It is in this chapter that you will use techniques adapted for combination forms as well as specialized wet and thermal styling techniques. These techniques will help you create more inspired and personalized designs that will earn your clients' loyalty.

The fourth chapter moves into long hair design, covering both basic and advanced techniques. You will learn to work with the hair in a completely different way than in Chapters 2 and 3. However, you will discover that the techniques you learned in Chapters 2 and 3 are often used to prepare the hair for long hair design services.

ADAPT AS A DESIGNER

Pages 380-381 of this coursebook give a brief preview of what it means to adapt a wet and thermal hair design or long hair design. As skills improve, designers move beyond producing results to composing and personalizing new wet, thermal and long hair designs.

Now you are ready to learn about temporarily changing the hair's form, texture and direction through hair design. Dive into *Hair Design, A Designer's Approach* with enthusiasm and confidence in yourself and your teachers to prepare for a successful career.
Enjoy the journey.

EXECUTIVE MANAGEMENT

Melanie Kopeikin
President

Robert Passage
Chairman & CEO

Guy Harrington
Vice President,
Domestic Sales and Field Education

Judy Rambert
Vice President,
Education and Research

Jan Laan
Vice President,
International Business Development

Robert Sieh
Senior Vice President,
Finance and Operations

Judie Maginn
Vice President, Global Marketing
and Business Development

PRODUCTION

John Bernin
Digital Media Manager

Deidre Glover
Editorial Associate

Eileen Dubelbeis
Program Development Coordinator

Sabine Held-Perez
Senior Director, Program Development

Jen Eckstein
Marketing Manager

Melissa Holmes
Program Development Associate

Brian Fallon
Educational Content Supervisor

Amy Howard
Program Development Coordinator

Anna Fehr
Educational Technology Manager

Joanna Jakubowicz
Graphic Design Associate

Janet Fisher
Senior Director, Instructional Support

Matt McCarthy
Production Manager

Vic Piccolotto
Program Development Associate

Denise Podlin
New Products Manager

Benjamin Polk
Editorial Associate

Tina Rayyan
Production Director

Markel Richards
Program Development Associate

Rick Russell
Graphic Design Associate

Maureen Spurr
Editorial Manager

Vasiliki A. Stavrakis
Education and Research Director

Csaba Zongor
Graphic Design Associate

Robert Richards
Fashion Illustrations

Richard Weaver
Graphic Design Consultant

THE POSSIBILITIES OF HAIR DESIGN

UNDERSTANDING THE WIDE RANGE OF TRANSFORMATIONS POSSIBLE IN HAIR DESIGN INSPIRES YOUR CREATIVITY

FOLLOWING THIS LESSON

YOU WILL BE ABLE TO:

Identify the types of hair design transformations possible in the areas of wet, thermal and long hair design

Explain the elements of form, texture and direction and how they relate to hair design

Summarize a series of design decisions that will lead to the desired wet and thermal hair design result

Compare the changes in volume and expansion that occur when creating different wet and thermal designs

Summarize a series of design decisions that will lead to the desired long hair design result

Compare the changes in placement of volume and directional emphasis that occur when creating different long hair designs

Hair design is about the finish of a design composition. Whether offered as a stand-alone service, or in conjunction with another salon service, hair design is important because the techniques you use will determine how your clients look when they leave the salon.

Chapter 1, The Possibilities of Hair Design, will open your eyes and mind to the amazing transformations hair design has to offer, helping you see and think as a true designer.

1.1 HAIR DESIGN: UP CLOSE AND PERSONAL

Hair design is a temporary change in form, texture and direction that is achievable through wet and thermal design as well as long hair design techniques.

To provide unique and interesting hair design services, you need to understand the transformations that are possible and to sharpen your observational skills to analyze the design you envisioned before creating it.

HAIR DESIGN TRANSFORMATION

The transformations you create in hair design can range from subtle to dramatic while suiting the needs of a range of clients. Hair design services are provided for three main purposes:

- To complete another service with hair design
- To perform a weekly or biweekly service for a client who does little or no styling at home
- To create a design for a special occasion

DESIGN AS A FINAL PHASE OF SALON SERVICES

When a hair design service is performed as a completion phase of another salon service, commercial finishes will usually be used in order to show the results. It is important to ensure the client is pleased with the initial service and given the opportunity to check and approve it before finishing. Although you have been working toward a specific vision for your client, keep in mind that most clients don't see it come to life until the finishing phase. You will want to take extra care to ensure that the client is pleased with what he or she sees and that the finished hair design matches what you both agreed upon.

Finishing a hair design with wet, thermal or long hair design techniques can accentuate a client's look after completion of another service such as a sculpture.

DESIGN FOR WEEKLY OR BIWEEKLY SERVICES

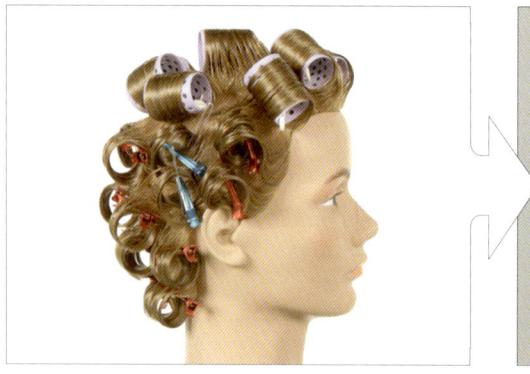 

In many cases, clients who receive a weekly hair design service will be more mature and wear styles that require a wet setting or styling with thermal irons. These clients often expect to do little or no maintenance and the goal is to create a hair design that lasts until the next appointment.

Clients with tightly curled hair, who receive thermal pressing services, often visit the salon every two weeks to avoid more frequent application of intense heat to their hair.

Clients with relaxed hair may desire a wet set on rollers. Since relaxed hair tends to be drier and may require less frequent shampooing, it is often possible to book these appointments two weeks apart.

DESIGN FOR SPECIAL OCCASIONS

Special occasions, such as weddings or proms, may lead clients to make appointments solely for a wet, thermal or long hair design service. You may want to create a special look for your client that captures a more dramatic feeling than she would normally wear. Special attention to the proportions of the design relative to the client and what she will be wearing is required to create a successful design.

The casual look achieved by air forming for subtle volume and indentation can be transformed by using a smaller round brush or setting the hair on hot rollers.

Long hair design is a service area that allows for amazing yet temporary transformations, as these images show. In this example, straightened uniform lengths were twisted and then the ends were secured into loops for this formal, yet youthful, design.

BRINGING HAIR DESIGN INTO FOCUS

Applying these basic and detailed levels of observation is an important step in seeing and thinking about a hair design before creating it.

Like many other hair designers, you will find many inspirations for hair designs from images around you, such as:

- Fashion magazines
- Movies
- TV shows
- Images a client brings to the salon

When you start to focus on a specific design, it is important to carefully observe and analyze the characteristics of the desired look. At first glance you need to identify the overall form. Looking closer, you need to assess texture and direction.

   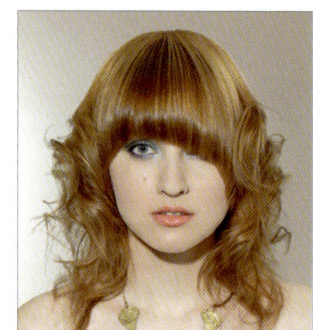

FORM

The overall form or shape of a design is determined by the degree and placement of volume and/or indentation.

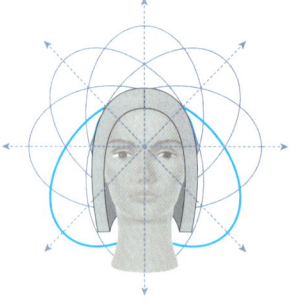 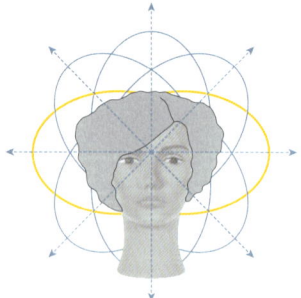 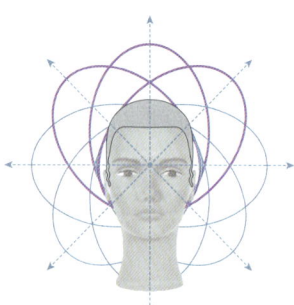

TEXTURE

The texture of a hair design can be identified as straight, wavy, curly or a combination. Note that the texture speed can vary in wavy and curly hair.

STRAIGHT

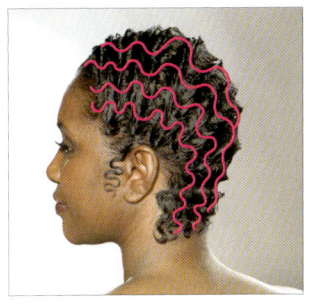

WAVY

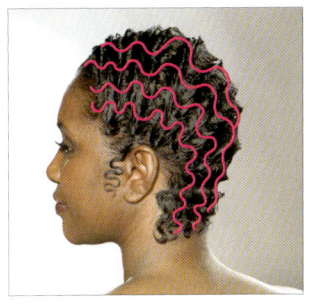

CURLY

COMBINATION

DIRECTION

Directions for the design overall as well as within can be identified using any lines from the celestial axis.

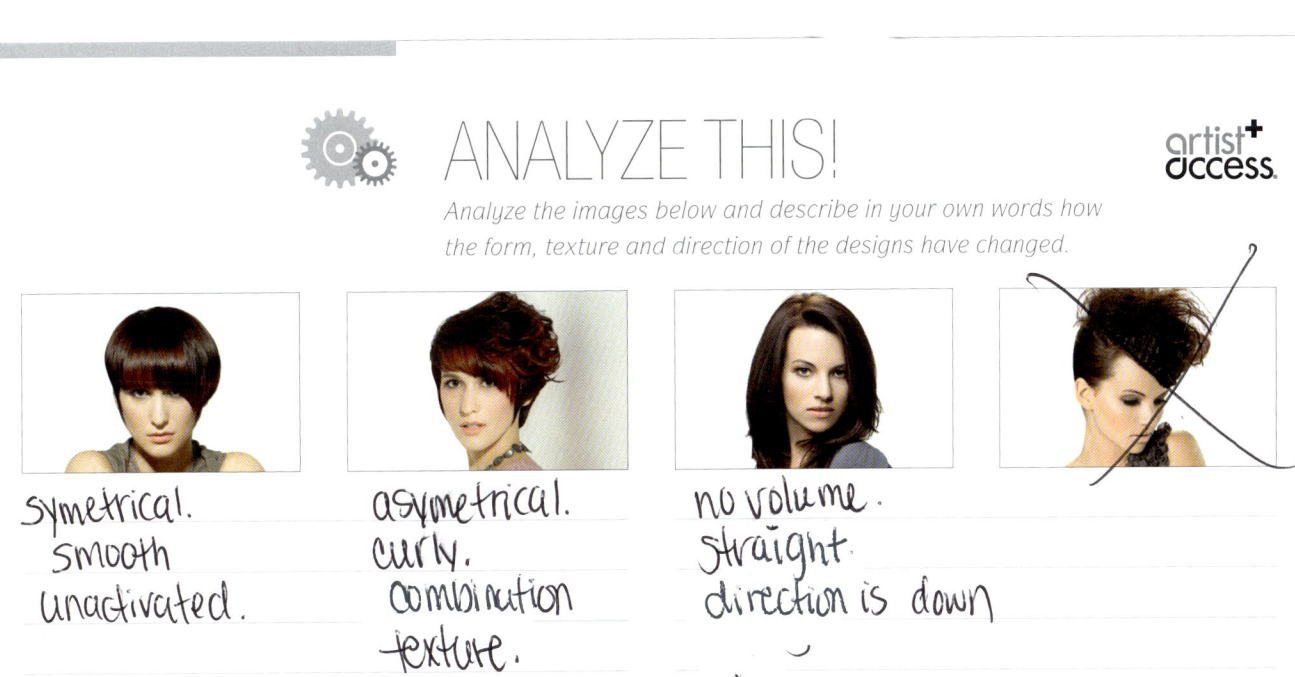

ANALYZE THIS!

Analyze the images below and describe in your own words how the form, texture and direction of the designs have changed.

artist⁺ access.

symetrical.
smooth
unactivated.

asymetrical.
curly.
combination
texture.

no volume.
straight.
direction is down

1.2 WET AND THERMAL HAIR DESIGN: THE BIGGER PICTURE

To ensure that your wet and thermal design changes produce the desired outcome, you will need to consider many of the same things that you think about for a hair sculpture:

- Facial shape
- Body structure
- Hair qualities

WET AND THERMAL HAIR DESIGN DECISIONS

Before creating a hair design, it is important to consult with your client so that both of you agree on the final look of the wet or thermal design. Once this is agreed upon, you can begin to make the series of design decisions that will determine the steps to make this happen.

VOLUME AND EXPANSION

One of the key characteristics of a design is the placement of volume and expansion. These placement options are greatly influenced by the sculpted form of the client's hair. As a designer you'll be able to choose from a series of wet and thermal design techniques that may either strengthen or diminish the distinguishing characteristics of the sculpted form.

SOLID FORM DESIGN CHOICES

Sleek, smooth finishes showcase the strong perimeter and unactivated texture, which are typical for a solid form sculpture.

Soft movement and texture give fullness and soften the perimeter. Note that this particular design has an old-world glamour feeling.

Curled texture designs show greater volume and expansion, along the perimeter. Lengths appear to be shorter when curled texture is added.

GRADUATED FORM DESIGN CHOICES

The contrasting textures of the graduated form are emphasized by smooth, unactivated designs.

The inherent width and expansion of the graduated form can be accentuated by keeping the interior lengths close to the head and expanding the weight area with a faster texture.

With curlier, more activated finishes, the expansion of the form will be the greatest at the weight area or ridge line.

INCREASE-LAYERED FORM DESIGN CHOICES

When increase-layered sculptures are styled with less volume and texture, the elongation of the form remains constant and directional movement is accentuated.

Adding volume and movement will expand the overall form while more clearly showing where layers fall.

Longer increase-layered lengths offer great options to introduce designs featuring more texture and volume in selected areas.

UNIFORMLY LAYERED FORM DESIGN CHOICES

Adding even volume throughout expands the form and makes the rounded shape more evident.

When adding volume in the interior and indentation in the exterior, the silhouette of the uniformly layered form can be changed completely.

Maximum expansion, roundness and activation are achieved when adding curly texture.

COMBINATION FORM DESIGN CHOICES

The basic lines of this combination form are more obvious with a smooth finish.

When air forming the ends with an indentation technique, the texture of the sculpted form becomes more evident.

The style can be completely tranformed when adding large curling iron texture to the longer lengths.

SHAPE CHOICES

As you analyze the movement and direction in the design that you and your client have chosen, you can begin to determine whether specific shapes need to be used to create the desired effects. Depending on the techniques you use, you may work with specific, clearly sectioned, geometric shapes to create the patterns and directions in which the hair should move. In other instances, as you gain experience in hair design, you may need the shape only for reference or as a more general guide.

STRAIGHT SHAPES

Straight shapes include:

- Rectangles
- Squares
- Triangles
- Trapezoids

Usually hair within a straight shape moves in one direction without curves. Straight shapes are often used in combination with curved shapes in hair design.

RECTANGLE

Parallel distribution is used within a rectangle. When analyzing a design, the hair within a rectangle shape will usually move in one direction.

TRIANGLE

Triangle shapes can be used effectively to adapt to the shape of the head. Parallel or radial distribution can be used in a triangle shape. Bases will often be staggered within a triangle shape to adapt to the width of the shape.

CURVATURE SHAPES

Curvature shapes imply movement or motion in the hair either in a clockwise or counterclockwise direction. Curved lines or waves will usually be the result of working with curvature shapes, such as:

- Circles
- Ovals
- Oblongs

Generally, only portions of these shapes are used within a hair design.

CIRCLE

The circle shape, or part of it, is most often used at the hairline to create curvature movement. Half of the movement will move away from the face, and the other half of it will move toward the face.

OBLONG

Oblongs are used to create wavy movements within a design. These waves can move in a variety of directions but are most often worn from a part or moving away from the face.

DESIGN PRINCIPLES

Design principles can be used to describe all of the elements evident in a hair design. The texture will usually be the primary aspect influenced by your choice of design principles.

REPETITION OF TEXTURE

ALTERNATION OF TEXTURE

PROGRESSION OF TEXTURE

CONTRAST OF TEXTURE

CHANGE THE WET AND THERMAL HAIR DESIGN, CHANGE THE EFFECT

When working with salon clients, designers frequently offer them different styling alternatives. In many cases, the finish that is chosen and created can depend on the mood of the client or the image and personality he or she wants to express that day.

Finishing with air-forming techniques for soft volume and an under-bevel effect creates lots of shine and allows us to see the colors as well as the layered texture. Scrunch-drying creates more expansion and texture, which also make lengths appear shorter.

In this example a curling iron was used to create the feminine and elegant finish. When a more sophisticated look is desired, volume air-forming techniques can be applied.

IDENTIFY THE MOVEMENT, DRAW THE SHAPE

artist⁺access

Assess the image below, then use a pencil to draw the movements you have identified on the head form provided. Finally, draw the shape(s) you would use to section the hair in order to imply the various movements.

Rollers
be rolled away
from the
face....

1.3 LONG HAIR DESIGN: THE BIGGER PICTURE

More than most other services, long hair design requires awareness of the occasion for which the design is being created. Understanding the long hair design decisions you need to make and how each affects the final result will allow you to choose the technical steps necessary to make your long hair designs a success.

LONG HAIR DESIGN DECISIONS

Designers and clients need to be in agreement on the mood or impression to be portrayed by the long hair design. Should it be sophisticated and glamorous? Soft and romantic? Totally "done up," or a little on the casual side? As you consult with your client, you will begin to formulate the design vision, which includes what kind of form, direction and texture you'll want to create.

Based on this vision, you then need to choose the shapes and techniques needed to achieve the desired look.

POSITION OF VOLUME

Long hair designs usually have a focal point—where the main emphasis of volume or mass is placed. Since the eye is drawn to this area, you'll need to make sure that the positioning of volume helps to create a flattering overall shape for the client. Altering the size of a specific element will also change the proportion of the overall design. Be sure to carefully observe your work from various angles to ensure eye-pleasing results when viewed from various directions. In long hair design, trends and fashions may figure into placement of volume as well.

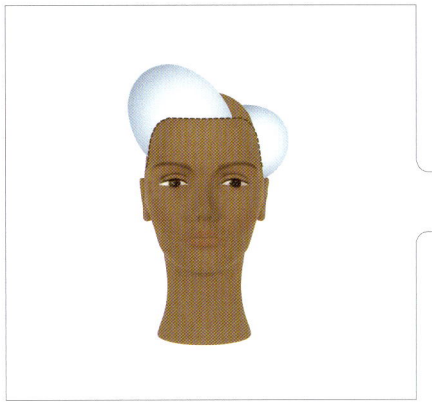 

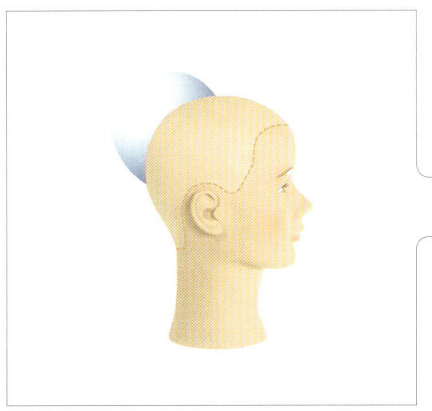 

DIRECTION

The direction of the form is determined by the position of shapes or volume within the design. The lines of the celestial axis can be used to analyze the overall direction of a long hair design as well as the various directions within a long hair design.

OVERALL DIRECTION

It is important to remember that the overall direction of a design may be significantly different when analyzed from various angles.

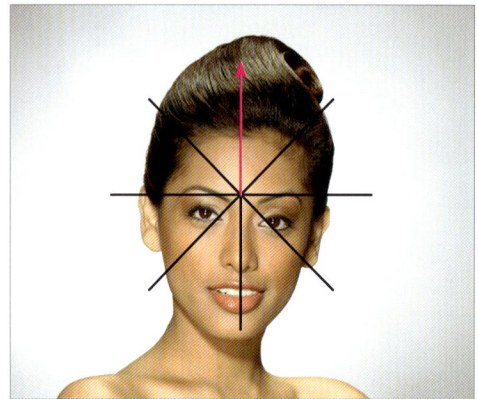 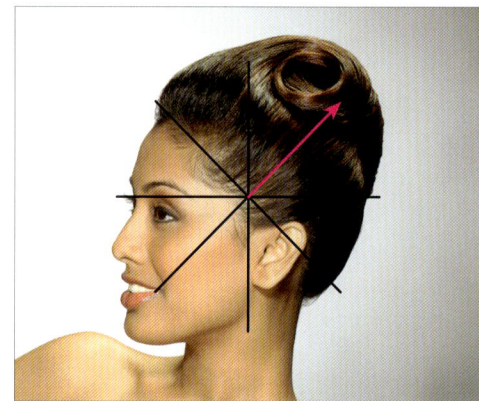

Vertical emphasis from the front view often creates a diagonal emphasis from the profile view.

Designs that place emphasis at the nape, which appear to have a vertical emphasis from behind. From the side, the emphasis is diagonal.

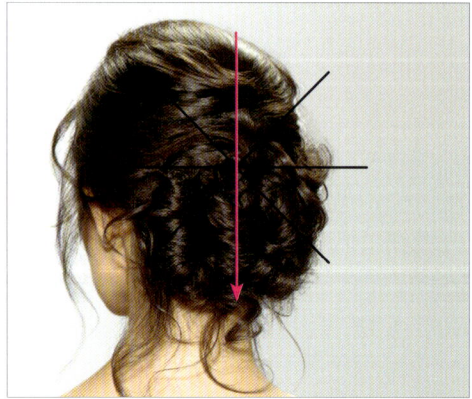 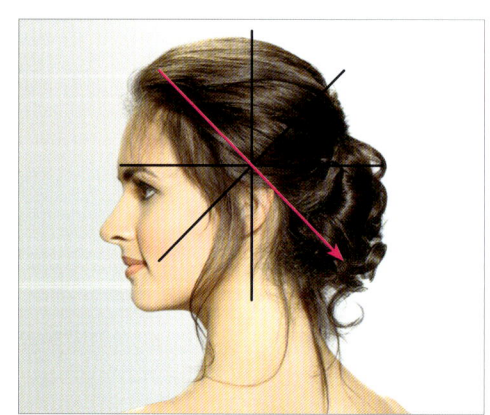

DIRECTIONS WITHIN THE FORM

The directions within the form imply motions and play an important part in the dynamics of a design. The hair may move in various directions within a design, drawing the eye to various focal points or simply through the design.

Forming multiple loops uniform in size and positioning them to move into various directions create interest without overwhelming the eye.

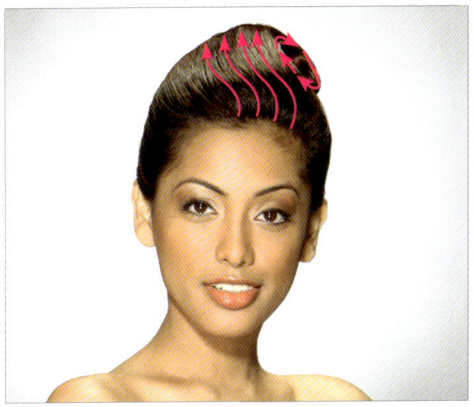

Sweeping the lengths from the fringe area upward in a clockwise movement helps to incorporate them into the remainder of the design.

Clockwise and counterclockwise knots are positioned along either side and lead the eye to the nape where several knots are positioned closely together.

In this braid design the eye is led along the lines of the distribution, which converge along the center back.

DESIGN PRINCIPLES

In long hair design you will apply your knowledge of the design principles primarily in relation to shape, size and texture.

Remember that the design principles also apply to the techniques that you use to prepare the hair for long hair designing. Whether you use rollers for a wet set, hot rollers or thermal irons, you can choose to use the same diameter throughout, progress in size from one diameter to another or create various degrees of contrast or alternation.

REPETITION OF TEXTURE

ALTERNATION OF DIRECTION

PROGRESSION OF SHAPE

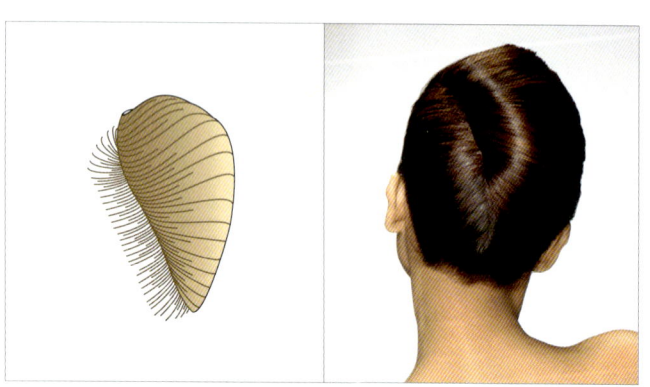

CONTRAST OF SHAPE

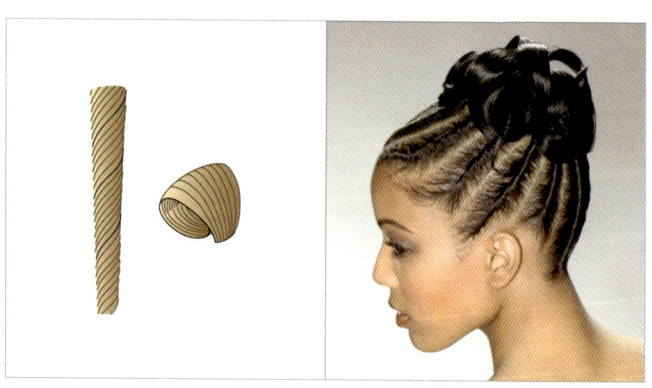

CHANGE THE LONG HAIR DESIGN, CHANGE THE EFFECT

Because the creative options in long hair design are almost infinite, you can create some truly remarkable transformations. In addition to this, your training as a hair designer enables you to make the most appropriate and effective design choices for your clients. By asking the right questions and carefully listening to the answers, you will be able to create long hair designs that meet and exceed your clients' expectations.

A client wanting to convey a soft and romantic image for an afternoon garden party can portray a much different image with a structured, classic long hair design for a formal affair.

 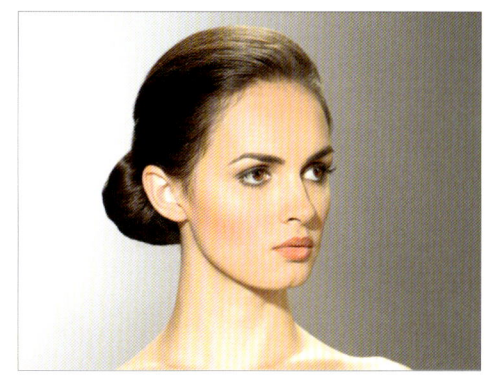

Expansion positioned at the crown with all the hair traveling to that same area gives a more mature appearance, while intricate texture created with knots along the sides and nape creates a more youthful image.

By dramatically changing the texture and placement of volume, a client can feature a classic and elegant look, but with a different long hair design can project a feminine unstructured image.

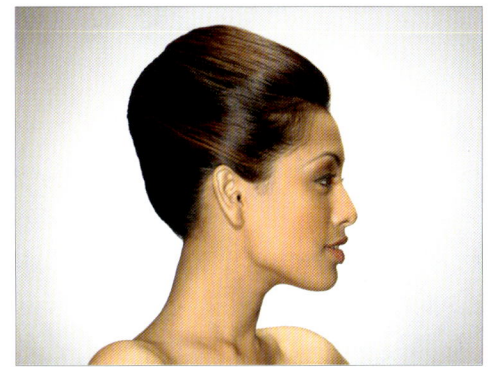 

WHAT'S THE PRINCIPLE?

artist⁺ access.

Look closely at the illustrations provided below, then match them to the appropriate design principle. Note that the first design principle has already been completed.

ALTERNATION	CONTRAST	REPETITION	PROGRESSION
Two or more units repeating in a sequential order	Units with opposite qualities	All units are identical	Continuous series of proportional steps

FORM

SHAPE

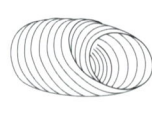 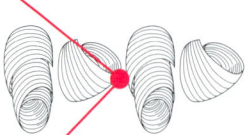  

SIZE

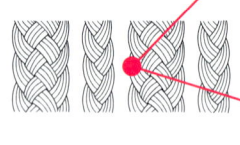  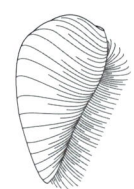 

DIRECTION

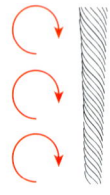 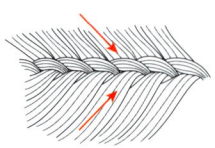 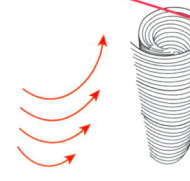 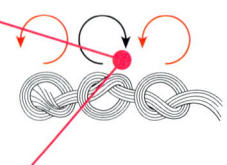

TEXTURE

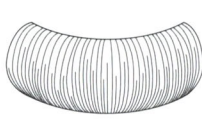  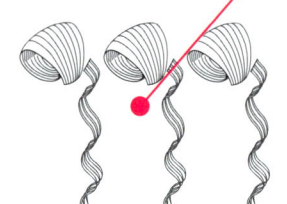 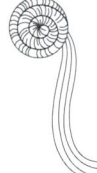

VOICES OF SUCCESS

"Not until I worked in a salon for a while did I realize how important it is to finish a client's hair design really well. The finish very often makes or breaks how well the client likes the hair sculpture or color he or she received that day."

THE DESIGNER

"One of the greatest things about long hair design is that it allows my students to be so creative. I love to coach them along the way and see how they use their eyes to assess their work, and then apply the right techniques to achieve their desired result."

THE EDUCATOR

"I used to leave the salon and couldn't wait to wash my hair. Not because I didn't like my haircut, but because the way it was styled just wasn't me. Thankfully, the designer I see now really understands how I like to look, and we decide together how she will style my hair. The best thing is—she even gives me tips so I can achieve the same look at home!"

THE CLIENT

IN OTHER WORDS

When you understand the creative, technical and emotional aspects of hair design, you will be better able to satisfy your clients with wet, thermal and long hair designs that have a positive impact on their image.

Circle the letter corresponding to the correct answer.

1. Hair design is a temporary change in:
   a. shape
   b. volume
   c. design principle
   d. form, texture and direction

2. Which of the following is not one of the main purposes of hair design services:
   a. drying the hair
   b. regular upkeep
   c. special occasions
   d. completion of another service received

3. Shapes within hair design are grouped into the following two main categories:
   a. angular and round
   b. squares and triangles
   c. circles and rectangles
   d. straight and curvature

4. Curvature shapes are used to imply movement in either of the following two directions:
   a. up and down
   b. straight and curved
   c. clockwise and counterclockwise
   d. diagonal forward and diagonal back

5. Oblongs used within a design create:
   a. volume
   b. a distinct part
   c. wavy movements
   d. movement of half the hair toward the face

LESSONS LEARNED

- Hair design encompasses the areas of wet, thermal and long hair design.

- The characteristics of a hair design are form, texture and direction and their relationship with one another.

- A series of design and procedural decisions needs to be made before beginning a hair design service.

- Choosing different wet and thermal design techniques influences the volume and expansion within a design.

- The placement of volume in a long hair design changes the directional emphasis.

- Aside from technical ability, it takes creativity and listening skills to create successful hair designs.

BASIC WET AND THERMAL HAIR DESIGN

CREATING PREDICTABLE WET AND THERMAL DESIGN RESULTS REQUIRES A STEP-BY-STEP PROCESS

FOLLOWING THIS LESSON

YOU WILL BE ABLE TO:

Describe the five procedural steps used to set hair

Describe the five procedural steps used to finish hair

Explain the importance of guidelines for ensuring client comfort and satisfaction when performing a wet or thermal hair design service

Explain various wet and thermal hair design options for the four basic forms

Demonstrate the knowledge and ability to perform various wet and thermal hair designs on the four basic forms

Imagine that you have produced a good hair sculpture and color for a new client. Now it is time to style the hair and the overall success of the salon service is in your hands—literally.

With an in-depth knowledge of the setting and finishing procedures, combined with refined technical skills, you will be able to create a hair design that meets—if not exceeds—your client's expectations.

Chapter 2, Basic Wet and Thermal Hair Design, will give you all you need to be prepared for the requests and needs your clients may express about their wet and thermal designs.

2.1 ESSENTIAL WET AND THERMAL HAIR DESIGN TECHNIQUES

As fashions change, the fundamental techniques in wet and thermal design will prove to be essential to your success as a designer. Even the simplest finishes require an understanding and mastery of the techniques and tools used in wet and thermal design.

It is the combination of technical knowledge and skill together with a client-centered approach that will help create predictable, client-pleasing wet and thermal design results.

PREDICTABLE WET AND THERMAL HAIR DESIGN RESULTS

Throughout this chapter you will learn to work with a variety of tools such as blow dryers, curling irons and rollers. Although the tools are quite different, each is applied in a systematic and consistent method by following procedural steps that lead to predictable results.

These procedures fall into two main categories: setting and finishing.

SETTING PROCEDURES

Once a designer has visualized the finished wet or thermal design, the procedures used to set the hair are:

- Distribute
- Mold
- Scale
- Part
- Apply

When performing a wet design like a roller set, each of these steps is performed separately in sequential order. When creating a thermal design, some of the steps are combined.

WET-SETTING PROCEDURES

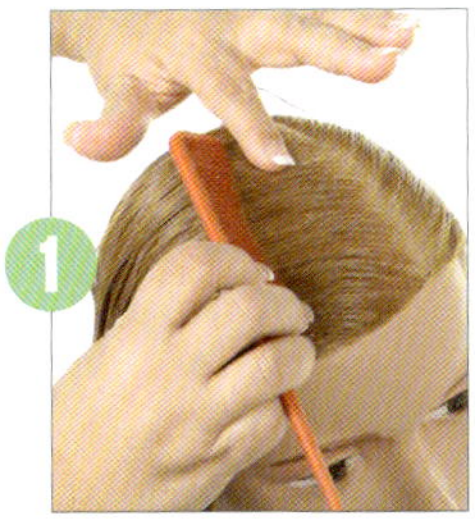

DISTRIBUTE

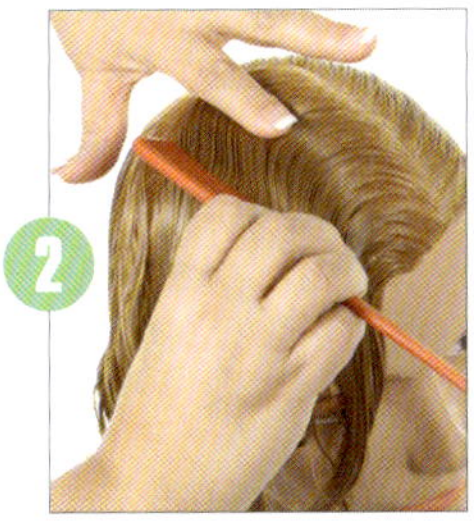

MOLD

SCALE

PART

APPLY

In this example of a roller set the hair is distributed (1) in parallel lines. It is then molded (2) in curved directions and scaled (3) in an oblong shape. The hair within the oblong shape is parted (4) diagonally to create bases upon which rollers are applied (5).

THERMAL SETTING PROCEDURES

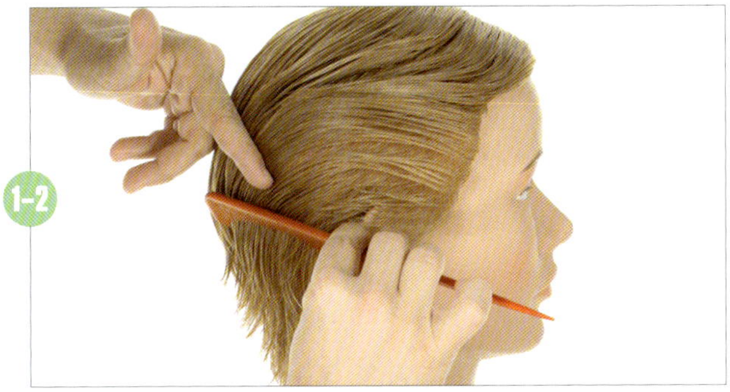

DISTRIBUTE/MOLD

SCALE/PART/APPLY

In this example of an air forming procedure distributing (1) and molding (2) the hair are combined into one step prior to actually drying the hair. Scaling (3) and parting (4) happen while a 9-row brush is applied (5) to the hair, in continuous fluid motions.

① DISTRIBUTE

The direction of the distribution and whether it is parallel (from many points of origin) or radial (from one point of origin) are determined by the directions identified in the desired design.

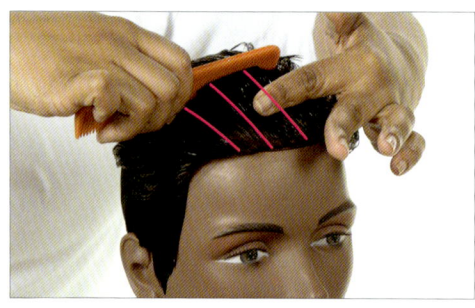

Parallel distribution involves the use of the teeth of a tail comb.

Radial distribution involves using the tip of the tail comb first, and then refining the distribution with a small section of the teeth of the tail comb.

② MOLD

By molding the hair, designers continue to map out how the hair is supposed to move when the design is completed. When molding, the hair is essentially combed to reflect the straight or curved lines that will be featured in the finished look.

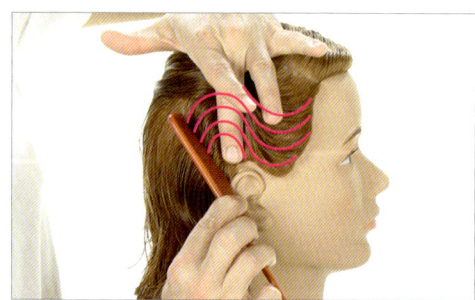

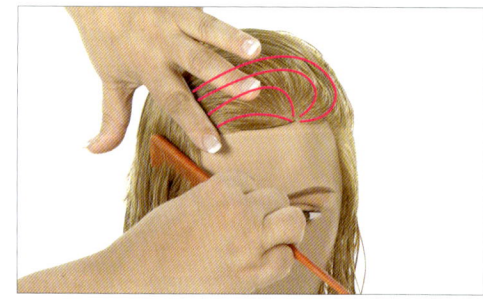

③ SCALE

Scaling involves separating the hair into various geometric shapes, each representing an area of the head in which a specific movement is supposed to be achieved. Designers use geometric terms to describe the shapes of these scaled sections.

The tip of a tail comb is used to scale out a shape. Pay careful attention that the previously established distribution and molding are not disturbed.

4 **PART**

Parting the hair involves creating the individual bases, or partings, to which the hair design tool and technique will be applied. The sizes of these bases are determined by the diameter of the tools chosen.

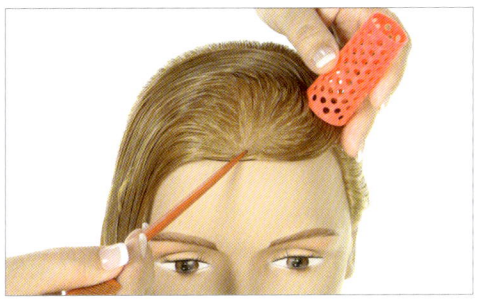

In wet hair designs the tip of the tail comb is used to part the hair.

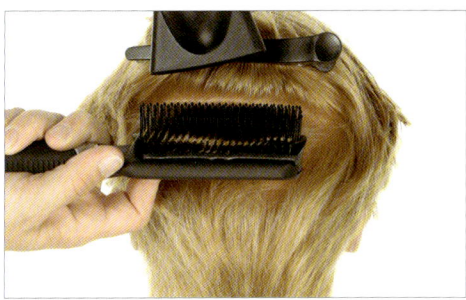

When air forming, the brush is most often used to part the hair.

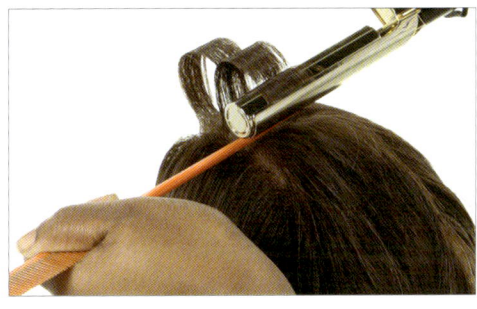

When working with curling or flat irons, the tail comb is most commonly used to part the hair.

5 **APPLY**

In hair design, applying directly refers to how the design tool, whether it be a brush, roller, thermal iron or even a pincurl, is used. Base control plays an important role when applying tools since it immediately determines whether volume or indentation is created and how strong either effect will be.

  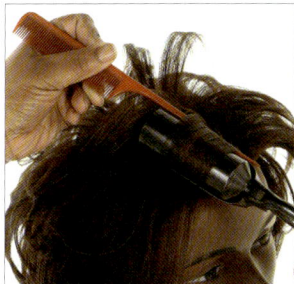

It is equally important to choose base controls carefully whether you are air forming or designing a roller or curling iron set.

FINISHING PROCEDURES

The steps used to finish a design are:

- Relax
- Dry mold
- Backcomb or backbrush
- Define the form
- Detail

Regardless of the tools and methods used to set the hair, these finishing techniques are applicable to most wet and thermal designs. Just like setting techniques, some of the finishing techniques may be combined or even omitted, depending on the desired character or feeling of the design as well as how long the design is intended to last.

FINISHING PROCEDURES FOR CLASSIC DESIGNS

RELAX

DRY MOLD

BACKCOMB/ BACKBRUSH

DEFINE THE FORM

DETAIL

In this example of finishing a classic design, the hair is first relaxed (1) with two cushion brushes. It is then dry molded (2) to assess the movement of the hair. Afterward the hair is backbrushed (3) to give support and blend bases. The form is then defined (4) with a cushion brush and detailed (5) with a wide-tooth tail comb.

FINISHING PROCEDURES FOR CASUAL DESIGNS

RELAX

DEFINE THE FORM

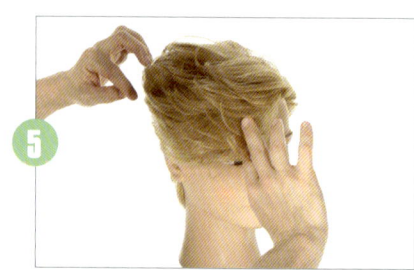
DETAIL

In this example of a casual design, steps that provide additional support, such as dry molding and backbrushing, are not performed. Casual designs are not typically meant to last as long as classic designs. After air forming the hair is relaxed (1) and the form is defined (4). Often the fingers are used to detail (5) the design.

1 RELAX

After the hair is set and completely dry, it is usually necessary to break up the set directions.

In classic designs created with roller sets, the hair is relaxed with cushion brushes.

In more contemporary or casual designs, the hair is often relaxed using the fingers.

2 DRY MOLD

During dry molding, designers direct and guide the hair into the desired final direction to assess where additional support may be needed.

3 BACKCOMB/BACKBRUSH

Often clients require designs that can last several days, or they desire additional volume and expansion in certain areas. These clients benefit from backcombing or backbrushing. While backcombing creates the strongest support, both techniques are popular, especially among mature clients or clients who desire a classic stylized finish.

Backcombing is performed from underneath the strand.

Backbrushing is performed on top of the strand.

DEFINE THE FORM

Designers ensure that the wet and thermal design techniques used so far have produced a well-balanced form, as well as flattering movements and overall texture. Depending on the desired look, designers use various combs, brushes and even their fingers to define the form.

  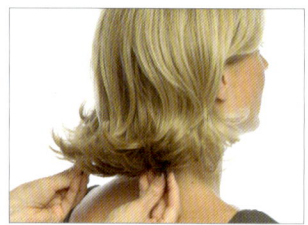

 DETAIL

Detailing is performed to make sure every hair sits just right, the texture shows enough interest and that it has the right amount of shine. It is mainly during this phase that designers will use finishing products to help realize their vision and make it last.

 # WHAT'S GOING ON?

artist⁺ access

Analyze the images below and determine which setting or finishing procedure step is shown.

SETTING PROCEDURES

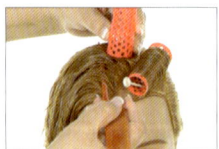   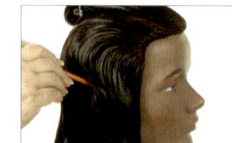 

FINISHING PROCEDURES

PRACTICE MAKES PERFECT 01
STRAIGHT VOLUME – AIR FORMING

The focus of this exercise is to provide practice in the techniques commonly used to air form medium-short to medium-long sculptures. The result will be smooth, shiny lengths with a slight bevel-under effect at the ends.

Practice this exercise to build rhythm, skill and accuracy using:

- Horizontal partings
- 9-row brush
- Volume air-forming techniques

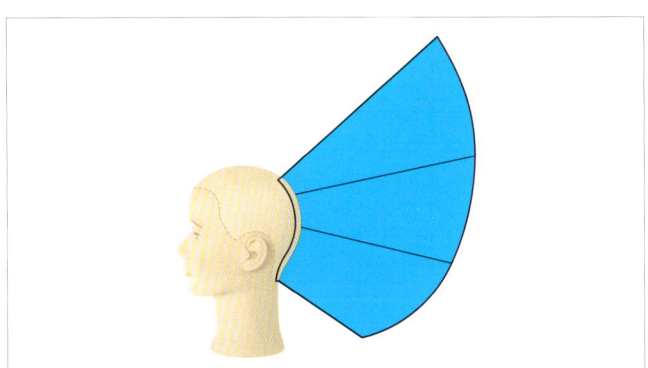

This exercise is performed on straight, solid lengths on a rectangle component.

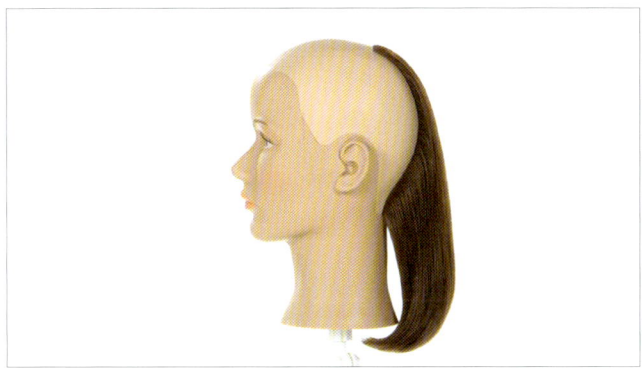

Air forming with a 9-row brush creates an unactivated, silky texture.

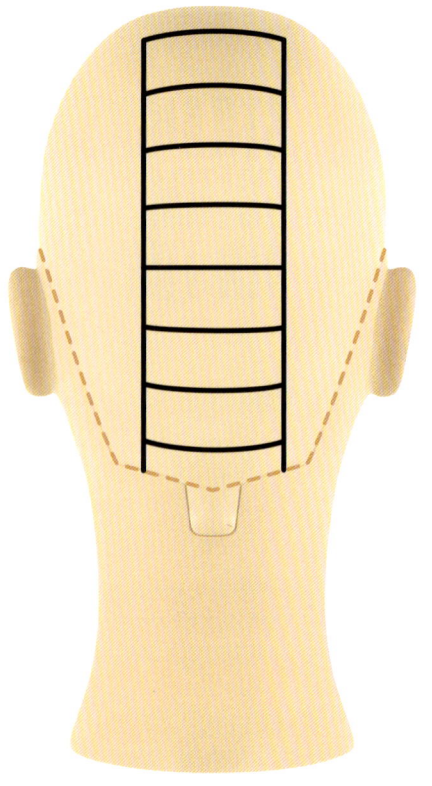

The art shows horizontal partings used throughout the exercise.

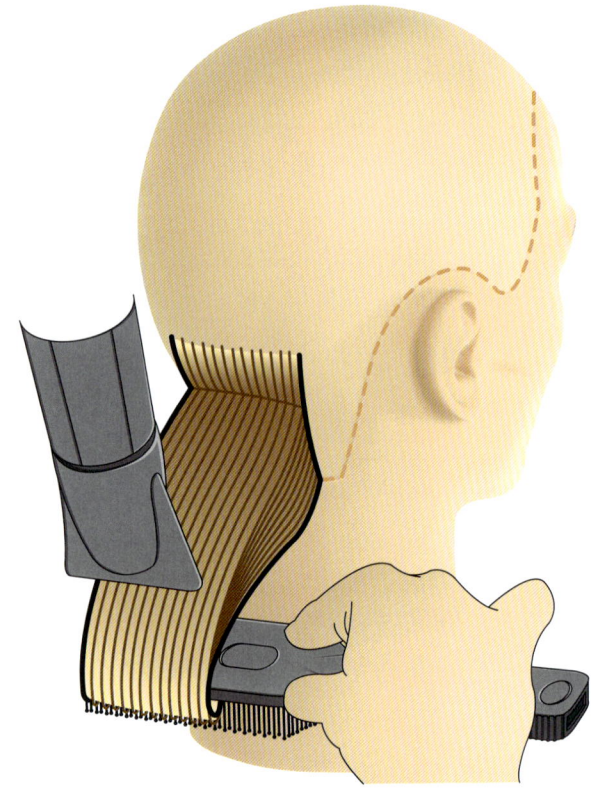

To achieve a sleek and shiny finish, the brush and concentrator are both positioned parallel to the partings.

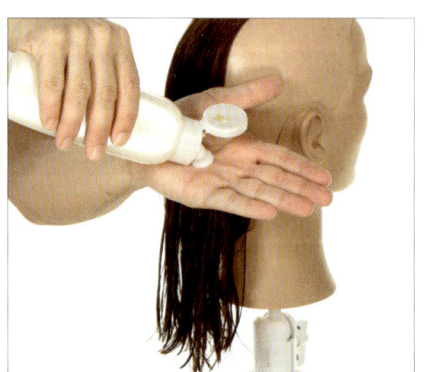

01–02 Begin by applying a styling cream or lotion evenly through hair from base to ends to create support.

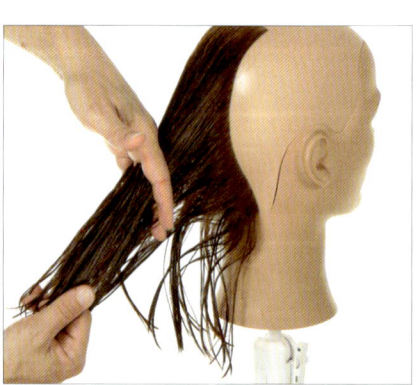

03 Remove approximately 75% of moisture using your fingers to control the lengths. Note that the airflow is directed toward the ends, as not to disturb the hair cuticle.

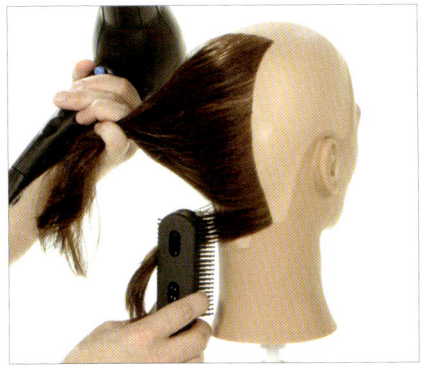

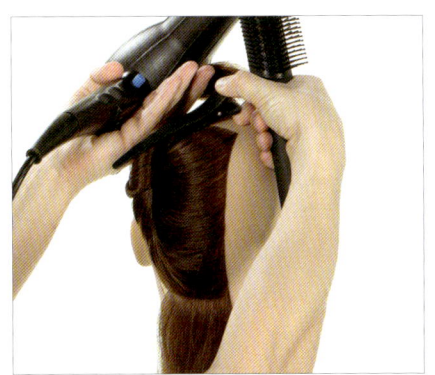

04–05 Attach the concentrator to the nozzle of the blow dryer. Distribute the hair horizontally to one side and use the tip of the 9-row brush to release a parting in the nape parallel to the horizontal form line. Twist remaining lengths upward and secure with a clip.

NOTE: *To increase efficiency, trained designers often keep the blow dryer in their hand while parting.*

06 Position the brush horizontally to pick up the hair at the base, using only the first few rows of the brush. Air form from base to midstrand by moving the brush away, using low projection for a small amount of volume.

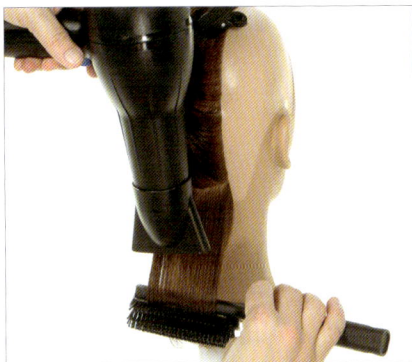

07 Then, position the brush under the strand and air form from the midstrand to the ends using a curved movement to achieve a subtle bevel-under effect.

08 Note that the blow dryer nozzle is used to control the hair after it is released and then picked up again with the brush.

09 Release the next horizontal parting and repeat the same technique. Direct the airflow to follow the cuticle to allow maximum shine.

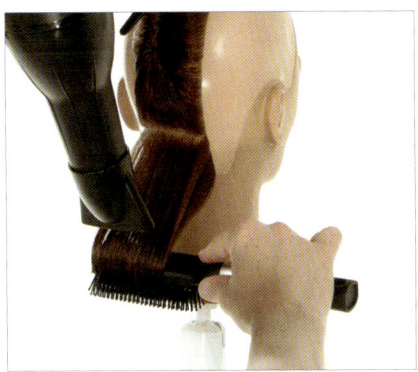

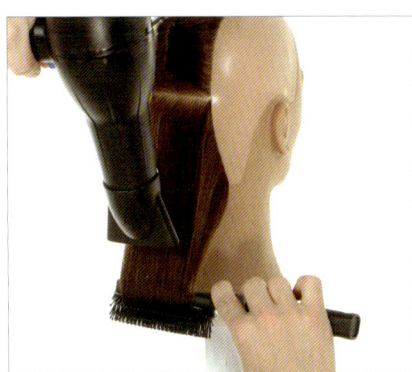

10 Then, incorporate the previously air-formed lengths and air form again from the midstrand to the ends. Use a curved motion to reinforce the slightly curved end texture and to blend the bases.

11 As you work upward, maintain low projection and remember to air form from base to midstrand first, and then midstrand to ends.

12 Then, incorporate the previously air-formed lengths to enhance the curved end texture. Continue to join air-formed lengths while working toward the crest.

13 Air form for subtle volume and a bevel-under effect while working in the upper portion of the rectangle component.

14–15 As you reach the top, maintain natural distribution and low projection to air form from the base to midstrand, then from the midstrand to the ends. Accentuate the curved end texture by gradually joining more and more of the previously air-formed lengths.

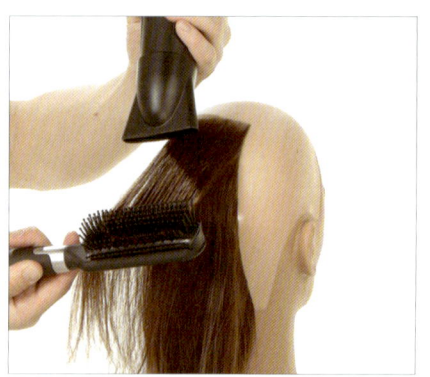

16 As an option, the blow dryer may be held by the nozzle for comfort.

17 The same air-forming techniques are used.

18 The finish shows straight, smooth texture with a slight underbevel.

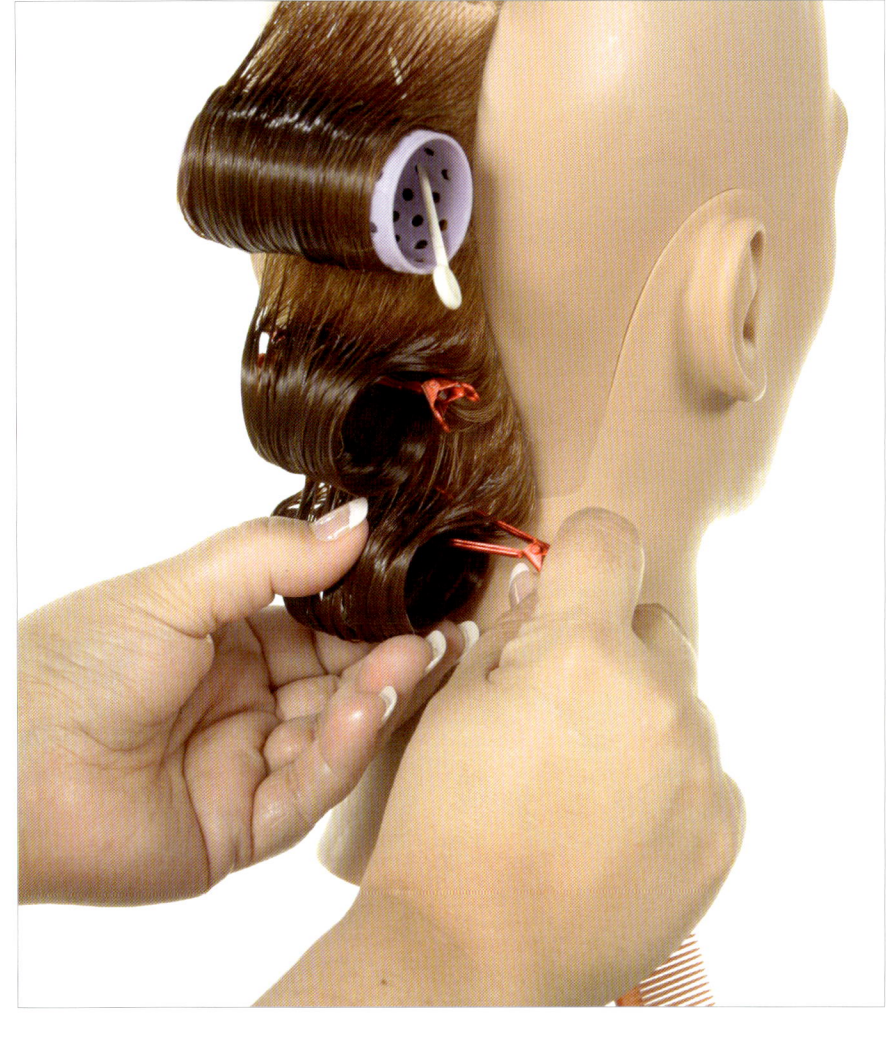

PRACTICE
MAKES PERFECT 02
STRAIGHT VOLUME/ BASE CONTROLS – ROLLERS/PINCURLS

The focus of this exercise is to provide practice in straight volume roller and pincurl setting techniques and various base controls. These techniques are generally used in the salon for clients with short to medium lengths to achieve curls and straight volume with varying degrees of base strength.

Practice this exercise to build rhythm, skill, speed and accuracy in wet setting and finishing for various base controls with rollers and pincurls.

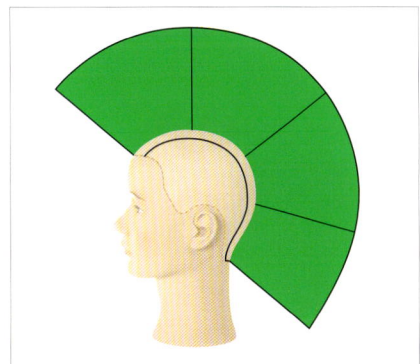

This exercise is performed on straight, uniform layers on a silhouette component.

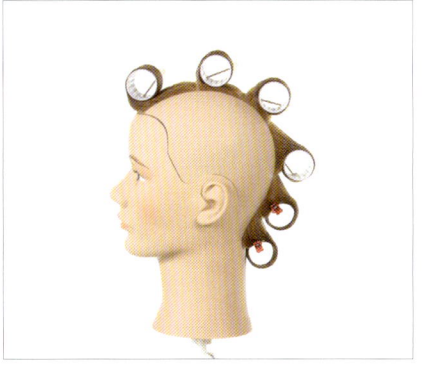

The same roller diameter is used to set two diameters (2x) overdirected, 1½x overdirected, 1x on base and 1½x underdirected base controls. Pincurls are used to set 1½x underdirected and 1x half-off base controls in the nape.

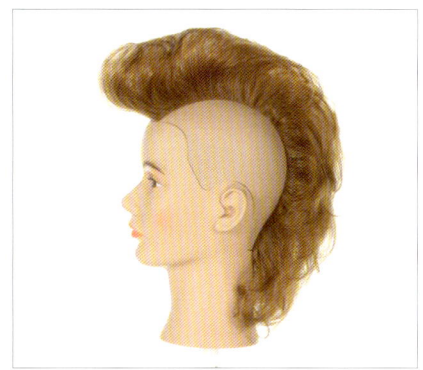

The use of various base controls creates different degrees of base support and volume throughout the silhouette component.

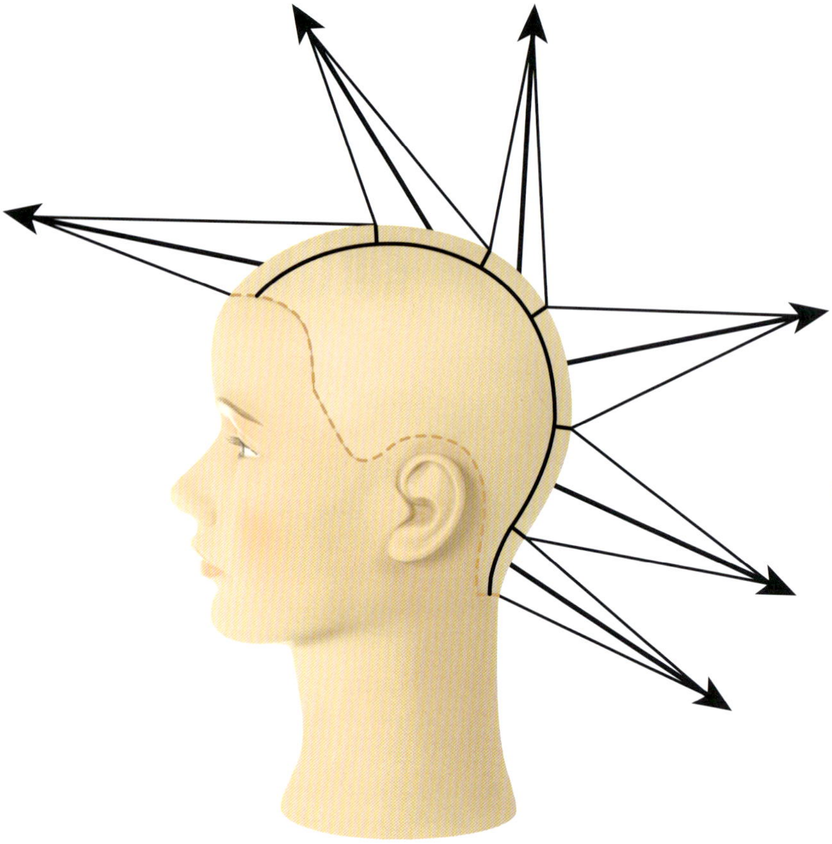

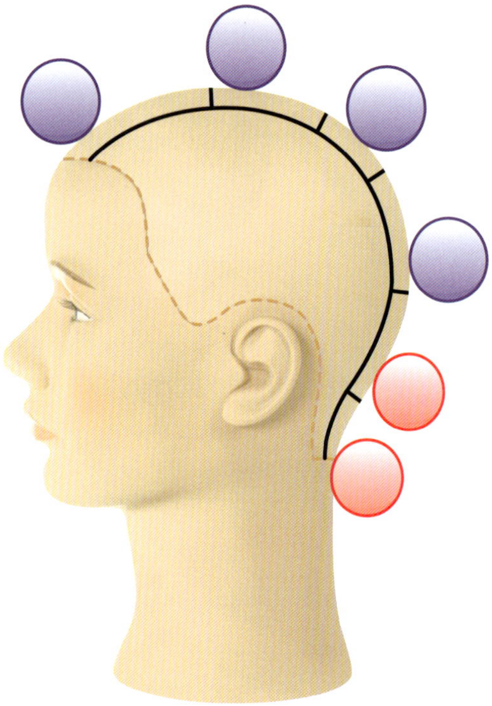

The art shows the projection angles used to achieve the various base controls for this exercise. The same projection is used whether setting the hair on a roller or forming a pincurl.

The art shows horizontal partings used to create different base sizes with rollers and pincurls set to move away from the face.

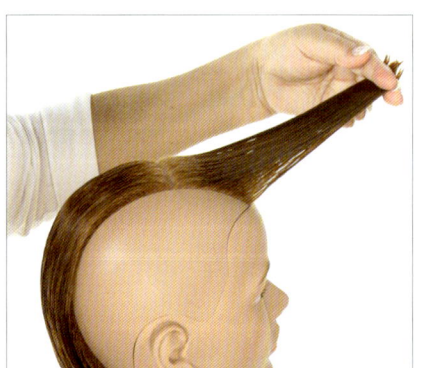 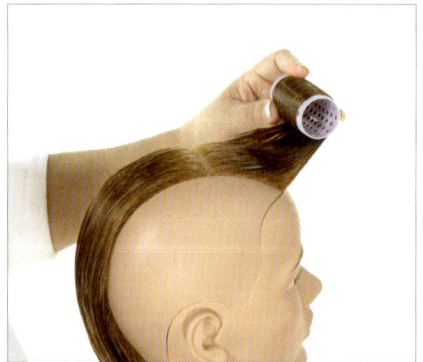 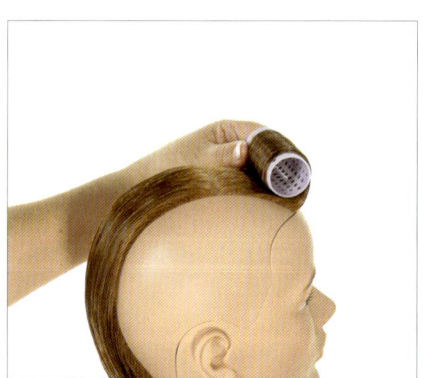

01–02 Beginning at the front of the silhouette component, measure and part a 2x base. Distribute and project the hair 45° above the center of the front base. Wrap the ends around the roller and use both hands to roll with even tension toward the base.

03 Position the roller in the upper portion of the base, creating an overdirected base control.

04 Use a pick to secure the roller with its forces.

05–06 Measure and part a 1½x horizontal base. Project the hair at 45° above the center of the base. Wrap the ends around the roller. Roll the hair with even tension toward the base, keeping the roller parallel to the horizontal parting. This angle will automatically position the roller in the upper portion of the base. Use a pick to secure the roller.

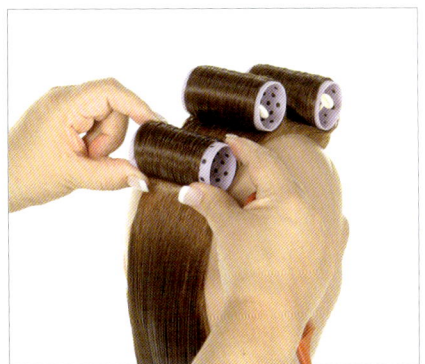

07 Next, release a 1x base and project 45° above the center of the base to achieve on-base control.

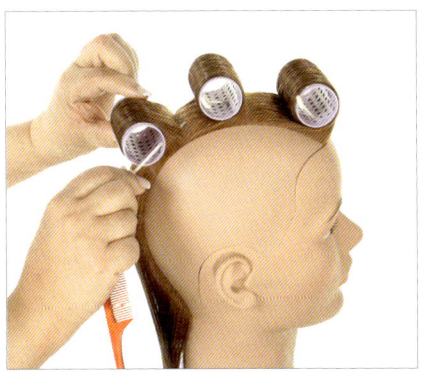

08 The roller is positioned within its base, encompassing the entire area.

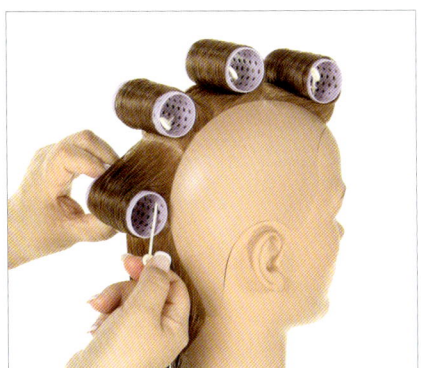

09 Measure, part and apply the next roller to create 1½x underdirected base control. Project 90° from the center of the base to position the roller in the lower portion of the base.

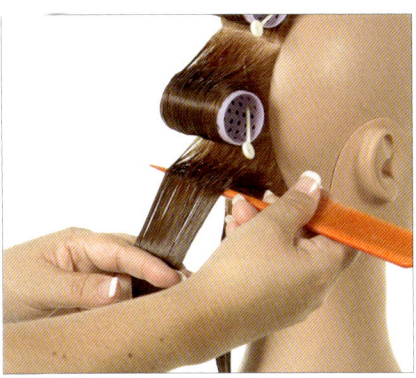

10 Next, release a 1½x base and project at 90° from the center of the base. Form a pincurl, reinforcing the arc with the tail of the comb.

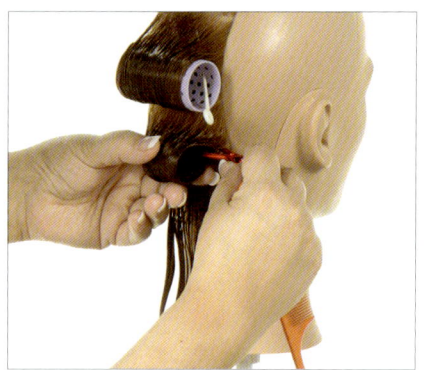

11 Form the circle and position it at the lower portion of the base. Hold the circle between your fingers and secure with a clip.

NOTE: *Pincurls of this width can be secured with clips from both sides.*

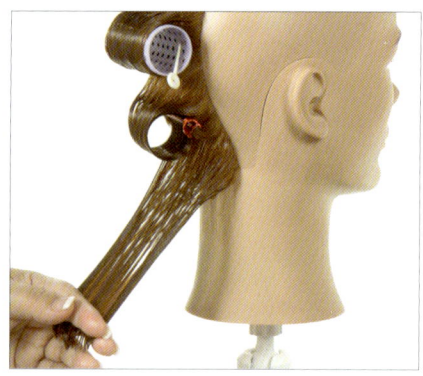

12 Project the last approximate 1x base at about 90° from the center of the base to create half-off base control.

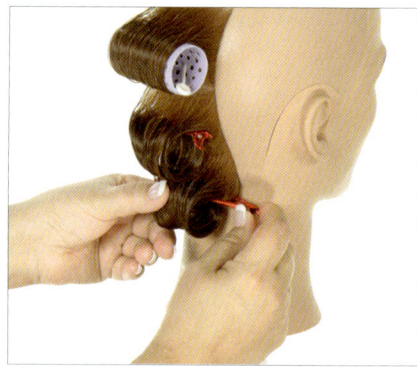

13 Form and position the pincurl to sit half-off base and secure.

14 The completed set incorporates multiple base controls using rollers and pincurls.

15 Once the hair is dry, remove the rollers and pincurl clips. Relax the hair using two cushion brushes. Start at the nape and work upward.

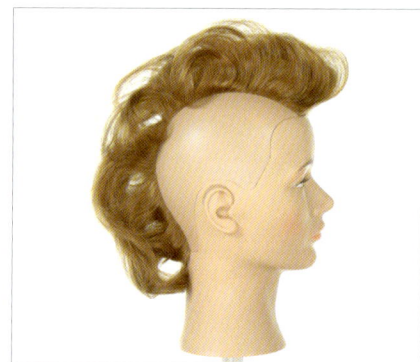

16 After dry molding, notice the different effects at the base.

VOLUME BASE CONTROLS

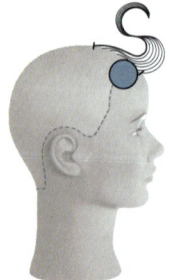

OVERDIRECTED
Exaggerated direction and volume, reduced base strength

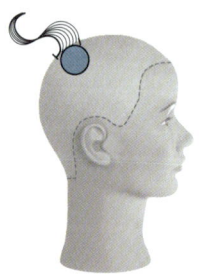

ON BASE
Maximum volume, maximum base strength

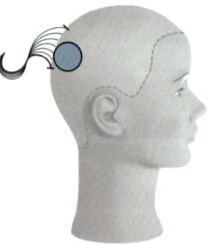

UNDERDIRECTED
Reduced volume and base strength

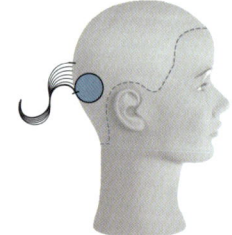

HALF-OFF BASE
Less volume, less base strength

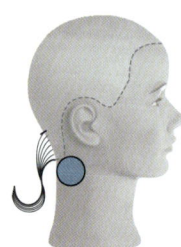

OFF BASE
Least volume, least base strength

17–18 Hold the hair with even tension and backbrush with two strokes on the top of the hair for medium support at the base. Backcombing can also be used to create the base support and to blend the bases. Then smooth the surface of the hair so that the backbrushing is not visible.

NOTE: *Refer to the DVD for additional information on backcombing and backbrushing.*

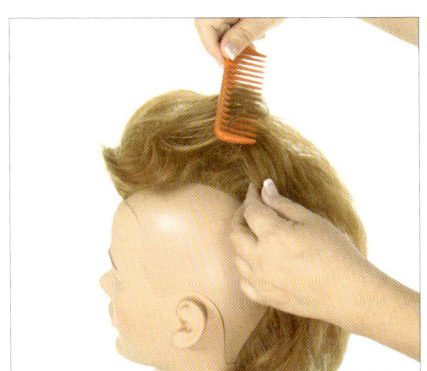
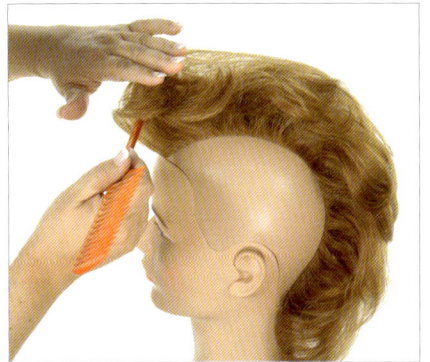
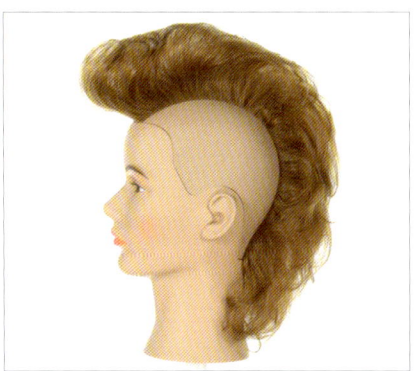

19 To create a textured finish, use a wide-tooth comb.

20 Use the tail of the comb to reinforce the overdirection at the front hairline.

21 The finish shows highly activated texture with varying degrees of base lift, volume and expansion.

STRAIGHT VOLUME AND INDENTATION – AIR FORMING

The focus of this exercise is to provide practice in the techniques most often used in the salon for air forming with a medium-diameter round brush using straight volume and indentation.

Practice this exercise to build rhythm, skill, speed and consistency using:

- Horizontal partings
- Medium-diameter roundbrush
- Half-off base control
- Volume air-forming techniques
- Indentation air-forming techniques

This exercise is performed on straight, uniform layers on a silhouette component.

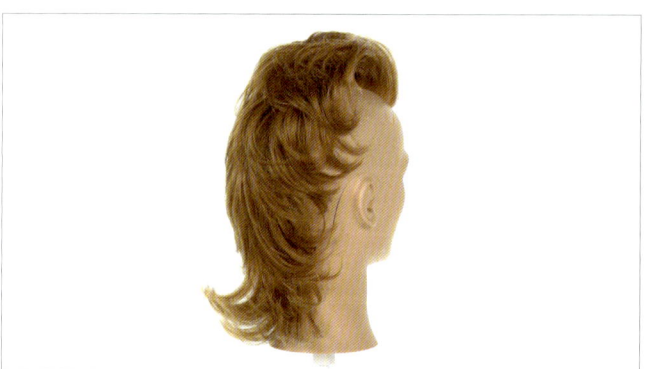

Air forming with a medium-diameter round brush creates a soft texture and blended bases. Half-off base control is used throughout this exercise.

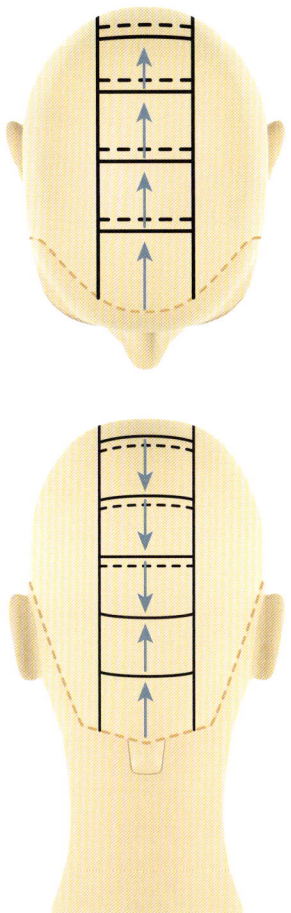

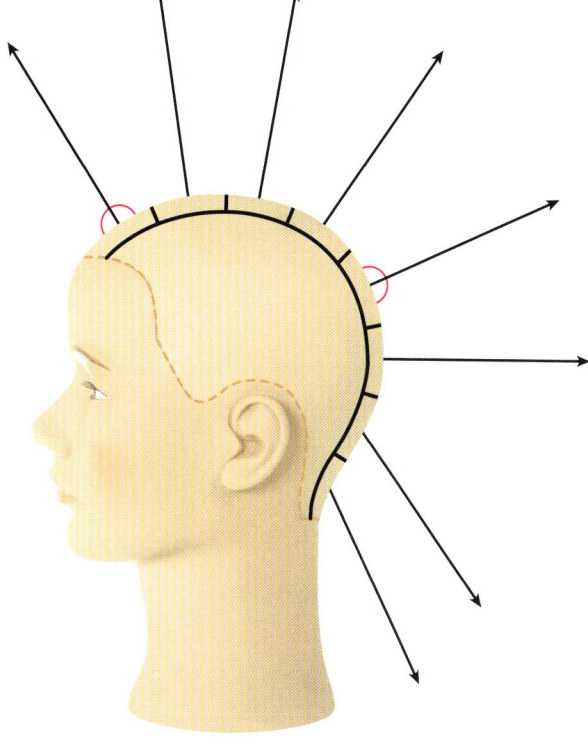

The art shows the partings and direction used. One-diameter (1x) bases are air formed with half-off base control. Note that small portions of previously airformed partings are carried over to the following to blend bases.

For consistent volume, each parting or base will be projected 90° from the center of its base. To achieve indentation in the nape area, two partings are projected at a low angle.

01 Apply a styling mousse and air form to remove excess moisture using a vent or 9-row brush. Position the blow dryer directly behind the hair and keep the airflow parallel to the brush.

02 Begin round brushing at the nape. Create indentation by positioning the brush on top of the strand.

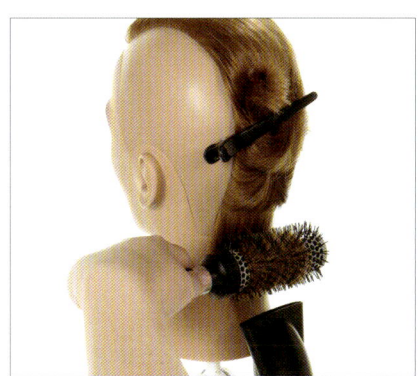

03 Keep the base flat and rotate the brush upward to secure the ends. Direct the airflow to follow the brush.

04–05 Release the next parting. Dry the base flat and turn the ends upward. Secure with a clip for control.

06 Create volume by placing the round brush under the strand to lift the base of the next parting. Rotate the ends under. Use a repetitive motion to dry the base, midstrand and ends.

07 Combine the top portion of the previous section to blend the bases while drying.

08–09 Practice approximately 1x half-off base volume control as you work upward. Blend each new section to the previous one.

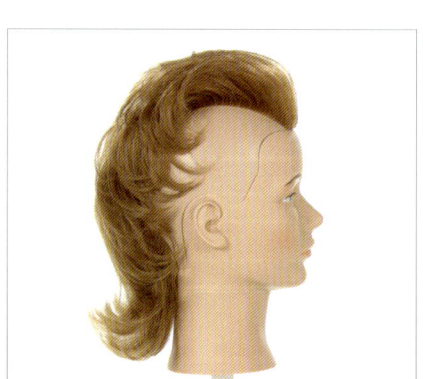

10 Air form the last base at the front hairline with 1x half-off base volume control.

11 Define and detail the form using a large-tooth tail comb.

12 The finish shows a combination of volume and indentation that results in fullness with a flip effect.

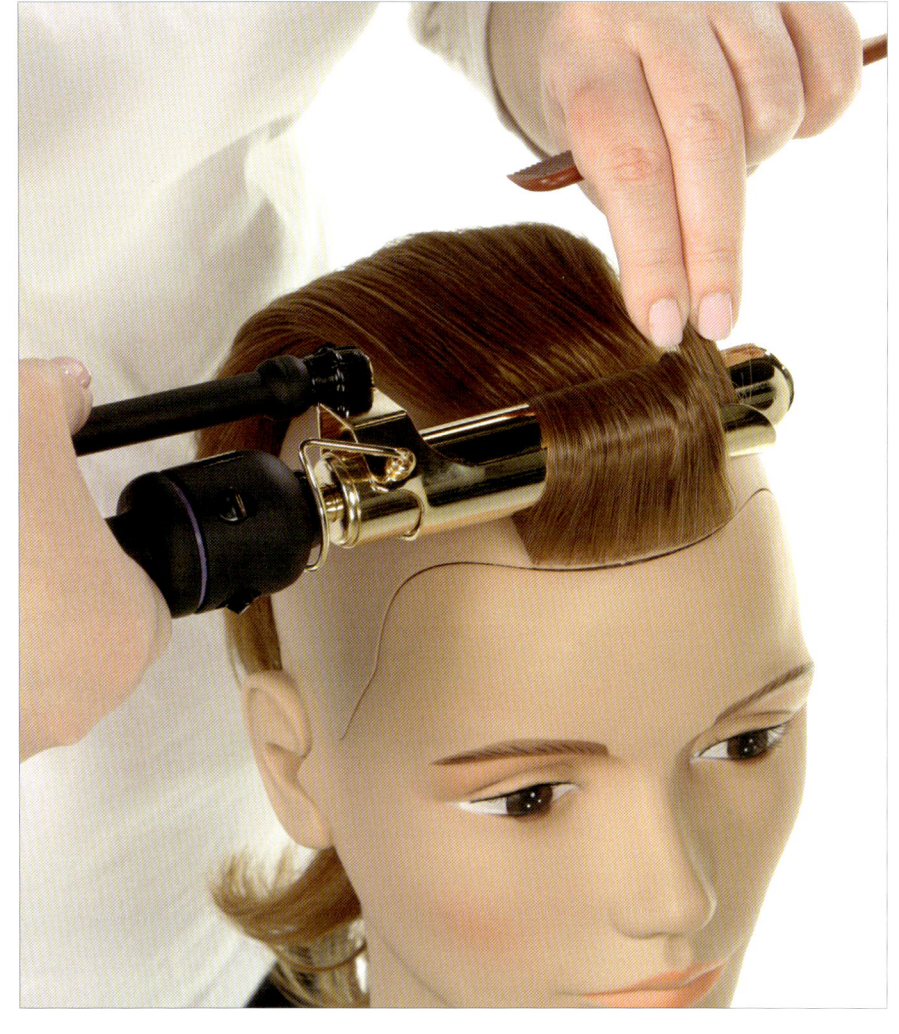

STRAIGHT VOLUME AND INDENTATION – CURLING IRON SET

The focus of this exercise is to provide practice in the techniques most often used in the salon with curling irons for straight volume and indentation. The result will give clients added support, volume and texture.

Practice this exercise to build rhythm, skill, speed and consistency while working with a curling iron and various base controls.

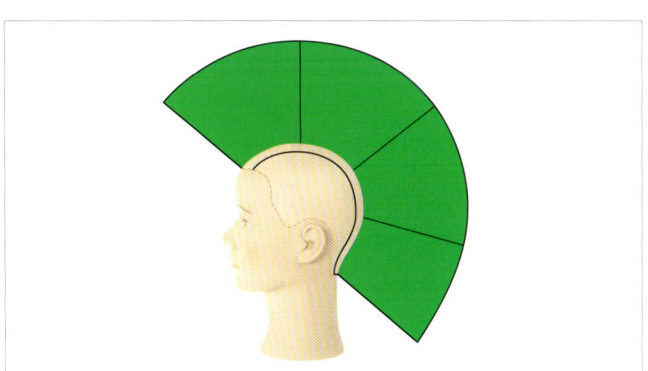

This exercise is performed on straight, uniform layers on a silhouette base component.

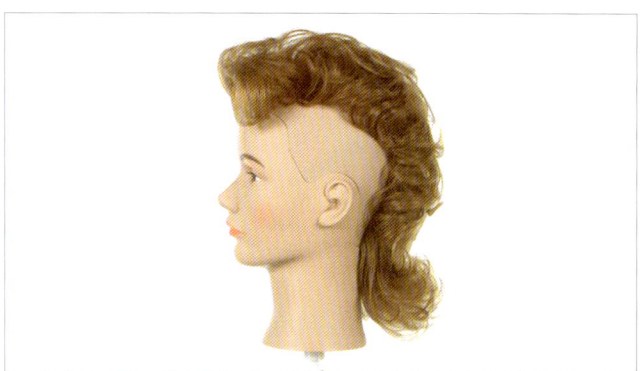

Curling iron sets are performed on dry hair, which has been air formed or dried under the dryer. As with rollers or round brushes, the diameter of the iron influences the resulting curl pattern.

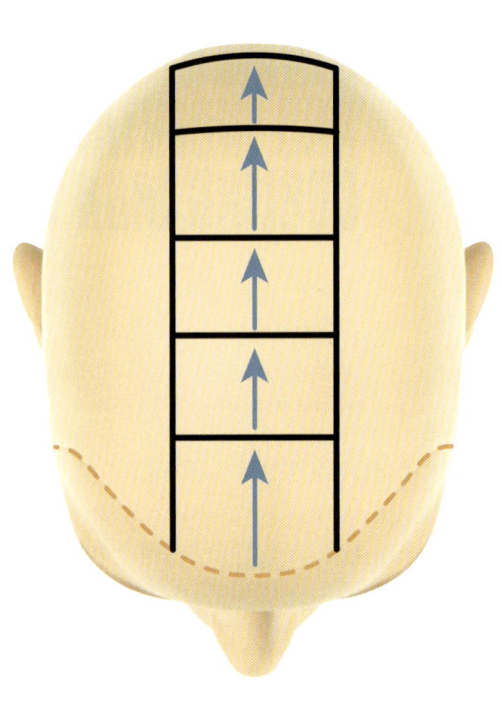

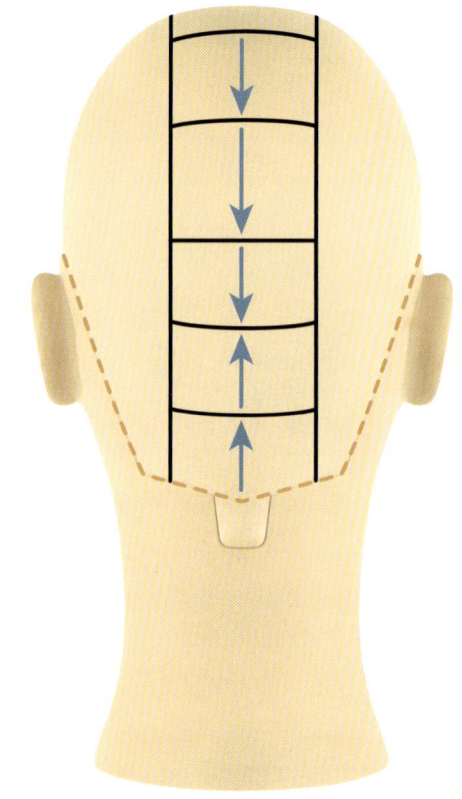

The art shows the parting pattern, different base sizes and directions you will use.

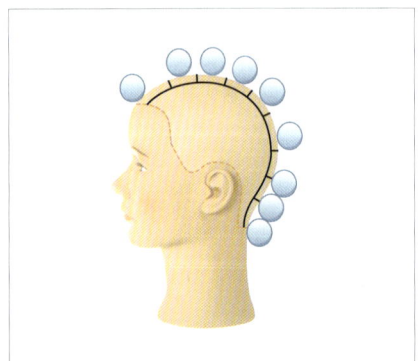

Each parting or base will be projected at a different angle from the center of its base to achieve a decreasing amount of volume and indentation.

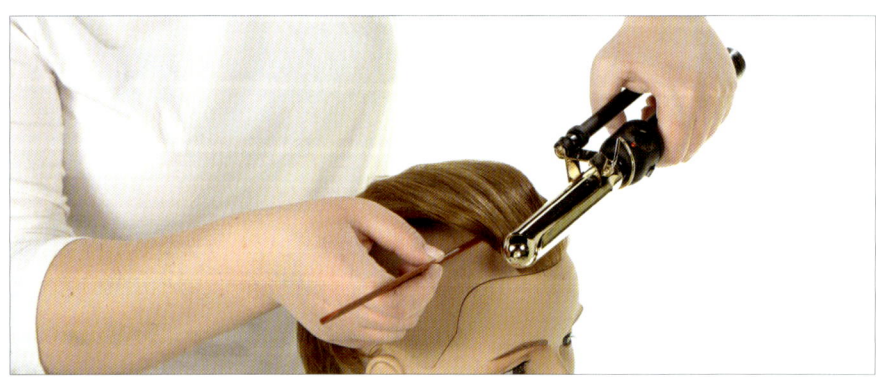

01 Measure a one-and-a-half (1½x) base using the diameter of the curling iron as a guide.

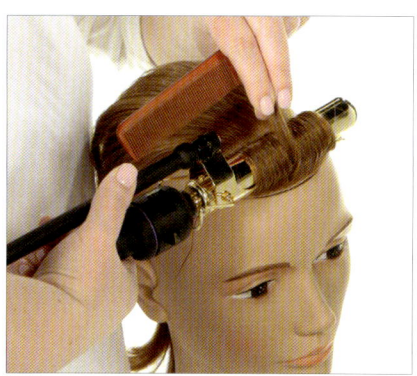

02–03 Insert the curling iron at the base of the parting and direct it forward to create an overdirected base volume control. Turn the iron to guide the strand under and around the barrel. Continue turning until the entire strand is around the iron and the curl is positioned at the front of the base.

04 Note that you may also guide the ends through the center of the parting.

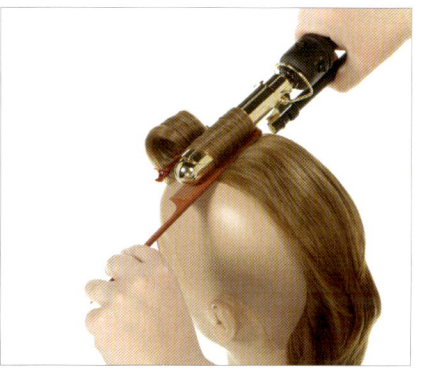

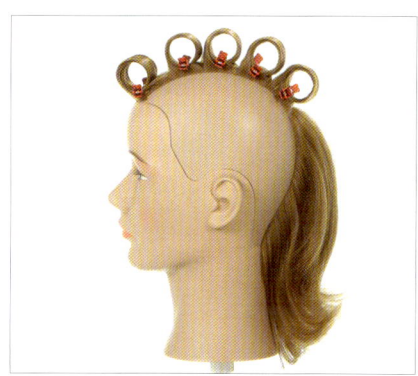

05 Place a comb under the iron to protect the scalp from heat. Release the curl and secure with a clip.

06 Next, create a 1x on-base control by distributing and projecting the hair at a 45° angle from the center of the base.

07 Repeat the same 1x on-base volume curling-iron technique for the next three partings.

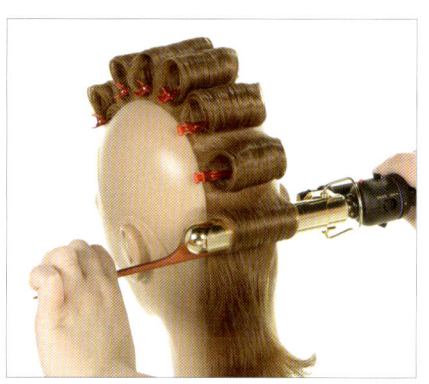

08 Then apply underdirected base volume control with a 1½x parting.

09 Curl the next parting, creating a 1x half-off base volume control.

10 Reverse the position of the iron to create indentation. Keep the 1x base flat and rotate the iron upward as you guide the ends into the iron.

INDENTATION BASE CONTROLS

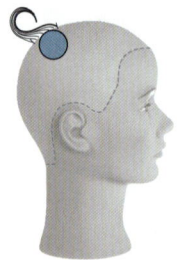

ON BASE
Maximum base strength and volume

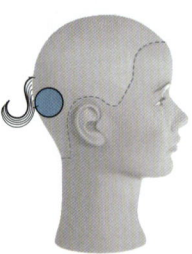

HALF-OFF BASE
Medium base strength, allowing more curl mobility

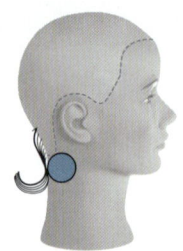

OFF BASE
Minimum base strength, maximum curl mobility

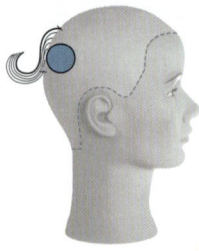

UNDERDIRECTED
Medium base strength, strong curl flare

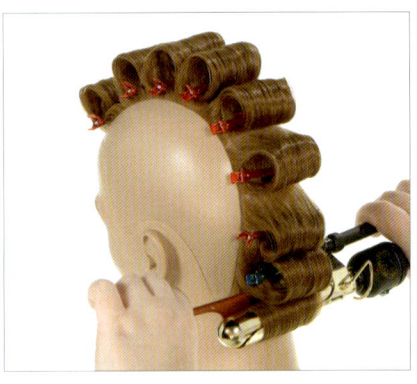

11 Repeat the same indentation curling-iron technique with 1x half-off base control.

12 Clips may be used to control the curls as the hair cools.

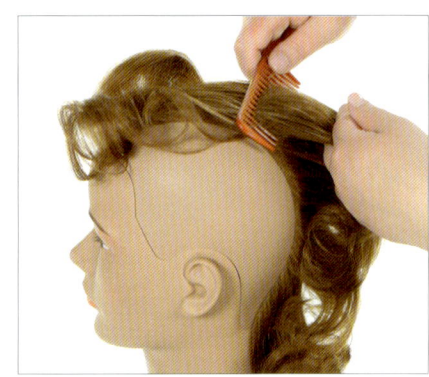

13 Relax and dry mold the hair while observing the results of each base control.

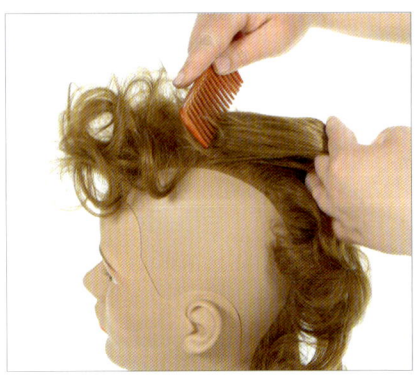

14 Lightly backcomb the hair surface with a large-tooth tail comb. Use long strokes on top of the hair surface, beginning at the front hairline working toward the nape.

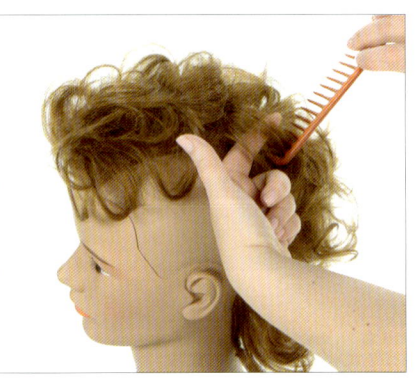

15 Define and detail the hair using your fingers and the tail comb.

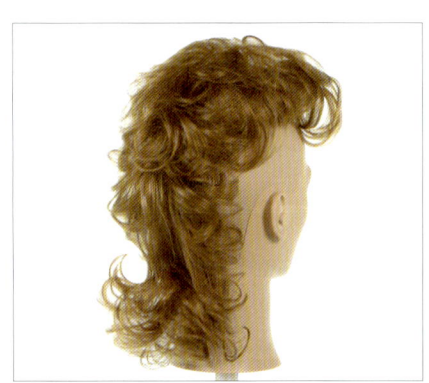

16 Using curling-iron techniques can help you achieve various degrees of volume and indentation as well as additional texture within a design.

STRAIGHT VOLUME – PRESS AND CURL

The focus of this exercise is to provide practice in temporarily straightening tightly curled hair using the thermal hard-pressing technique. The result will be straight lengths with a subtle movement and bevel-under effect.

Practice this exercise to build skill and accuracy using:

- Horizontal partings
- Appropriate heat temperature
- Pressure
- Comb manipulation

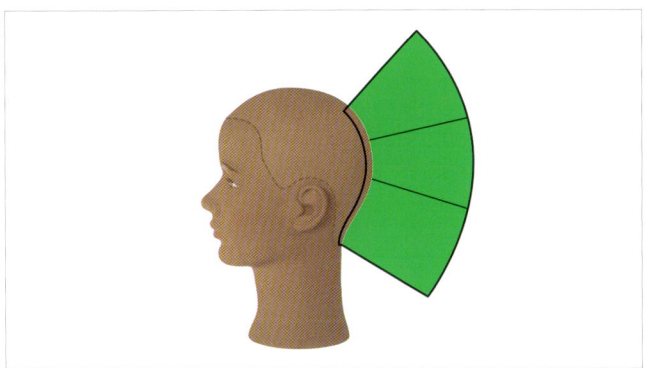

This thermal hard-pressing technique is demonstrated on the back portion of the tightly curled uniform silhouette component.

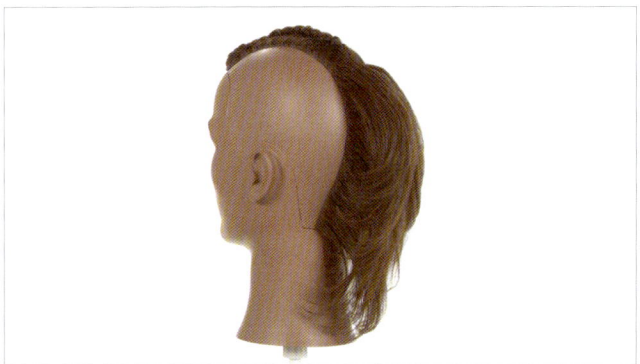

The finish shows thermally straightened lengths, which were finished using a curling iron.

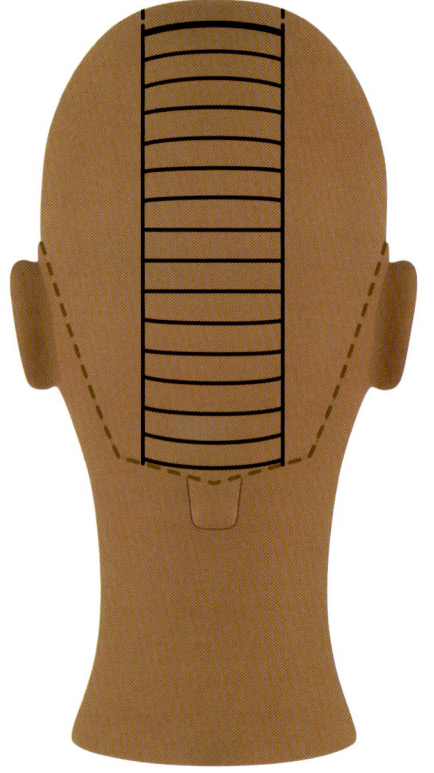

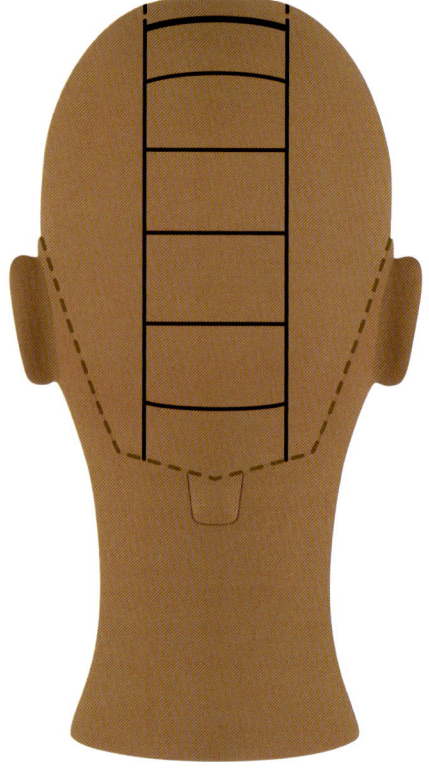

The art shows ¼" (.6 cm) horizontal partings used throughout the pressing portion of this exercise.

The art shows one-diameter (1x) horizontal partings used throughout the curling portion of this exercise.

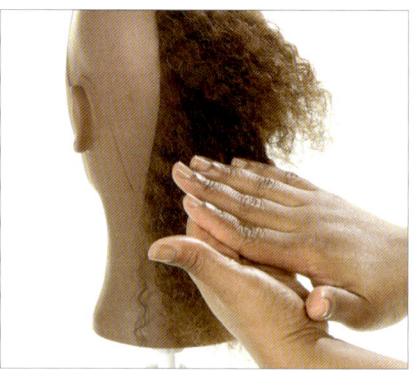

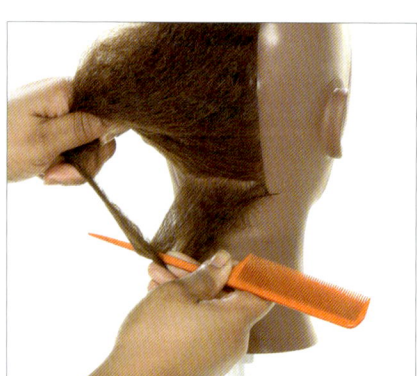

01–02 Apply pressing cream or oil from base to ends on damp pre-shampooed lengths. Apply product in sections to ensure even application. Note that pressing cream or oil may also be applied onto clean, dry hair.

03 Starting in the nape, use a tail comb to part the hair using ½" (1.25 cm) horizontal partings. The remainder of the hair is clipped up and out of the way.

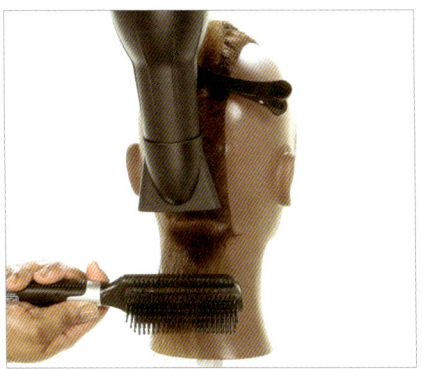

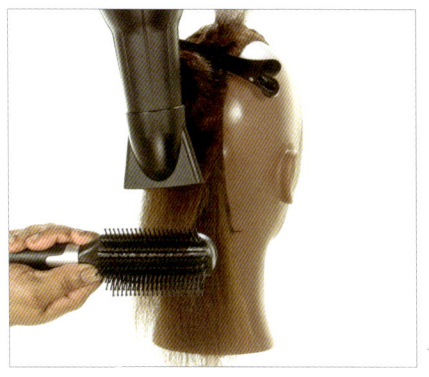

04 Air form on the highest heat setting and stretch the hair while drying with the 9-row brush. Turn the brush down air forming from base to midstrand and then from midstrand to ends.

05–06 Release the next horizontal parting. Continue to air form the hair from base to midstrand and then from midstrand to ends, removing as much curl as possible. Work to the top and complete air forming.

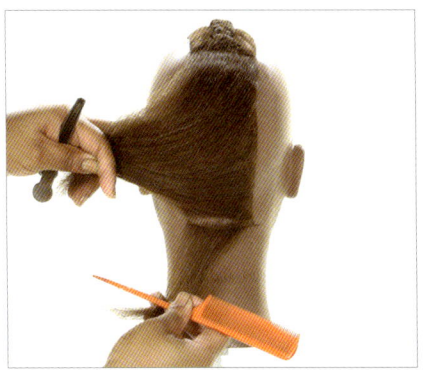

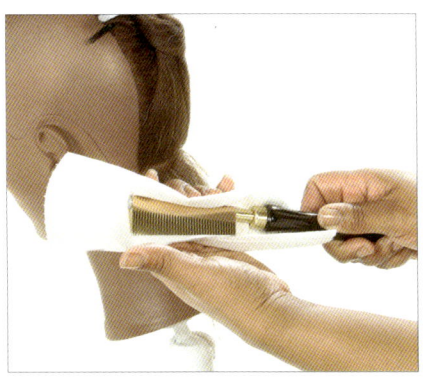

07 Return to the nape. Part the hair using ¼" (.6 cm) horizontal partings with a tail comb. You may apply pressing cream or oil if necessary as you press.

08 Place the pressing comb in the heating element. Test the temperature of the pressing comb on a white paper towel. If the paper stays white, you can safely proceed without damaging the hair.

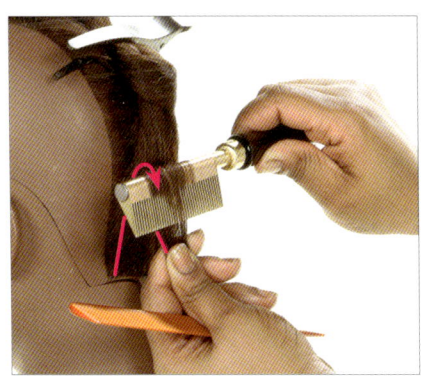

09–10 Insert the teeth of the comb underneath the strand near the base. Control the ends of the hair with the opposite hand. Turn the pressing comb and press the hair using the spine as you work upward from base to ends. Slowly feed the hair through the teeth of the comb while working toward the ends. Repeat using the same technique.

11 Then, insert the teeth on top of the strand near the base. Turn the pressing comb and press the hair from base to ends. Slowly feed the hair while working toward the ends.

12–13 Release another ¼" (.6 cm) horizontal parting and clip the remaining hair up and out of the way. After testing the temperature, press twice on both sides of the strand. Maintain even tension along the entire strand as you press toward the ends.

14 Use more heat and/or tension if not enough curl is being removed.

 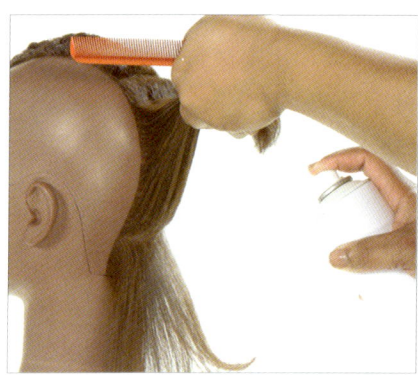 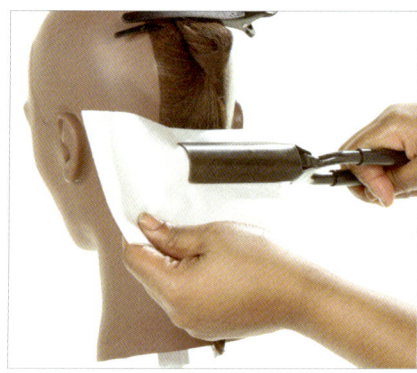

15 Use the same hard-press techniques as you complete the last parting.

16 Apply holding spray to the hair to assist with support. Apply to the hair section by section.

17 Place the marcel curling iron in the heating element. Test the temperature of the marcel curling iron on a piece of white paper towel.

 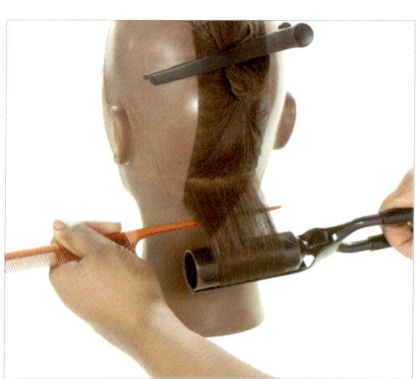

18 Starting in the nape, release a 1x horizontal parting. Clip the remaining lengths up. Smooth the base by placing the barrel of the curling iron at the base and turning the iron while applying pressure.

19 Then, position the curling iron away from the base and turn the iron so the shell is at the bottom. Slide down the strand using a tail comb to hold lengths at a lower projection angle. Turn the curling iron downward to create a slightly curved texture.

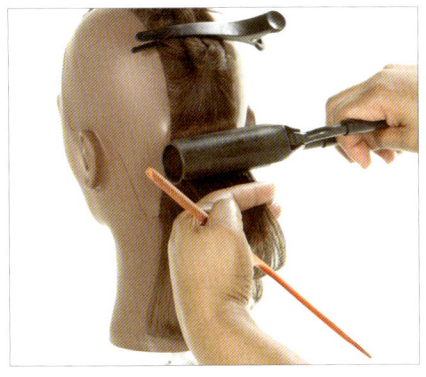
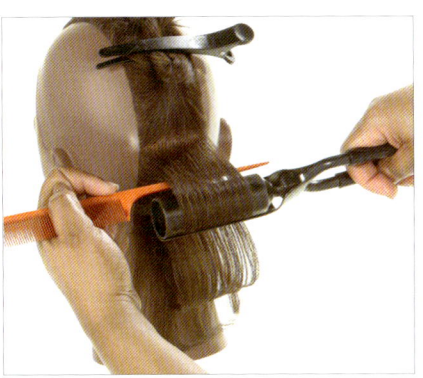

20–21 Continue to first smooth the base, then curl away from the base to the ends as you work upward. Be sure to hold the tail comb at the angle of the desired base position.

When a pressing comb or a marcel iron is too hot, it will cause discoloration on the white paper towel. If this happens, allow the comb or iron to cool, then retest before applying to the hair.

22 Repeat on the last parting.

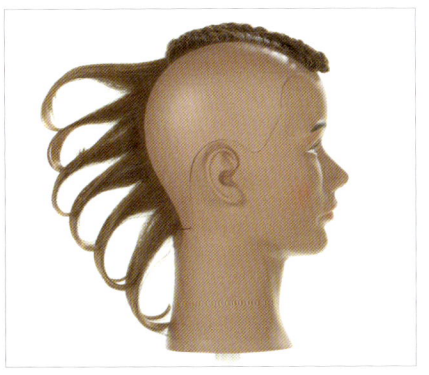

23 Here we see the finished component with uniform base control and sizes.

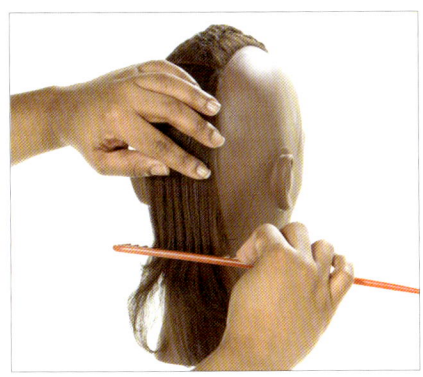

24 Relax the curls with a wide-tooth tail comb to help blend the bases and remove splits.

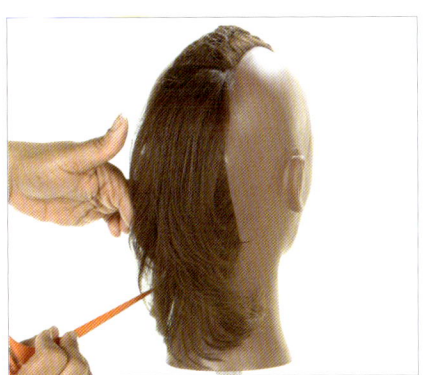

25 Using the tail of a comb, define and detail.

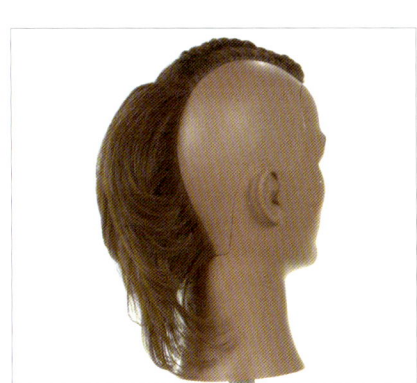

26 The finish shows straight hair with curved end texture. The result of this technique looks great on layered lengths for slight activation.

CURVATURE VOLUME/HALF-CIRCLE – ROLLERS

The purpose of this exercise is to provide practice in wet setting curvature volume in a half-circle shape. Practice is also provided in finishing techniques to reflect the set movement.

Practice this exercise to build rhythm, skill, speed and consistency to:

- Distribute radially
- Mold counterclockwise
- Scale a half-circle
- Part triangle-shaped bases
- Set with on, half-off and off base controls
- Relax
- Backbrush
- Define the form

This exercise is performed on uniform lengths.

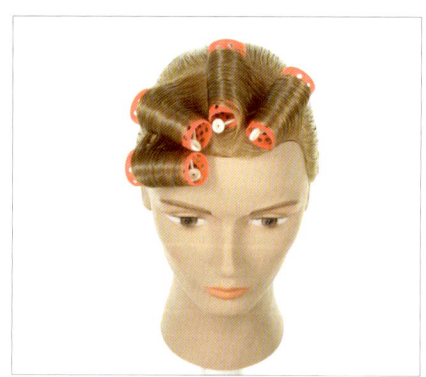

On-base, underdirected, half-off and off-base controls are used to set the counterclockwise half-circle.

Curvature volume moves equally away from and then toward the face.

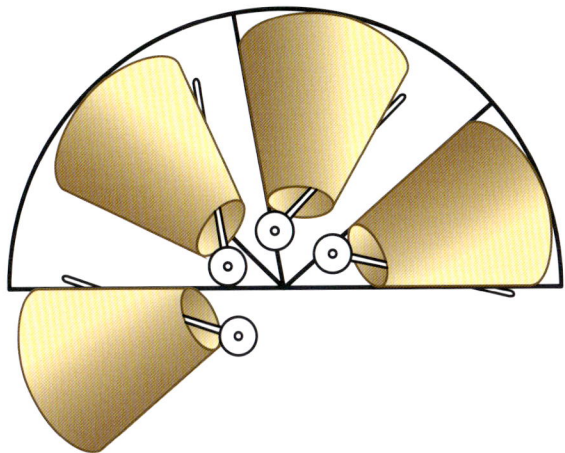

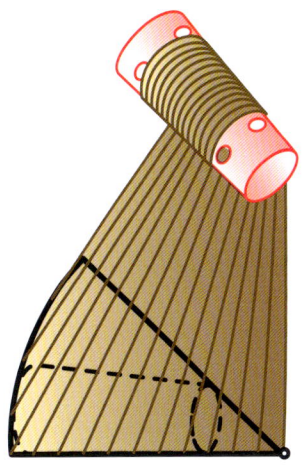

Cone-shaped rollers are used to set the half-circle shape. Keep in mind the three rules for setting cone-shaped rollers: 1) set each cone-shaped roller one diameter (1x) away from the point of origin, 2) set each roller parallel to its lower parting, and 3) secure each roller with its forces.

When setting cone-shaped rollers, the small end of the roller is angled toward the point of origin. Then the roller is rolled toward the back of the shape.

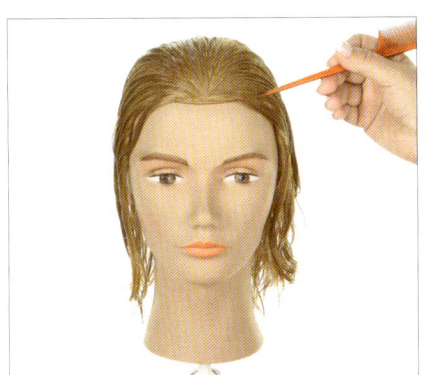

01 Use the tip of the tail comb and distribute from a center point of origin using radial distribution.

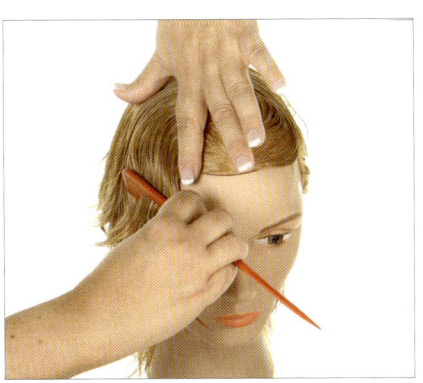

02 Then place your finger approximately 1" (2.5 cm) away from the point of origin and mold a half-circle in a counterclockwise direction.

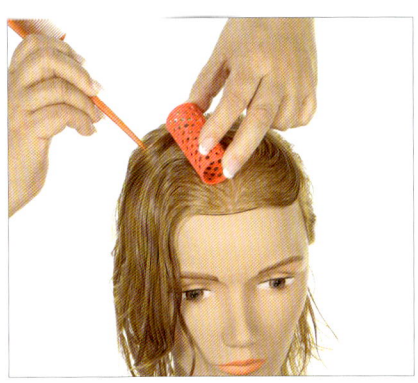

03 Use the diameter of the small end of the roller plus the length to scale the shape.

04 Here we see the completed molding and scaling of the half-circle shape.

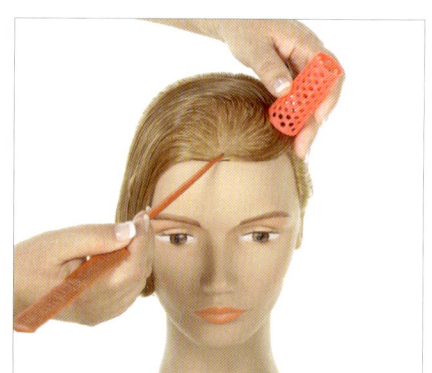

05–06 Measure a 1x base area with the large end of the cone-shaped roller at the perimeter. Then, part from the point of origin to the outside of the shape. Project the hair at 45° above the center of the base. Angle the roller toward the point of origin, then roll it down and toward the back of the shape. Secure with a pick at the small end of the tool.

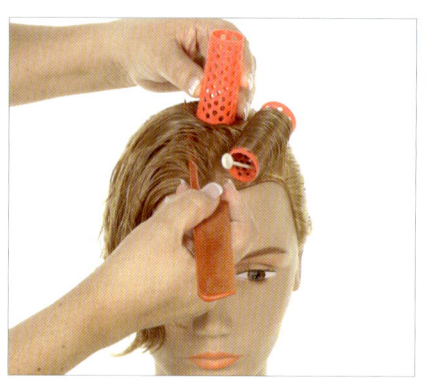

07 Next, measure a 1½x base, using the large end of the cone-shaped roller at the perimeter of the half-circle shape.

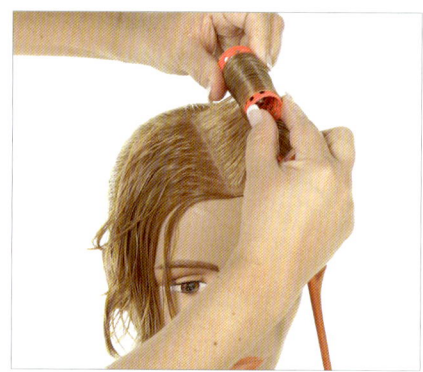

08 Project 90° from the center of the base and wrap the roller downward to create 1½x underdirected base control.

09 Measure and part the next 1x base. Project 90° from the center of the base and wrap downward to achieve half-off base control.

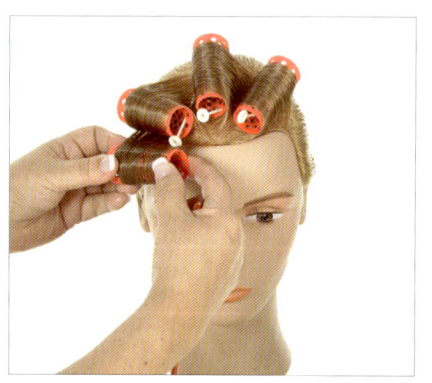

10 Project the last base 45° below the center to achieve off-base control.

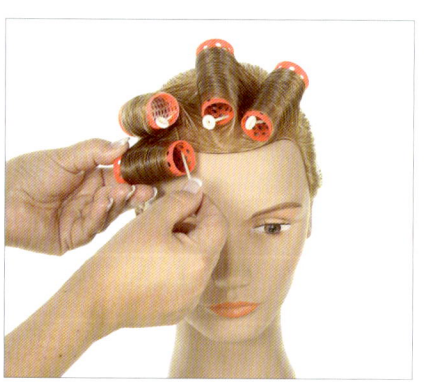

11 Continue to secure each roller at the small end with the forces.

12 Here we see the completed half-circle set on rollers.

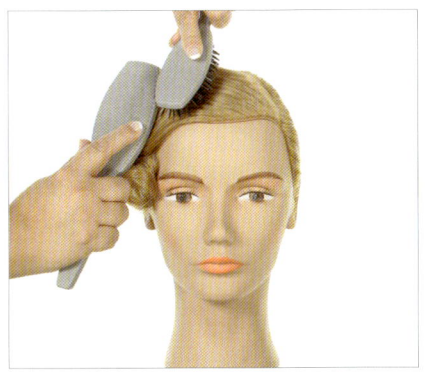

13 After it has completely dried and cooled, use two cushion brushes to relax the hair.

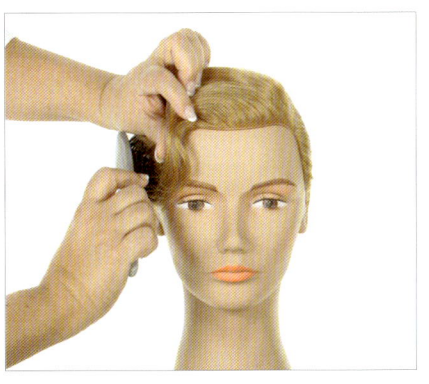

14 Dry mold the hair to reinforce the lines of the half-circle shape.

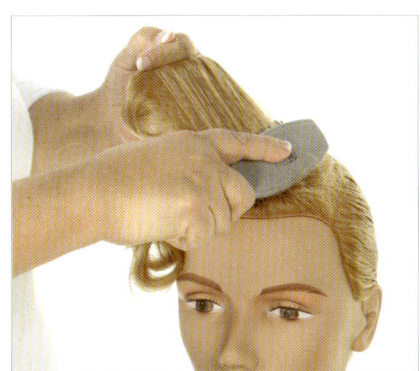

15 Backbrush for medium support (2 strokes) and to blend the bases following the direction of the set.

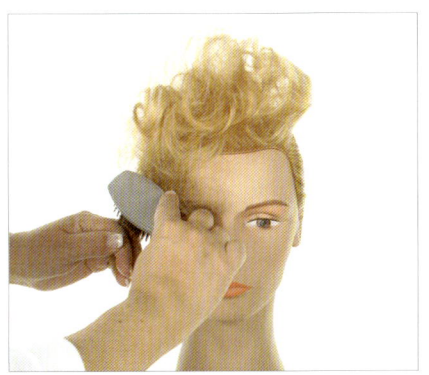

16 Use a lower projection angle for diminished volume to reflect the off-base control used.

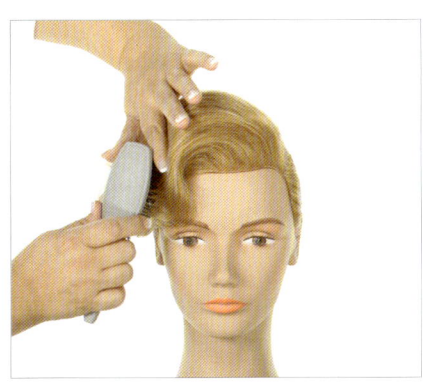

17 Use the cushion brush to define the form, following the lines of the half-circle shape.

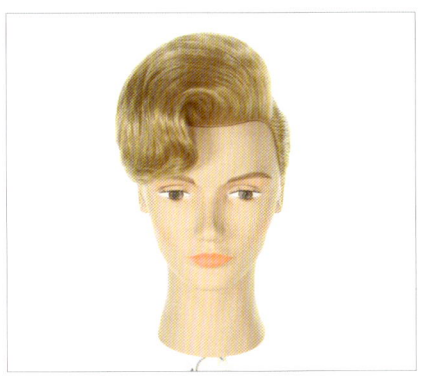

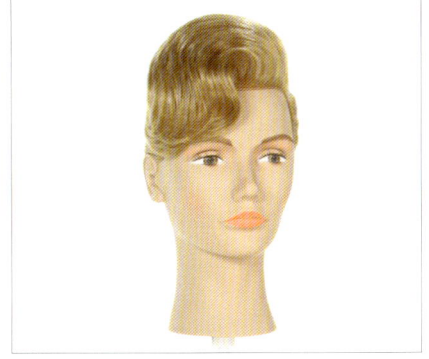

18–19 The half-circle shape positioned at the center front hairline creates equal movement away from and toward the face.

CURVATURE VOLUME/HALF-OVAL – PINCURLS

The purpose of this exercise is to provide practice in the techniques most often used to set a half-oval shape using pincurls.

Practice this exercise to build rhythm, skill, speed and consistency to:

- Mold and scale a fast-to-slow counterclockwise half-oval
- Set the shape using fast, medium and slow-speed pincurls with on-base, half-off and off-base controls
- Backcomb and finish to reflect the set movement

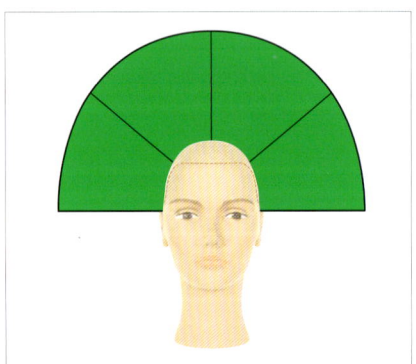

This exercise will be performed on uniformly layered lengths.

On-base, half-off and off-base controls are used to set fast, medium and slow-speed pincurls in the half-oval shape.

A fast to slow half-oval results in a curvature movement that moves mostly toward the face.

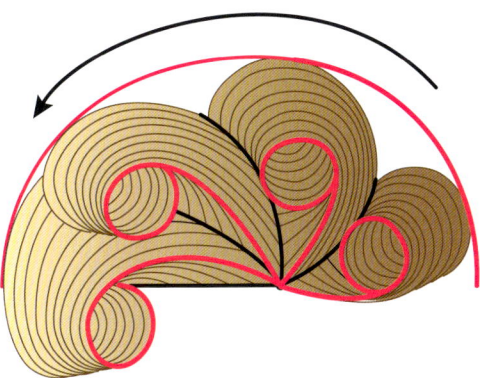

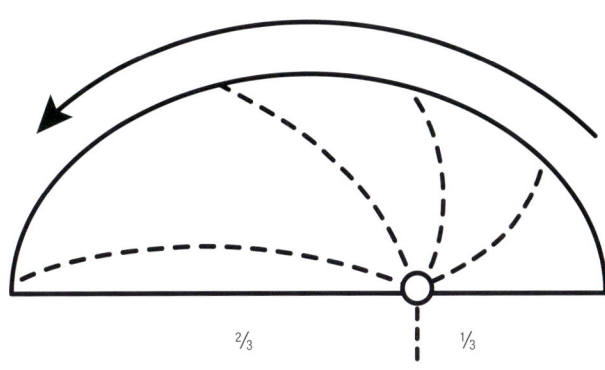

²/₃   ¹/₃

Remember that an oval consists of unequal radii from one point of origin. Short radial lines create fast speeds because they travel a shorter distance. Longer radii create slower speeds because they travel a longer distance.

The proportion of this oval is ⅓ fast to ⅔ slow, and it moves in a counterclockwise direction. With the fast-to-slow speed oval, a smaller amount of hair moves away from the face.

NOTE: *With a slow-to-fast speed oval, more hair moves away from the face.*

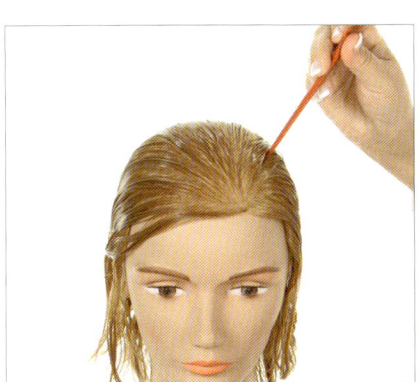

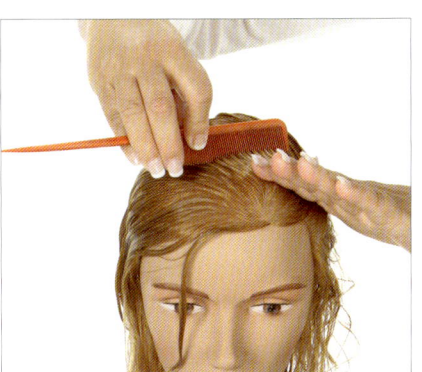

01 Beginning with a point of origin above the center of the left eyebrow, distribute the lengths using radial distribution.

02–03 Mold a ⅓ fast to ⅔ slow counterclockwise half-oval moving first away from the face and then toward the face. Note that while molding, the finger is positioned closer to the point of origin for faster speed and farther away for slower speed.

04 Use the tail of the comb to scale out the half-oval shape.

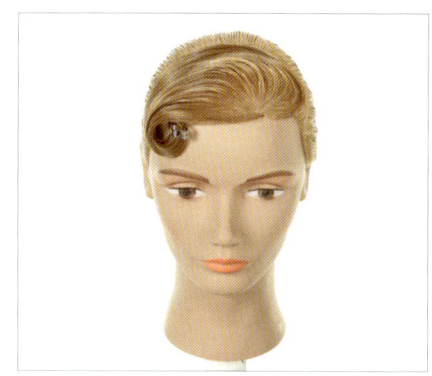

05 Here we see the complete molded and scaled half-oval.

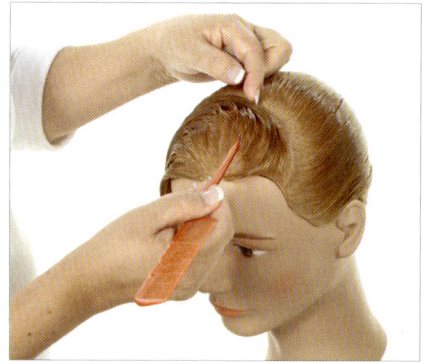

06 Take a slightly curved or crescent-shaped parting.

07 Distribute then reinforce the arc of the pincurl with the tail of the comb.

08–09 Form a fast-speed volume pincurl using an on-base control. Secure the pincurl in the first direction. The diameter of the pincurl should reflect the diameter of the base at the perimeter of the shape.

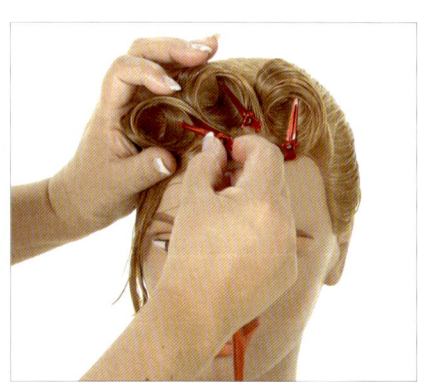

10 Set the next two pincurls using one-diameter (1x) half-off base control. The circle sits farther from the point of origin, creating medium-speed pincurls.

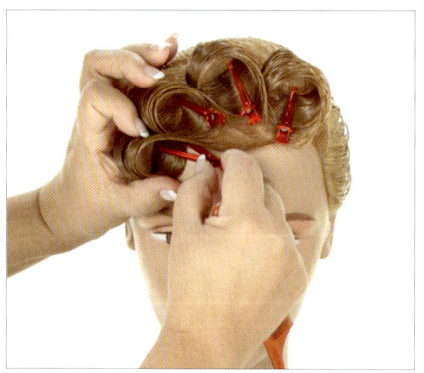

11 Set the last slow-speed pincurl using 1x off-base control.

12 Here we see the completed half-oval pincurl set. Compare the distance from the point of origin to the outer perimeter of the fast, medium and slow-speed pincurls.

13 After the hair has dried and cooled completely, relax the set using two cushion brushes.

14 Dry mold following the movement of the half-oval shape.

15–16 Use the one-stroke backcombing technique for light base support. Use a large-tooth tail comb and backcomb in the direction of the set. For stronger support a fine-tooth tail comb may be used.

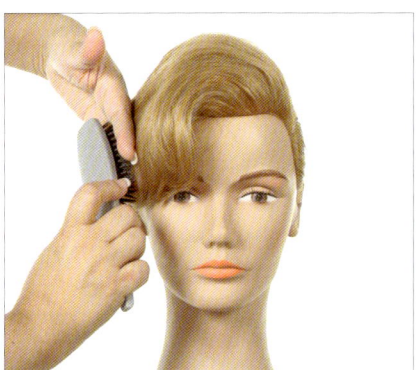

17 Define and detail the form with a small cushion brush.

18 The finished design reveals a half-oval that moves from fast to slow in a counterclockwise direction.

GUIDELINES FOR CLIENT-CENTERED WET AND THERMAL HAIR DESIGNS

Client-centered guidelines are designed to help you maintain the integrity and health of your client's hair and to enhance your client's comfort and satisfaction. Combining your experience with predictable wet and thermal design results and client-centered guidelines will ensure exceptional results and a pleasant service experience for your clients.

PROCEDURAL GUIDELINES

The following chart will help you ensure your client's comfort and safety during the wet and thermal hair design service.

DESIGN STEP	CLIENT CONSIDERATIONS
DISTRIBUTE/MOLD 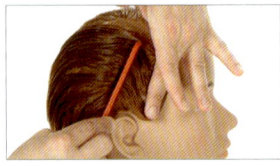	• Face client toward mirror and describe why you are distributing and molding hair in desired direction • Reiterate how distribution and molding pattern serves as a blueprint for the finished design
PART/APPLY 	• Explain how partings you choose help control the hair and how base controls help create volume and fullness in the right areas • Give tips and hints on how he or she could apply some of your design techniques at home
BACKBRUSH/BACKCOMB 	• Show areas where additional support is needed and how it can be created by backbrushing or backcombing • Advise on how aerosol hairspray should be used to add more support
DEFINE THE FORM 	• Give client a hand mirror and turn his or her back toward a large mirror • While defining the form of a design, explain that it is important to assess the finished look from various angles to ensure a balanced form from all directions
DETAIL 	• Teach how to use proper styling products during this final stage of finishing • Recommend styling products for at-home care to help achieve same great look between salon visits

COMMUNICATION GUIDELINES

The following chart will help you respond to some of the most common client cues in a way that encourages client trust and open communication.

CLIENT CUE	DESIGNER RESPONSE
"My scalp gets itchy when I use mousse to style my hair."	*"Could you please explain to me how you are applying the mousse at home? One great way you can apply mousse without touching the scalp is to put it between the bristles of a vent brush and brush it in. This not only avoids contact with the scalp, but also helps distribute it much more evenly."*
"What can I do to protect my hair from the heat of my curling iron?"	*"I recommend a thermal protectant as a finishing product. Thermal protectants come in a variety of forms, such as sprays, lotions and creams. They contain moisturizing additives that protect against heat from curling irons as well as blow dryers. In addition, these products often lend shine and style support. Let me show you the one I think would be best for your hair…"*
"I always have trouble using hairspray. I get too much in one area and the rest of my hair doesn't hold."	*"Make sure to check the instructions on the container, which most product companies provide. On average, hairspray should be held at least 10" (25 cm) to 12" (30 cm) away from the hair while spraying. This allows the product to be applied to a wider area, not in a concentrated area, which prevents over-saturation. Also, you can opt for an aerosol spray. It usually feels dryer and leaves the hair more workable after it has been applied."*
"I really don't know what to do about the cowlick in the back of my head. The hair in that area just does whatever it wants."	*"The design I created for you today should help you incorporate your cowlick. In addition, let me show you what I do when I style your hair to tame this cowlick. I'll turn you with your back toward the mirror and let you hold this small mirror so you can watch while I share my techniques with you. With a bit of practice I am sure this cowlick won't give you any more problems."*
"I really wouldn't mind my curly hair if I just knew what to do with it. It always seems to get frizzy."	*"There are a few different things you can do to make your curls look great. While your hair is still wet, apply a curl cream that contains moisture. As you apply it, twist individual strands of hair and either diffuse your hair or let it air dry in this formation. Once it's dry, distribute a silicone-based product during this final stage of finishing, using your fingers. Let me show you the products I recommend for you, and how to use them."*

2.2 SOLID FORM

The solid form is a classic example of a timeless, striking hair sculpture. It has earned a permanent place as a reliable staple in the repertoire of successful hair designers. After taking a look at the common wet and thermal design options available for solid form lengths, you'll have the opportunity to study and practice various techniques frequently used on these designs in the salon.

SOLID FORM DESIGNING

Common wet and thermal design techniques for the solid form include volume or indentation on the ends. By temporarily introducing a different texture, you can also dramatically change the appearance of a solid form design.

FORM OPTIONS

Solid form shapes generally tend to expand most along the perimeter due to the concentration of weight. This is a result of the longer interior and shorter exterior lengths falling to the same level. Keep in mind that by adding volume and/or texture while designing on a solid form, lengths appear to be shorter.

TEXTURE OPTIONS

Although smooth and sleek finishes are popular and best showcase the characteristics of the solid form sculpture, the solid form's longer interior lengths are ideal for featuring a variety of texture patterns.

  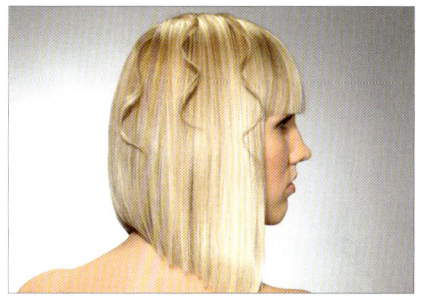

The addition of waves around the face can add a touch of glamour.

Spiral curls can dramatically change a person's appearance and soften the angularity of a solid form.

For an edgy effect, different—even angular—textures can be introduced overall or to selected strands.

DIRECTION OPTIONS

The longer lengths of solid forms are often designed from a center or side part. Designing solid lengths back off the face requires backcombing and/or finishing techniques. A fringe is incorporated if lengths are worn toward the face.

CENTER PART

SIDE PART

AWAY FROM THE FACE

TOWARD THE FACE

STRAIGHT VOLUME – AIR FORMING

This smooth, sleek design is one of the most popular in salons today. Altering base controls while air forming with the round brush and using the straight volume technique affects the degree of volume and curved end texture.

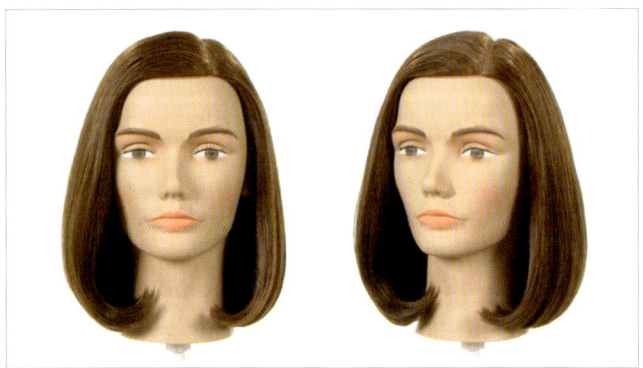

Air forming with medium- and large-diameter round brushes expands the form and adds fullness along the perimeter of this solid design.

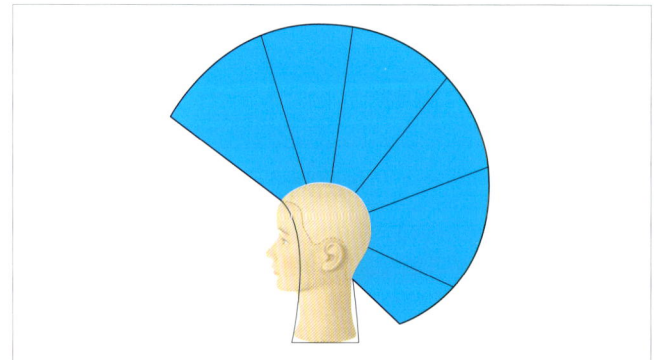

This exercise will be performed on a horizontal solid form.

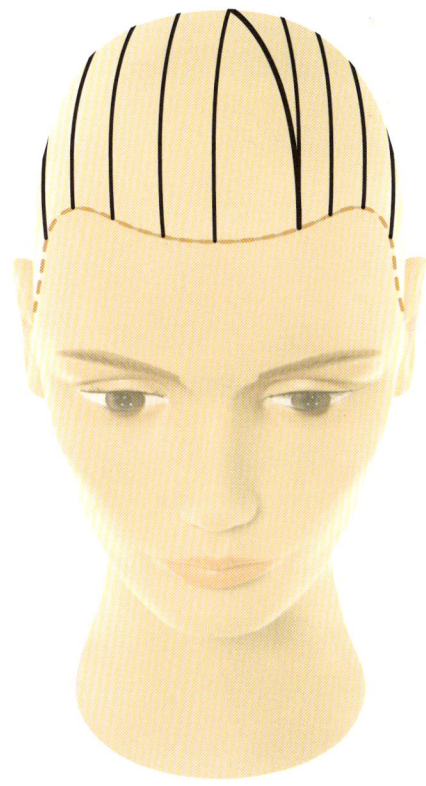
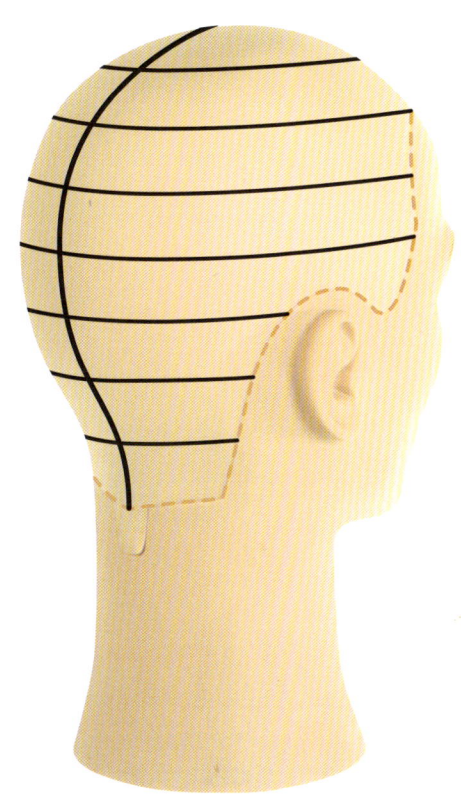

The head is sectioned from a side part to the crown, and from the crown to the center nape. Horizontal partings will be used throughout the service.

01 Apply styling mousse to towel-dried hair to help create support.

02 Air form to remove most of the moisture using your fingers to control the hair. As an option, you may also use a large vent brush. Then section the hair with a side part.

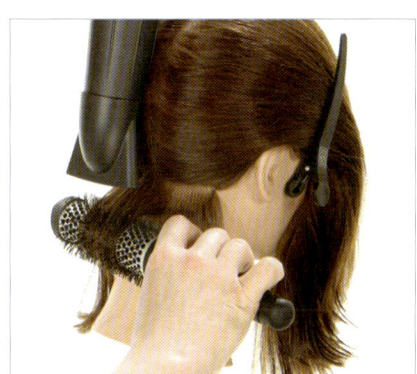

03 Begin at the nape, and position a medium-size round brush underneath the hair to create base lift. Direct the airflow on top as you dry the base, midstrand, then the ends using half-off base volume control.

05 Release the next horizontal parting. Take a small portion of the previously air-formed lengths to reduce splits. Start at the center to help blend the center part. Work from the center to each side.

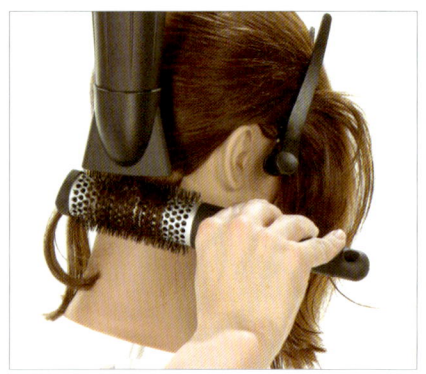

04 Work from the center toward one side, directing the airflow toward the ends. Repeat on the opposite side.

06 Continue to use half-off base control and the same air-forming technique.

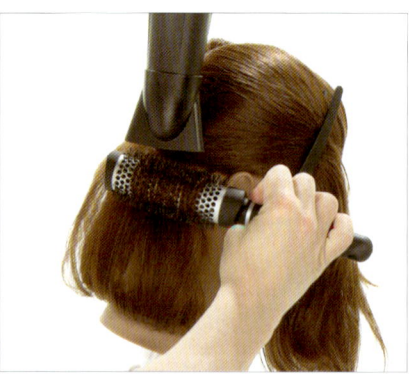

07 Rotate the brush toward the base as you continue to direct the airflow over the hair to reinforce the curl.

08 The art shows the partings extending over the ear to the front hairline.

10 Work to the front hairline using the same air-forming technique. Direct the airflow to follow the cuticle of the hair.

09 Switch to a larger-diameter round brush. Reduce base lift by using medium projection for an off-base control. Work from the center to one side.

11 Then, work from the center toward the opposite side using medium projection. Check for symmetry before continuing.

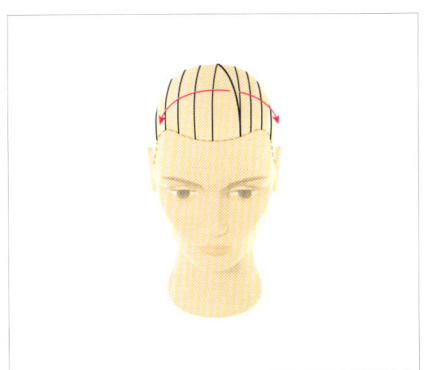

12 Work toward the top using the same technique. Release a parting on both sides and work from the center to either side.

13 Continue the horizontal parting pattern for the remaining top lengths.

14 At the top on the light side, use the same base control and air-forming technique.

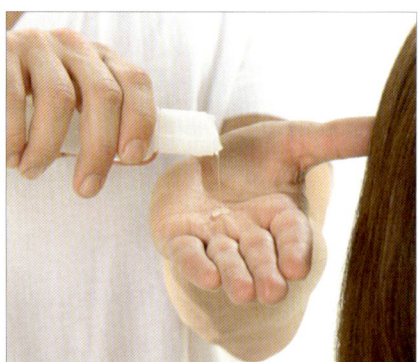

15 On the heavy side, adjust the base size and brush position to create the base lift desired. Here half-off base control is used. Continue until you reach the side part.

16–17 Add a small amount of silicone gloss when air forming is complete. Distribute the product evenly in your hands. Apply it to the hair working from the ends upward.

18–19 The finish shows a smooth surface with the perimeter weight of the solid form accentuated by end texture with a bevel-under effect.

DESIGN DECISIONS *WORKSHOP 01*

STRAIGHT VOLUME – AIR FORMING

artist+ access

Draw or fill in the boxes with the appropriate answers.

STRUCTURE

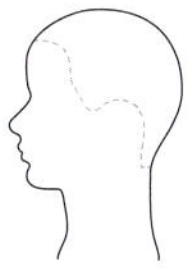

FORM/TEXTURE

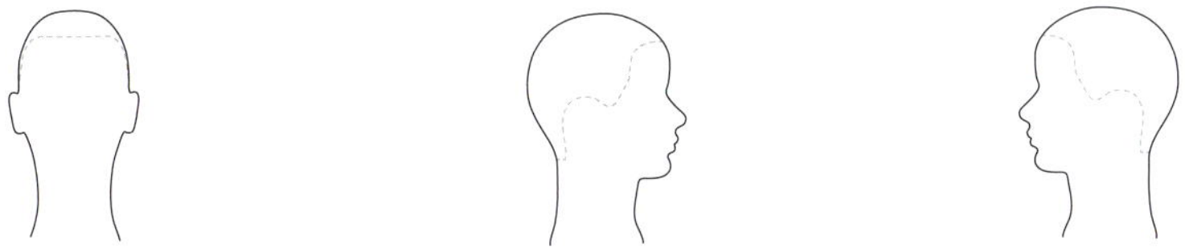

DIRECTION

AIR-FORMING PATTERN

COMB-OUT/FINISH

☐ RELAX ☐ DRY MOLD ☐ BACKCOMB/BACKBRUSH ☐ DEFINE THE FORM ☐ DETAIL

TOOLS/PRODUCT CHOICE

Educator Signature

Date

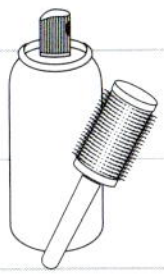

STRAIGHT VOLUME – CURLING IRON

This variation creates face-framing waves on solid lengths by positioning a few curls along either side of the side part. This technique creates curls that undulate into a wave pattern on longer lengths, creating very soft, feminine surface texture.

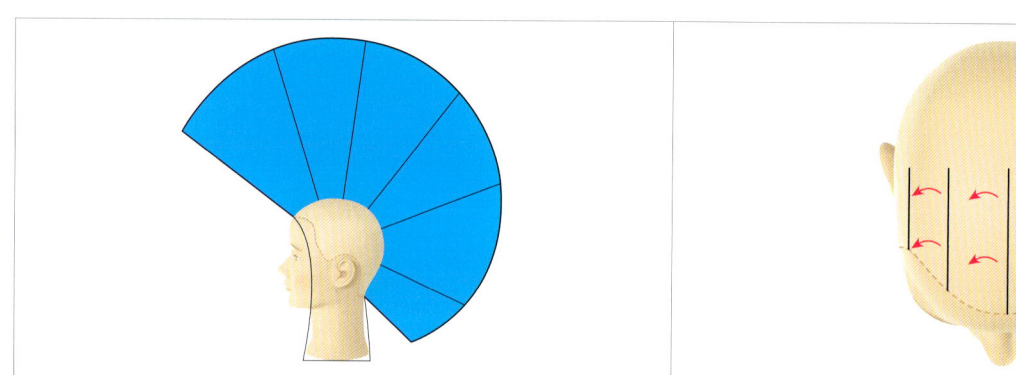

This design is created from a side part. On the heavier side of the part, one-diameter (1x) half-off base control is used to create barrel curls, extending to the recession area of the head. The curls were clipped for base support and to reinforce the curl while cooling. On the lighter side, 1½x half-off base control is used. The hair is relaxed and then defined using a large-tooth tail comb.

HAIR DESIGN RUBRIC *WORKSHOP 01*
STRAIGHT VOLUME – AIR FORMING

This rubric is a performance assessment tool designed to measure your ability to **create** *Pivot Point hair designs.*

	LEVEL 1 *in progress*	LEVEL 2 *getting better*	LEVEL 3 *entry-level proficiency*
PREPARATION			
• Assemble hair design essentials	☐	☐	☐
CREATE			
• Shampoo, condition and apply styling mousse to towel-dried hair	☐	☐	☐
• Air form to remove most of the moisture using fingers or large vent brush to control hair; section with side part	☐	☐	☐
• Create base lift using medium-diameter round brush underneath hair in nape	☐	☐	☐
• Direct airflow on top, drying base, midstrand and ends	☐	☐	☐
• Enforce curl by rotating brush toward base, directing airflow toward ends	☐	☐	☐
• Air form next partings using same technique; take small portion of previously air-formed lengths to reduce splits	☐	☐	☐
• Air form partings extending to side front hairlines using larger-diameter round brush; use medium projection for half-off base control, ensuring symmetry from side to side	☐	☐	☐
• Air form remaining top lengths using same techniques taking horizontal partings; begin at the center and work to either side	☐	☐	☐
• Adjust base size and brush position to create base lift on heavier side	☐	☐	☐
• Add small amount of silicone gloss for added shine	☐	☐	☐
• Define form and smooth surface	☐	☐	☐

TOTAL POINTS = _____ + _____ + _____

TOTAL POINTS _____ ÷ HIGHEST POSSIBLE SCORE 36 X 100 = _____ %

Record your time in comparison with the suggested salon speed.

To improve my performance on this procedure, I need to:

_____   _____   _____
Student Signature   Educator Signature   Date

STRAIGHT VOLUME AND INDENTATION – AIR FORMING

The "flip" has been a classic design over the years. The indentation can vary from a subtle flick to a more pronounced flip. Altering the amount of indentation can make this design look classic and sophisticated, or youthful and sporty, depending on the length of the hair and the desired result.

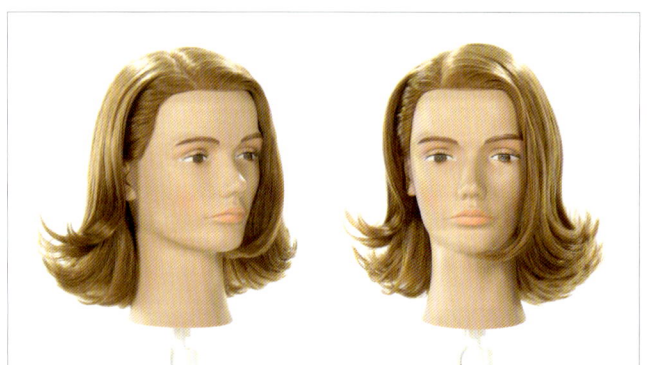

The finish shows volume and indentation achieved by air forming with a round brush to create an expanded form with a soft "flip" effect along the perimeter of this solid form.

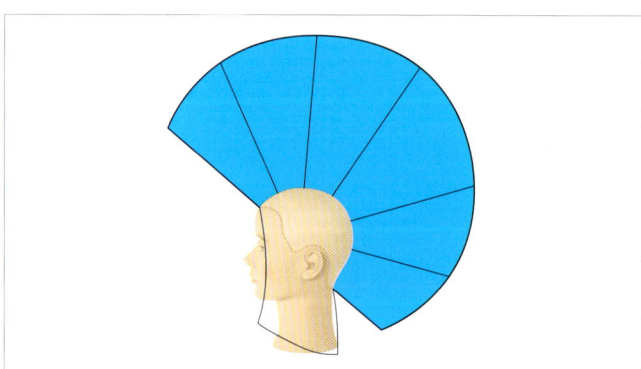

This hair design has been created on a diagonal-back/convex solid form.

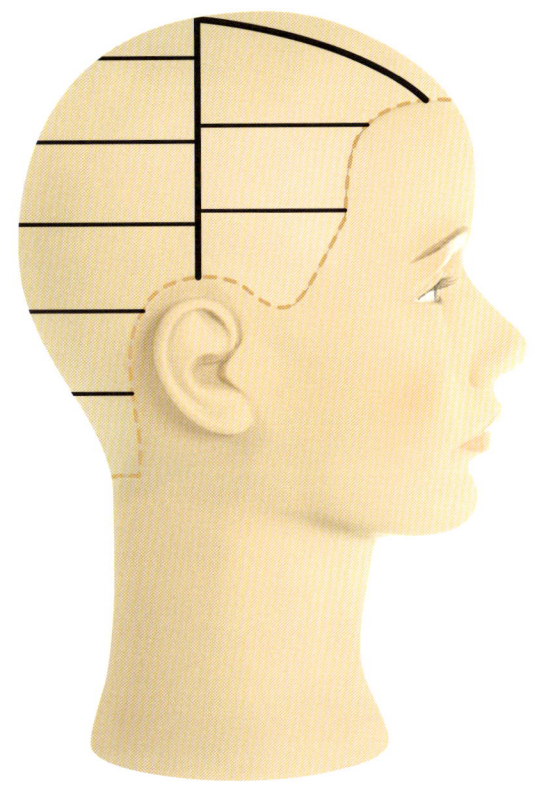
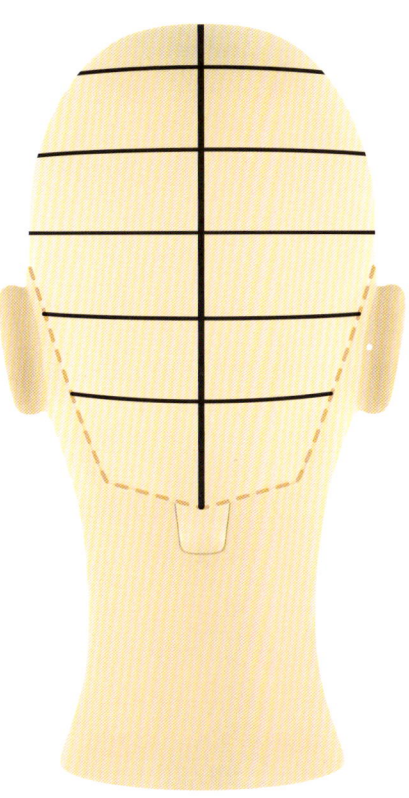

The art shows that the hair is sectioned with a side part from the front hairline to the crown, and then from the crown to the center nape. Then it is sectioned from the crown to the top of each ear. One-diameter (1x) horizontal partings are used throughout the exercise.

01 Apply styling mousse to towel-dried hair to create support and volume.

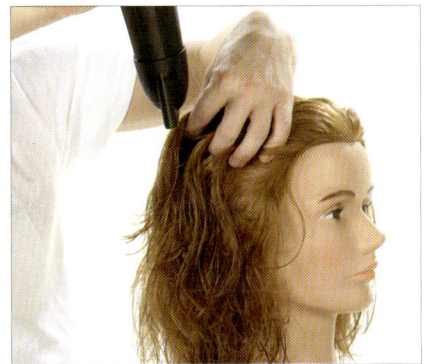

02–03 Air form the hair to remove excess moisture using your fingers. You may work with or without a nozzle on the blow dryer at this point. Then use a paddle brush to continue removing excess moisture while smoothing the hair.

04 The art shows the back and sides are air formed in both volume and indentation.

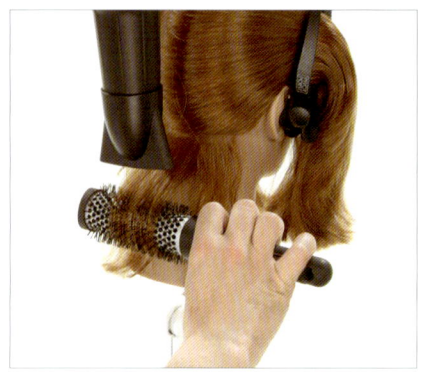

05 Begin at the nape with a medium-diameter round brush. Position the brush under the strand using low projection to create base lift.

06 Then position the brush on top of the strand and roll the ends upward to create indentation. Position the blow dryer below the brush to allow the airflow to follow the direction of the cuticle and to help keep the hair on the brush while air forming.

07 Work from the center to one side, then from the center to the other side to help eliminate splits due to the center sectioning line.

08 Work upward, air forming the base first for volume, then the ends for indentation. Use a small section of the previously air-formed hair to help blend the bases.

09 At the crest, switch to a larger-diameter round brush.

10 Continue to position the brush under the strand to create volume at the base.

11 Then position the brush on top of the strand to create indentation at the ends, directing the airflow from below.

12 Air form the crown for volume. Project the hair according to the volume desired.

13 Position a self-adhering roller half-off base to reinforce the shape as the hair cools. Note that the diameter of the roller corresponds to the diameter of the round brush.

  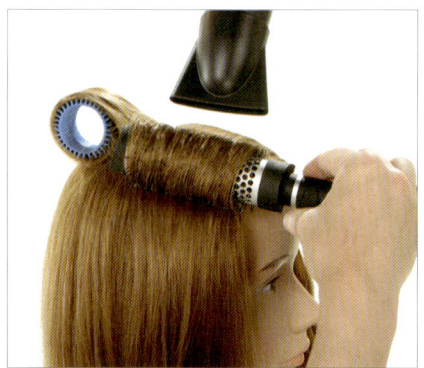

14–15 Move to the lighter side. Air form volume for base lift. Then turn each section upward to create indentation. Watch the height of the flipped texture and adjust how far you roll the brush upward so that the side blends to the back.

16 When you reach the last section, air form for volume only.

17 Then subdivide the hair and position self-adhering rollers, using half-off base control.

18 On the heavier side, continue to air form for both volume and indentation. Air form to create an equal amount of indentation on both sides.

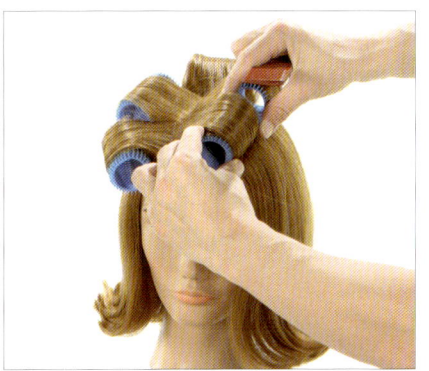

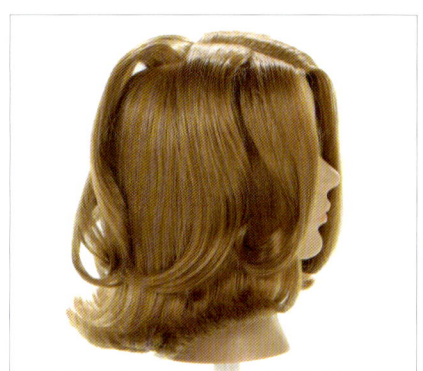

19–20 Subdivide the last section and air form for volume only. Position self-adhering rollers half-off base. You may apply additional heat with the blow dryer to strengthen the curl. After heat is applied, allow the hair to cool on the rollers.

21 Remove the rollers and relax the hair with a large wide-tooth comb starting at the crown working forward.

22 To create additional volume you may choose to backcomb in the interior, blending bases as you work through the area that was set on rollers.

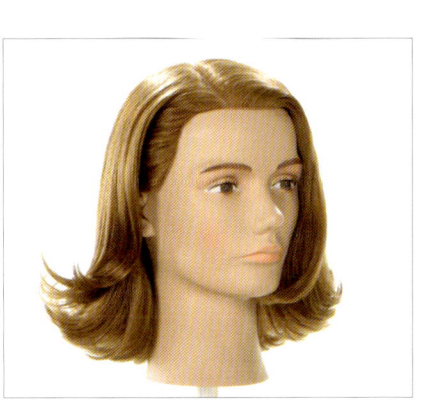

23–24 The finished hair design shows fullness through the top of the design with indentation along the perimeter.

STRAIGHT VOLUME AND INDENTATION – AIR FORMING

Draw or fill in the boxes with the appropriate answers.

STRUCTURE

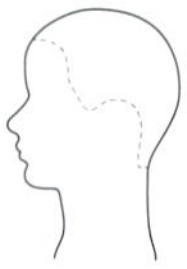

FORM/TEXTURE

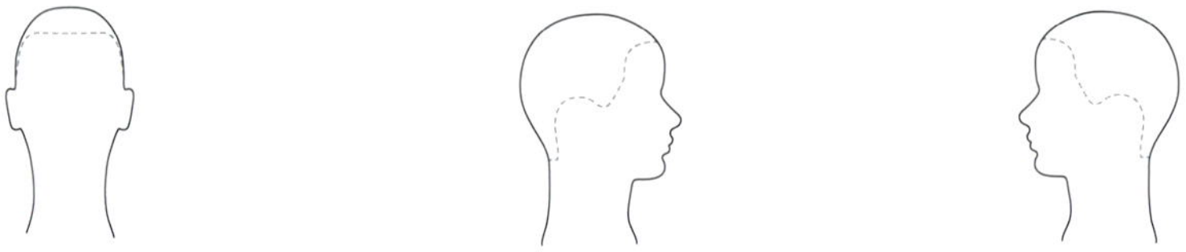

DIRECTION

AIR-FORMING/SETTING

COMB-OUT/FINISH

☐ RELAX   ☐ DRY MOLD   ☐ BACKCOMB/BACKBRUSH   ☐ DEFINE THE FORM   ☐ DETAIL

TOOLS/PRODUCT CHOICE

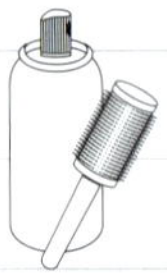

_____   _____
Educator Signature   *Date*

HAIR DESIGN RUBRIC *WORKSHOP 02*

STRAIGHT VOLUME AND INDENTATION – AIR FORMING

This rubric is a performance assessment tool designed to measure your ability to ***create*** *Pivot Point hair designs.*

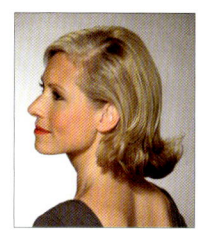

	LEVEL 1 *in progress*	LEVEL 2 *getting better*	LEVEL 3 *entry-level proficiency*
PREPARATION			
• Assemble hair design essentials	☐	☐	☐
CREATE			
• Shampoo, condition and apply styling mousse to towel-dried hair	☐	☐	☐
• Section side part from front hairline to the crown and subdivide back from crown to center nape	☐	☐	☐
• Air form beginning at nape with horizontal partings; position medium-diameter round brush under strand, creating base lift, and then on top of strand, rolling ends upward creating volume at base and indentation at ends	☐	☐	☐
• At the crest, air form using larger-diameter round brush and dry in indentation, working up back of head from center to either side	☐	☐	☐
• Air form for volume at crown, projecting hair according to desired volume	☐	☐	☐
• Position a large self-adhering roller at crown using approximately half-off base control, reinforcing shape as hair cools	☐	☐	☐
• Air form sides creating base lift and then indentation with round brush	☐	☐	☐
• Blend into back flip, adjusting how far brush is rolled upward	☐	☐	☐
• Air form at top for volume only with round brush	☐	☐	☐
• Subdivide hair and position self-adhering rollers on lighter side of part with half-off base control	☐	☐	☐
• Air form heavier side for volume and indentation with round brush	☐	☐	☐
• Subdivide last section and air form volume; position self-adhering roller half-off base, applying heat if needed	☐	☐	☐
• Remove rollers and relax hair	☐	☐	☐
• Backcomb connecting each section; work through set area	☐	☐	☐

TOTAL POINTS = _____ + _____ + _____

TOTAL POINTS _____ ÷ HIGHEST POSSIBLE SCORE 45 X 100= _____ %

Record your time in comparison with the suggested salon speed.

To improve my performance on this procedure, I need to:

Student Signature

Educator Signature

Date

2.3 GRADUATED FORM

Often clients will ask for volume in specific areas, which can be achieved when graduated forms are combined with the appropriate setting and finishing techniques. With the large variety of styling tools and products, graduated finishes can take on an array of looks, which makes designing them even more exciting. After exploring a few samples of design possibilities for the graduated form, it will be your turn to learn about and create some of the standard designs for this form.

GRADUATED FORM DESIGNING

When it comes to wet or thermal designing on a graduated form, the options are as versatile as the graduated sculpture itself. Depending on the line of inclination, the graduated sculpture features volume and expansion that can be created above the perimeter or even in the interior.

FORM OPTIONS
Graduated forms have a weight area that creates a natural expansion above the perimeter form line.

The shape of graduated forms varies but generally expands upward, creating a variety of effects ranging from width at the sides to expansion overall, to height within the design, just to name a few.

  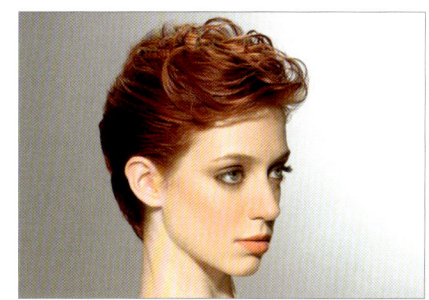

TEXTURE OPTIONS

The textural contrast between an unactivated interior and activated exterior is most visible when graduated forms are finished in a smooth and sleek fashion. Other texture options, such as curls, can result in beautiful texture along the strand and make the textural contrast that is inherent to the graduated sculpture less obvious.

Straight, unactivated finishes best showcase where the two textures of the graduated form meet.

Subtle waves can be reminiscent of a specific era.

Curls can lend texture to soften the otherwise angular appearance of the graduated form.

DIRECTION OPTIONS

The interior lengths of the graduated form determine the possible direction of the design. For example, with longer interior lengths the design needs to be worn with a distinct part, and shorter interior lengths give the option to wear the hair away from or toward the face.

CENTER PART

SIDE PART

AWAY FROM THE FACE

TOWARD THE FACE

CURVATURE AND STRAIGHT VOLUME – ROLLERS AND PINCURLS

Curvature and straight volume combine with the diagonal-forward graduated form to create a classic design with fluid movements.

The finish shows a voluminous shape with structured, curved lines that flow into activated perimeter end texture.

The complete roller and pincurl set features a counterclockwise half-circle at the front, expanded circles at the sides and a bricklay pattern in the back. Notice that the set progresses from the large-diameter rollers at the top, to medium-diameter rollers in the back and small-diameter rollers and pincurls at the sides and in the nape area.

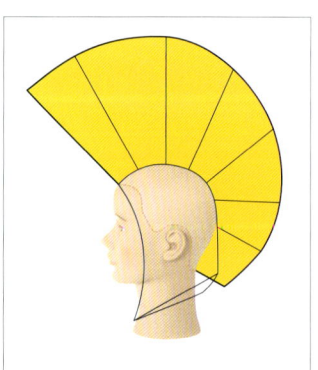

The structure graphic shows the diagonal-forward graduated form used for this roller and pincurl design.

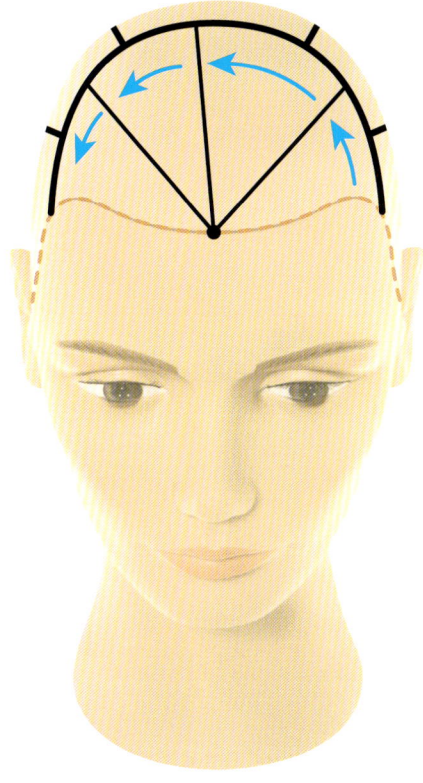 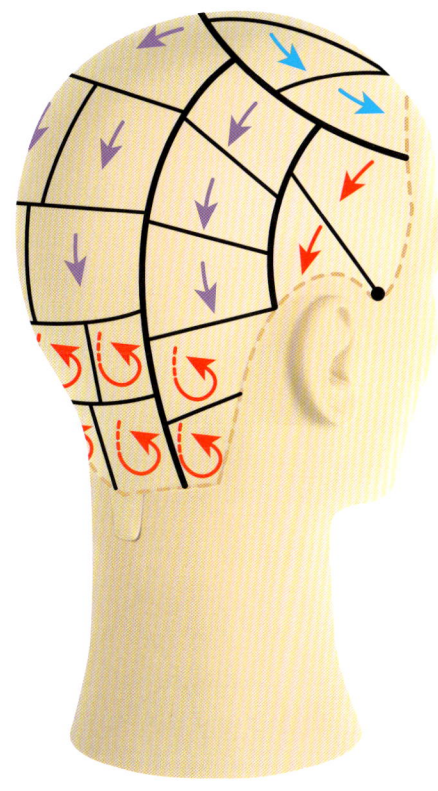

The art shows a counterclockwise half-circle in the fringe area set with large-diameter rollers.

The expanded circles on the sides progress from small-diameter rollers in the inner circle to medium-diameter rollers in the outer circle. The bricklay pattern in the back is set with medium-diameter rollers, and small pincurls are used in the nape area to accommodate the short lengths.

 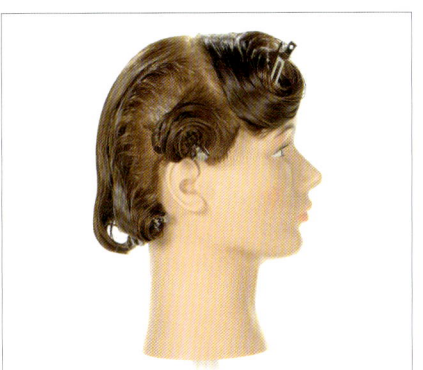 

01 Apply styling gel evenly through clean, wet hair. Distribute, mold and scale a counterclockwise half-circle with the point of origin at the center front hairline. Secure the ends in a flat, circular shape.

02 Distribute, mold and scale an expanded circle on the right side. Secure the ends and repeat the same techniques on the left side.

03 In the back, mold the remaining lengths straight down and secure under.

Refer to DVD for more information on molding and scaling the expanded circle.

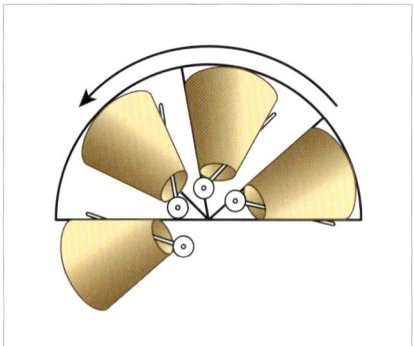

04 The art shows the half-circle set with one diameter (1x) on base, 1½x underdirected, 1x half-off and 1x off-base control. Position each roller parallel to its parting and 1x away from the point of origin.

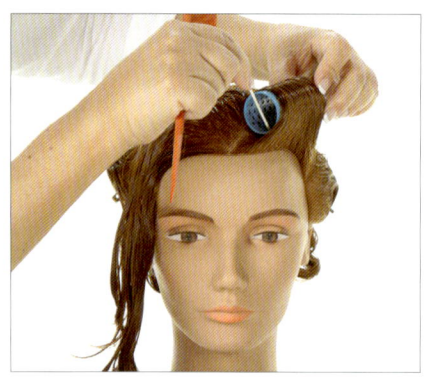

05 Part and apply the first large-diameter cone-shaped roller using 1x on-base control and secure through the small end of the roller. Then part and apply the second roller with 1½x underdirected base control.

06 Next, part and apply the third roller with 1x half-off base control and the final roller with 1x off-base control.

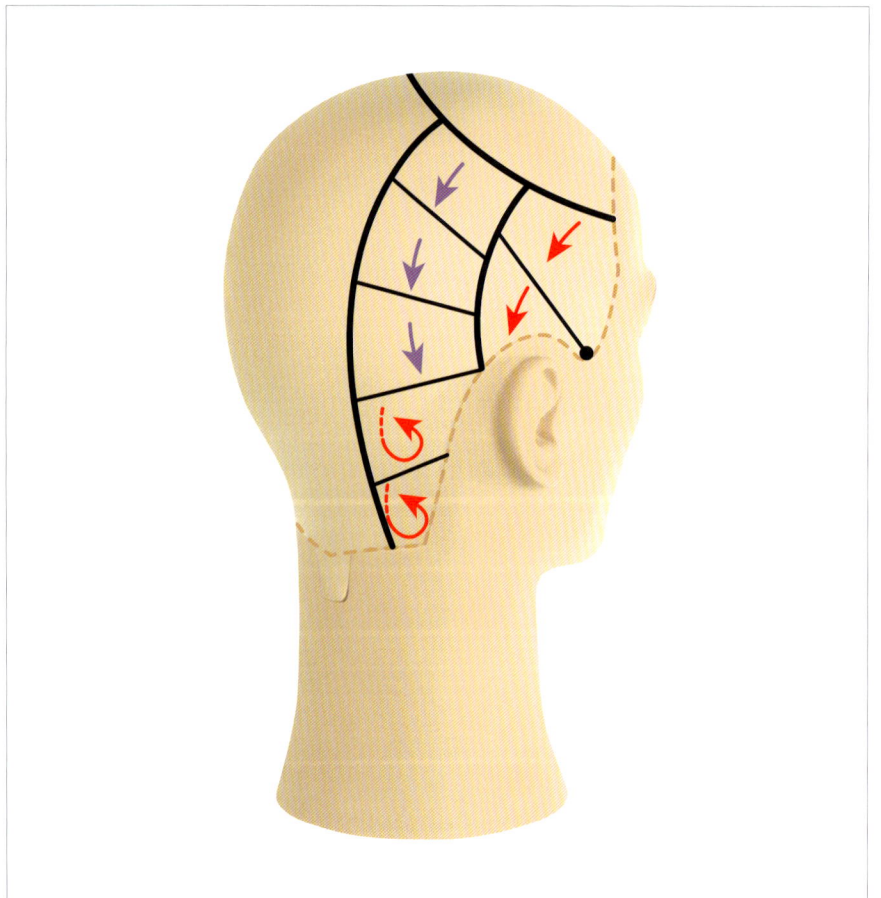

07 The inner circle has triangle-shaped bases while the outer circle has trapezoid-shaped bases created from the same point of origin. The inner circle rollers are positioned 1x away from the point of origin and the trapezoid-shaped bases are equal to the length of the roller. All rollers are positioned parallel to the parting.

08 Beginning at the inner circle on one side, part and apply the first small-diameter conical roller with 1x half-off base control.

09 Apply the second roller of the inner circle using the same technique.

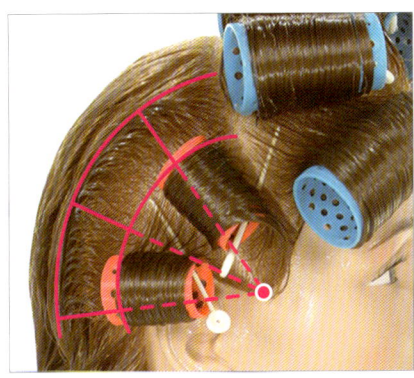

10 Use the inner circle's point of origin to create the trapezoid-shaped bases of the outer circle.

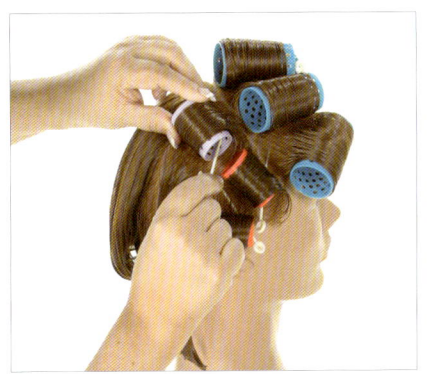

11 The outer circle is set on medium-diameter conical rollers using 1x half-off base control.

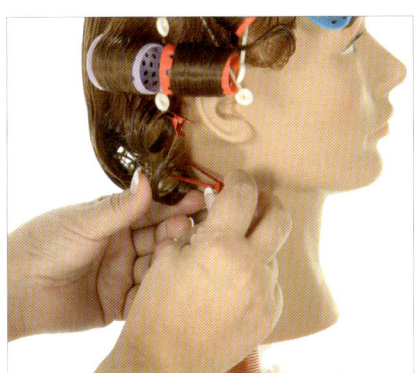

12 Set the last two partings with volume pincurls.

13 Observe the expanded circle roller and pincurl portion of the set.

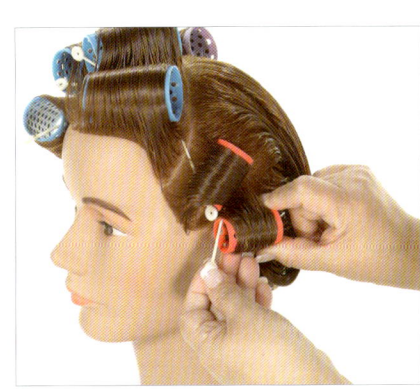

14 Move to the other side and set the inner circle with the small-diameter conical rollers using 1x half-off base control.

15 Then set the outer circle with medium-diameter conical rollers and use 1x half-off base control. Complete the outer circle with pincurls.

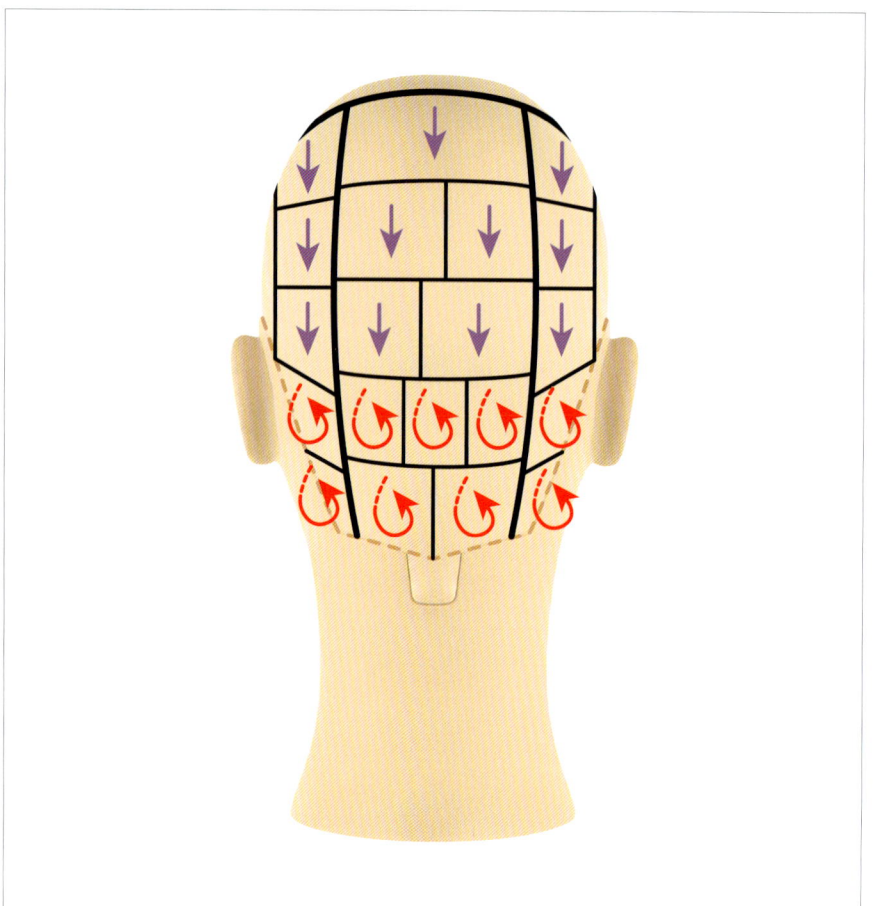

16 The art shows how the bricklay pattern is used to fill the remaining section in the back. Medium-diameter cylindrical rollers will be used with a progression to small pincurls in the nape area.

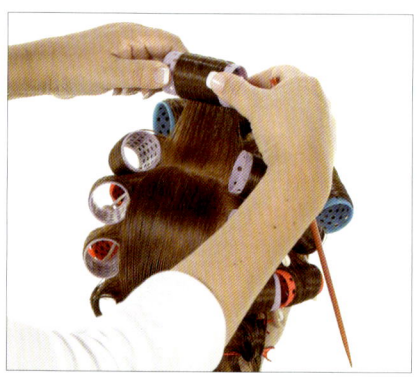

17 Begin at the top of the back section using the one-two bricklay method. Part and apply the first medium-diameter roller with 1x on-base control.

18 Position the roller within its base and secure.

19 Part and apply the next row using 1x on-base control and two shorter rollers.

20 In the third row, use 1x half-off base control. Adapt the roller lengths to fit the area and stagger the base partings.

21 The roller set portion of the design is complete. The last two rows will be set with volume pincurls.

22 Continue to use the bricklay pattern with 1x half-off base control to set three volume pincurls across the next row. The diameter corresponds to the small-diameter roller.

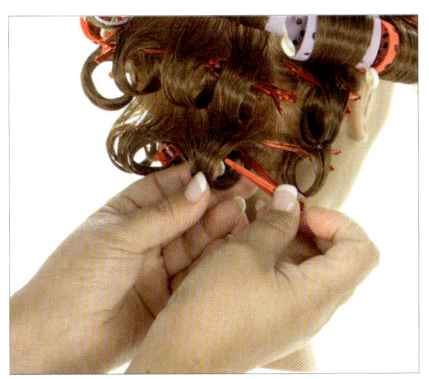

23 Complete the last row. Continue to stagger the bases to avoid splits.

24 The completed set features curvature volume in the front and on each side with straight volume in the back.

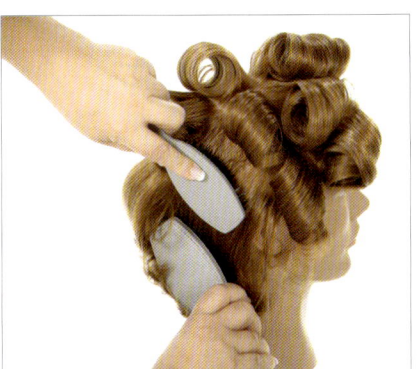

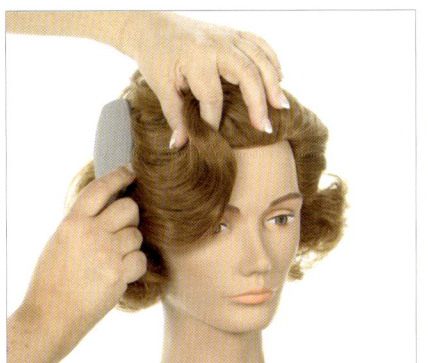

25–26 After the hair has dried and cooled, relax the set with two cushion brushes, working upward from the nape to the sides and then the top. Then, dry mold by retracing the design directions.

 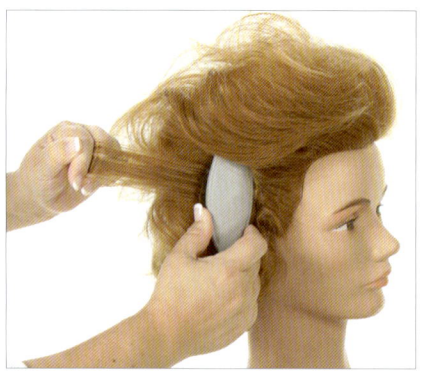 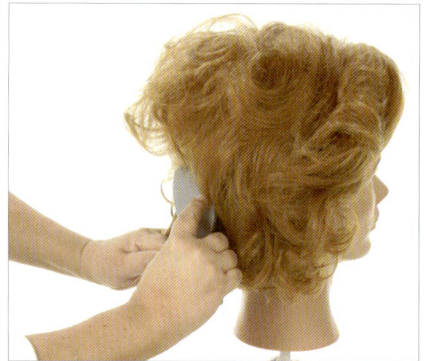

27–28 Use a one-stroke technique and begin backbrushing the half-circle, following the direction in which it was set. Then smooth the top surface. Use the same technique to backbrush the expanded circle in the direction of the set on either side.

29 Continue to the back using the one-stroke backbrushing technique throughout the design.

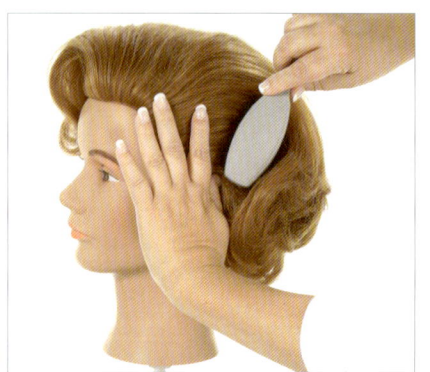

30 Define the form by following the pattern that was set and smooth the surface. Then, use a wide-tooth comb to add surface texture and definition.

31–32 The finish shows curvature volume half-off the face and half toward the face, blending to straight volume in the back, with perimeter texture creating this classic style.

DESIGN DECISIONS *WORKSHOP 03*
CURVATURE AND STRAIGHT VOLUME – ROLLERS AND PINCURLS

Draw or fill in the boxes with the appropriate answers.

STRUCTURE

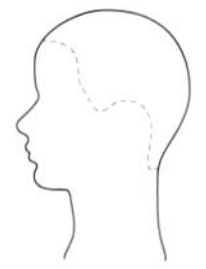

FORM/TEXTURE

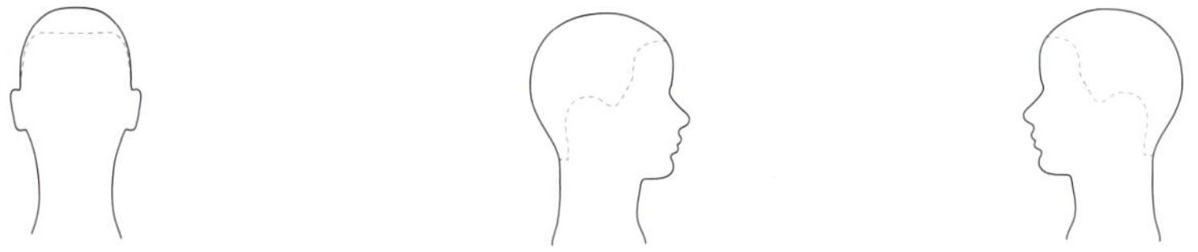

DIRECTION

MOLDING/SCALING

SETTING PATTERN

COMB-OUT/FINISH

☐ RELAX

☐ DRY MOLD

☐ BACKCOMB/BACKBRUSH

☐ DEFINE THE FORM

☐ DETAIL

TOOLS/PRODUCT CHOICE

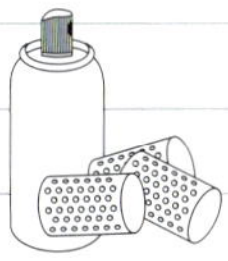

Educator Signature

Date

HAIR DESIGN RUBRIC *WORKSHOP 03*

CURVATURE AND STRAIGHT VOLUME – ROLLERS AND PINCURLS

This rubric is a performance assessment tool designed to measure your ability to *create* Pivot Point hair designs.

	LEVEL 1 *in progress*	LEVEL 2 *getting better*	LEVEL 3 *entry-level proficiency*
PREPARATION			
• Assemble hair design essentials	☐	☐	☐
CREATE			
• Shampoo, condition and apply styling gel evenly through hair	☐	☐	☐
• Distribute, mold and scale a counterclockwise half-circle at front hairline; secure in a flat, circular shape	☐	☐	☐
• Distribute, mold and scale expanded circles on both sides	☐	☐	☐
• Mold remaining back lengths straight down and secure under	☐	☐	☐
• Part from point of origin and apply 4 large-diameter conical rollers parallel to partings within half-circle; set with 1x on-base, 1½x underdirected, 1x half-off and 1x off-base control	☐	☐	☐
• Part from point of origin and apply small-diameter conical rollers parallel to parting within inner circle with 1x half-off base control on one side	☐	☐	☐
• Part from same point of origin and apply medium-diameter conical rollers in outer circle using 1x half-off base control	☐	☐	☐
• Place 1x half-off base volume pincurls in last 2 partings of outer circle	☐	☐	☐
• Repeat the same technique on other side	☐	☐	☐
• Set remaining straight shape in bricklay pattern using medium-diameter cylindrical rollers with 1x on-base control for first 2 rows, 1x half-off base control for next row and pincurls set with half-off base control in nape	☐	☐	☐
• Relax set using cushion brushes	☐	☐	☐
• Dry mold entire set, retracing directions within design	☐	☐	☐
• Backbrush using a one-stroke technique following direction of set; begin at half-circle, then move to sides and back	☐	☐	☐
• Define form following set pattern, and smooth surface using a brush	☐	☐	☐
• Detail and smooth surface using large-tooth comb	☐	☐	☐

TOTAL POINTS = _____ + _____ + _____

TOTAL POINTS _____ ÷ HIGHEST POSSIBLE SCORE 48 X 100 = _____ %

Record your time in comparison with the suggested salon speed. _____

To improve my performance on this procedure, I need to: _____

_____ _____ _____
Student Signature   *Educator Signature*   *Date*

WORKSHOP 04
CURVATURE VOLUME AND INDENTATION – AIR FORMING

This classic graduated form is coupled with off-the-face curved movement, creating a wave pattern that blends to a smooth nape. This classic style creates expansion above the crest and will complement a variety of facial shapes.

The finish shows smooth movements and maximum expansion. Combining volume and indentation air-forming techniques creates soft movement and textural interest in the fringe.

A more textured finish shows slightly less expansion.

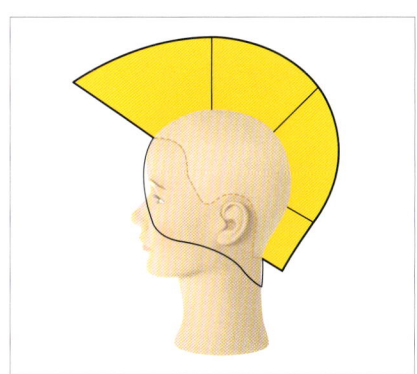

The structure graphic shows the graduated form this design is created on.

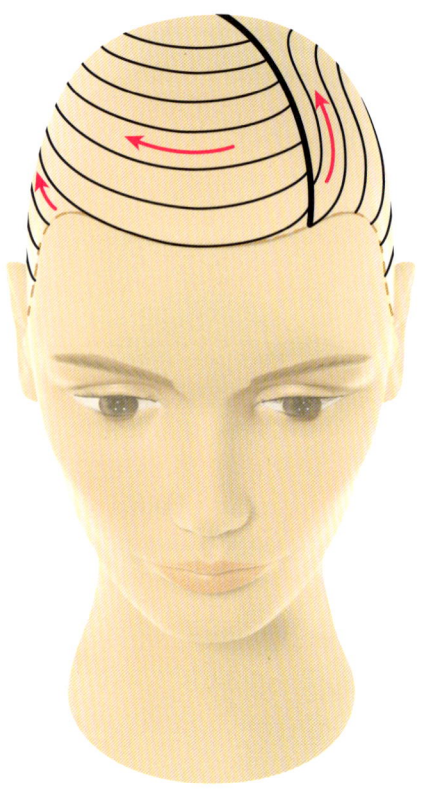 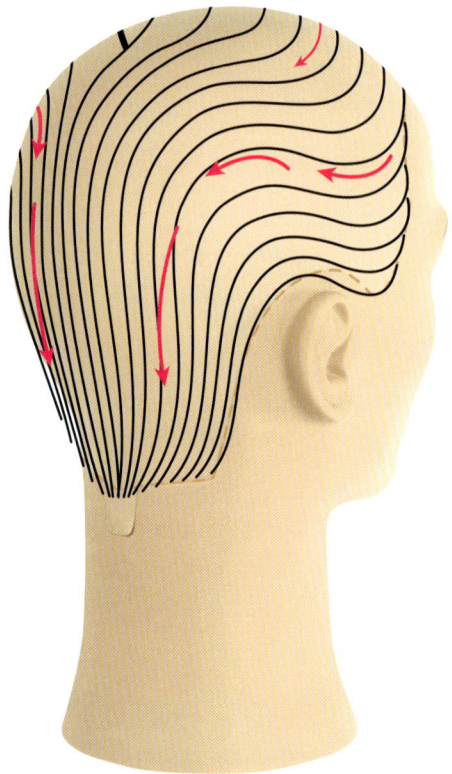

The art shows the various directions within this design. Note how the sides curve from the front hairline to the center nape, following along the shape of the hairline. The top moves in curved lines from a side part.

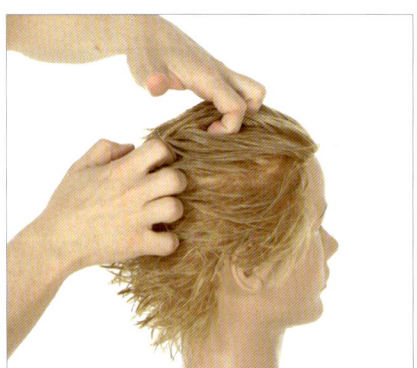 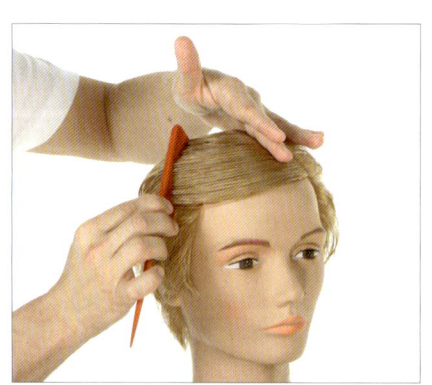 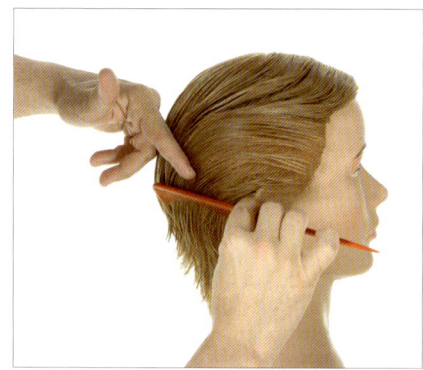

01 Apply a styling cream to clean, wet hair by rubbing it between your hands and raking it through the hair with your fingers. Comb through to distribute it evenly.

02 Part on the side from the center of the eye to the center of the crown. Mold the hair on the heavier side of the part with curved, parallel distribution that blends into the sides.

03 Mold the sides using curved, parallel distribution from the front hairline, curving around the ear and into the nape.

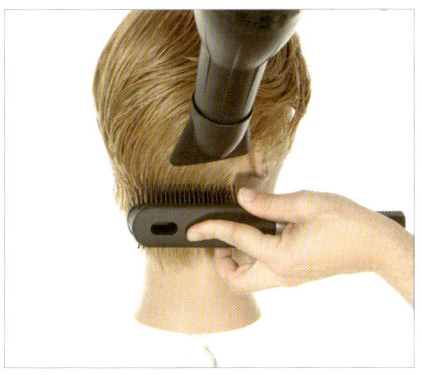

04–05 Air form, beginning in the nape with a 9-row brush, following the molding direction and directing the airflow from base to ends using the concentrator for control. Air form for closeness on both sides of the nape using the same technique.

06 Move to the sideburn and temple area on the heavier side and air form following the molded direction. Direct the hair back, blending into the nape.

07 Then air form the same area to create subtle volume, using the 9-row brush and horizontal partings.

08 Move to the opposite side and repeat the same techniques. First air form to reinforce the molded direction, then use horizontal partings to create subtle volume.

09 In the back crest area, section a rectangle shape and secure the lengths up. Air form the hair right below the secured area using the 9-row brush to lift the hair from the base.

10 Then, direct the ends of the hair toward the center to blend into the previously air-formed areas.

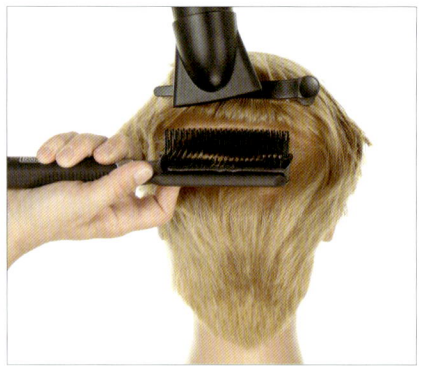

11 Release a horizontal parting and use the same techniques with the 9-row brush.

12 Then use a medium-diameter round brush with half-off base control to increase volume and add end texture above the crest. Begin in the center of the parting and move to one side, incorporating a portion of the previous base to avoid splits.

13 You may choose to switch hands, which may allow you to more easily create the desired effect with less physical strain.

14 Work upward through the crown area. First use the 9-row brush to create base lift. Then use the medium-diameter round brush with half-off base control to create volume with curved end texture.

15 As you work from the crown to the apex area, use the round brush with on-base control to increase volume.

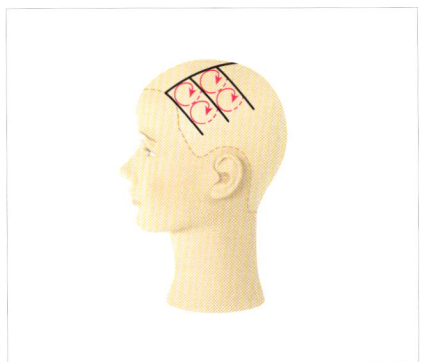

16 The art shows the diagonal-back partings and the indentation technique used, and the direction in which the hair is styled on the lighter side.

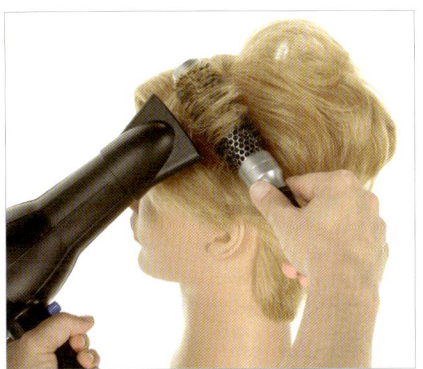

17 Move to the lighter side of the interior and direct the lengths back with the medium-diameter round brush and diagonal-back partings.

18 Work from above the ear toward the front hairline of this section using the same technique.

19 Blend the lighter side into the crown area and back by gliding your fingers through the hair while directing the airflow from the front hairline toward the back.

20 At the top, begin at the hairline using the 9-row brush and horizontal partings. Use the brush to lift the lengths up and dry the base, working from the fringe toward the apex area.

21 Then release a vertical parting and project the lengths at 90° using the medium-diameter round brush with on-base control along the side part to create volume.

22 Next, use the round brush with diagonal-back partings and the indentation technique to create movement that curves from the sides toward the crown. Start near the apex and work toward the front hairline.

23 As you air form each parting, incorporate a small portion of the exterior to blend.

24 Continue using the same techniques until you reach the front hairline.

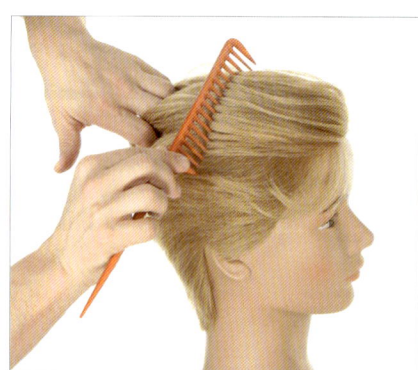

25 Using the wide-tooth tail comb and your fingers, direct the hair back following the molded directions and blending the sections.

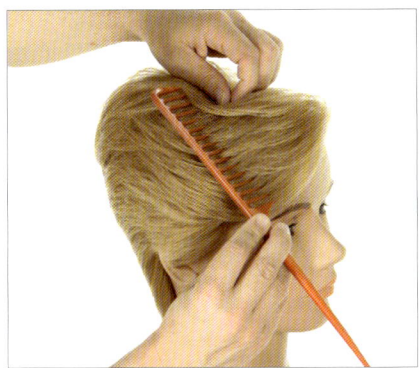

26 Push the hair toward the face, creating volume at the hairline, and continue to detail the texture as desired. Note that you may use hairspray as needed or desired.

27 To create a variation of this style, use styling pomade and rub the product between your hands. Then, glide your fingers through the hair following the directional pattern of the design.

28 Detail the design as desired using your fingers.

30 The finish shows more texture detail with slightly less expansion.

29 A smooth nape with expansion above the crest area and a textured wave in the fringe is the result of combining volume and indentation air-forming techniques on this graduated form.

CURVATURE VOLUME AND INDENTATION – AIR FORMING

Draw or fill in the boxes with the appropriate answers.

STRUCTURE

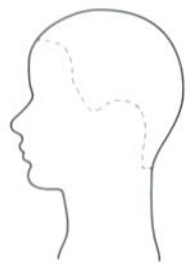

FORM/TEXTURE

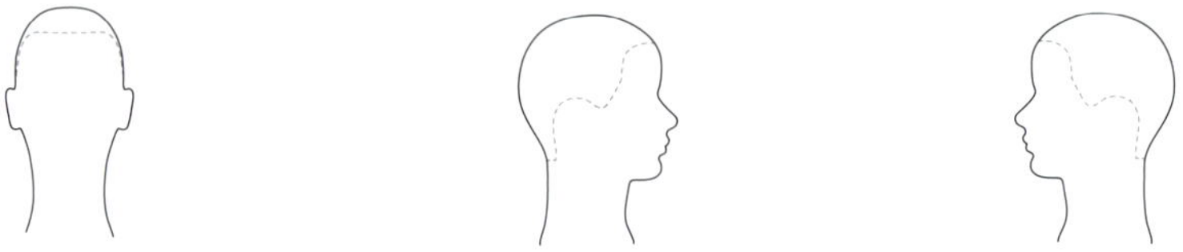

DIRECTION

AIR-FORMING PATTERN

STRUCTURE

COMB-OUT/FINISH

- ☐ RELAX
- ☐ DRY MOLD
- ☐ BACKCOMB/BACKBRUSH
- ☐ DEFINE THE FORM
- ☐ DETAIL

TOOLS/PRODUCT CHOICE

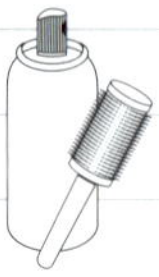

_____
Educator Signature

Date

HAIR DESIGN RUBRIC *WORKSHOP 04*

CURVATURE VOLUME AND INDENTATION – AIR FORMING

This rubric is a performance assessment tool designed to measure your ability to *create* Pivot Point hair designs.

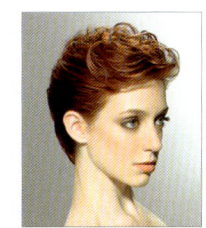

	LEVEL 1 *in progress*	LEVEL 2 *getting better*	LEVEL 3 *entry-level proficiency*
PREPARATION			
• Assemble hair design essentials	☐	☐	☐
CREATE			
• Apply styling cream to clean, wet hair; distribute evenly	☐	☐	☐
• Mold top from side part with curved, parallel distribution, and mold sides with curved, parallel distribution from front hairline to nape	☐	☐	☐
• Air form for closeness at nape with 9-row brush following molded pattern	☐	☐	☐
• Air form heavier side at sideburn and temple area, first following molded direction using the 9-row brush; then use horizontal partings and the 9-row brush to create subtle volume	☐	☐	☐
• Repeat techniques on opposite side	☐	☐	☐
• Section rectangle shape in back crest area and secure lengths up	☐	☐	☐
• Air form horizontal parting under secured area with 9-row brush to lift hair from base	☐	☐	☐
• Direct ends of hair toward center to blend into previously air-formed areas	☐	☐	☐
• Release a horizontal parting; air form using 9-row brush to create subtle base lift; direct ends toward center to blend	☐	☐	☐
• Release another parting and repeat same techniques	☐	☐	☐
• Air form using medium-diameter round brush and half-off base control to increase volume and add end texture; air form at center then move to one side, incorporating a portion of previous base; repeat on other side	☐	☐	☐
• Air form throughout rectangle shape at crown, first using the 9-row brush with horizontal partings lifting base; then use a round brush to create volume and curved end texture	☐	☐	☐

CURVATURE VOLUME AND INDENTATION – AIR FORMING

	LEVEL 1 *in progress*	LEVEL 2 *getting better*	LEVEL 3 *entry-level proficiency*
• Incorporate part of previous base to avoid splits	☐	☐	☐
• Continue using same techniques, working upward to crown area	☐	☐	☐
• Air form with on-base control as you work from crown toward apex area to increase volume	☐	☐	☐
• Air form using diagonal-back partings and medium-diameter round brush, working from above ear to front hairline on lighter side; then glide fingers through hair while directing airflow from front hairline toward back to blend	☐	☐	☐
• Air form at top, beginning at hairline working toward apex; use horizontal partings and 9-row brush to lift and dry base	☐	☐	☐
• Air form vertical parting adjacent to side part with medium-diameter round brush to create volume	☐	☐	☐
• Air form heavy side using round brush with diagonal-back partings and indentation technique; incorporate small portion of exterior with each parting to blend; work from apex area to hairline	☐	☐	☐
• Distribute hair back following molded directions with fingers and wide-tooth comb; push hair toward face in fringe area to create volume; detail as desired	☐	☐	☐

COMB-OUT VARIATION:

• Distribute styling pomade evenly through hair with hands following the design's directional pattern	☐	☐	☐
• Detail using fingers as desired	☐	☐	☐

TOTAL POINTS = _____ + _____ + _____

TOTAL POINTS _____ ÷ HIGHEST POSSIBLE SCORE 63 X 100 = _____ %

÷ HIGHEST POSSIBLE SCORE/VARIATION 69 X 100 = _____ %

Record your time in comparison with the suggested salon speed.

To improve my performance on this procedure, I need to:

Student Signature   *Educator Signature*   *Date*

WORKSHOP 05

STRAIGHT VOLUME AND INDENTATION – PRESS AND CURL

Pressing and curling is a way to temporarily straighten tightly curled hair for clients who want to avoid chemical straightening. Once the hair has been pressed straight, it can be curled with marcel irons in any design desired.

A refined look that features added support and volume in the interior and sides and soft, modern indentation at the nape is achieved.

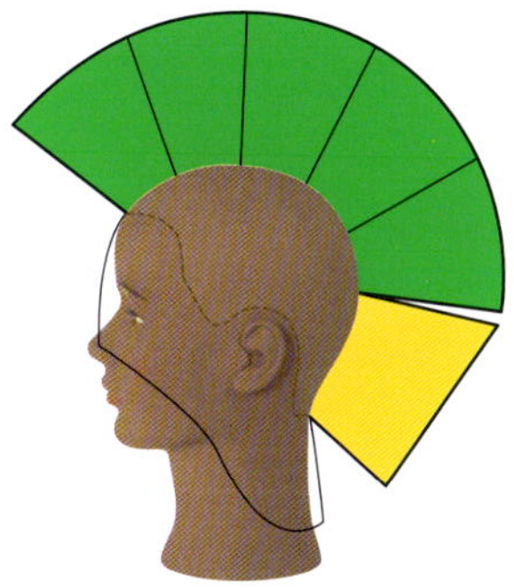

This design will be performed on tightly curled hair with graduated exterior and crest lengths and some uniform layers in the interior.

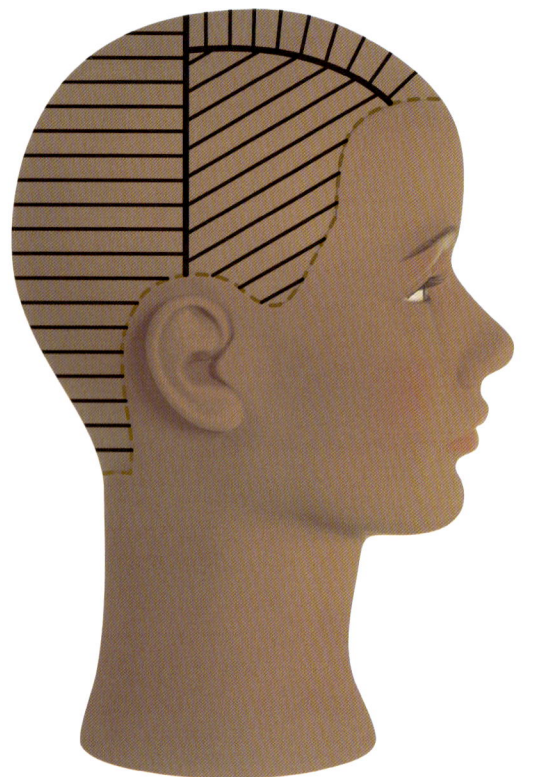
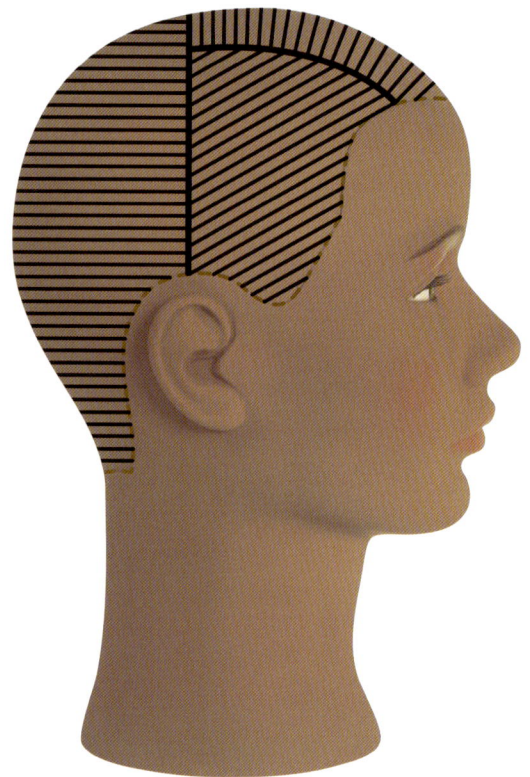

The art shows that the head will be sectioned in five sections to perform the air forming and pressing portion of the service. Horizontal partings will be used in the back and top sections. Diagonal-back partings will be used on the sides. For initial air forming, ½" (1.25 cm) partings will be used, while ¼" (.6 cm) partings will be used to press the hair.

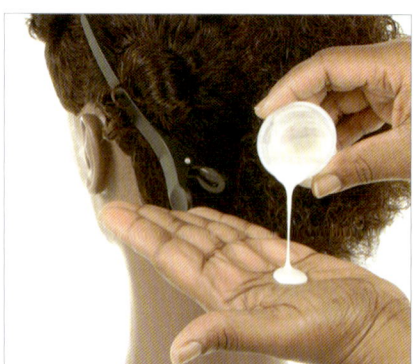
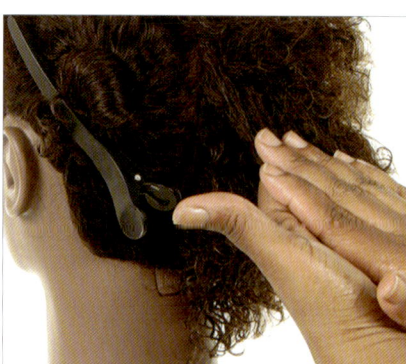
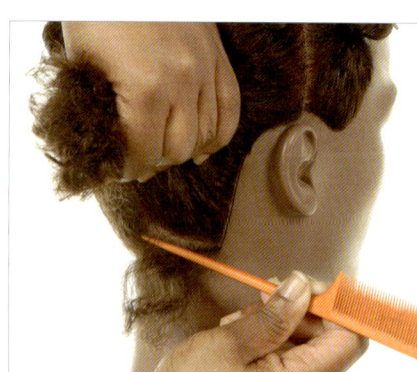

01–02 Section the head and begin in the right back section by applying pressing cream or oil to freshly shampooed, damp hair. Distribute the cream evenly in your hands and apply it from base to ends. Work from the bottom hairline to the top of the head. For better control, subsection horizontal partings as you work up the section. Repeat in the remaining sections.

03 Starting in the nape on the right side, use a tail comb to release a ½" (1.25 cm) horizontal parting. Clip the remainder of the hair up and out of the way.

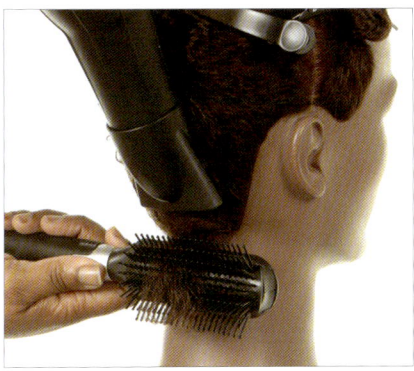 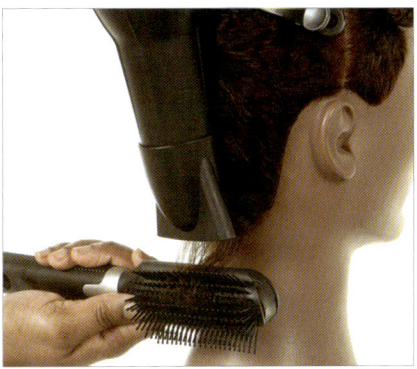

04–05 Air form on the highest heat setting and use a 9-row brush with tension to stretch the hair and reduce the natural curl pattern. Air form from base to midstrand, and then midstrand to ends, maintaining consistent heat and airflow.

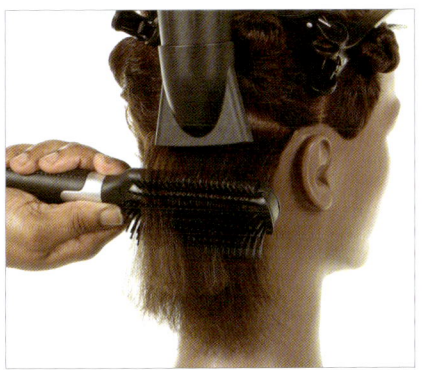 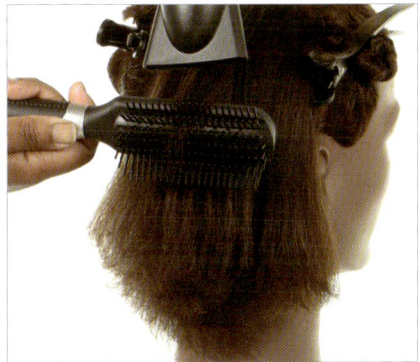

06–07 Continue to air form the hair from base to midstrand and then midstrand to ends taking ½" (1.25 cm) partings for control and removing as much curl as possible. Work to the top of the section and repeat on tho back left section.

  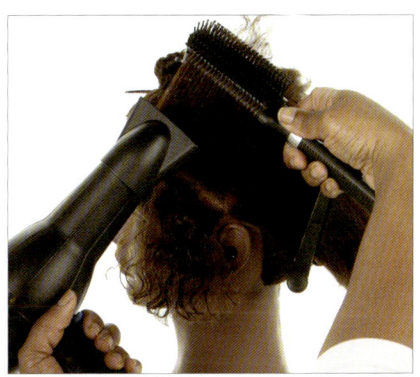

08 Move to the left side and take a ½" (1.25 cm) diagonal-back parting at the top of the section.

09 Air form from base to midstrand and then from midstrand to ends, directing the hair up and away from the face to avoid a split between the back and side sections.

10 Work to the front hairline. Repeat on the opposite side section.

11–12 Move to the top section and begin at the crown, taking horizontal ½" (1.25 cm) partings. Direct the hair back and away from face, drying from the base to the midstrand and then from midstrand to ends. Continue until you reach the front hairline.

13 Prior to applying the pressing comb to the hair, test the temperature on a white paper towel. If the paper stays white, the comb is cool enough to be used.

14 Begin at the nape and release a ¼" (.6 cm) horizontal parting. Insert the teeth of the comb underneath the strand near the base. Control the ends with the opposite hand. Turn the pressing comb and press the hair using the spine as you work from base to ends. Slowly feed the hair through the comb while working toward the ends. Repeat the same technique one more time along the strand.

15 Then insert the teeth on top of the strand near the base. Turn the pressing comb and press the hair using the spine as you work downward, slowly feeding the hair through to the ends. Repeat one more time along the strand.

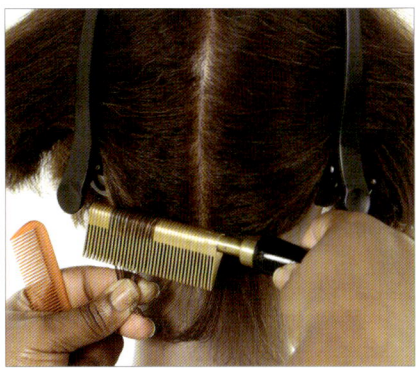 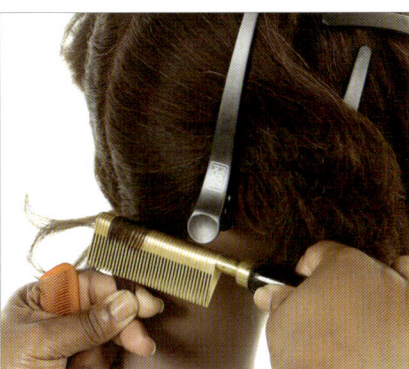

16–17 Continue the pressing technique, working from the center to the left side of the parting. Then work from the center to the right side of the parting.

18–19 Work toward the crown. Begin at the center of each ¼" (.6 cm) parting, working toward the left side and then from the center to the right side. First press each parting upward two times, then press downward two times, using the spine of the pressing comb while holding the ends of the hair with the opposite hand. Continue to slowly feed the hair through the comb as you straighten it from base to ends.

20–21 Release a ¼" (.6 cm) diagonal-back parting at the top of the side section. First press the parting downward two times, then press the parting upward two times.

22 Remember to use the back or spine of the comb for the actual pressing. As partings become wide, subdivide them for better control.

23 Repeat throughout the opposite side section.

24 In the top section, take horizontal partings beginning at the crown. Stand behind the client and press forward two times using the spine of the comb.

25 Then press with the comb backward two times.

26–27 Work toward the front, making sure to reheat the pressing comb when needed.

28 To complete the pressing technique, work around the hairline beginning at the front and working to the nape. Comb and press from the base toward the ends to ensure even straightening.

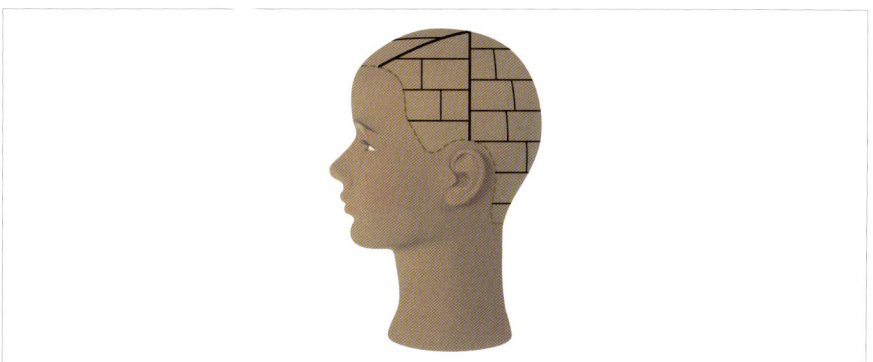

29 The art shows horizontal partings used across the back and sides for the curling portion of this service. The width of a parting is determined by the diameter of the marcel curling iron used. Partings are subdivided when they become wider while working to the top.

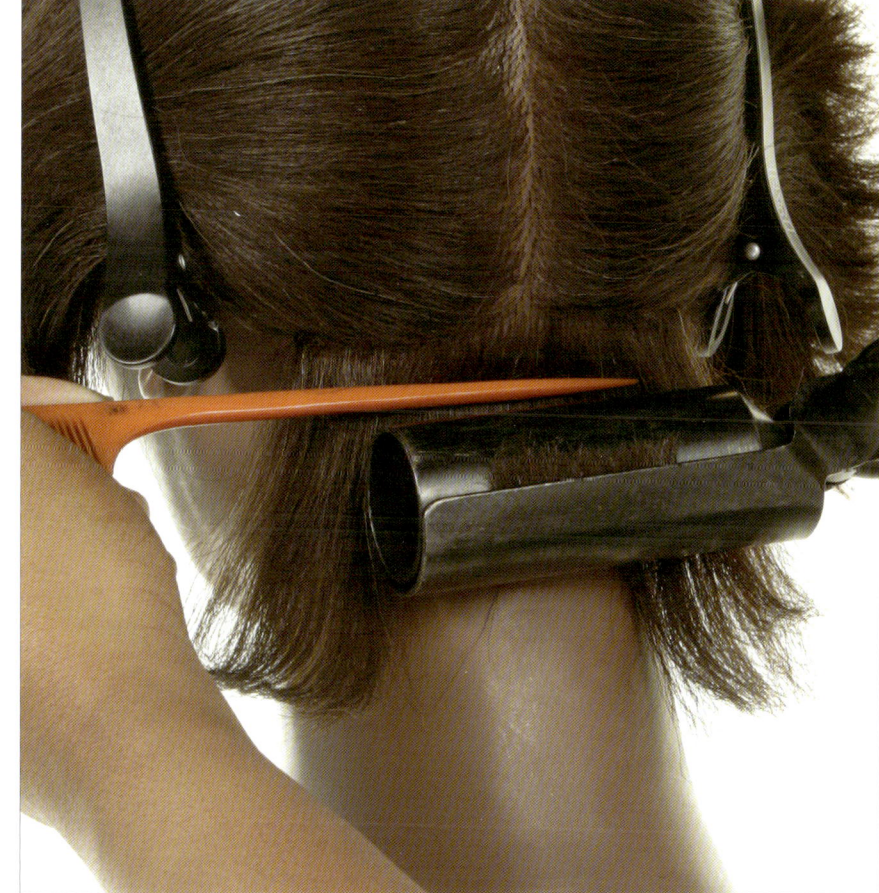

30 Place the marcel curling iron in the heating element. Test the temperature of the marcel curling iron on a white paper towel.

31 Starting at the nape, release a one–diameter (1x) parting, using the marcel curling iron as a guide. Clip the remaining lengths up. Smooth the base by placing the barrel of the curling iron on top of the strand. Then insert the strand between the barrel and the shell of the iron, which is positioned underneath the hair. Turn the iron upward for indentation, while working from midstrand to ends.

32 Continue to create indentation until you reach the crest area.

33–34 At the crest area, position the curling iron so that the shell is on top of the strand. Slide down the strand with tension and turn the curling iron under to create volume with slightly curved end texture. Extend partings to the front hairline until you reach the recession area.

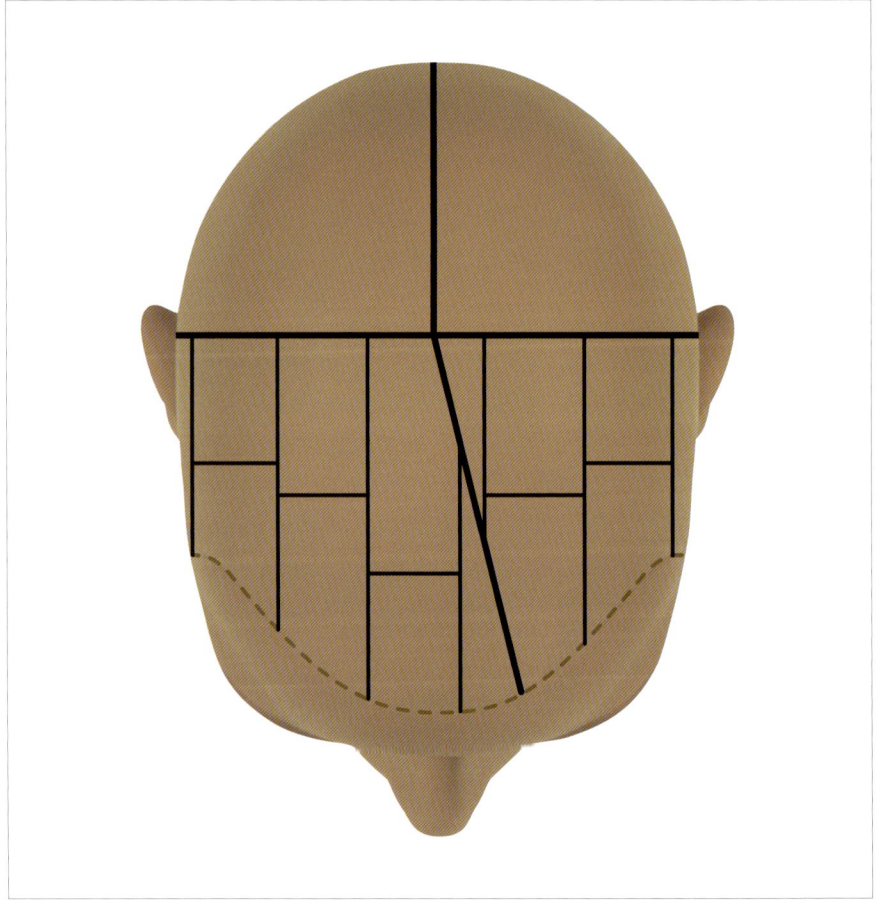

35 Continue toward the top of the head, working from the center back to the left front hairline and then to the front right hairline.

36 The art shows 1x horizontal partings used in the top, which is sectioned with a diagonal side part. A bricklay pattern is used to subdivide partings for control.

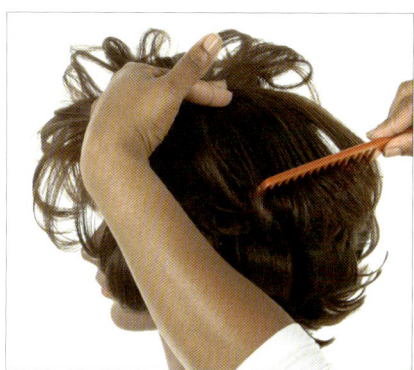

37–38 Adjust the projection angle of the hair to achieve the desired volume throughout the top of the head.

39 Relax the curls with a wide-tooth tail comb to help blend the bases. Backcomb lightly along the surface for added volume and movement.

40 Using the tail of the comb, define and detail the hair as desired.

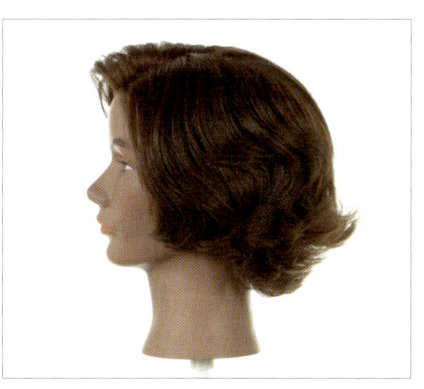

41 The finish shows a feminine shape with volume in the interior and indentation in the exterior. This technique results in a great design on graduated lengths for a modern style.

STRAIGHT VOLUME AND INDENTATION –
PRESS AND CURL

artist⁺
access.

Draw or fill in the boxes with the appropriate answers.

STRUCTURE

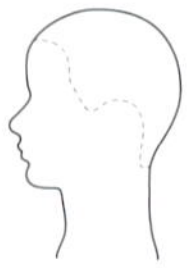

FORM/TEXTURE

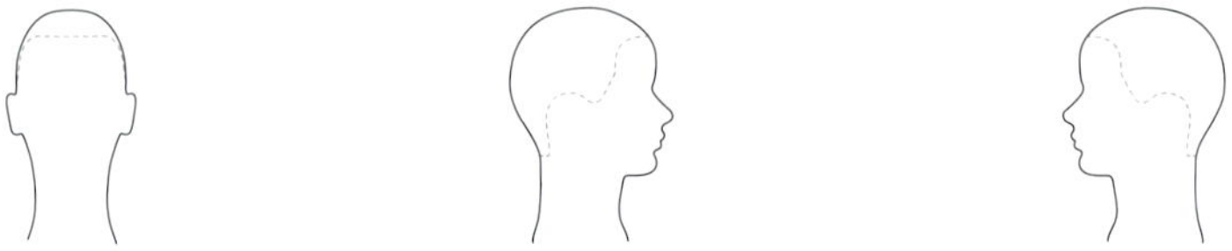

DIRECTION

AIR-FORMING PATTERN

PRESSING PATTERN

CURLING PATTERN

COMB-OUT/FINISH

- [ ] RELAX
- [ ] DRY MOLD
- [ ] BACKCOMB/BACKBRUSH
- [ ] DEFINE THE FORM
- [ ] DETAIL

TOOLS/PRODUCT CHOICE

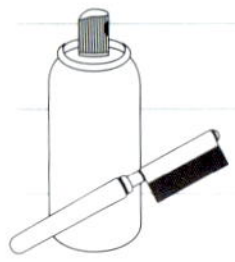

Educator Signature

Date

VARIATION 02
STRAIGHT VOLUME – PRESS AND CURL

In this design variation, a conventional straightening iron, marcel straightening iron and marcel curling iron are used to achieve a modern, silky texture on tightly curled hair. This technique is great for clients who have had a chemical service, since using the straightening iron causes less pressure with lower temperature on the hair.

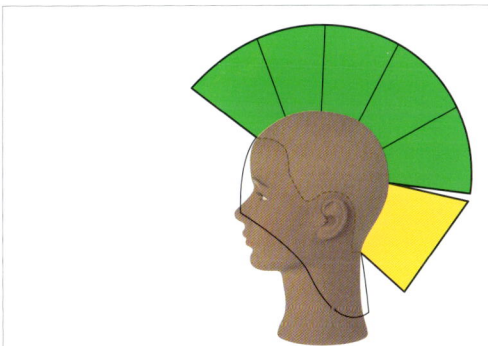

After air forming the shampooed and conditioned lengths to reduce the curl pattern, ¼" (.6 cm) horizontal partings are used to straighten/press the hair. If using a marcel straightening iron, test the heat of the iron on a white paper towel. Place the iron at the base of the parting and smooth the hair using moderate pressure. Place a tail comb at the base, then follow with the iron and straighten lengths from base to ends using low projection. If using a conventional straightening iron, place it at the base and smooth all the way to ends. Continue taking ¼" (.6 cm) partings throughout the head as you work from the nape to the top. Then use horizontal partings with a volume technique and a marcel curling iron to achieve soft volume and movement from a side part.

HAIR DESIGN RUBRIC *WORKSHOP 05*

STRAIGHT VOLUME AND INDENTATION –
PRESS AND CURL

This rubric is a performance assessment tool designed to measure your ability to
create *Pivot Point hair designs.*

	LEVEL 1 *in progress*	LEVEL 2 *getting better*	LEVEL 3 *entry-level proficiency*
PREPARATION			
• Assemble hair design essentials	☐	☐	☐
CREATE			
• Shampoo, condition and apply pressing cream to towel-dried hair; distribute pressing cream using horizontal partings working from base to ends	☐	☐	☐
• Section hair into five sections for air forming	☐	☐	☐
• Air form using the 9-row brush from base to midstrand then midstrand to ends taking ½" (1.25 cm) horizontal partings in back	☐	☐	☐
• Air form side sections from top to front hairline taking ½" (1.25 cm) diagonal-back partings; direct hair up and away from face	☐	☐	☐
• Air form remaining top lengths from crown to front hairline taking ½" (1.25 cm) horizontal partings; direct hair back away from face, drying from base to midstrand then midstrand to ends	☐	☐	☐
• Test temperature of pressing comb prior to applying on hair	☐	☐	☐
• Take ¼" (.6 cm) partings beginning at nape, inserting teeth of pressing comb underneath strand near base; turn pressing comb and press hair from base to ends; repeat technique	☐	☐	☐
• Insert teeth of pressing comb on top of same strand; turn comb and use spine as you work downward	☐	☐	☐
• Feed hair slowly through comb working from base to ends; repeat technique up to crown	☐	☐	☐
• Take ¼" (.6 cm) diagonal-back partings on sides pressing each parting upward and downward 2 times; work from top of sides to front hairline	☐	☐	☐
• Take ¼" (.6 cm) horizontal partings on top; stand behind client and press forward 2 times and backward 2 times, working from crown to front hairline	☐	☐	☐
• Work around hairline pressing from base to ends	☐	☐	☐
• Test temperature of marcel curling iron prior to applying on hair	☐	☐	☐
• Release 1x partings at nape; place barrel of marcel curling iron on top of strand and smooth; turn iron upward for indentation	☐	☐	☐
• At crest area, position marcel curling iron shell on top of strand; turn iron under to create volume	☐	☐	☐
• Adjust projection toward top for more volume	☐	☐	☐
• Relax curls with wide-tooth tail comb to blend bases and remove splits	☐	☐	☐
• Backcomb lightly for added volume and movement as needed	☐	☐	☐
• Define and detail hair with tail comb	☐	☐	☐

TOTAL POINTS = _____ + _____ + _____

TOTAL POINTS _____ ÷ HIGHEST POSSIBLE SCORE 60 X 100 = _____ %

Record your time in comparison with the suggested salon speed.

To improve my performance on this procedure, I need to:

Student Signature   Educator Signature   Date

2.4 INCREASE-LAYERED FORM

After reviewing some of the ways in which design options affect the form and texture of an increase-layered form, you'll be ready to learn about the techniques and tools used to create increase-layered designs that are in high demand among a range of customers.

INCREASE-LAYERED FORM DESIGNING

The increase-layered form offers styling versatility that makes it popular in the salon. While clients can enjoy the beauty of long hair, increase layers give the opportunity to create volume in the interior, expand the shape overall or experiment with a variety of textures.

FORM OPTIONS

The elongated shape of the increase-layered form is a result of shorter interior lengths and longer exterior lengths. Expansion can be created throughout the form while maintaining an elongated silhouette with no discernible build-up of weight.

Keep in mind that with all sculpted forms, the client's existing hair texture and density, as well as the design techniques chosen, influence the amount of expansion in the finished design.

TEXTURE OPTIONS

The basic lines of the sculpted increase-layered form are most evident when designed in a simple and smooth fashion. Longer lengths lend themselves well to a variety of temporary texture changes, which can range from soft and feminine waves to highly activated, more or less natural-looking curls. Note that these longer lengths even give the option to place texture along selected areas of the strand.

Smooth finishes with subtle end texture work well to emphasize how much and where in the sculpture texture activation appears.

Soft, curved movement can create an ultra-feminine feeling.

Enhancing a client's natural curl texture and refining it with product can be all that's needed for a fun, casual, yet still feminine look.

DIRECTION OPTIONS

In general, increase-layered forms offer great opportunities to feature directional movement and texture. Increase-layered forms featuring longer interior lengths will require a center or side part. Many clients enjoy the versatility of shorter interior lengths, which allow design direction options such as wearing the hair completely away from or toward the face.

CENTER PART

SIDE PART

AWAY FROM THE FACE

TOWARD THE FACE

WORKSHOP 06
STRAIGHT VOLUME – AIR FORMING FORWARD

Directional movement toward the face creates a soft look on this elongated form. This design is ideal for clients who want to spend minimal time on their long hair and maintain a refined style with curved end texture.

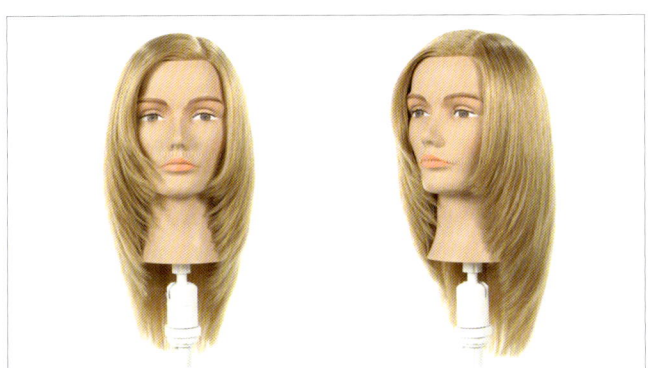

This smooth finish was achieved by using a 9-row brush to create volume and a round brush to enhance the texture of the increase-layered form.

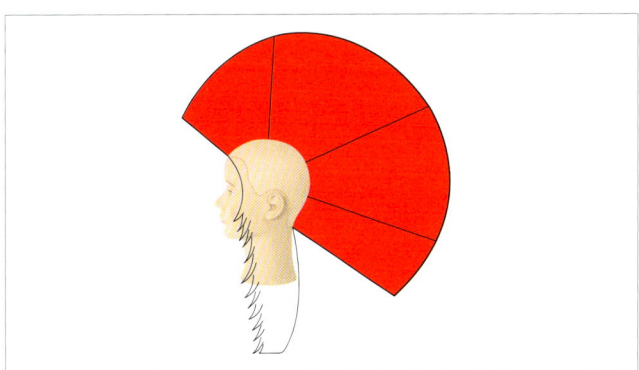

This air-formed design is created on an increase-layered form that positions the shortest lengths along the face.

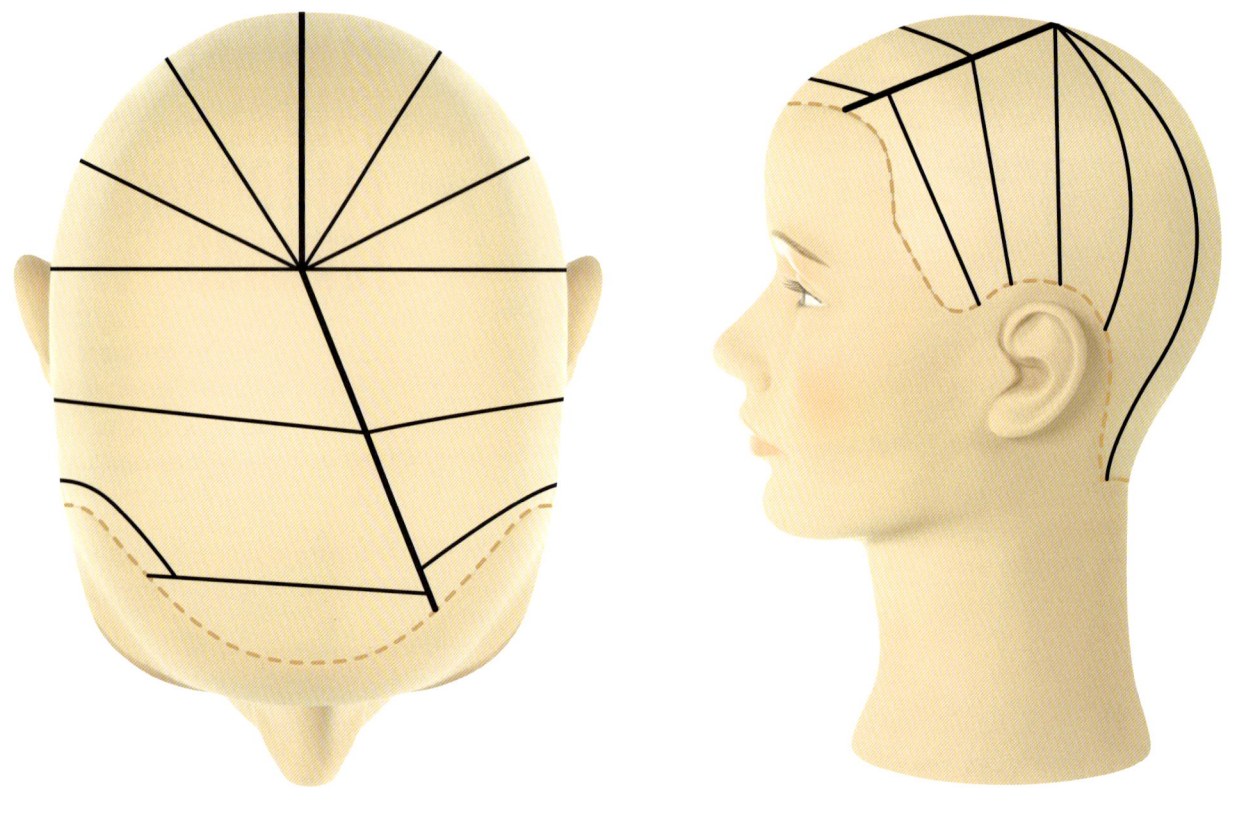

The art shows a side part from the front hairline to the crown and pivotal partings in the back. Steep diagonal-back partings that reflect the front hairline are used to air form the sides.

01–02 Begin by distributing a small amount of thickening cream evenly throughout the hair.

03 Remove excess moisture by using your fingers to control the hair while air forming.

04 Starting on the lighter side, release a parting parallel to the front hairline. Lift the hair at the base using a 9-row brush for maximum volume. Dry the base first.

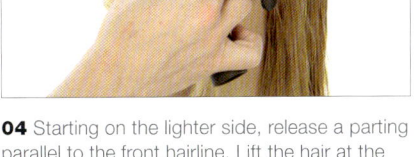

05 Then use a curved movement to create curved end texture while drying midstrand to ends.

06–07 Continue to lift and dry the base first for maximum volume. Then dry the midstrand to the ends using a curved movement. Air form from the top to the perimeter as you work toward the back.

08 Combine all the hair on the brush and air form with the same technique to ensure all the hair ends are moving in the same direction.

09 Release pivotal partings in the back and continue to air form the base first, then midstrand to ends.

10 Work toward the center back to complete this side.

11–12 Move to the heavier side and release a parting parallel to the front hairline. Lift the hair for maximum volume. Dry the base first, then midstrand and ends. Work to the ear with steep diagonal back partings.

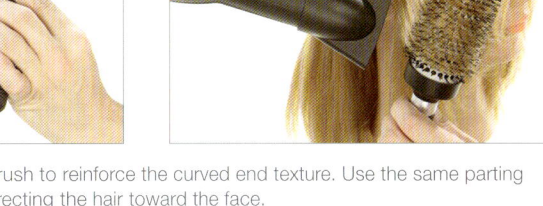

13 Release pivotal partings in the back and continue to air form. Work to the center back to complete this side.

14–15 Switch to a large round brush to reinforce the curved end texture. Use the same parting pattern with a larger base size, directing the hair toward the face.

16 For subtle lift and volume at the face, use the round brush to direct the hair up, away from the face, while directing the airflow along the base and midstrand.

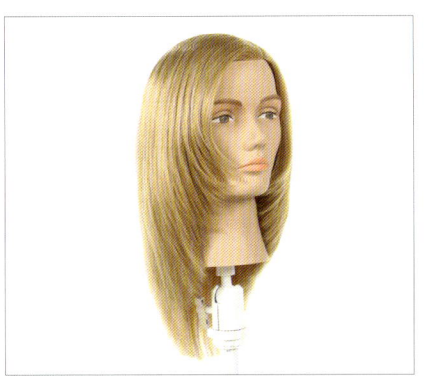

17–18 The finish displays soft, curved end texture that frames the face and beautifully showcases the texture of the increase-layered form.

DESIGN DECISIONS *WORKSHOP 06*

STRAIGHT VOLUME – AIR FORMING FORWARD

Draw or fill in the boxes with the appropriate answers.

STRUCTURE

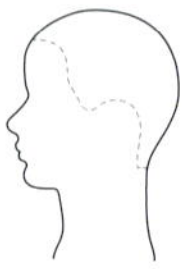

FORM/TEXTURE

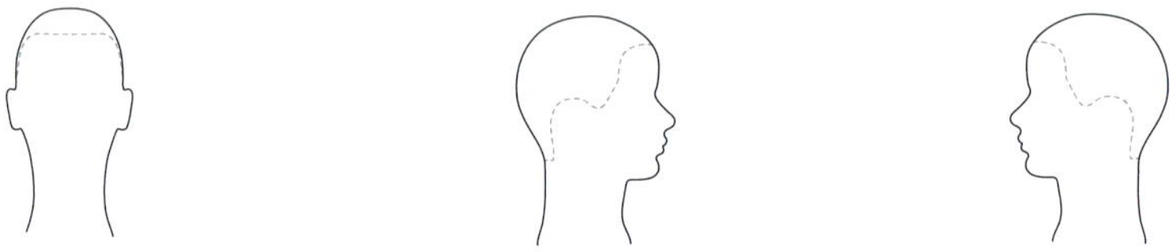

DIRECTION

AIR-FORMING PATTERN

COMB-OUT/FINISH

☐ RELAX ☐ DRY MOLD ☐ BACKCOMB/BACKBRUSH ☐ DEFINE THE FORM ☐ DETAIL

TOOLS/PRODUCT CHOICE

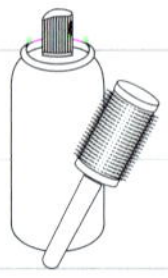

Educator Signature

Date

VARIATION 03
STRAIGHT VOLUME – AIR FORMING FORWARD

For added volume and texture, first air form the hair with a round brush, then set it for straight and curvature volume with self-adhering rollers. A progression of roller diameters is chosen to relate to the increase-layered lengths.

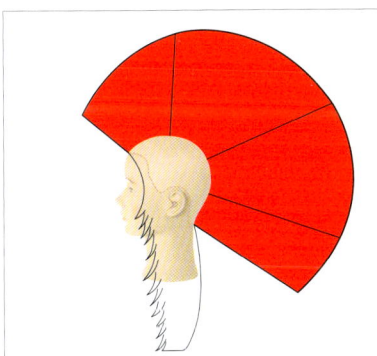
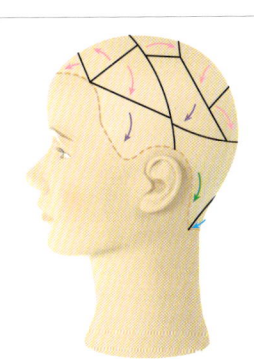

A half-circle with the point of origin above the left eye is used to position self-adhering rollers at the front. The size of the rollers is determined by the length of the hair and the desired amount of surface texture. In the crown, a roller is positioned half-off base for moderate volume. Through the remaining area, trapezoid-shaped and triangular bases are used to position self-adhering rollers. Note that the base controls gradually diminish from half-off base to off base toward the perimeter. As an option, the set hair can be placed under a hooded dryer or air formed for several minutes. The result shows fullness and directional movement toward the face.

HAIR DESIGN RUBRIC *WORKSHOP 06*

STRAIGHT VOLUME –
AIR FORMING FORWARD

This rubric is a performance assessment tool designed to measure your ability to **create** *Pivot Point hair designs.*

	LEVEL 1 *in progress*	LEVEL 2 *getting better*	LEVEL 3 *entry-level proficiency*
PREPARATION			
• Assemble hair design essentials	☐	☐	☐
CREATE			
• Shampoo, condition and apply thickening cream	☐	☐	☐
• Remove excess moisture using fingers to control hair	☐	☐	☐
• Air form beginning on lighter side of parting using 9-row brush to lift hair at the base for maximum volume	☐	☐	☐
• Air form midstrand to ends, moving 9-row brush in a curved motion to create curved end texture	☐	☐	☐
• Combine all the hair on 9-row brush and air form to ensure all hair ends move in same direction	☐	☐	☐
• Air form from top to perimeter, working toward center back using same technique	☐	☐	☐
• Repeat same air-forming procedures on opposite side	☐	☐	☐
• Air form with round brush using same parting pattern, creating additional curved end texture	☐	☐	☐
• Use round brush to direct the hair at fringe away from face, directing airflow along the base and midstrand	☐	☐	☐
• Define and detail using fingers and light hairspray	☐	☐	☐

TOTAL POINTS = _____ + _____ + _____

TOTAL POINTS _____ ÷ HIGHEST POSSIBLE SCORE 33 X 100 = _____ %

Record your time in comparison with the suggested salon speed.

To improve my performance on this procedure, I need to:

_____

Student Signature   *Educator Signature*   *Date*

WORKSHOP 07
DIRECTIONAL VOLUME – AIR FORMING

Some clients have facial features and shapes that can benefit from volume moving away from the face. This air-formed design creates soft-looking curved end texture throughout, which produces a very feminine appearance.

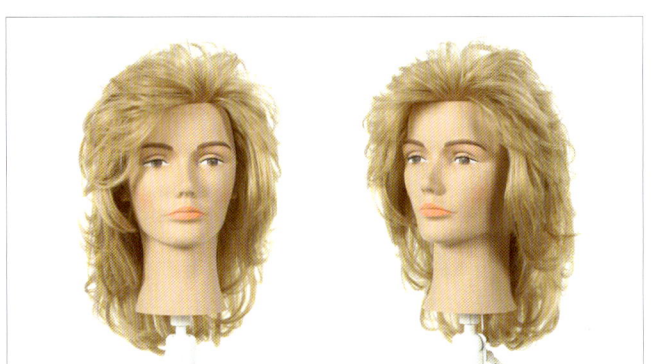

This finish was created using a medium round brush to produce additional texture and volume on the longer lengths.

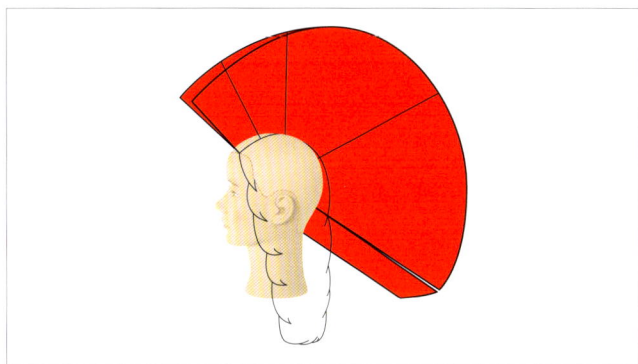

This exercise will be performed on an increase-layered form.

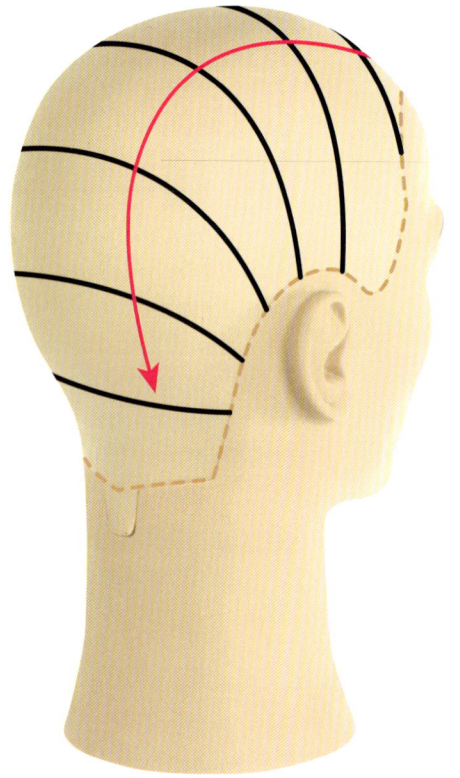

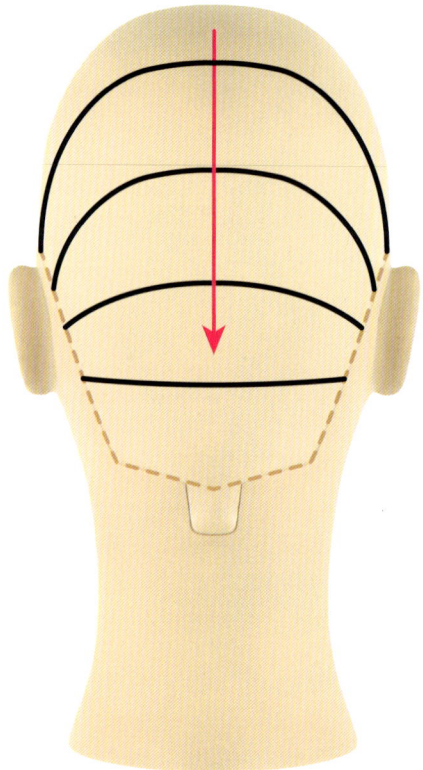

The art shows that lengths will be air formed back away from the face using horizontal, diagonal-forward and vertical partings. Note that this parting pattern follows the curve of the head.

01 Begin by applying styling mousse evenly through the lengths for control and support.

02 Remove excess moisture from the hair using a vent brush.

03–05 Begin at the nape and release a horizontal parting. Position a medium-diameter round brush underneath the hair and project at 90° to create a half-off base control. Air form from base to ends by slightly turning the brush in a curved movement. Rotate the brush at the ends, then roll the brush up to the base and direct the heat on the top of the brush. Allow the lengths to cool, then release.

06 Work from the center to either side. Carry a small portion from the center over to either side to avoid splits.

07 The art shows that horizontal and diagonal-forward partings will be used for the area slightly behind the ear. Due to the curve of the head, the diagonal-forward partings will transition to vertical partings in the area at the top and in front of the ear.

 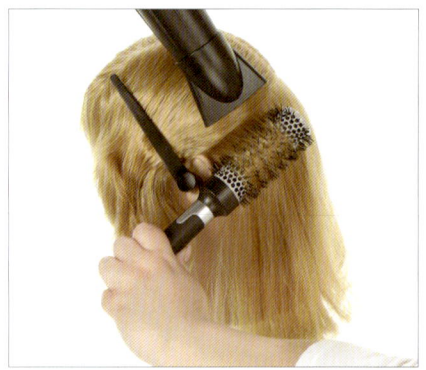 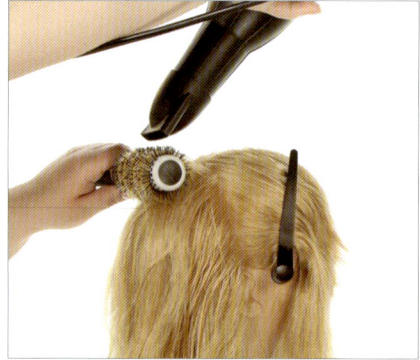

08–09 Stagger the bases as you work upward, continuing to use half-off base control. Use diagonal-forward partings as you reach the area slightly behind the ear.

10 As you work toward the crown, be sure to maintain a half-off base position by projecting the lengths at 90° from the center of the base.

12 Work across the top of the head using the same technique.

11 Use vertical partings at the sides, directing the lengths back away from the face. Use the airflow to help control the ends around the brush.

13 Blend the top lengths with both sides.

  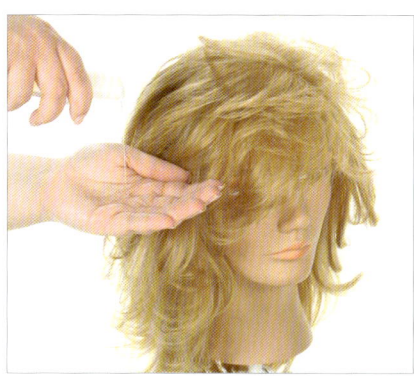

14–15 At the fringe area, air form lengths back off the face. Again, use the airflow to control ends around the brush. Then take a small portion of the fringe and air form lengths toward the face. Rotate the brush at the ends, roll lengths up to the base and gently release.

16 Next, apply a silicone-based product onto your hands and distribute it evenly.

17 Using your fingers, define the direction and end texture as you creatively position the lengths.

18–19 The finish shows a soft, totally activated, curved end texture with lengths moving away from the face.

DIRECTIONAL VOLUME – AIR FORMING

Draw or fill in the boxes with the appropriate answers.

STRUCTURE

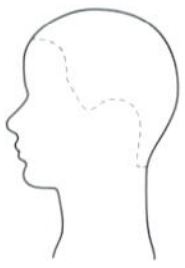

FORM/TEXTURE

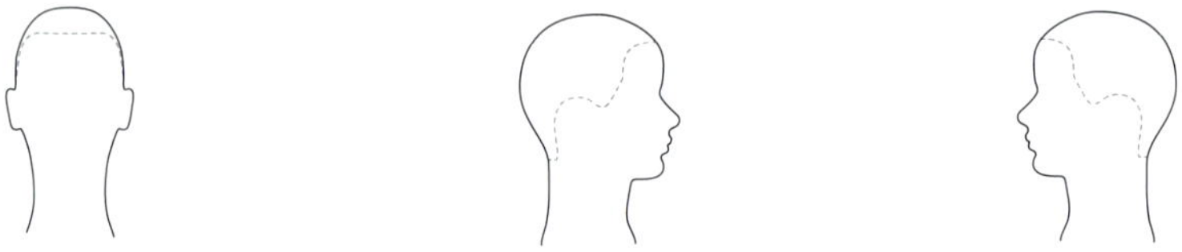

DIRECTION

AIR-FORMING PATTERN

COMB-OUT/FINISH

☐ RELAX   ☐ DRY MOLD   ☐ BACKCOMB/BACKBRUSH   ☐ DEFINE THE FORM   ☐ DETAIL

TOOLS/PRODUCT CHOICE

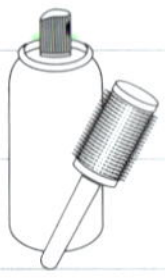

Educator Signature

Date

HAIR DESIGN RUBRIC *WORKSHOP 07*

DIRECTIONAL VOLUME – AIR FORMING

This rubric is a performance assessment tool designed to measure your ability to **create** *Pivot Point hair designs.*

	LEVEL 1 *in progress*	LEVEL 2 *getting better*	LEVEL 3 *entry-level proficiency*
PREPARATION			
• Assemble hair design essentials	☐	☐	☐
CREATE			
• Shampoo, condition and apply styling mousse	☐	☐	☐
• Remove excess moisture using vent brush	☐	☐	☐
• Release horizontal parting in nape; air form volume using half-off base control from base to ends; start in nape using medium-diameter round brush; slightly turn brush in curved movement	☐	☐	☐
• Rotate brush at ends; roll brush up to base; direct heat on top of brush; allow hair to cool, then release	☐	☐	☐
• Air form working from center to either side using small portion of center to avoid splits	☐	☐	☐
• Stagger bases working upward; follow curve of head using diagonal-forward partings behind ears and same air-forming techniques	☐	☐	☐
• Maintaining half-off base position in crown, air form from center to either side	☐	☐	☐
• Air form sides using vertical partings, working from center to either side directing lengths back off the face	☐	☐	☐
• Air form top first, blending to either side	☐	☐	☐
• Air form fringe lengths away from face using same technique	☐	☐	☐
• Release a small portion of fringe and air form toward face	☐	☐	☐
• Apply silicone-based product and distribute evenly	☐	☐	☐
• Define direction and end texture using fingers	☐	☐	☐

TOTAL POINTS = _____ + _____ + _____

TOTAL POINTS _____ ÷ HIGHEST POSSIBLE SCORE 42 X 100 = _____ %

Record your time in comparison with the suggested salon speed. _____

To improve my performance on this procedure, I need to: _____

_____   _____   _____
Student Signature   Educator Signature   Date

WORKSHOP 08
CURVATURE AND STRAIGHT VOLUME – ROLLERS

Expanded ovals are used to create gentle curved movement in this design. Finger styling creates a piecier look that retains the curl formation. This option is especially effective for clients with relaxed hair.

The expanded oval technique, also referred to as the indirect technique, is used to set the sides. A rectangle encompasses the top, and a bricklay pattern is used to set the remaining shape in the back. The off-the-face rectangle blends with the top movement of the ovals for a flattering design with most of the hair moving away from the face.

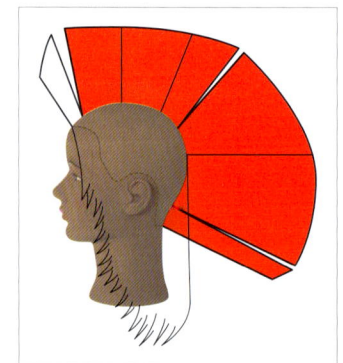

This design is set on increase layers that were sculpted using the planar technique in the interior.

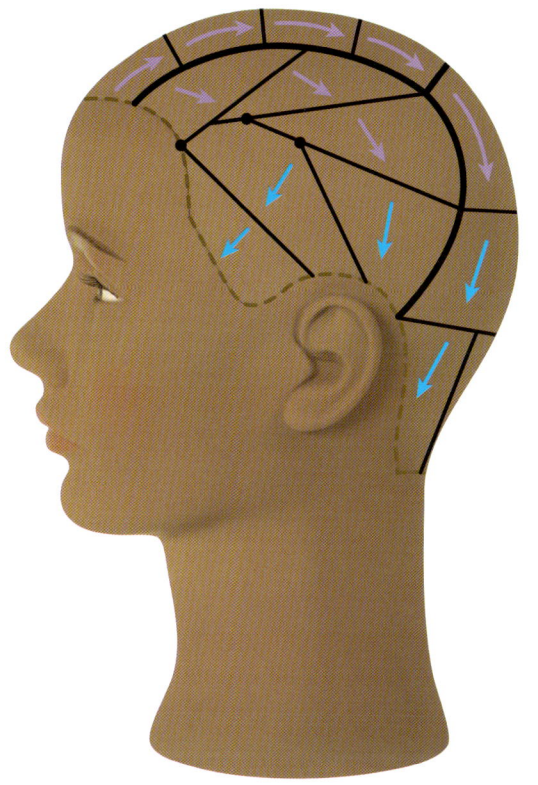
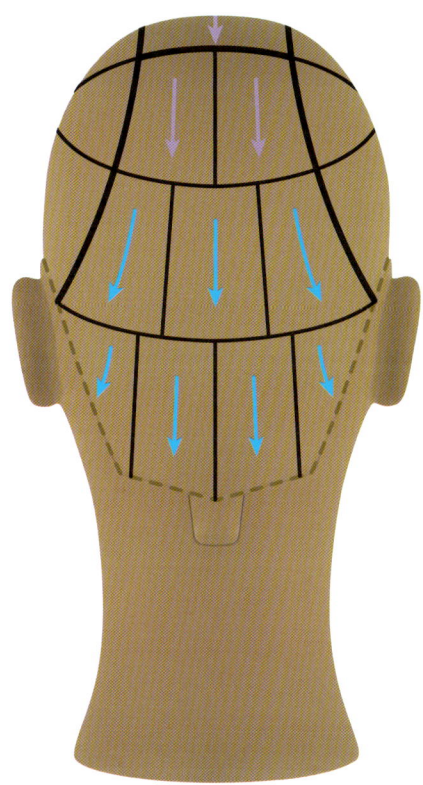

The art shows the sectioning and parting pattern used in this exercise. Expanded ovals are set on either side using one-diameter (1x) half-off base control throughout. A straight rectangle at the center top is also set using half-off base straight control. A bricklay pattern is used to set the remainder of the hair, with diminished volume toward the nape.

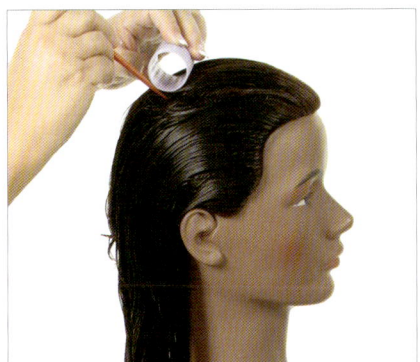

01 Mold and scale a rectangle from the front hairline to the crown. Use the length of the roller and scale the length of the rectangle to equal four diameters of the roller.

02 Mold a fast-to-slow counterclockwise expanded oval on the right side of the head.

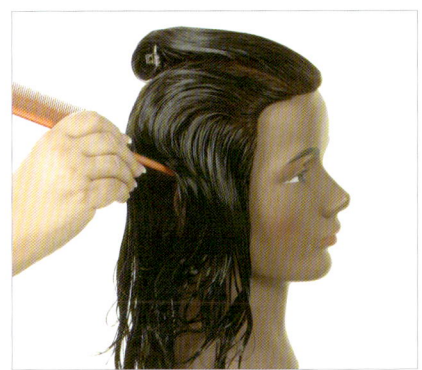

03 Then use the tail comb to scale the expanded oval shape in preparation for the indirect technique.

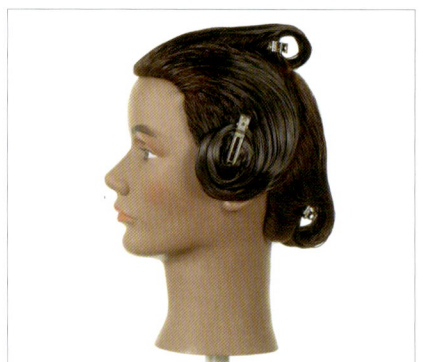

04 Mold and scale a fast-to-slow clockwise expanded oval on the opposite side.

05–06 Begin setting the rectangle-shaped section at the front hairline using a cylindrical roller. Measure and part a 1x horizontal base. Project approximately 90° from the center of the base, wrap the ends around the roller and roll downward with even tension. Position the roller half-off base.

08 Set the remaining (three) rollers in the rectangle shape, positioning each roller half-off base.

07 Use a pick to secure the roller.

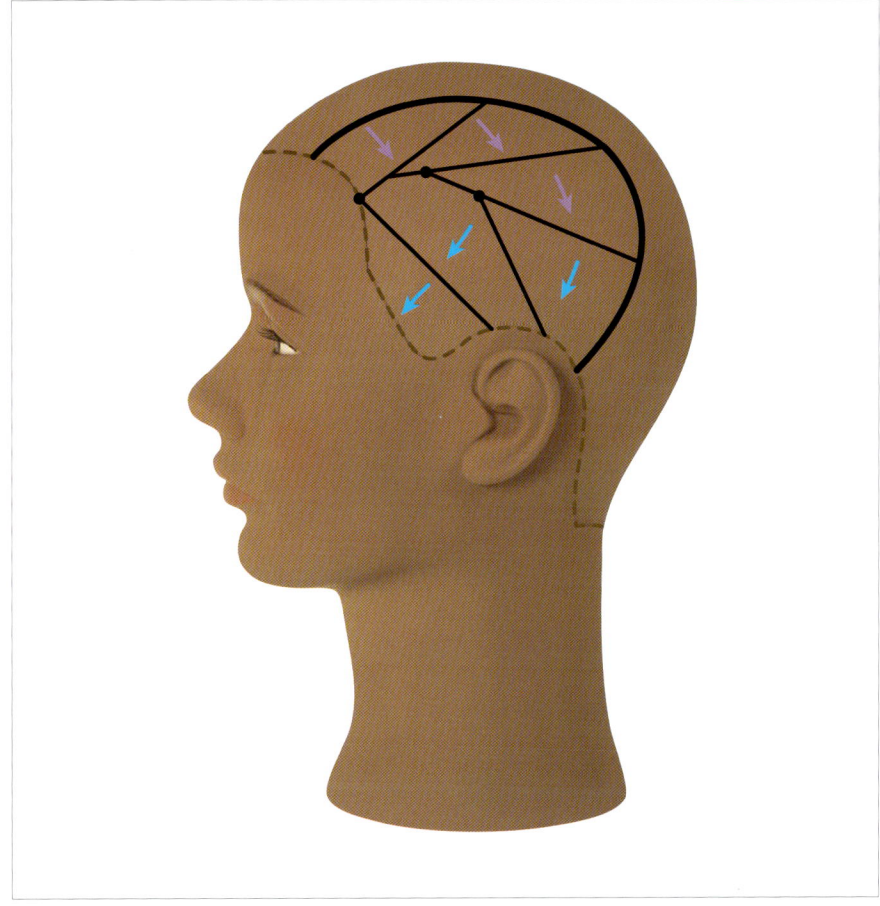

10 Measure the first base using the diameter plus the length. Use half-off base control and position the roller 1x from the point of origin.

09 The art shows the parting pattern that will be used to set the expanded ovals using the indirect technique with cone-shaped rollers. After the first roller is set, each new point of origin will be located at the front bottom corner of each previous roller. All rollers in this shape are set with 1x half-off base control and 1x from their various points of origin.

11 Secure at the small end of the cone-shaped roller.

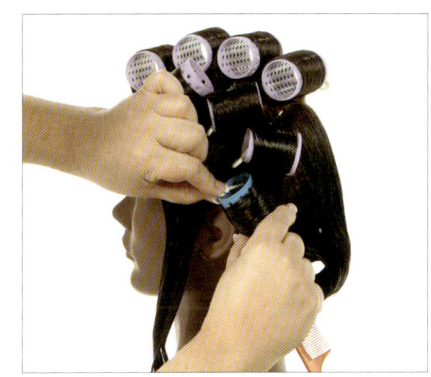

12–13 Measure the next base using the front bottom corner of the first roller as the point of origin. Use 1x half-off base control, positioning the roller parallel to the parting. Set the next roller. Again use the front bottom corner of the previous roller as the point of origin.

14 Use a larger-diameter roller to complete the perimeter of the shape.

15–16 Return to the original point of origin. Measure and part a 1x base using the larger-diameter roller. Use half-off base control, positioning the roller parallel to the parting. Pick to secure at the smaller end of the roller.

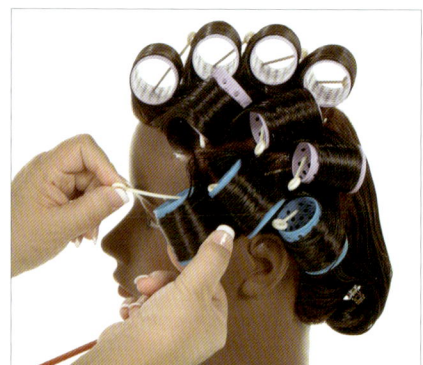

17 Use the original point of origin to set the last roller to complete the shape.

18 Here we see the completed expanded oval. Note that the larger-diameter rollers correspond to the longer lengths in the exterior.

19 Set the expanded oval on the opposite side. Begin at the point of origin and use the indirect technique.

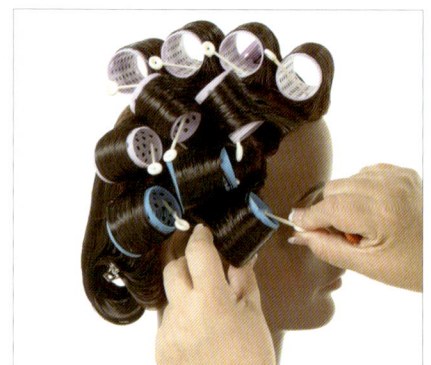

20 Complete the shape setting each cone-shaped roller half-off base.

22 Set the first two rollers using the smaller-diameter size with 1½x underdirected base control for diminished volume.

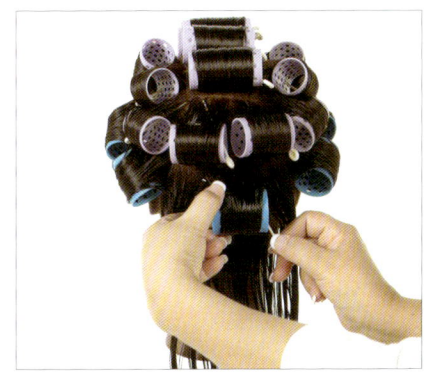

23 Use the larger-diameter roller and 1½x half-off base control to set the next row. Begin setting this row at the center, staggering the bases.

21 The art shows the horizontal bricklay pattern that will be used to set the remainder of the lengths in the back of the design using cylindrical rollers. Note that the rollers at either side of the nape hairline are set at angles to conform to the curves of the head, and to blend with the movement of the expanded oval shape.

24 Work from the center to either side to complete this row.

25 Set the last row using 1½x off-base control. Stagger the bases and set the rollers on each side at angles.

26 The bricklay pattern in the back of the design creates neutral direction with diminishing volume toward the nape.

27 Allow the hair to dry and cool completely before removing the rollers.

28 Use your fingers to rake through the hair to relax the set. Do not comb or brush the hair at this point.

29 After applying a silicone-based shine product, use your fingers to arrange the hair for a loose, tousled effect.

30 You may choose to relax the set more fully and backcomb slightly to blend the bases. Clients can create similar styling options as the set relaxes.

31–32 The finish shows loose curls with a flattering movement away from the face in the interior. Depending on the client's wishes, the expanded oval movement can be more or less apparent in the finished design.

DESIGN DECISIONS *WORKSHOP 08*
CURVATURE AND STRAIGHT VOLUME – ROLLERS

Draw or fill in the boxes with the appropriate answers.

artist+
access.

STRUCTURE

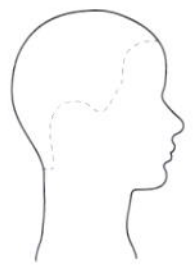

FORM/TEXTURE

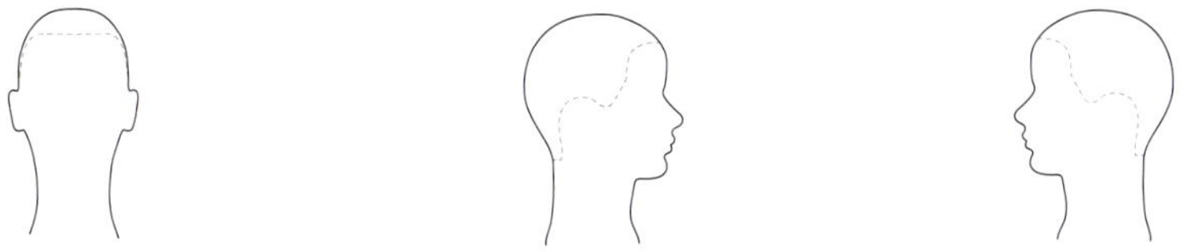

DIRECTION

MOLDING/SCALING

SETTING PATTERN

COMB-OUT/FINISH

- ☐ RELAX
- ☐ DRY MOLD
- ☐ BACKCOMB/BACKBRUSH
- ☐ DEFINE THE FORM
- ☐ DETAIL

TOOLS/PRODUCT CHOICE

Educator Signature

Date

HAIR DESIGN RUBRIC *WORKSHOP 08*

CURVATURE AND STRAIGHT VOLUME – ROLLERS

This rubric is a performance assessment tool designed to measure your ability to **create** *Pivot Point hair designs.*

	LEVEL 1 *in progress*	LEVEL 2 *getting better*	LEVEL 3 *entry-level proficiency*
PREPARATION			
• Assemble hair design essentials	☐	☐	☐
CREATE			
• Shampoo, condition and apply appropriate styling product	☐	☐	☐
• Mold/scale rectangle at center top, measuring the length of roller for width and 4 diameters for length	☐	☐	☐
• Mold/scale fast-to-slow counterclockwise expanded oval on right side	☐	☐	☐
• Mold/scale fast-to-slow clockwise expanded oval on left side	☐	☐	☐
• Set rectangle using 1x horizontal bases with cylindrical rollers and half-off base control; work from front hairline to crown	☐	☐	☐
• Set expanded oval using cone-shaped rollers; measure first base 1x plus length and use 1x half-off base control; position roller 1x from point of origin	☐	☐	☐
• Measure next 3 bases from front bottom corner of each previous roller and set with 1x half-off base control, 1x from point of origin; use larger-diameter roller to complete perimeter of shape	☐	☐	☐
• Return to original point of origin and use 1x half-off base to set remainder of shape with larger-diameter rollers	☐	☐	☐
• Repeat the same procedure on the opposite side	☐	☐	☐
• Set remaining shape using bricklay technique and cylindrical rollers; work from top, setting first row with 1½x underdirected base control with smaller-diameter rollers	☐	☐	☐
• Set next row 1½x half-off base with larger-diameter rollers	☐	☐	☐
• Set last row 1½x off-base, angling rollers at nape hairline to blend with movement of expanded oval	☐	☐	☐
• Use fingers to relax set	☐	☐	☐
• Apply silicone shine product and arrange with fingers for tousled effect	☐	☐	☐
COMB-OUT VARIATION			
• Relax set more fully	☐	☐	☐
• Backcomb slightly to blend bases	☐	☐	☐

TOTAL POINTS = _____ + _____ + _____

TOTAL POINTS _____ ÷ HIGHEST POSSIBLE SCORE 45 X 100 = _____ %

÷ HIGHEST POSSIBLE SCORE/VARIATION 51 X 100 = _____ %

Record your time in comparison with the suggested salon speed.

To improve my performance on this procedure, I need to:

Student Signature   Educator Signature   Date

2.5 UNIFORMLY LAYERED FORM

In the area of wet and thermal design the uniformly layered form is highly versatile, which is part of the reason why it will always be popular. After taking a look at some of the ways in which the uniformly layered form can be designed, you'll be ready to learn about and practice design techniques that create uniformly layered hair design finishes ranging from trendy or casual to classic and elegant.

UNIFORMLY LAYERED FORM DESIGNING

Just like the other basic forms, there are many options available when designing uniform layers. A thorough client consultation will ensure that the design choices you make will please your clients and lead to a successfully finished look.

FORM OPTIONS

Uniformly layered forms have consistent lengths throughout creating equal expansion. However, the circular shape can be altered depending on the lengths of the hair, and the position and amount of volume.

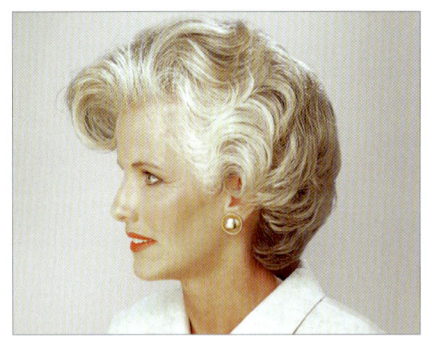

Consistent volume base controls throughout will enhance the circular shape.

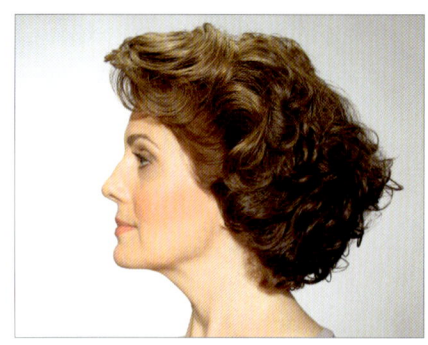

With maximum volume in the interior, but closeness in the exterior, the form can almost appear similar to a graduated sculpture.

When volume and indentation techniques are combined, the resulting shape can be very different.

TEXTURE OPTIONS

When it comes to the texture for uniformly layered forms, shorter uniformly layered lengths lend themselves more to sporty or product-driven finishes. Medium lengths may be designed for classic as well as casual finishes. Longer uniformly layered lengths offer nearly the same texture options as increased layers, featuring a variety of temporary textures.

Finger-styling combined with the right product creates a progressive look that highlights the sculpted texture.

Waves at the front with large curly texture throughout the rest of the shape create a classic look.

Irregular curls add texture as well as fullness throughout.

DIRECTION OPTIONS

When designing, keep in mind that longer uniformly layered forms require a part. Since all lengths in this design are uniform, the position of the part is flexible and can be changed easily, allowing clients to change things up a bit. Shorter uniformly layered forms can be designed in all directions and are usually worn without a distinct part to display the activated end texture.

SIDE PART

MULTIPLE DIRECTIONS

AWAY FROM THE FACE

TOWARD THE FACE

WORKSHOP 09
STRAIGHT AND CURVATURE VOLUME – AIR FORMING

This uniform structure is accentuated by straight and curvature volume air-forming techniques, creating varying movements and textures within the design.

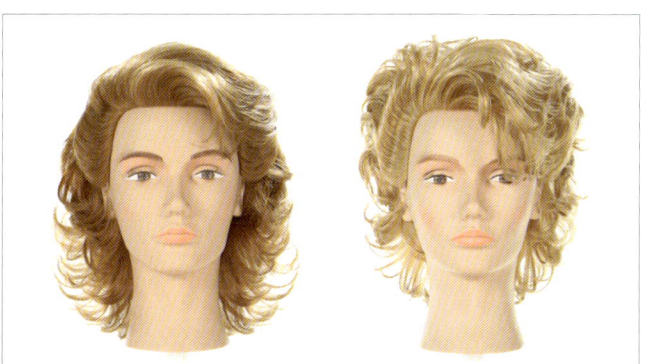

The finish shows a variety of directions and movements in a slightly elongated shape on the longer uniformly layered form.

NOTE: *The same techniques applied on a shorter uniform sculpture create a rounder, more voluminous shape.*

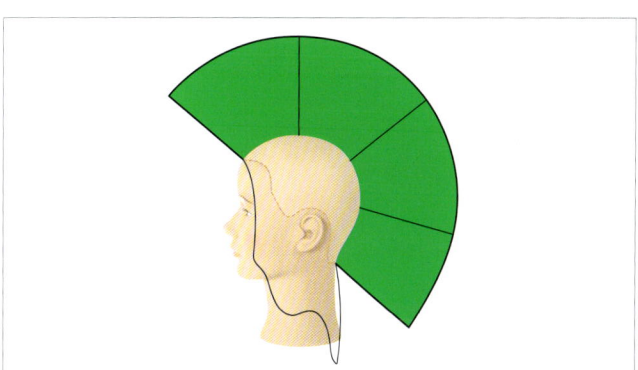

The structure graphic shows the uniformly layered form used in this exercise.

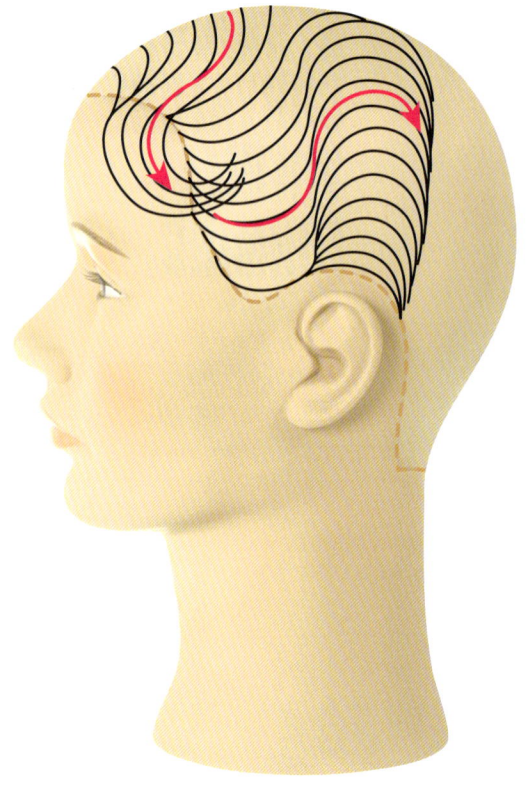

The art shows the design direction for the alternating oblongs molded on each side.

Note how the fringe moves off the face in curved lines.

01 Use a light styling mousse to give the hair flexible hold.

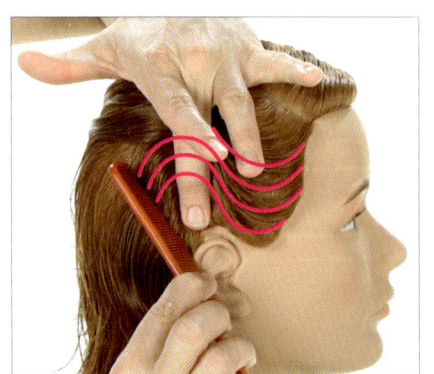

02 Distribute and mold vertical alternating oblongs on each side. Secure the ends into a flat circular shape in the second direction of the last oblong. Then direct the top back away from the face and secure.

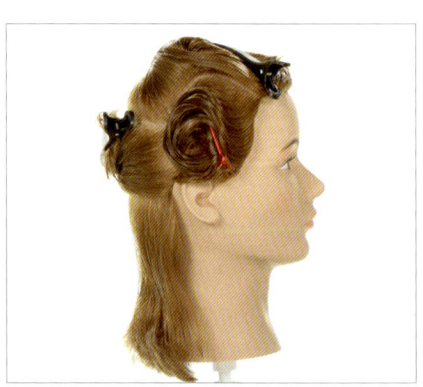

03 Finally, subsection the back horizontally at the occipital area and the upper crest.

04–05 Begin in the nape using the 9-row brush to lift vertical partings at the base. Focus the airflow on the base to create base lift. Then release the crest section and repeat the same technique.

06 Release a horizontal parting in the nape the same width as the round brush. Tilt the head slightly and air form for volume and curved end texture, starting at the center and moving to one side.

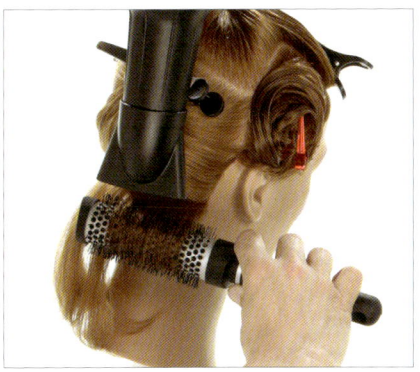

07 Then repeat on the other side. Carry over part of the previously dried center to prevent splits.

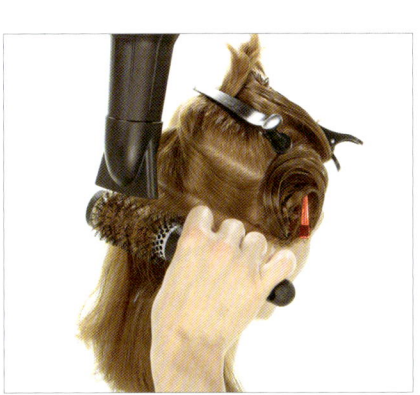

08 Once you reach the lower crest, air form each parting with a volume technique using a medium round brush first.

09 Then, using a small-diameter round brush, turn the ends upward and air form to create indentation. Work to the top of the crest section.

10 Alternating oblongs are air formed at the sides. Use the round brush to create parallel curved lines. To reinforce the second direction of the oblong, direct the airflow in the center of the first shape.

11 Next, part in the first direction of the second oblong and air form the lengths with a small-diameter round brush to create volume. Be sure not to disturb the first oblong.

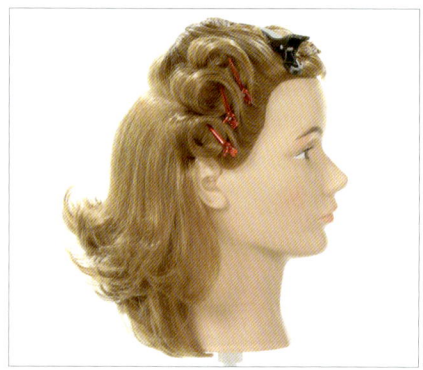

12 Secure the ends, allowing the curl to cool in the desired shape for extra support. Repeat throughout the oblong.

13 Repeat on the opposite side. First reinforce the directions of the oblongs, then air form the ends with a volume technique and secure.

14 Return to the crown area and use the medium-diameter round brush to create maximum volume. Work until you reach the apex.

15 In the fringe area the hair will be air formed away from the face first, then toward the face, creating a half-circle.

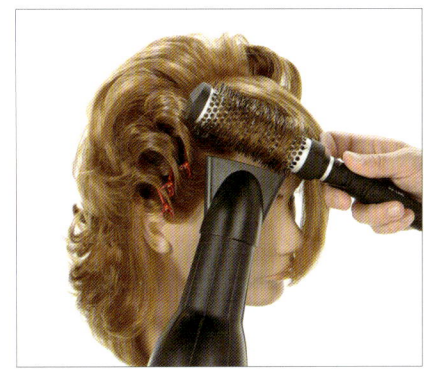

16 To achieve a curvature volume effect, air form the first and second parting for a one-and-a-half diameter (1½x) overdirected base control.

17 Then air form the last parting using on-base volume control.

18 Relax and dry mold the design. Then lightly backcomb from underneath using a wide-tooth tail comb.

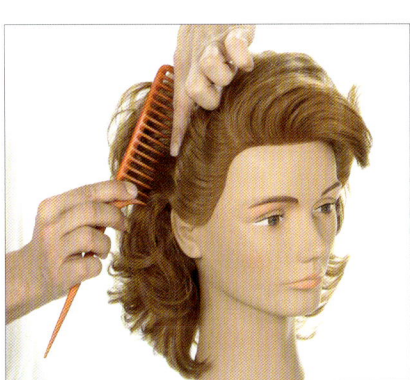

19 Define the form using your fingers to secure directions within the design when necessary. Detail to separate the texture.

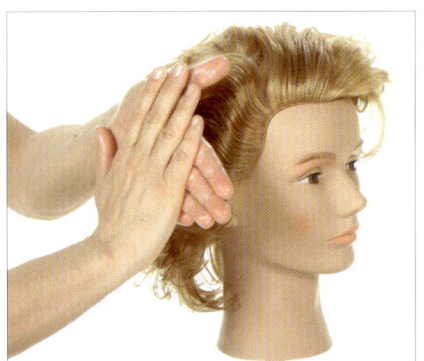

20 On a shorter uniform sculpture, rub a small amount of light pomade between your palms and fingers to ensure even distribution.

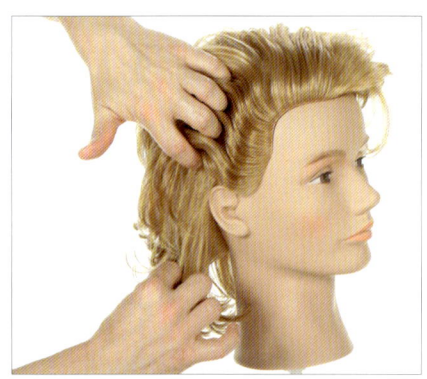

21 Then work the product through the hair following the design's directions to create a refined textured look.

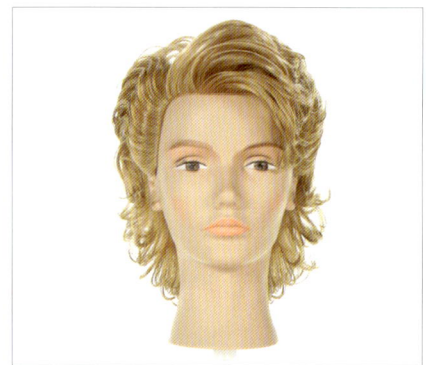

22 This finish shows the same techniques applied to a shorter uniformly layered form. This design has more volume and a more textured look.

23–24 The finish shows a classic shape with a variety of textures, volume and indentation, which can be modified to suit a wide range of clients.

DESIGN DECISIONS *WORKSHOP 09*

STRAIGHT AND CURVATURE VOLUME – AIR FORMING

artist+access.

Draw or fill in the boxes with the appropriate answers.

STRUCTURE

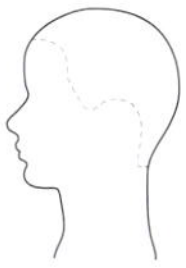

FORM/TEXTURE

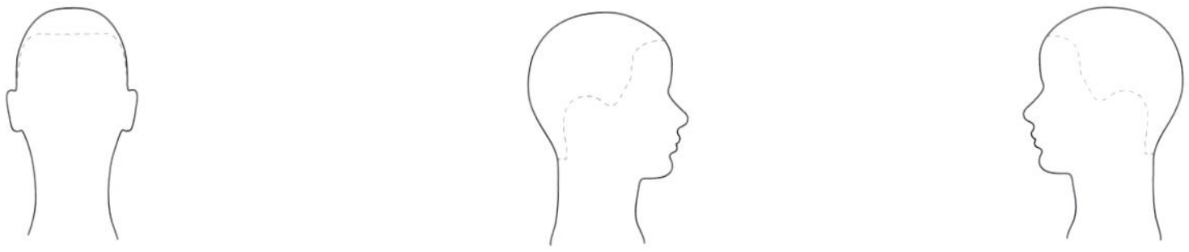

DIRECTION

MOLDING/SCALING PATTERN

AIR-FORMING PATTERN

COMB-OUT/FINISH

☐ RELAX

☐ DRY MOLD

☐ BACKCOMB/BACKBRUSH

☐ DEFINE THE FORM

☐ DETAIL

TOOLS/PRODUCT CHOICE

Educator Signature

Date

STRAIGHT AND CURVATURE VOLUME – AIR FORMING

This rubric is a performance assessment tool designed to measure your ability to **create** *Pivot Point hair designs.*

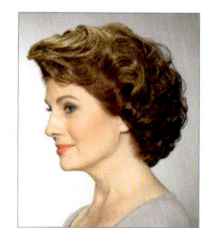

	LEVEL 1 *in progress*	LEVEL 2 *getting better*	LEVEL 3 *entry-level proficiency*
PREPARATION			
• Assemble hair design essentials	☐	☐	☐
CREATE			
• Shampoo, condition and apply a light styling mousse	☐	☐	☐
• Mold vertical alternating oblongs on each side and secure the ends into flat circular shape in second direction of last oblong; direct top back away from face and secure	☐	☐	☐
• Subsection horizontally in back at occipital area and upper crest	☐	☐	☐
• Air form at base in nape area using 9-row brush and vertical partings; release crest section and repeat same technique	☐	☐	☐
• Release horizontal parting in nape with same width as round brush used; tilt head slightly forward	☐	☐	☐
• Air form to create volume and curved end texture; start at center, working to one side then the other; carry over part of previously dried center to prevent splits; work upward	☐	☐	☐
• Air form volume with medium-diameter round brush first, then use small-diameter round brush to create indentation; work from lower crest to top of crest section	☐	☐	☐
• Air form oblong on one side using small-diameter round brush; direct airflow in center of shape	☐	☐	☐
• Reinforce second oblong by directing airflow into center of shape	☐	☐	☐
• Part in first direction of second oblong, air form with small-diameter round brush and secure curl to cool in desired shape; do not disturb first oblong; repeat on opposite side	☐	☐	☐
• Air form in crown area with medium-diameter round brush for maximum volume; work to apex	☐	☐	☐
• Air form top half-circle shape with curvature volume using medium-diameter round brush and 1½x overdirected base control for first and second parting; air form last parting using on-base volume control	☐	☐	☐
• Relax and dry mold design; use wide-tooth comb and lightly backcomb from underneath	☐	☐	☐
• Define form using fingers to secure directions when necessary; detail to separate texture	☐	☐	☐

COMB-OUT VARIATION

• Rub small amount of light pomade between palms and fingers and distribute evenly following the design's directions to create refined textured look	☐	☐	☐

TOTAL POINTS = _____ + _____ + _____

TOTAL POINTS _____ ÷ HIGHEST POSSIBLE SCORE 45 X 100 = _____ %

÷ HIGHEST POSSIBLE SCORE/VARIATION 48 X 100 = _____ %

Record your time in comparison with the suggested salon speed. _____

To improve my performance on this procedure, I need to: _____

_____   _____   _____
Student Signature   *Educator Signature*   *Date*

WORKSHOP 10
DIRECTIONAL VOLUME AND INDENTATION – AIR FORMING

Clients with shorter uniform lengths usually prefer a look that is trendy and easy to maintain. This air-formed design is versatile and can be worn to look casual or fashionable.

This highly textured look features a side part and slightly curved end texture throughout. Volume and indentation are air formed to accentuate the texture of the sculpture.

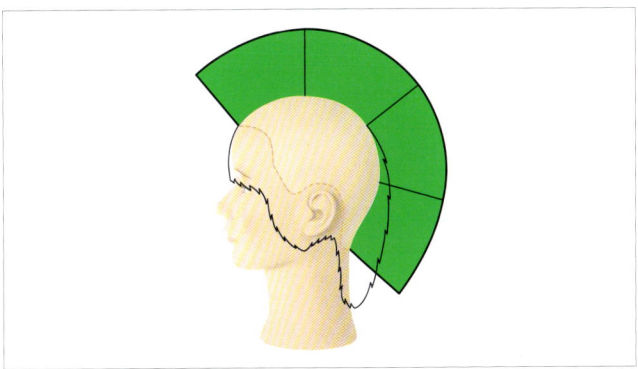

This exercise will be performed on a short uniformly layered form.

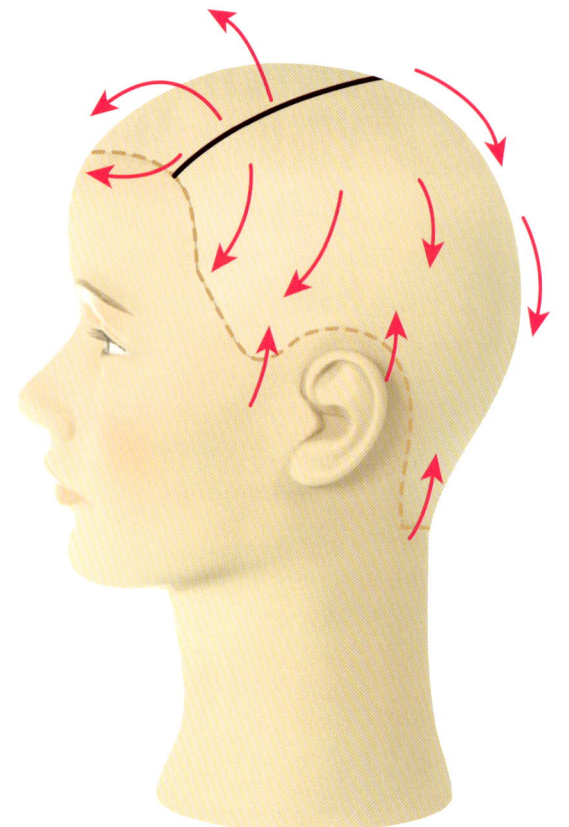
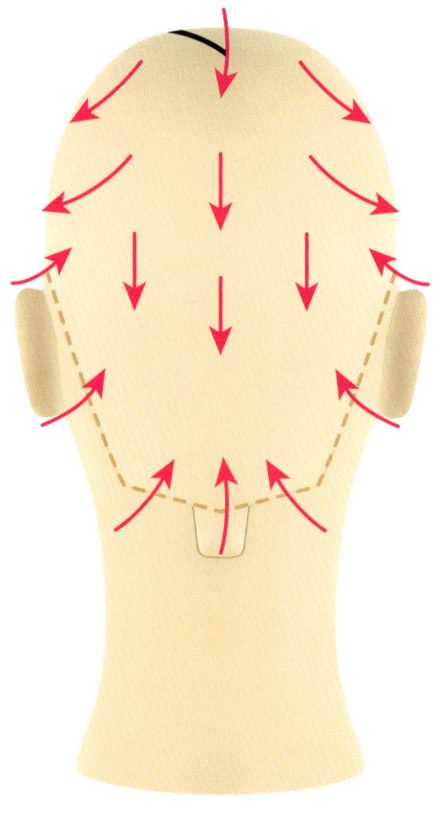

The art shows the various directions in which the hair will be air formed. Note that the design incorporates a side part on the left side.

01 Begin by applying styling cream from base to ends with your fingers.

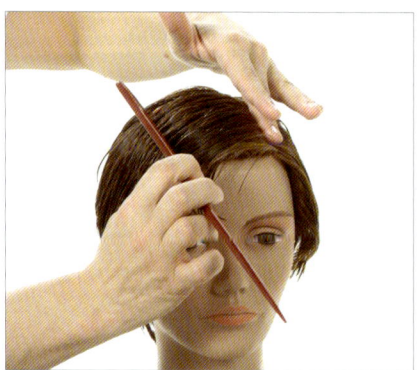

02 Next, create a side part from the center of the left eye to the crown. Then, use a wide-tooth tail comb to distribute into the intended directions of the design. Work from the front hairline to the sides.

03 Then, distribute the crown area using radial distribution. Distribute the nape downward.

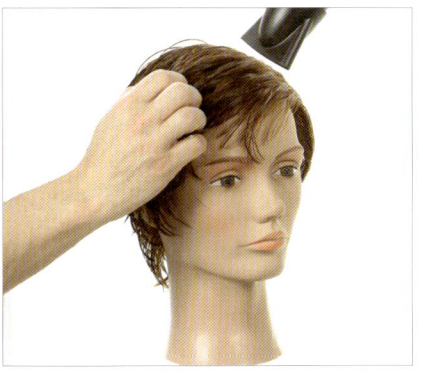 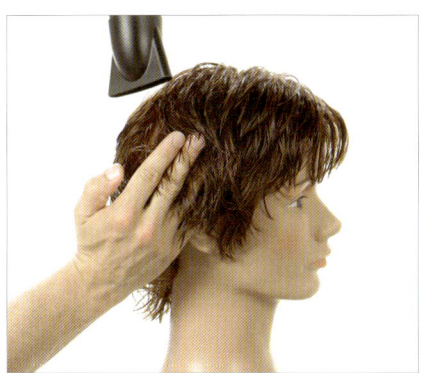 

04–06 Pre-dry the hair starting at the front of the heavier side. Air form with the blow dryer set on medium temperature and speed for control. Lightly manipulate the lengths using your fingers in the direction of the design to completely dry the hair. Manipulate the base for lift and support, and the ends for desired movement and direction. Then, move to the crown and use the same technique working toward the nape. Direct the airflow at the nape and perimeter upward for a slight indentation.

07 Some clients may choose to wear this more casual, low-maintenance look. This "finger-finish" works especially well when hair has subtle, wavy texture.

08 The art shows that the back will be air formed using horizontal and diagonal-back brush positions.

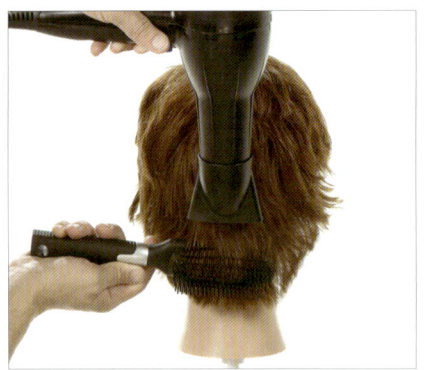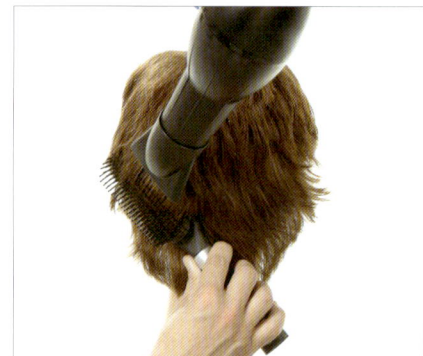

09–11 Starting just above the center nape, position a 9-row brush horizontally and air form volume from base to ends using a curved movement to smooth the ends and reinforce the curved direction. Work from the center to either side. Air form using a diagonal-back brush position at the sides.

12 Next, air form the perimeter, directing the airflow from underneath the strand and turning the brush upward for indentation.

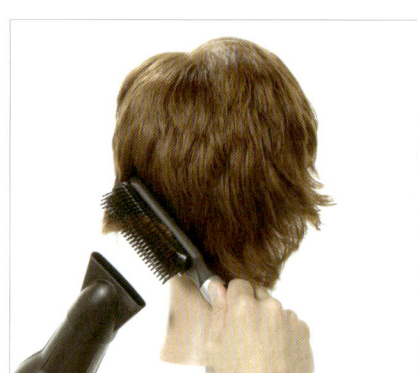

13 Then, position the brush diagonal back on either side of the nape and continue to create subtle indentation.

14 Next, move to the front of the heavier side and air form to create volume using a diagonal brush position.

15 Then air form the ends of the fringe for a subtle bevel-under effect.

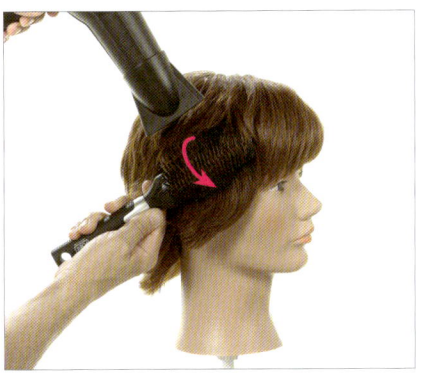

16 Now, move to the side and air form for volume, starting above the ear using a diagonal-back brush position. Continue using this technique until you reach the top.

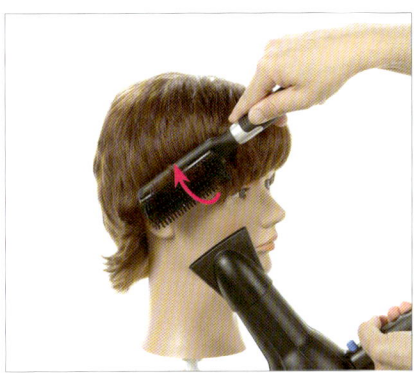

17 Air form the side perimeter, directing the airflow from underneath the strand to create indentation.

18 Repeat on the opposite side. Air form volume starting above the ear working to the top. Then, air form indentation at the side perimeter.

19 Next, air form to blend between volume and indentation and break up the texture using your fingers. Start below the nape and direct the airflow upward. Work around the head and slightly move the dryer back and forth as you work to the sides and toward the top.

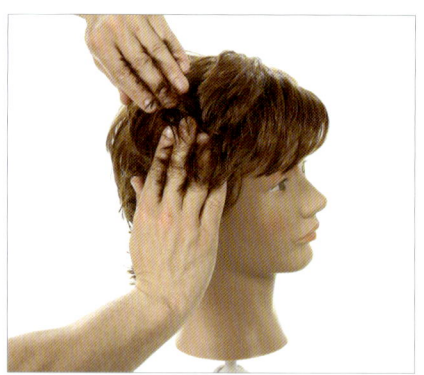
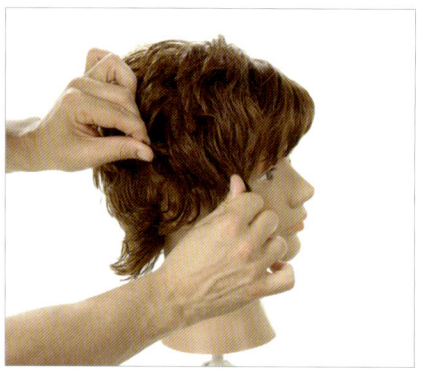

20–21 Apply a silicone-based finishing product, distributing it evenly through the hair. Then use your fingers to define the direction and texture of the design.

22 Scrunch the ends to enhance the activated texture.

23 Smooth the fringe to create textural contrast in the design.

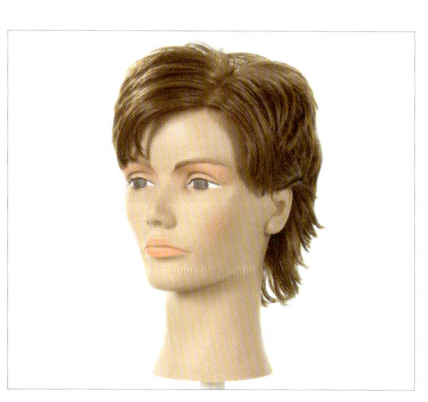

24–25 The finish shows a highly textured, air-formed design that showcases the uniformly layered form. The hair can also be tucked behind the ears for an easy styling option.

02

DIRECTIONAL VOLUME AND INDENTATION – AIR FORMING

Draw or fill in the boxes with the appropriate answers.

STRUCTURE

FORM/TEXTURE

DIRECTION

AIR-FORMING PATTERN

COMB-OUT/FINISH

☐ RELAX ☐ DRY MOLD ☐ BACKCOMB/BACKBRUSH ☐ DEFINE THE FORM ☐ DETAIL

TOOLS/PRODUCT CHOICE

Educator Signature

Date

DIRECTIONAL VOLUME AND INDENTATION – AIR FORMING

This rubric is a performance assessment tool designed to measure your ability to **create** *Pivot Point hair designs.*

	LEVEL 1 *in progress*	LEVEL 2 *getting better*	LEVEL 3 *entry-level proficiency*
PREPARATION			
• Assemble hair design essentials	☐	☐	☐
CREATE			
• Shampoo, condition and apply styling cream	☐	☐	☐
• Create a side part from center of left eye to crown	☐	☐	☐
• Distribute in direction of design using parallel distribution from front hairline to sides; then from crown to nape using radial distribution	☐	☐	☐
• Air form heavier side using fingers to manipulate base for lift and ends for movement; work in direction of design	☐	☐	☐
• Air form crown using same technique; work toward nape	☐	☐	☐
• Air form nape and perimeter upward for indentation	☐	☐	☐
• Air form volume, starting above nape using 9-row brush along a horizontal line in center and diagonal-back lines on sides	☐	☐	☐
• Work toward top using same technique	☐	☐	☐
• Air form perimeter nape for slight indentation; use horizontal brush position at center, diagonal back at sides; direct airflow from underneath	☐	☐	☐
• Air form volume starting at front of heavier side using diagonal brush position; work up to side part	☐	☐	☐
• Air form ends of fringe under	☐	☐	☐
• Air form volume starting above ear on one side using a diagonal-back brush position; work toward top; air form indentation at perimeter	☐	☐	☐
• Repeat same techniques on the opposite side	☐	☐	☐
• Blend directions using fingers to control lengths and directing airflow up, moving dryer back and forth	☐	☐	☐
• Apply silicone-based product and distribute evenly	☐	☐	☐
• Define direction and texture using fingers	☐	☐	☐
• Scrunch the ends and smooth the fringe for textural contrast	☐	☐	☐

TOTAL POINTS = _____ + _____ + _____

TOTAL POINTS _____ ÷ HIGHEST POSSIBLE SCORE 54 X 100 = _____ %

Record your time in comparison with the suggested salon speed.

To improve my performance on this procedure, I need to:

_____ _____ _____
Student Signature   Educator Signature   Date

WORKSHOP 11
CURVATURE VOLUME – CIRCLE WRAP

The circle wrap is commonly performed after a relaxer service. It provides the longevity and movement of a wet set with the smoothness of a thermal design. This service is essentially a molded set and requires a hood dryer. The flat iron can be used after the wrap is combed out to provide an even silkier, more polished texture.

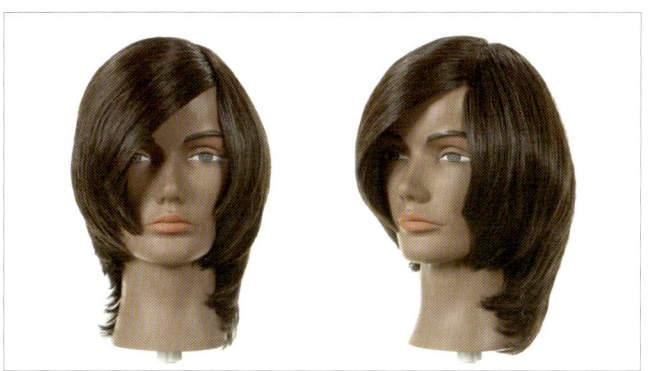

The finish shows uniform lengths that conform to the head, frame the face and display smooth texture.

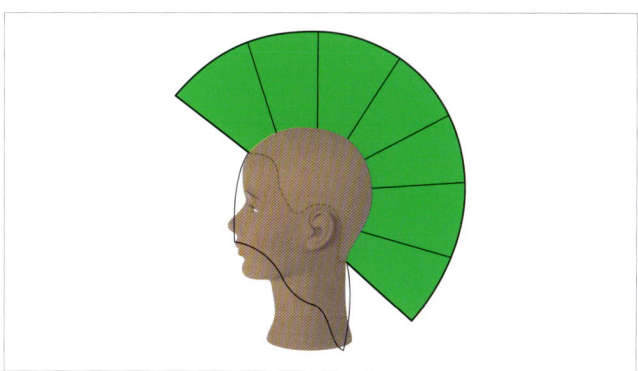

This design is created on a uniformly layered form.

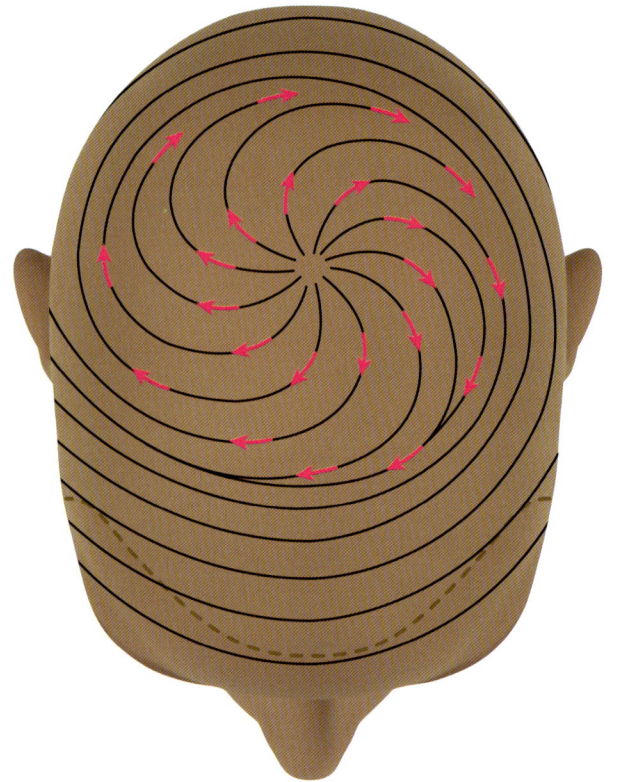
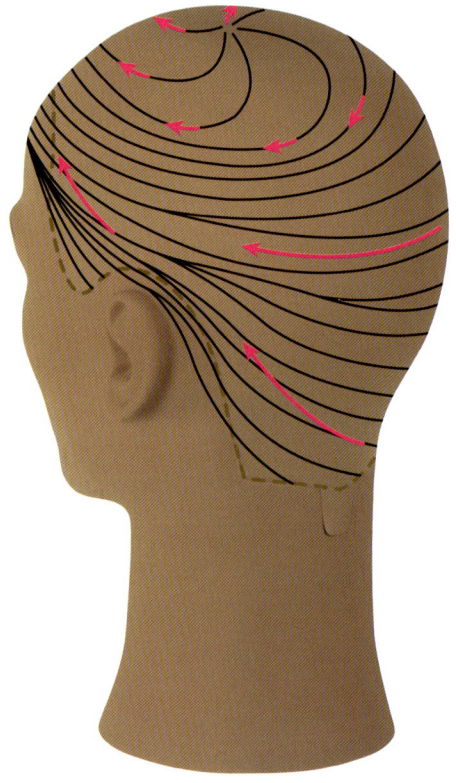

The art shows the distribution and molding direction used in this design. Note that radial distribution is used with a point of origin just behind the apex, while the hair is molded in a circular, clockwise direction.

01–03 After the hair is shampooed and gently towel-dried, apply a liberal amount of setting lotion throughout the hair. Distribute the product with a fine-tooth comb from base to ends.

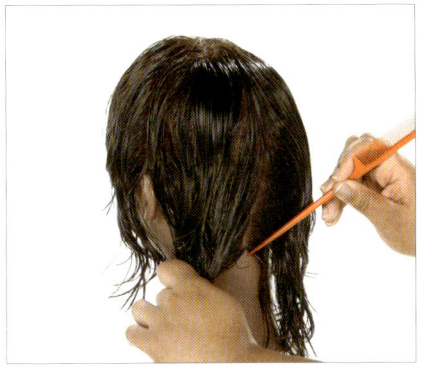

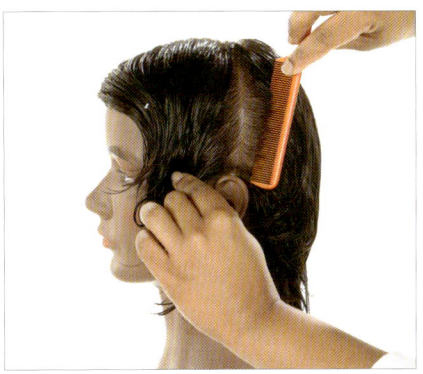

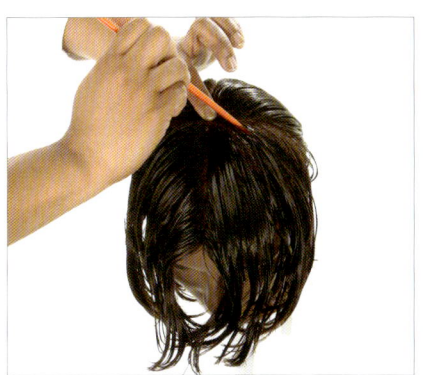

04–05 Section the hair from the front hairline to the center nape. Next, section from just behind the apex to each ear, establishing the location of the point of origin for the design.

06 Beginning in the front-left quadrant, distribute the hair from the point of origin using radial distribution and the tail of the comb.

07 Continue to establish radial distribution through all remaining quadrants.

08 Next, use the first few teeth of the comb to refine the direction of the radial distribution prior to molding the hair.

09 Return to the back-left quadrant and protect the point of origin by placing your index finger approximately 1" (2.5 cm) away. Begin to mold a circle in a clockwise direction.

10 Continue to mold the hair around the head, maintaining tension so the hair stays smooth and controlled.

11 After a small complete circle has been molded around the top of the head, use the same molding technique to incorporate the hair below.

12 At the front, direct the lengths up and mold them along the front hairline to keep the hair off the face.

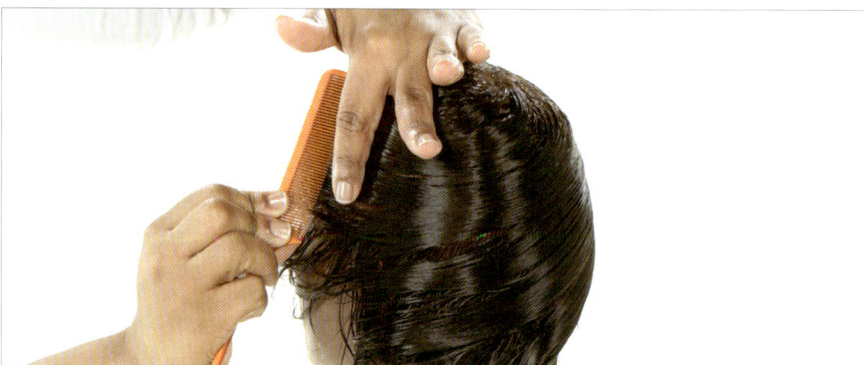

13–14 Distribute the hair from behind the left ear upward and blend it with the interior lengths that have already been molded. If needed, subdivide the hair to control the lengths and mold them to rest on top of the previously molded hair.

15 When you return to the front hairline, use the tip of the tail comb to direct the lengths up and around the face. Continue to incorporate the lengths into the previously molded hair. Use your index finger to support the molded direction as you work.

16 Follow the hairline down on the opposite side, and use the tip of the tail comb to lift the sideburn lengths around the ear.

17–18 Continue to use the same molding technique as you add subsequent hair from the exterior into the previously molded hair.

19 Continue to apply tension and reinforce the molded direction with your index finger to keep the hair smooth.

20–21 Continue to distribute and mold the hair in this manner until the entire set is completed and all the hair is smoothly incorporated.

22 Use the tail comb on the surface to lightly refine the circular molding.

23 As an option, position a paper strip around the hairline to keep the hair in place while under the hood dryer. The time your client spends under the dryer depends on the length, density and texture of hair.

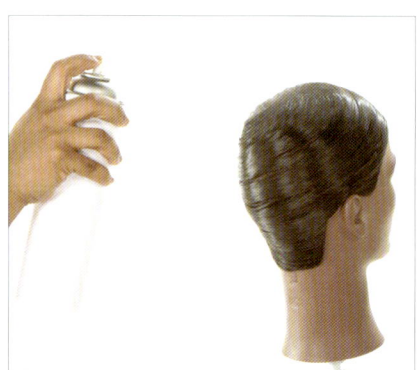

24 When the hair is completely dry, apply a shine-spray to loosen it.

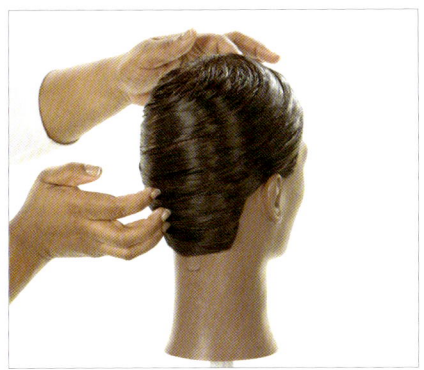

25 Use your fingers to loosen the surface and check to assure the hair has dried completely while it is still molded.

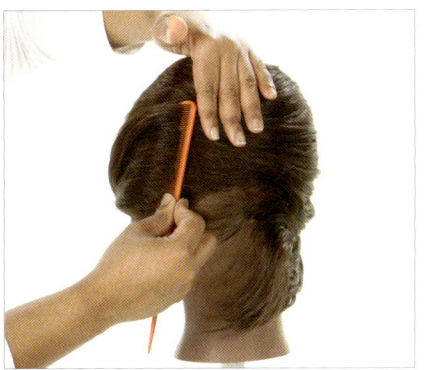

26 Next, use your tail comb to further relax the set while following the direction of the wrap.

27 Use a large-tooth tail comb to distribute the hair into the final finished direction.

28 Use the tip of the tail comb to define the form and detail the texture of the design.

29–30 The result of this circle wrap features smooth, silky lengths that conform to the head and frame the face.

DESIGN DECISIONS *WORKSHOP 11*

CURVATURE VOLUME – CIRCLE WRAP

artist+ access.

Draw or fill in the boxes with the appropriate answers.

STRUCTURE

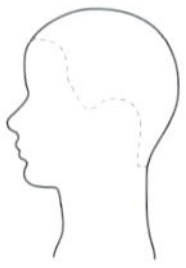

FORM/TEXTURE

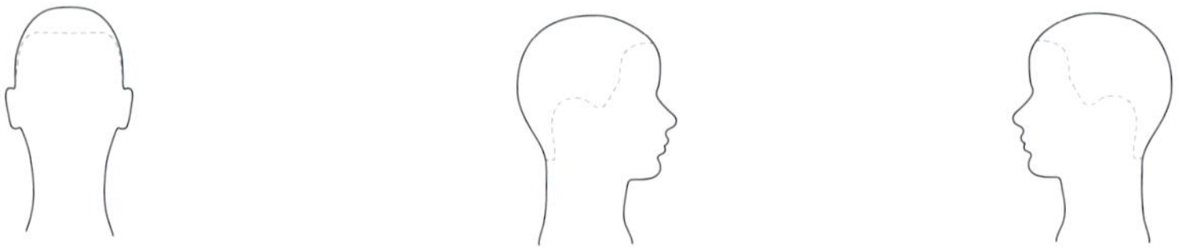

DIRECTION

MOLDING PATTERN

COMB-OUT/FINISH

☐ RELAX ☐ DRY MOLD ☐ BACKCOMB/BACKBRUSH ☐ DEFINE THE FORM ☐ DETAIL

TOOLS/PRODUCT CHOICE

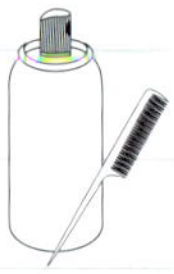

Educator Signature

Date

VARIATION 04
CURVATURE VOLUME – CIRCLE WRAP

This roller wrap variation creates a lot of body and movement, and is ideal for clients with previously relaxed hair. Clients appreciate how easy it is to take care of this style between salon visits.

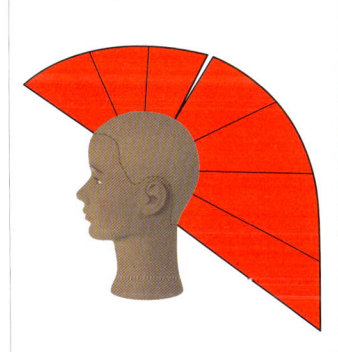
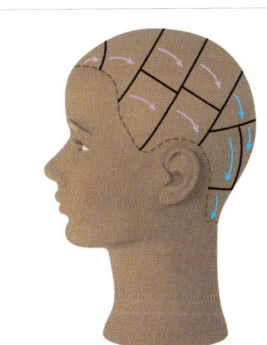

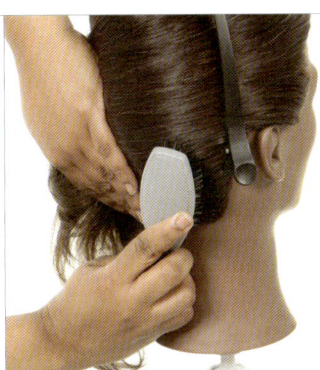

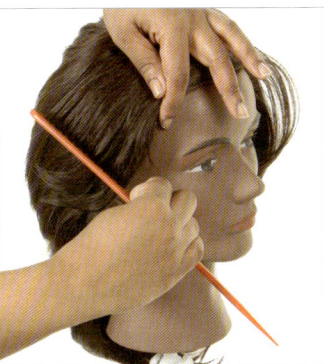

After the hair is towel-dried, setting lotion is applied and distributed from base to ends. Large rollers are used to set the hair in a bricklay pattern away from the face and allowed to dry. Then the set is relaxed using large and small cushion brushes to blend the bases. A vent brush is used with medium heat to direct the hair toward the face. This technique continues to blend the bases and loosen the curl while maintaining volume and support at the base. While wrapping the dry hair in the circular direction, contour clips are used to help keep it in place. You may choose to use a very light-hold hairspray to help control the lengths while wrapping. The hair is placed under a hood dryer for no longer than 5 minutes to further relax the set and reinforce the wrap direction. Afterward, the hair is allowed to cool, and then relaxed and detailed using a large-tooth tail comb.

HAIR DESIGN RUBRIC *WORKSHOP 11*

CURVATURE VOLUME – CIRCLE WRAP

This rubric is a performance assessment tool designed to measure your ability to **create** *Pivot Point hair designs.*

	LEVEL 1 *in progress*	LEVEL 2 *getting better*	LEVEL 3 *entry-level proficiency*
PREPARATION			
• Assemble hair design essentials	☐	☐	☐
CREATE			
• Shampoo, towel-dry and apply setting lotion, distributing from base to ends with a fine-tooth comb	☐	☐	☐
• Establish point of origin by sectioning from front hairline to center nape, and from just behind apex to each ear	☐	☐	☐
• Distribute hair from point of origin using radial distribution and tail of comb; begin at front-left quadrant	☐	☐	☐
• Establish radial distribution throughout remaining quadrants	☐	☐	☐
• Refine direction of radial distribution using first few teeth of tail comb	☐	☐	☐
• Mold a circle in clockwise direction while protecting point of origin with index finger; begin in back-left quadrant	☐	☐	☐
• Mold a small complete circle around top of head maintaining tension	☐	☐	☐
• Mold using same techniques to incorporate hair below	☐	☐	☐
• Direct lengths at the front up and along front hairline	☐	☐	☐
• Distribute hair behind left ear upward and blend with interior lengths	☐	☐	☐
• Direct lengths at front hairline up and around face using tip of tail comb	☐	☐	☐
• Lift sideburn lengths around ear using tip of tail comb while following hairline down opposite side	☐	☐	☐
• Mold subsequent hair from exterior into previously molded hair using same technique	☐	☐	☐
• Distribute and mold hair, applying tension and reinforcing molded direction with index finger, until all hair is smoothly incorporated	☐	☐	☐
• Refine circular molding lightly over the surface using tail comb	☐	☐	☐
• Position paper strip around hairline; place under hood dryer	☐	☐	☐
• Apply shine spray to loosen hair when completely dry	☐	☐	☐
• Loosen surface using your fingers to assure hair has completely dried while still molded	☐	☐	☐
• Relax set using tail comb following direction of wrap	☐	☐	☐
• Distribute hair into final finished direction using large-tooth tail comb	☐	☐	☐
• Define form and detail texture using tip of tail comb	☐	☐	☐

TOTAL POINTS = _____ + _____ + _____

TOTAL POINTS _____ ÷ HIGHEST POSSIBLE SCORE 66 X 100 = _____ %

Record your time in comparison with the suggested salon speed.

To improve my performance on this procedure, I need to:

_____

Student Signature   *Educator Signature*   *Date*

VOICES OF SUCCESS

"The finish of a hair design can make or break the way a client feels about the entire service. To make sure my clients look great every day, I like to share proven styling tips. After all, the way my clients look is my best advertisement."

THE DESIGNER

"I am so glad that I can teach my students a system that will lead them to predictable hair design results, matching the original vision they have for their clients!"

THE EDUCATOR

"I made it standard procedure in my salon that all designers ensure that their clients are completely satisfied with the way their hair is finished. It is important to all of us that our clients look and feel great when they leave."

THE SALON OWNER

IN OTHER WORDS

Following a step-by-step process to achieve predictable wet and thermal hair design results on the four basic forms is part of the strong foundation designers rely on for their career success.

LEARNING CHALLENGE

Circle the letter corresponding to the correct answer.

1. The standard procedures used to set hair in wet and thermal design are:
    a. comb, scale, part and apply
    b. distribute, mold, scale and apply
    c. distribute, mold, scale, part and apply
    d. distribute, mold, section, part and apply

2. The two types of distribution in wet and thermal hair designs are radial and:
    a. straight
    b. parallel
    c. curvature
    d. from one point of origin

3. The standard procedures used to finish a design are:
    a. relax, dry mold, backcomb or backbrush, detail
    b. distribute, dry mold, backcomb, define the form and detail
    c. relax, mold, backcomb or backbrush, define the form and detail
    d. relax, dry mold, backcomb or backbrush, define the form and detail

4. When designing solid forms, their shapes generally expand most:
    a. on the sides
    b. at the crown
    c. along the perimeter
    d. above the perimeter form line

5. When designing uniformly layered forms, maximum base volume control in the interior and close-fitted lengths in the exterior can create the illusion of:
    a. more length
    b. a solid form
    c. a graduated form
    d. an increase-layered form

LESSONS LEARNED

- The five setting steps that will produce predictable wet and thermal hair design results are: distribute, mold, scale, part and apply.

- The five finishing steps that will produce predictable wet and thermal hair design results are: relax, dry mold, backcomb or backbrush, define the form and detail.

- The volume and expansion within a wet and thermal hair design depend on using the proper base control.

- Remembering client-centered guidelines for wet and thermal hair designs ensures that clients appreciate everything you do during the service and are pleased with the results after the service.

ADVANCED WET AND THERMAL HAIR DESIGN

COMBINING ADVANCED DESIGN TECHNIQUES AND PATTERNS WITH A SYSTEMATIC APPROACH CREATES A WIDE RANGE OF HAIR DESIGNS

FOLLOWING THIS LESSON
YOU WILL BE ABLE TO:

Relate how form, texture and direction design options can affect the appearance of a combination form hair design

Explain the theory involved in using advanced wet and thermal design techniques and patterns, including flat-ironing, scrunch-drying and oblongs

Demonstrate the knowledge and ability to create a variety of advanced wet and thermal hair designs using advanced wet and thermal design techniques and patterns

As a professional hair designer, you may find yourself in a fast-paced, highly creative environment—maybe backstage at a fashion show—in which your advanced wet and thermal design skills would be critical.

Studying and practicing the techniques and designs presented in *Chapter 3, Advanced Wet and Thermal Hair Design* will bring you even closer to being ready for all the creative work opportunities hair design has to offer.

3.1 ADVANCED HAIR DESIGN TECHNIQUES

Designers who can offer finishes created with advanced wet and thermal hair design techniques will be able to follow current trends as well as create glamorous, classic styles, positioning themselves another notch above the competition.

The following pages will show how the wet and thermal design techniques can be used to successfully finish combination form designs. You will also see how alternating directions or wave patterns can be created in hair with a variety of advanced design techniques.

COMBINATION FORM DESIGNING

Design options for combination forms are abundant. In general, the sculpted form in the exterior greatly influences the silhouette or shape of the design, while the sculpted form in the interior greatly influences the texture options of the design.

Often solid or graduated lengths are positioned in the exterior to achieve a distinct perimeter, shape and weight buildup in some area of the form. These lengths are commonly combined with either increase or uniform layers in the interior. The layers disperse the weight in the interior while adding texture. This allows for volume and expansion at the top of the head as well as textural interest and directional movement along the surface of the style.

FORM OPTIONS

Shorter combination forms with layered interiors are versatile and offer numerous interior design options.

INCREASE/GRADUATION

Increase-layered/graduated combination forms offer the greatest expansion possibilities where the two structures meet, creating a weight area. Depending on the design techniques chosen and the volume achieved, this weight area can be accentuated.

Compare the forms and expansion in these two examples.

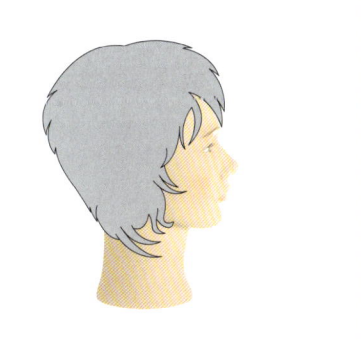

UNIFORM/GRADUATION

Uniform/graduated combination forms show expansion up to the area where the graduated and uniform lengths meet. The graduated lengths shift volume toward the interior where the uniform layers evenly distribute it, resulting in a rounded interior silhouette.

Compare the forms and expansion in these two examples.

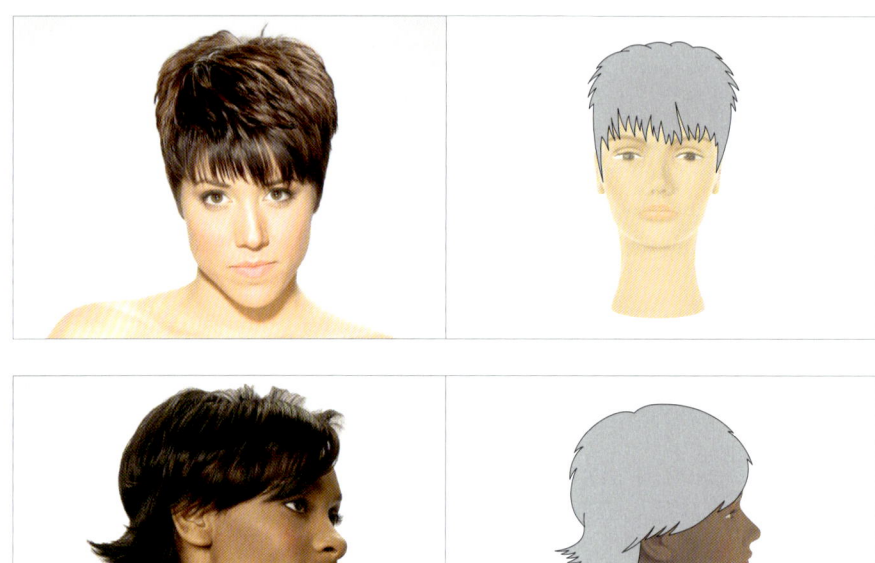

TEXTURE OPTIONS

Showcasing different textures on combination forms not only varies the form, but also changes the mood of the composition.

DIRECTION OPTIONS

Shorter to mid-length combination forms with shorter interior layers allow for unlimited design direction possibilities.

FREEFORM DESIGNS

It is important to remember that not all wet and thermal design compositions can be classified with specific geometric forms or design techniques. Some fall in a category simply known as "freeform." However, the term "freeform" may be misleading. These designs still require thorough consulting and planning in order to achieve outcomes that are just as predictable as the more classic finishes.

WHAT'S GOING ON?

artist⁺
access.

Imagine the hair design in the image to the left is one of your creations, and you are explaining it to one of your colleagues over the phone. Using the space provided, describe the form, texture and direction of the design.

SPECIALIZED TECHNIQUES AND PATTERNS

As times and hair trends change, so do the techniques and tools for wet and thermal hair design.

This section of the chapter includes some of the popular, in-demand techniques and design patterns used to create a variety of temporary effects. These range from super-straight, silky hair to natural-looking curly hair and classic, elegant waves.

FLAT-IRONING

Very straight, shiny hair has regained popularity over the past few years and flat-ironing can be the key to achieving the look. In the next section you will have the opportunity to learn and practice the essential skills needed to work with a flat iron and achieve ultra-smooth finishes.

PRACTICE
MAKES PERFECT 01
STRAIGHT VOLUME –
FLAT-IRONING

The focus of this exercise is to provide practice in air forming and flat-ironing techniques. This is a frequently performed service that is suitable for a variety of hair textures.

Practice this exercise to build rhythm, skill and accuracy using:

- Horizontal partings
- Flat-ironing techniques

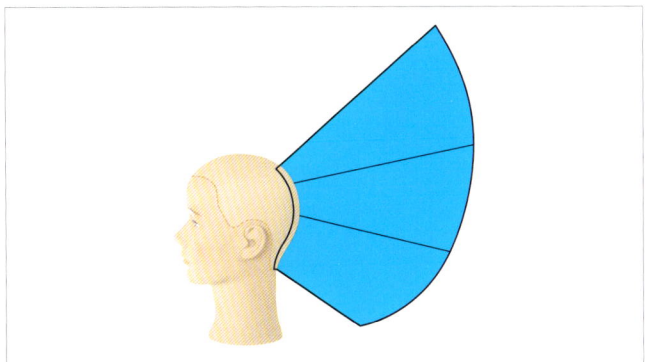

The structure graphic shows the solid form rectangle component used in this exercise.

The finish shows a smooth, unactivated surface without volume on the solid rectangle component.

The art shows ¼" (.6 cm) horizontal partings that will be used to flat-iron the hair. Finer partings will help avoid indentations near the base. You will work from the nape to the top of the rectangle component.

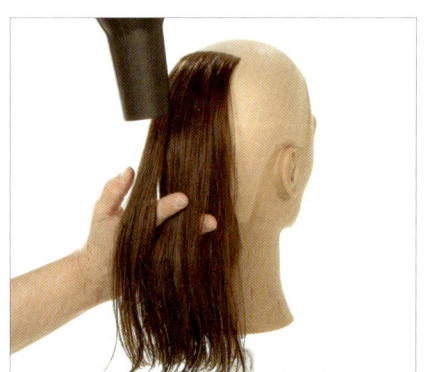

01 Distribute a small amount of light smoothing cream through wet hair. Then, remove approximately 75% of the moisture while running your fingers through the hair.

02 Air form the rectangle component using horizontal partings and a 9-row brush with the Straight Volume – Air Forming technique.

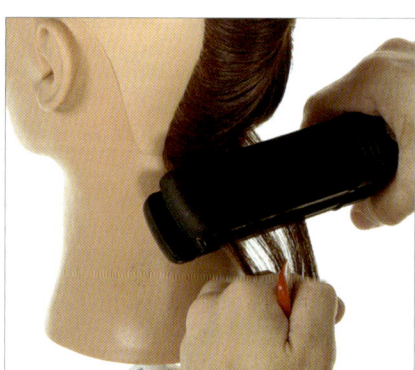

03 Project the first ¼" (.6 cm) horizontal parting at approximately 90° and comb to smooth. Then hold the parting loosely with your fingers and close the iron lightly, moving to the ends.

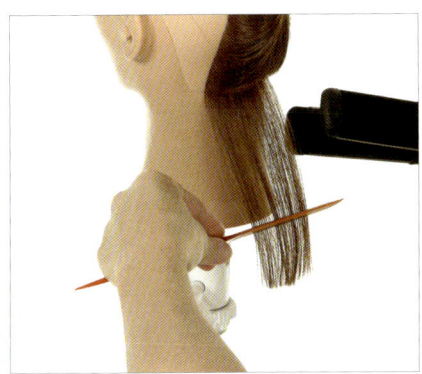

04 Allow the same parting to fall into the heat-resistant tail comb at the base. Slowly move the comb away from the base and insert the iron above the comb near the base.

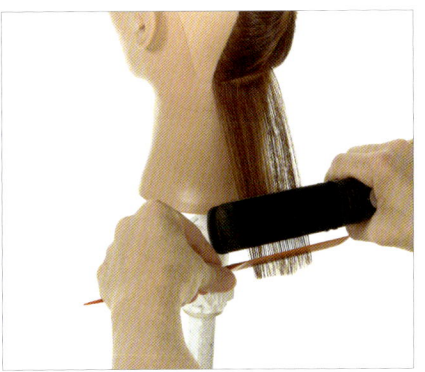

05 Guiding the hair with the comb, close the flat iron with slightly more pressure. Lower the parting to natural fall as you move to the ends.

Be sure not to move too slowly or too quickly and never allow the flat iron to sit on the hair without moving.

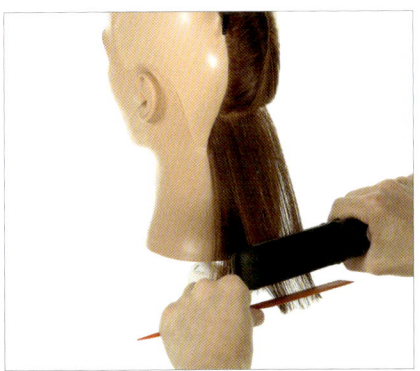

06 Release subsequent horizontal partings and continue using the same techniques as you work upward. Practice using fluid movements while passing the iron twice over each parting.

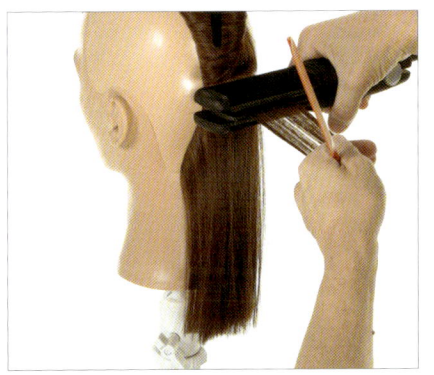

07 As you reach the crest area, continue to project at approximately 90° as the iron is closed and moved along the strand the first time.

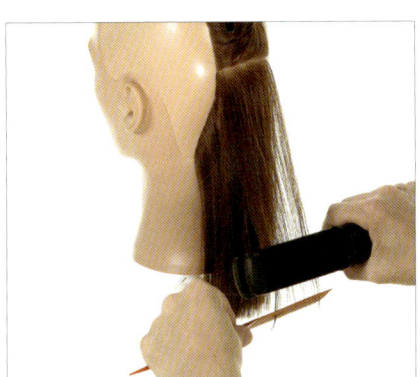

08 Lower the parting on the second pass to avoid volume at the base.

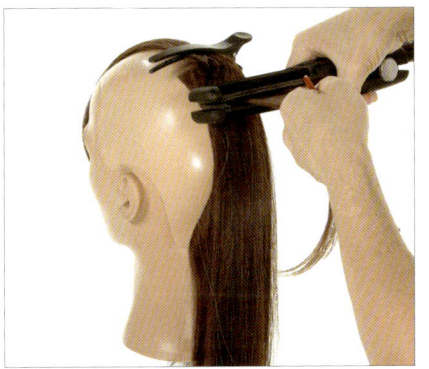

09 Continue using the same techniques as you work upward.

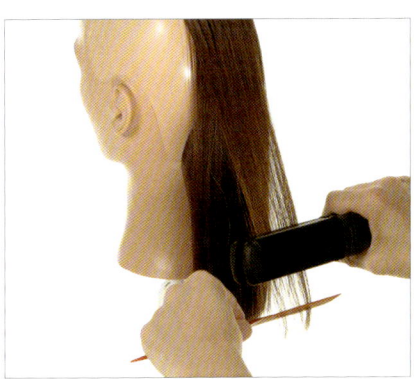

10 Complete the flat-ironing service, projecting the last parting at approximately 90° for the first pass and in natural fall for the final pass.

11 The finish shows straight, sleek lengths with less volume and more shine than air forming will generally achieve.

12–13 You may choose to bevel the ends under. Use the same flat-iron techniques, but slowly turn your wrist as you progress toward the ends. This creates a soft bevel-under effect.

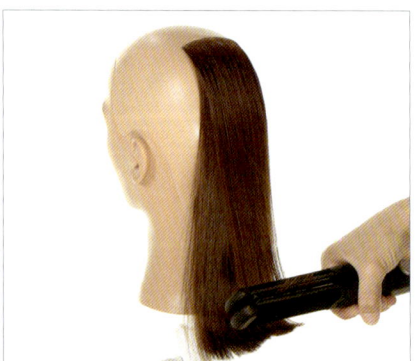 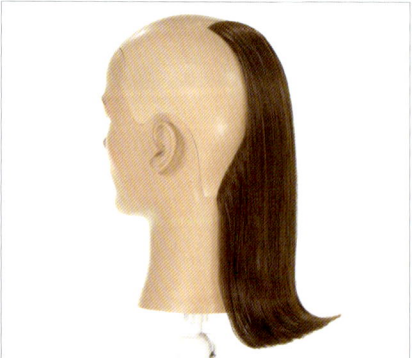

14–15 The ends may also be flipped up by turning your wrist upward as you reach the ends of the hair. Depending on the flat iron being used, the tip of the iron may be held with the opposite hand for control.

SCRUNCH-DRYING

As much as some clients may not like their curls, there are plenty of others who embrace them. This is a great opportunity for a designer to apply scrunch-drying techniques with the appropriate styling and finishing products to tame a wild mane and turn it into bountiful curls.

Additionally, scrunch-drying is fast and involves finger styling, so designers can teach their clients how to work with their curls successfully at home and boost retail sales.

TIPS AND TRICKS TO REMEMBER

WHEN SCRUNCH-DRYING

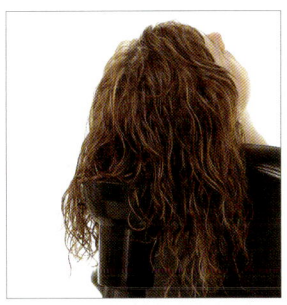

After applying a styling product, twist individual strands of hair and then scrunch-dry them to help calm tighter, more unruly curl textures.

Use a diffuser attachment and gentle, slow movements to manipulate the hair. Hair that is treated in a rough manner will look rough.

Let the client slide down in the salon chair and rest her head on the back of the chair while scrunching the top of the head. This allows the hair to fall freely while the curl formation is enforced.

Let the client tilt her head and lean forward to dry the exterior. This will boost volume, if desired.

OBLONGS

Giving hair a wavy, temporary texture has been an ancient skill in some of the world's most amazing historic eras. In the early 20th century, this look was popular and created through fingerwaves and pincurls. Over time, hair designers have found methods to create this wave formation with a variety of tools and techniques. However different these tools and techniques may appear, they all rely on the fundamental principles of working with oblongs or alternating oblongs.

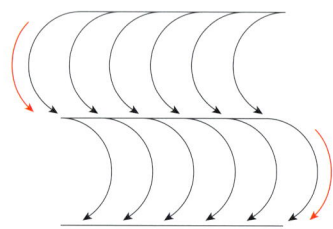

Two or more oblongs moving in alternating directions create wave patterns. Oblongs can be positioned horizontally, vertically or diagonally within a design.

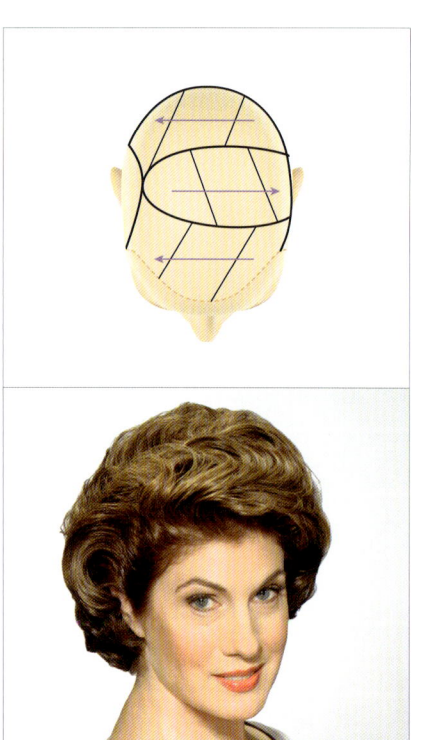

HORIZONTAL OBLONGS

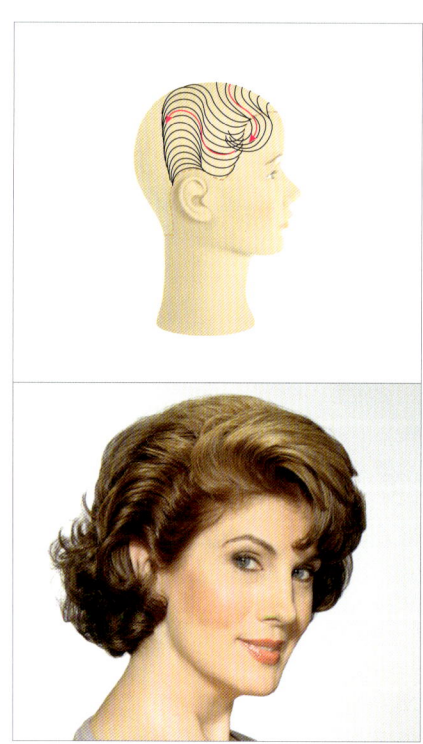

VERTICAL OBLONGS

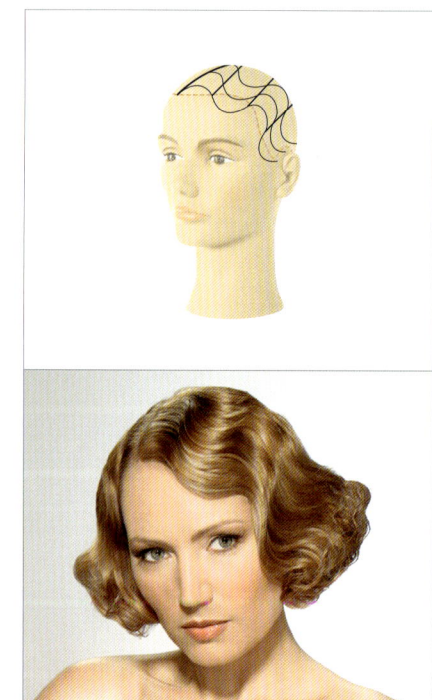

DIAGONAL OBLONGS

Volume and indentation oblongs are used to create waves and soft movements for contemporary and classic designs.

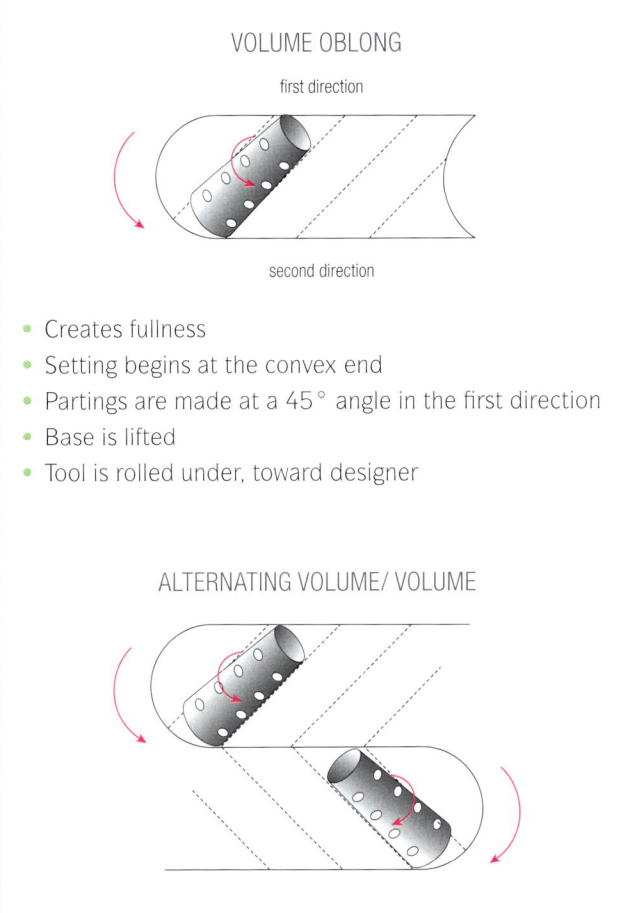

VOLUME OBLONG

- Creates fullness
- Setting begins at the convex end
- Partings are made at a 45° angle in the first direction
- Base is lifted
- Tool is rolled under, toward designer

ALTERNATING VOLUME/ VOLUME

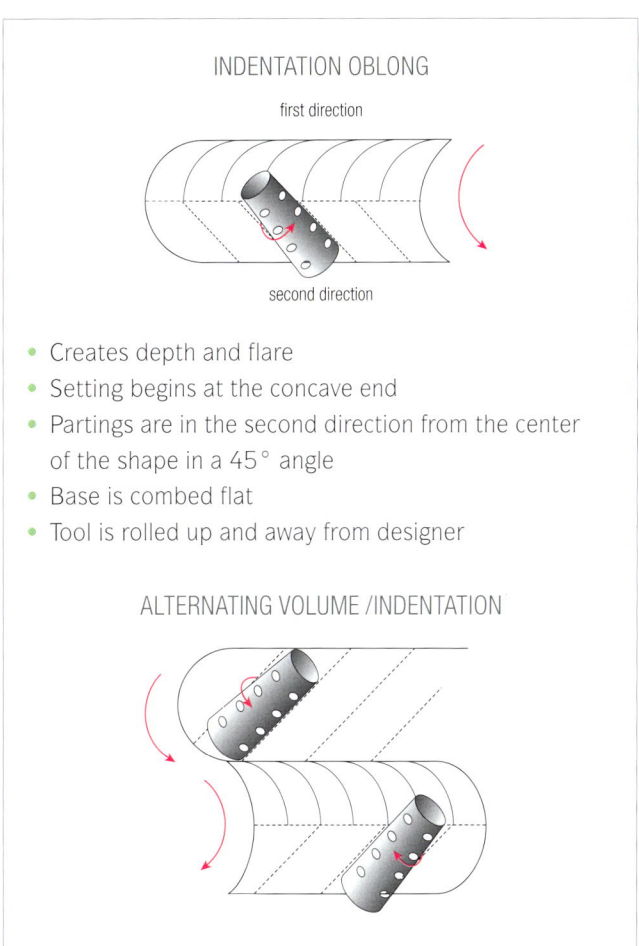

INDENTATION OBLONG

- Creates depth and flare
- Setting begins at the concave end
- Partings are in the second direction from the center of the shape in a 45° angle
- Base is combed flat
- Tool is rolled up and away from designer

ALTERNATING VOLUME /INDENTATION

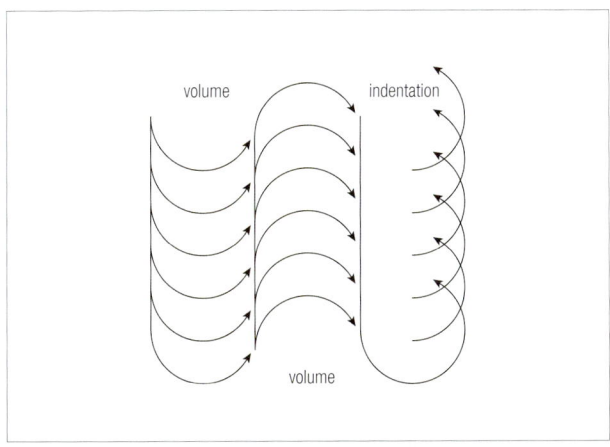

Often, designs incorporate both volume and indentation oblongs. In these instances, volume oblongs are used for most of the design, and an indentation oblong is set along the perimeter of the alternating oblong area.

PRACTICE MAKES PERFECT 02
ALTERNATING OBLONGS – ROLLERS

The purpose of this exercise is to provide practice in wet setting alternating oblongs for volume and indentation. Practice is also provided in finishing techniques to reflect the set movement.

Practice this exercise to build rhythm, skill, speed and consistency to:

- Use parallel distribution
- Mold and scale alternating oblongs
- Part rhomboid-shaped bases
- Use half-off base control
- Relax
- Backbrush
- Define the form

The finish features a combination of volume and indentation alternating oblongs set on rollers.

The completed set shows horizontal oblongs. Note that the first two rows are set with volume and the last row is set with indentation techniques.

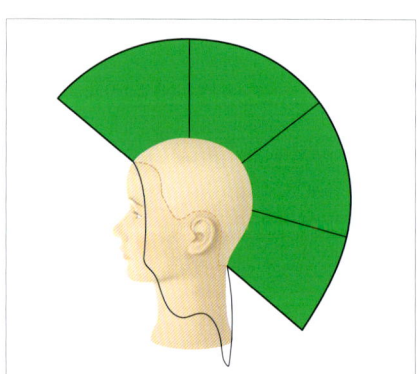

This exercise is performed on uniform lengths.

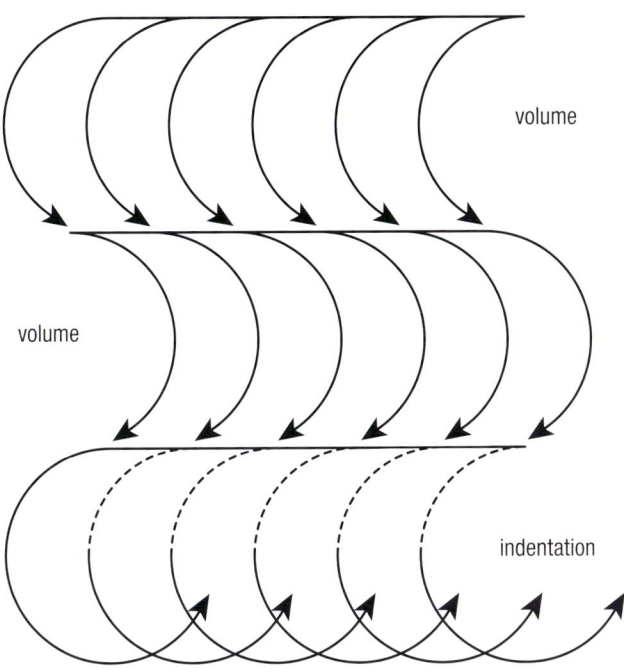

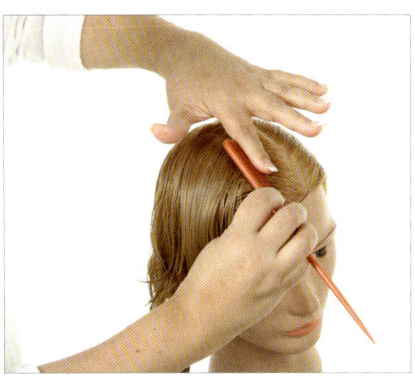

01 Start at the convex end and distribute the hair at a 45° angle toward the convex end. Place your finger in the center of the shape and comb through to the ends. Work to the concave end.

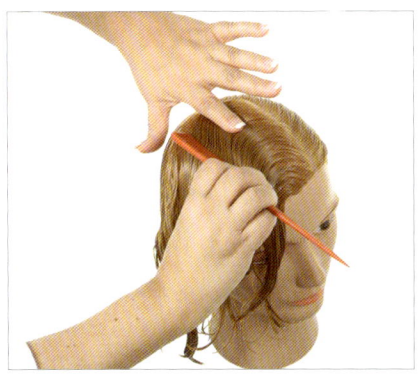

02 Mold the second direction starting at the concave end. Firmly place your finger in the middle of the oblong and direct the hair toward the concave end. Work to the convex end.

The art shows that the first two of the three horizontal oblongs will be set in volume and the last one will be set in indentation.

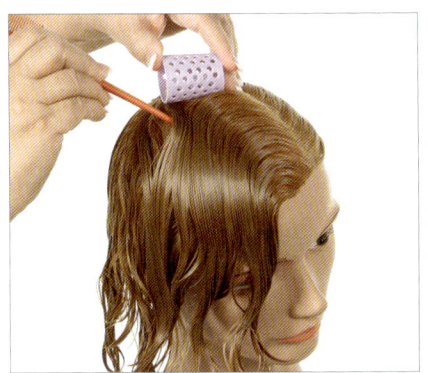

03–04 Mold and scale the two volume oblongs by positioning the roller in the first direction. Start at the convex end and move toward the concave end using the length of the roller as a guide.

05 For indentation, scale 1½ times the length of the tool to create a larger shape required for indentation.

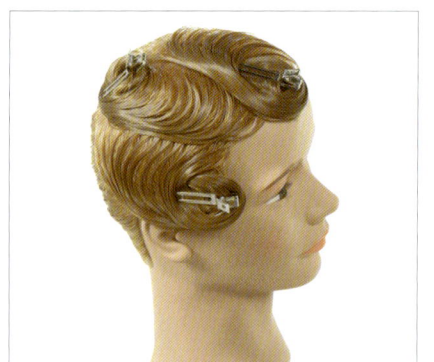

06 Mold, scale and use a clip to secure the three alternating oblongs.

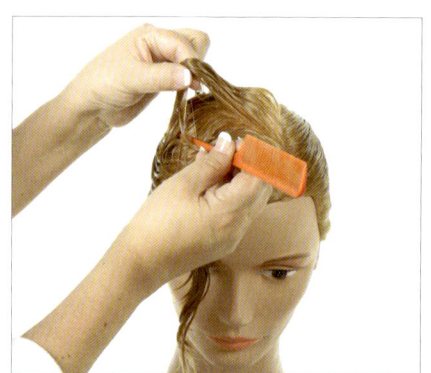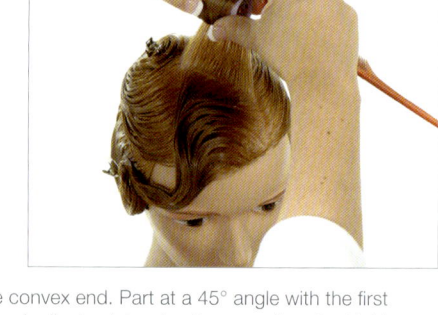

07–08 Begin setting the first volume oblong at the convex end. Part at a 45° angle with the first direction using the large diameter of the cone-shaped roller to determine the one-diameter (1x) base size. Position the roller parallel to the part, project the hair 90° and position the roller half-off base.

09 Position a pick to secure at the small end of the roller.

10 Repeat with the next two rollers, positioning each roller half-off base.

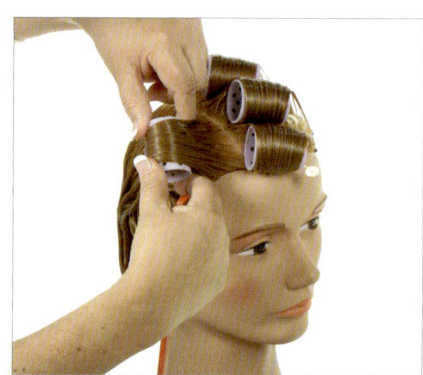

11 Move to the second oblong and part the hair in the first direction, again starting at the convex end. Project the hair at 90° and position the roller parallel to the part with half-off base control.

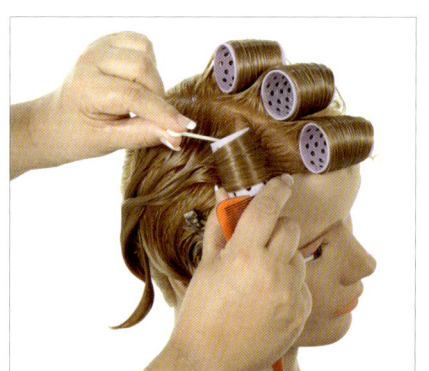

12 Position a pick to secure the roller.

13 Complete the second oblong.

14 Begin setting the indentation oblong at the concave end. Part with the second direction from the center of the shape.

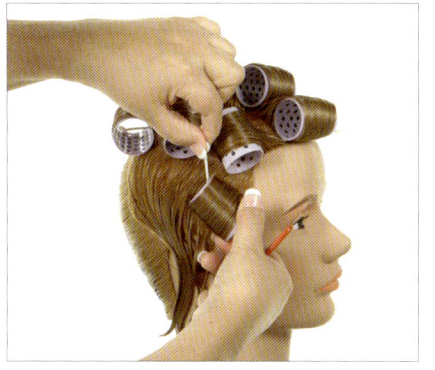

15–16 Position the roller at a 45° angle, keeping the first direction flat with low projection, and roll upward. Position the roller in the second direction, and position a pick to secure the roller.

17 Repeat on the next two rollers.

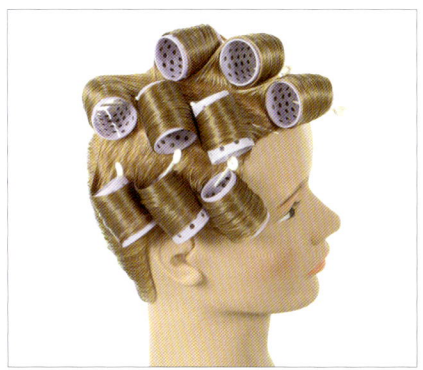
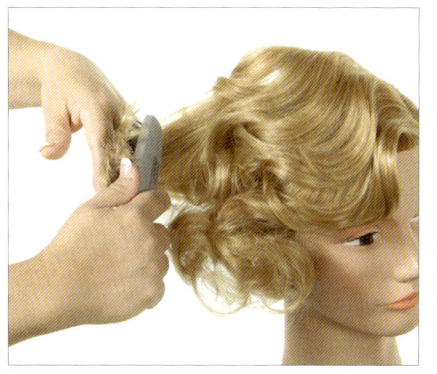

18 Note how the top half of the indentation oblong is left undisturbed. This is what creates the hollow space.

19 Relax and dry mold the design in the direction the hair was set.

20 Backbrush to create volume and to blend the bases.

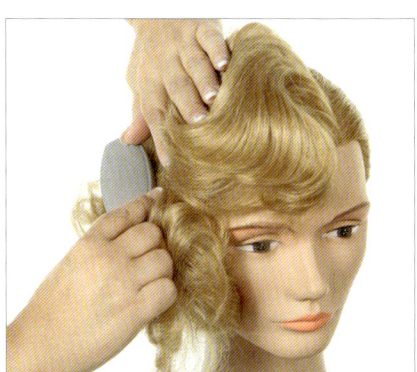

21 Then smooth the surface following the direction of the set. Define the form.

22 Use a wide-tooth comb to detail the form. You may also use the tail of the comb to reinforce the flare in the indentation.

23 The finish shows alternating oblongs with volume and indentation.

PRACTICE MAKES PERFECT 03
ALTERNATING OBLONGS – PINCURLS

The focus of this exercise is the application of flat, volume and indentation pincurls within alternating oblongs.

Practice this exercise to build rhythm, skill, speed and consistency to:

- Use parallel distribution
- Mold and scale alternating oblongs
- Part rhomboid-shaped bases
- Set flat volume and indentation pincurls
- Relax
- Backbrush
- Define

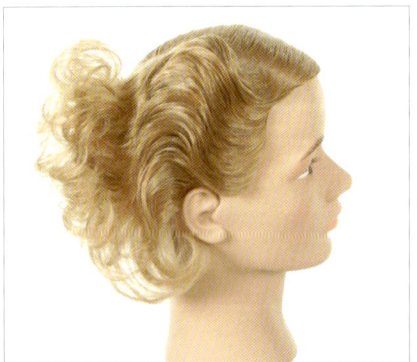

The finish shows alternating oblongs that feature closeness at the hairline, blend into volume and end with indentation and activated texture.

The completed set shows alternating oblongs set in flat, volume and indentation pincurls.

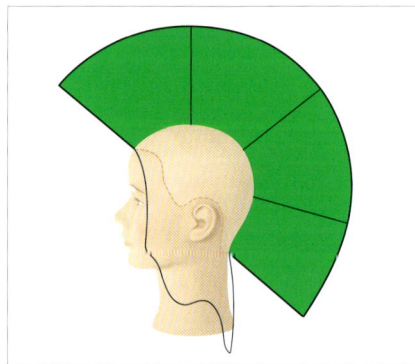

This alternating-oblong exercise is performed on uniformly layered lengths.

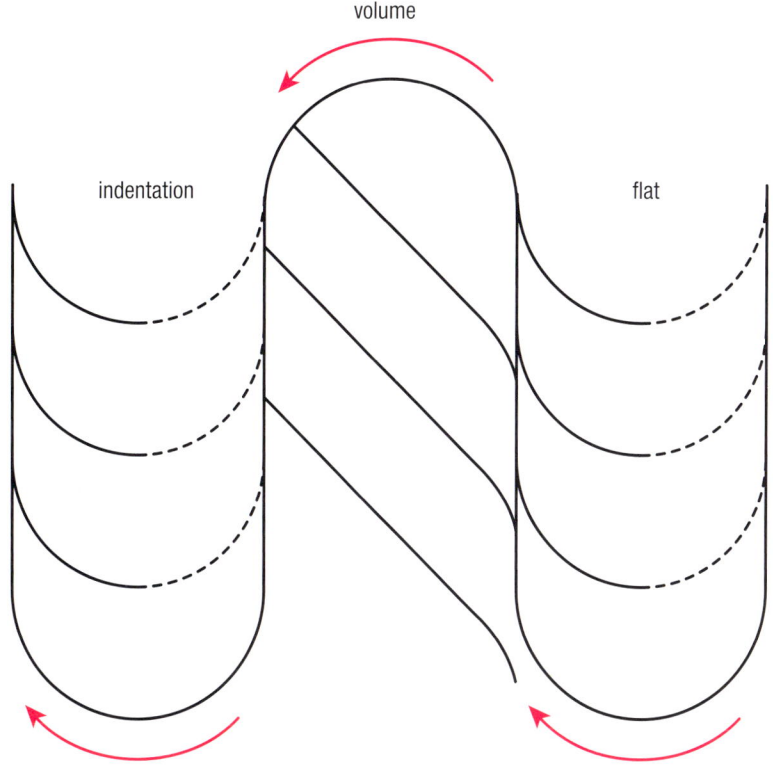

volume

indentation

flat

The art indicates the parting patterns that will be used to set vertical oblongs. Note that flat and indentation pincurls are parted from the center of the shape in the second direction, while volume pincurls are parted diagonally across the shape in the first direction.

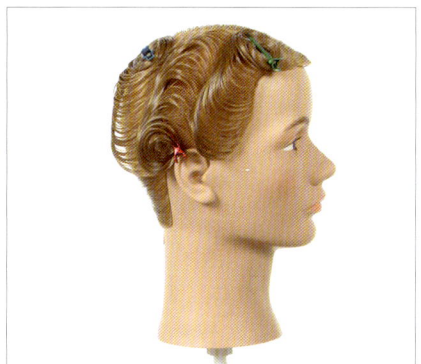

01 Mold and scale three vertical oblongs on the side of the head.

02 Begin setting the oblong at the front hairline in flat pincurls. To create the flat pincurls, begin at the concave end and part in the second direction.

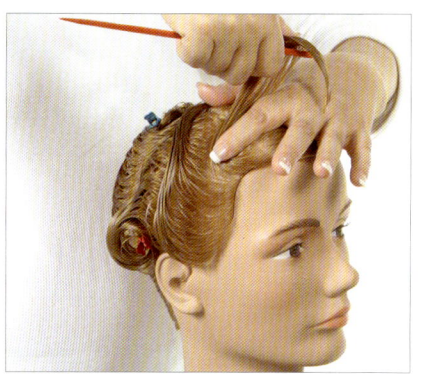

03 Place your fingers in the center of the shape to keep the center of the base flat. Then curve the arc and form the circle.

04 Position the circle in the front of the base.

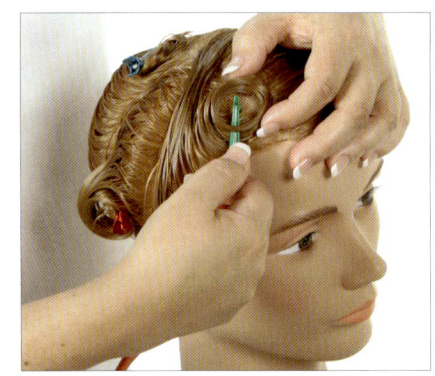

05 Secure across the circle with the second direction.

06 Repeat the same techniques to complete the oblong.

07 Set the next oblong with volume pincurls. Begin at the convex end and part with the first direction.

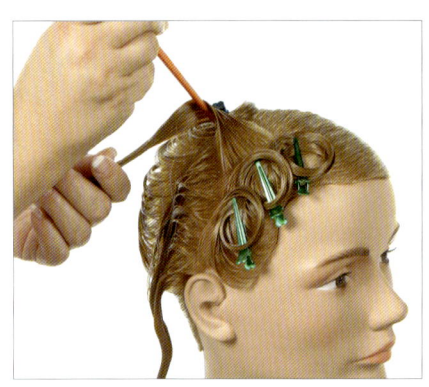

08 Create base lift with your comb, and reinforce the arc with the tail of the comb. Smooth the hair.

09 Form the circle around your finger, using one finger to hold the shape and the other hand to smooth the curl.

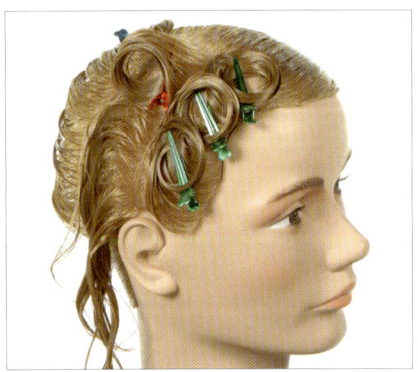

10 Secure parallel to the parting in the first direction.

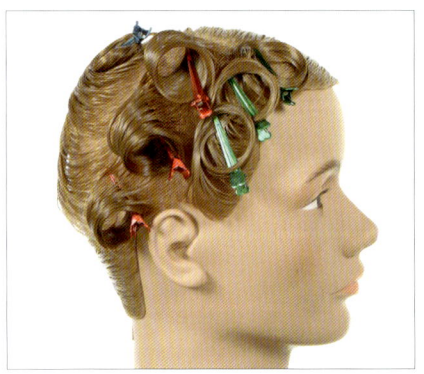

11 Repeat the same techniques to complete the pincurls in the volume oblong.

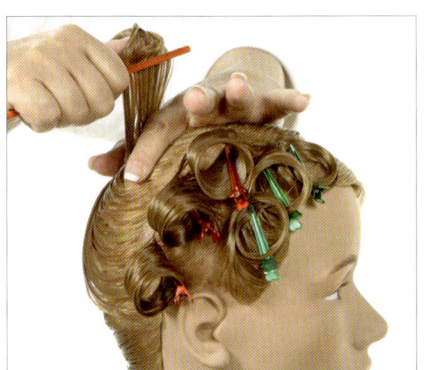

12 Set the last oblong with indentation pincurls. Begin at the concave end and part from the center of the shape with the second direction. Position your index finger in the center of the shape to avoid disturbing the first direction.

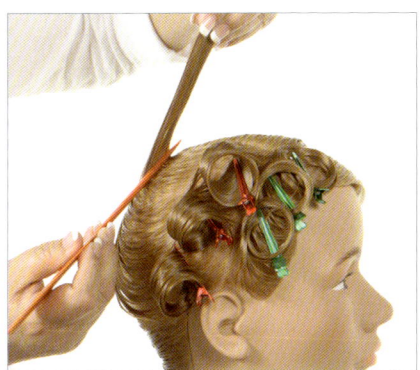

13 Keep the base flat, curve the arc and form the circle.

14 Smooth the hair and use your fingers to form a circle that turns up and away.

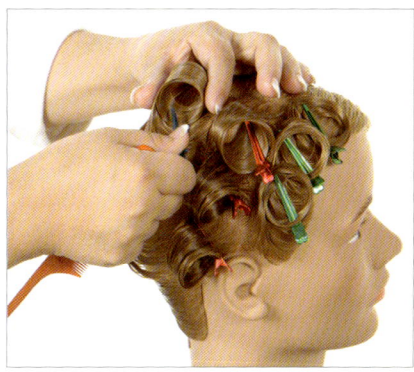

15 Position the pincurl in front of the base and secure through the circle in the second direction. Repeat these procedures to complete the shape.

16 Relax the hair using two cushion brushes to blend the pincurls and their partings.

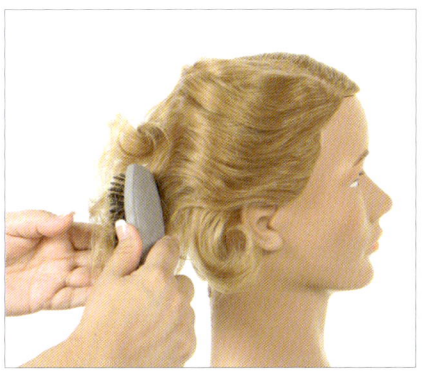

17 Using a cushion brush, dry mold to retrace the shapes and to reinforce the oblongs.

18 Begin backbrushing in the direction the hair was set. Be sure to connect each shape as you backbrush the surface of the hair.

19 Retrace the alternating oblongs as you smooth the surface. Then define the form holding the previous oblong to protect the shape.

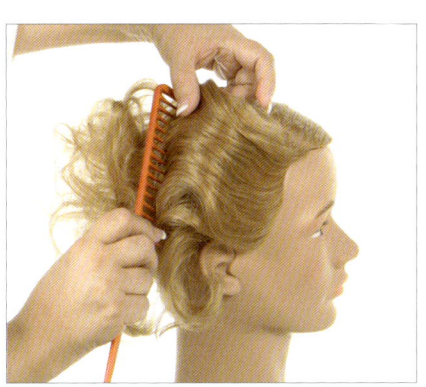

20 Use a large-tooth comb to define the texture and reinforce the waves.

21 The completed exercise features a wave pattern with flare at the ends that moves away from the face.

3.2 ADVANCED HAIR DESIGNS

At this stage in your wet and thermal hair design training, you are ready to learn about and practice some of the most requested techniques. Keep in mind that as trends evolve, your styling repertoire as a hair designer needs to grow. Taking all you've learned in basic wet and thermal designing and combining it with the patterns and techniques that follow will set you on the path to success.

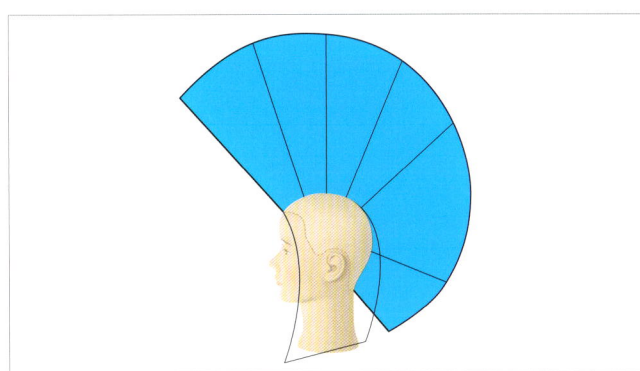

WORKSHOP 01

STRAIGHT VOLUME – AIR FORMING/ FLAT-IRONING

The flat-iron technique is used to minimize volume and create completely straight lengths. This technique is often popular with younger clients and is also beneficial to use prior to checking the accuracy of the solid form hair sculpture.

The finish shows very straight, unactivated lengths with minimal volume.

This exercise is performed on the diagonal-forward solid form sculpture.

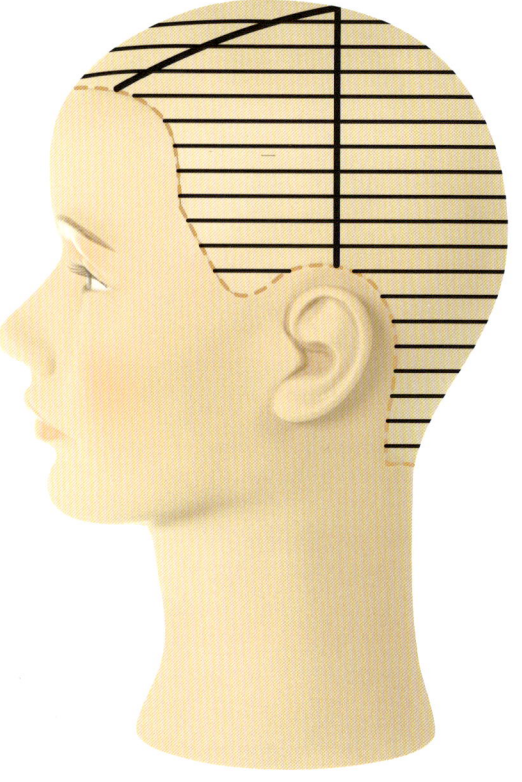

The art shows ¼" (.6 cm) horizontal partings used throughout the exercise with a side part over the left eye. Note that although the form line of this design is diagonal forward, horizontal partings are used to flat-iron the hair. This avoids any type of directional movement near the ends.

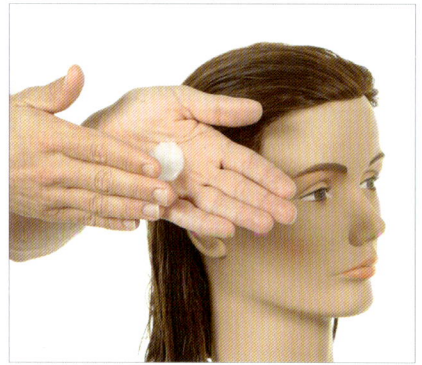
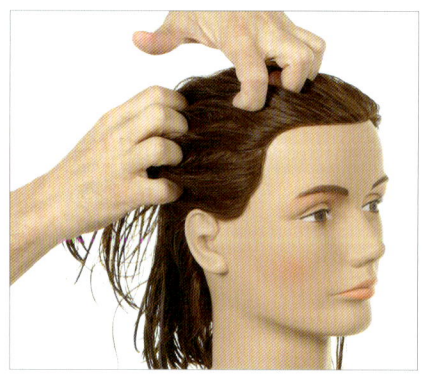
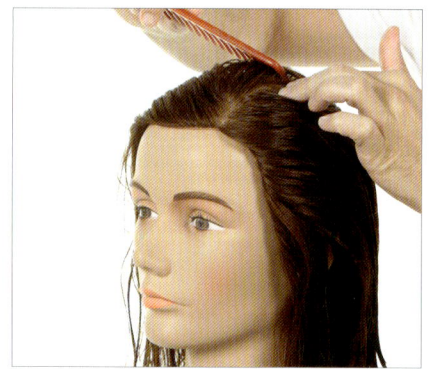

01–02 Apply a smoothing cream to the hair to soften the lengths and create minimum hold while still protecting the hair from the styling heat. Distribute through the lengths from base to ends.

03 Create a diagonal side part over the left eye extending to the center crown.

04 Air form the hair to remove excess moisture using your fingers to control the lengths.

05 Then air form using the 9-row brush to smooth the hair and direct the lengths in the intended direction. Dry the hair completely before proceeding.

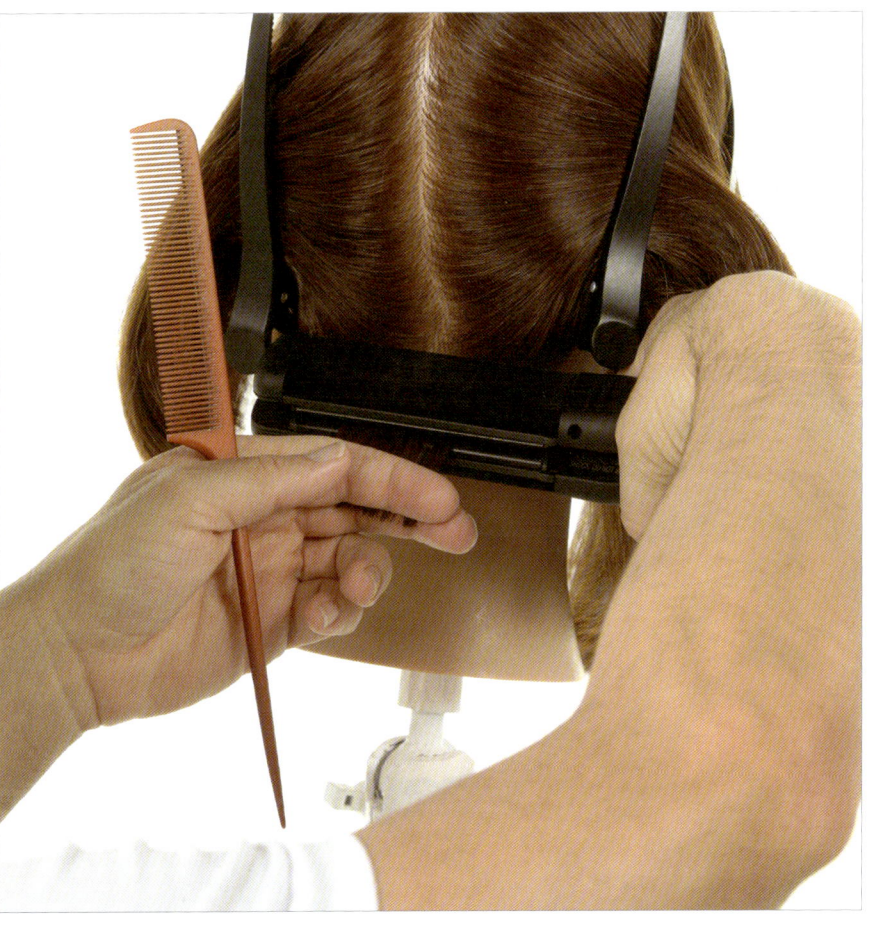

06 Begin the flat-iron service at the nape hairline. Release a ¼" (.6 cm) horizontal parting and position the head slightly forward. Begin at the center and project the hair 90° to allow the flat iron to be placed as close to the scalp as possible. This will eliminate any potential indentations from the flat iron. Close the iron with light, even pressure and move down the strand to the ends.

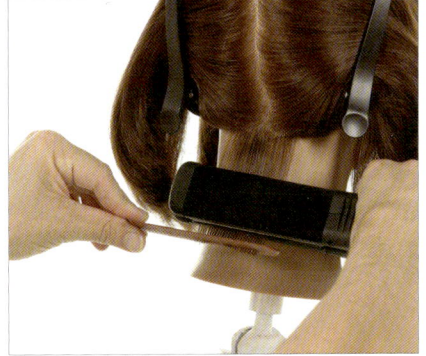

07–08 Position the teeth of the tail comb near the base as the flat iron moves toward the ends. Then, move the comb toward the ends and position the flat iron at the base. Close the iron with more pressure and follow the comb to the ends. Lower the projection angle to create minimal volume.

Some manufacturers offer a thinner flat iron. This will allow the iron to be positioned closer to the base, further eliminating the possibility of indentations.

The same technique is used with the smaller irons, alternating the placement of the comb and the iron.

09–10 Continue working up to the back. Extend partings all the way across to avoid splits. Continue to release ¼" (.6 cm) horizontal partings working from the center to either side. At the sides, make sure to direct the lengths in natural fall.

11 When working to the ends of the hair, position the flat iron to make the ends as straight as possible. Avoid turning the ends either up or down.

12 Work up to the crest. With the head positioned slightly forward, continue to project the hair at 90° when applying the flat iron the first time.

13 Then direct the lengths straight down to minimize volume and create completely straight lengths.

14 Continue working from the center to either side of each parting.

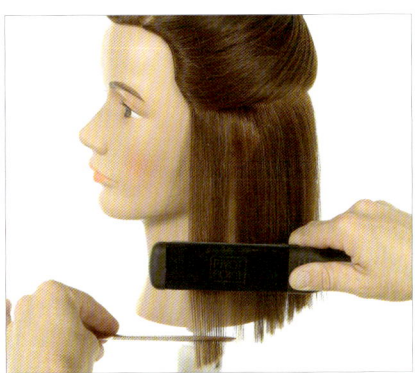

15 When you reach the area above the ear, extend the partings to the front hairline.

16 As you work over the curves of the head, remember to maintain 90° projection for the first application of the flat iron.

17 Then distribute the lengths straight down while applying more pressure to the iron. Continue to work from the center to each side.

18 Work toward the top of the head using the same flat-ironing techniques with ¼" (.6 cm) horizontal partings.

19–20 While working over the curves of the head, begin flat-ironing each parting using 90° projection and positioning the flat iron as close to the scalp as possible.

21 Then lower the projection to diminish volume and create extremely straight lengths.

22 To complete the service, apply a silicone gloss to smooth the hair. Apply the product from ends working toward the top.

23–24 The finished result shows smooth, unactivated lengths with no volume at the base and no curvature texture along the lengths.

DESIGN DECISIONS *WORKSHOP 01*

STRAIGHT VOLUME – AIR FORMING/FLAT-IRONING

Draw or fill in the boxes with the appropriate answers.

artist⁺ access.

STRUCTURE

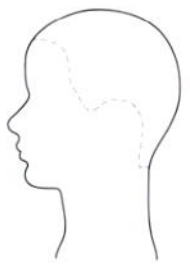

FORM/TEXTURE

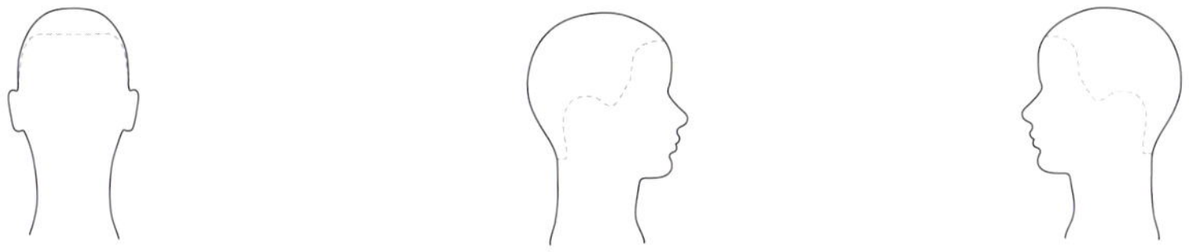

DIRECTION

AIR-FORMING PATTERN

FLAT-IRONING PATTERN

COMB-OUT/FINISH

☐ RELAX
☐ DRY MOLD
☐ BACKCOMB/BACKBRUSH
☐ DEFINE THE FORM
☐ DETAIL

TOOLS/PRODUCT CHOICE

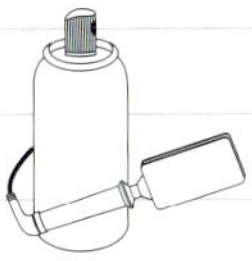

_____
Educator Signature

Date

HAIR DESIGN RUBRIC *WORKSHOP 01*
STRAIGHT VOLUME –
AIR FORMING/FLAT-IRONING

This rubric is a performance assessment tool designed to measure your ability to **create** *Pivot Point hair designs.*

	LEVEL 1 *in progress*	LEVEL 2 *getting better*	LEVEL 3 *entry-level proficiency*
PREPARATION			
• Assemble hair design essentials	☐	☐	☐
CREATE			
• Shampoo, condition and apply appropriate styling product to towel-dried hair	☐	☐	☐
• Section with side part from above left eye through to center of crown	☐	☐	☐
• Air form to remove most moisture using fingers first and then 9-row brush to control hair; work until completely dry	☐	☐	☐
• Release ¼" (.6 cm) horizontal parting at center nape hairline; project hair 90° and place flat iron close to scalp	☐	☐	☐
• Close iron with light, even pressure; move down strand	☐	☐	☐
• Repeat on the same strand, but close iron with more pressure; lower projection and move down strand	☐	☐	☐
• Work from the center to either side; work upward	☐	☐	☐
• Above ear, extend partings to front hairline; use same techniques	☐	☐	☐
• Work to top using same flat-ironing techniques; continue using 90° projection for first application; lower projection for second application	☐	☐	☐
• Apply silicone gloss working from ends toward top	☐	☐	☐

TOTAL POINTS = _____ + _____ + _____

TOTAL POINTS _____ ÷ HIGHEST POSSIBLE SCORE 33 X 100 = _____ %

Record your time in comparison with the suggested salon speed. _____

To improve my performance on this procedure, I need to: _____

_____   _____   _____
Student Signature   Educator Signature   Date

03

WORKSHOP 02
ALTERNATING OBLONGS – FINGERWAVES/ PINCURLS

Molded alternating oblongs can be used alone or combined with rollers or pincurls. The proportions of each technique may be customized to vary the amount of expansion and texture within the design. In this exercise molded alternating oblongs are used in the interior, and flat pincurls are used in the exterior to create this classic and glamorous design.

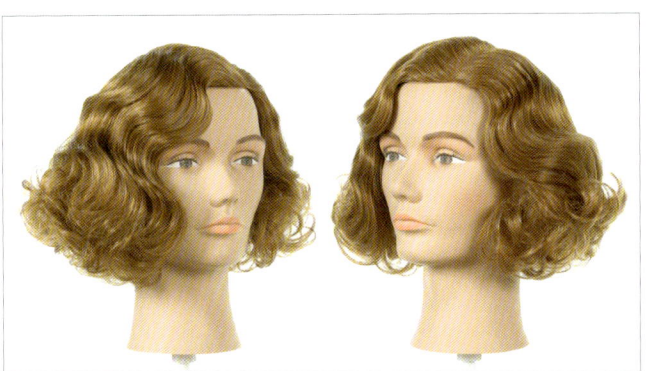

The finished design shows slightly diagonal fingerwaves off a side part with activated texture from flat pincurls that result in expansion through the exterior of the form.

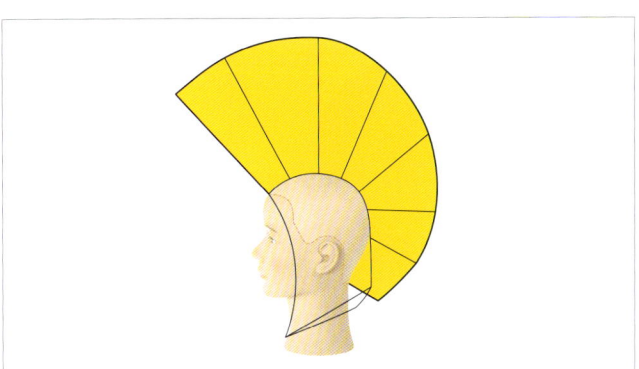

The structure graphic shows the diagonal-forward graduated form used in this exercise.

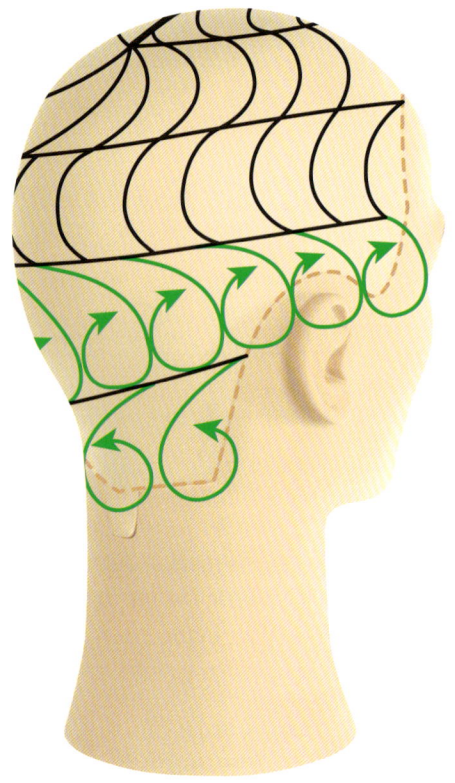

The art indicates the direction of the alternating oblong pattern. Flat pincurls are indicated by green arrows, which alternate in clockwise and counterclockwise directions.

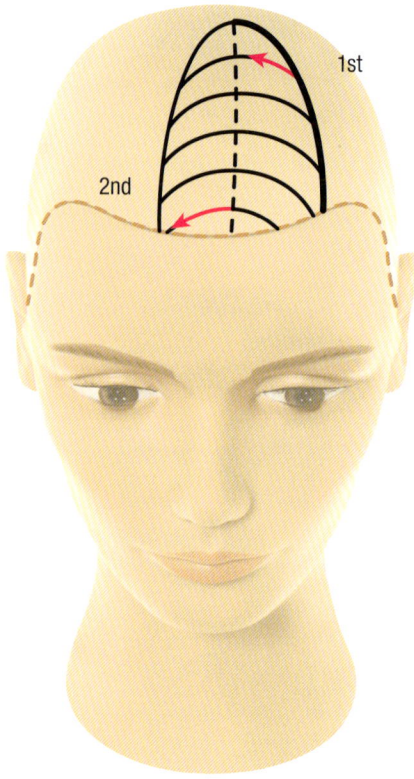

The art shows the first molded oblong created off a slightly curved and diagonal side part and the parallel C-shapes within it.

01–02 Distribute gel evenly through wet hair. Begin on the heavy side of the part and distribute the hair diagonally away from the face to prepare for the first direction.

03 Use the fine teeth of the molding comb and your index finger to mold the first direction, working from the convex end to the concave end of the oblong.

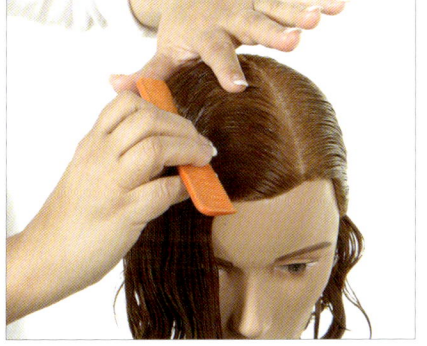

04 Press down firmly in the center of the oblong and distribute the hair in the second direction. Work from the concave end toward the convex end of the oblong.

05 Begin creating the ridge at the concave end using your index finger to protect the oblong. Gently slide the comb approximately 1" (2.5 cm) toward the concave end. Then flatten the comb and position your index and middle finger to control the ridge.

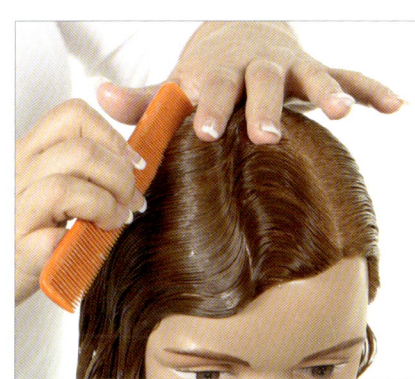

06 Then, turn the comb upright and distribute the lengths in the opposite direction. Use the fine teeth of the comb to refine the distribution of the hair at the base of the ridge. To avoid disturbing the oblong and the ridge, keep your palm off the head.

07 Continue to create the ridge as you work toward the convex end, connecting each section.

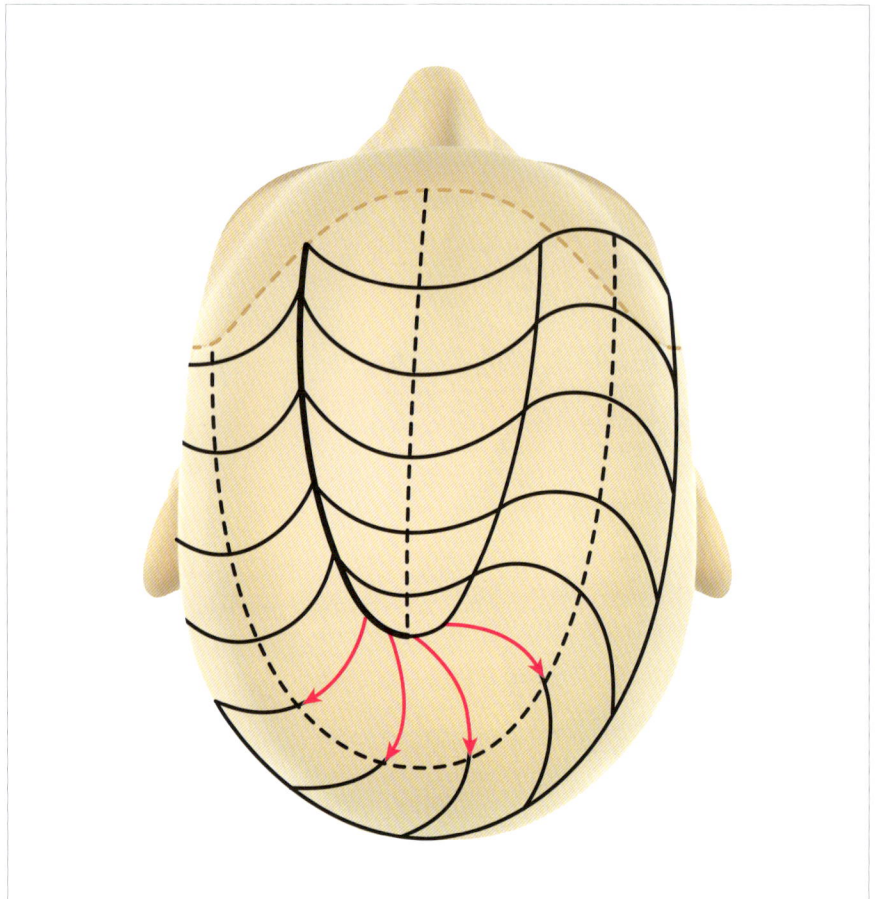

08 The art shows the second oblong pivoting in the crown around the back of the first oblong.

NOTE: *Avoid overdirecting the hair while working around the crown area.*

09 Note that the first direction for the next oblong is partially established. Continue molding the first direction around the crown to the front hairline.

10 Reinforce the second direction of this oblong beginning at the concave end. Work around the crown to the convex end.

11–12 Begin forming the ridge at the concave end. Move the comb toward the concave end. Flatten the comb, reposition your fingers, and distribute the lengths in the opposite direction. Work toward the back. Continue to create the ridge. Work to the convex end, keeping your palm off the hair to avoid disturbing the oblong and the ridge.

13 The first direction is already established for the next oblong. Reinforce the second direction working from the concave to the convex end.

14 Create the ridge beginning at the concave end using the same techniques. Strive for equally spaced waves throughout the design.

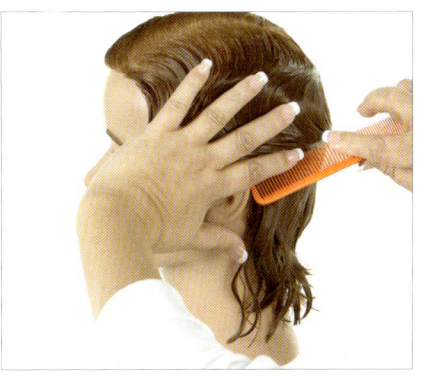

15 Mold the next alternating oblong working around the head until you reach the ear.

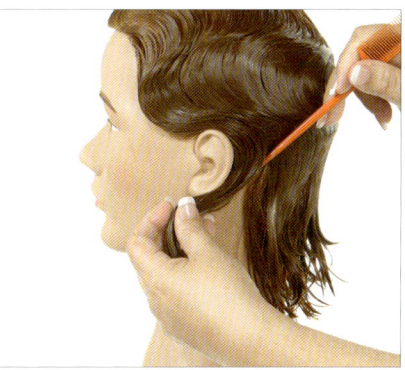

16 Set flat pincurls beginning at the concave end of the last oblong. Part curved bases from the center in the second direction. To avoid disturbing the ridge, do not scale the oblong.

17 Position all circles in front of their bases and secure in the second direction.

18 Work around the curve of the head to the convex end of the oblong using the same techniques. Note that the pincurls slightly overlap one another.

 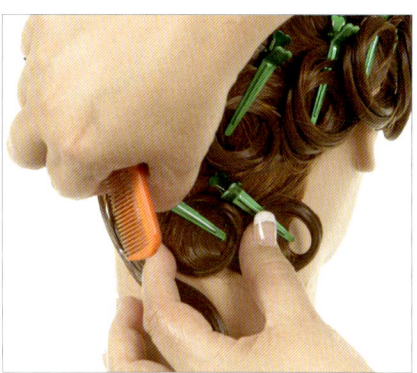 

19–20 Mold and scale the next oblong in the opposite direction. Begin setting flat pincurls at the concave end. Use curved partings taken in the second direction, from the center of the oblong. Part and secure in the second direction.

21 Note that the ridge is a connecting line between the alternating oblongs, and the pincurls finish the ends to create perimeter texture.

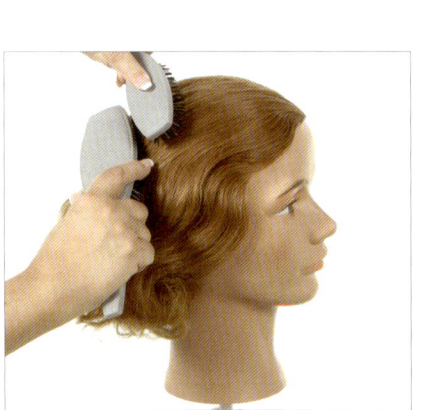

22 After the hair has dried completely, relax the set using two cushion brushes.

23 Define the form using a wide-tooth tail comb. Reinforce the waves by moving the comb and your fingers in alternating directions.

24 Continue to reinforce each oblong as you move around the head. In the perimeter, lift the hair to create additional expansion.

25 Fantasy pins and holding spray may be used to reinforce the wave movements.

26 The finish shows soft, undulating waves with a more activated texture along the perimeter.

27 Finishing an alternating oblong set for a more relaxed result can create an elegant, yet very current version of this design.

DESIGN DECISIONS *WORKSHOP 02*

ALTERNATING OBLONGS – FINGERWAVES/PINCURLS

Draw or fill in the boxes with the appropriate answers.

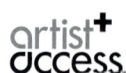

STRUCTURE

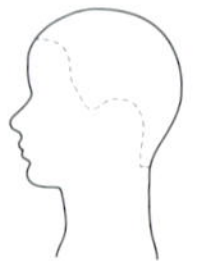

FORM/TEXTURE

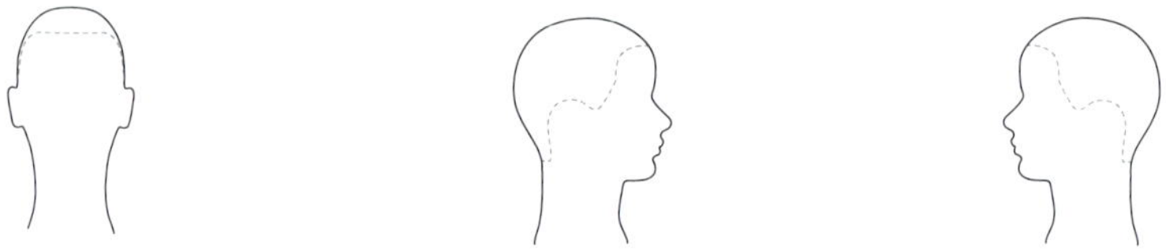

DIRECTION

MOLDING/PINCURL PATTERN

COMB-OUT/FINISH

☐ RELAX ☐ DRY MOLD ☐ BACKCOMB/BACKBRUSH ☐ DEFINE THE FORM ☐ DETAIL

TOOLS/PRODUCT CHOICE

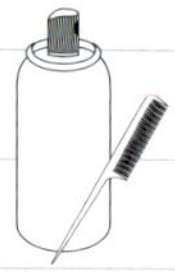

Educator Signature

Date

VARIATION 01
FINGERWAVE

In this variation, small, close alternating oblongs are molded to move off the face from the front hairline using a two-comb technique. This technique is especially effective for thicker, shorter, relaxed hair to create smaller waves with strong ridges.

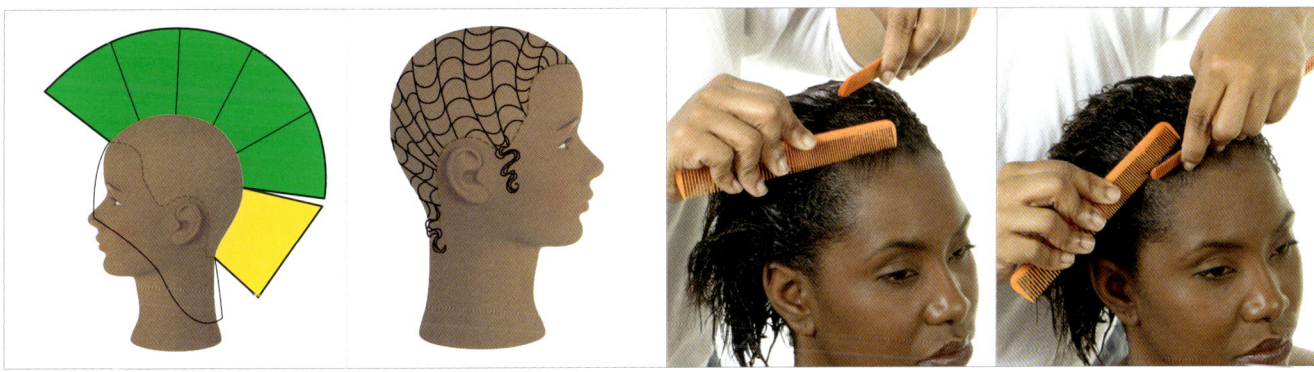

This variation is performed on a combination of uniform lengths over short graduation. Styling gel is applied liberally through the hair concentrating in the base area. The first direction is molded at the front hairline using the fine teeth of a molding comb. Then the first direction is supported with the spine of a second comb, and the first molding comb is used to distribute the hair into the second direction and to create the ridge. The combs are kept parallel to each other throughout the design, and the fine teeth are used to distribute the hair.

After the second direction is established, the spines of both molding combs are placed on either side of the ridge and moved in opposite directions to reinforce the ridge. The same technique is used to complete the oblong, working from the concave end to the convex end. Work toward the nape following the contour of the head. While working, styling product may be reapplied for better control and support.

HAIR DESIGN RUBRIC *WORKSHOP 02*

ALTERNATING OBLONGS – FINGERWAVES/PINCURLS

This rubric is a performance assessment tool designed to measure your ability to **create** *Pivot Point hair designs.*

	LEVEL 1 *in progress*	LEVEL 2 *getting better*	LEVEL 3 *entry-level proficiency*
PREPARATION			
• Assemble hair design essentials	☐	☐	☐
CREATE			
• Shampoo, condition and apply gel evenly through hair	☐	☐	☐
• Mold first direction of oblong from side part, and then second direction, placing index finger at center of shape	☐	☐	☐
• Create slightly diagonal ridge beginning at concave end; use wide teeth of molding comb to move hair toward concave end; work toward convex end; use fine teeth to refine	☐	☐	☐
• Mold first and second directions of next oblong, pivoting around crown area toward hairline on opposite side	☐	☐	☐
• Create ridge beginning at concave end, working around crown to convex end; keep palm off head to avoid disturbing ridge line	☐	☐	☐
• Fingerwave from one side of head to other using the same techniques; strive for equally spaced oblongs	☐	☐	☐
• Part curved bases in second direction from center of last (4th) oblong	☐	☐	☐
• Apply flat pincurls beginning at concave end; position in front of base and secure in second direction	☐	☐	☐
• Mold and scale oblong in opposite direction; part and position flat pincurls following same procedure	☐	☐	☐
• Relax dry set with cushion brushes	☐	☐	☐
• Define form with large-tooth comb, reinforcing waves and adding expansion	☐	☐	☐

TOTAL POINTS = _____ + _____ + _____

TOTAL POINTS _____ ÷ HIGHEST POSSIBLE SCORE 36 X 100 = _____ %

Record your time in comparison with the suggested salon speed.

To improve my performance on this procedure, I need to:

_____   _____   _____
Student Signature   *Educator Signature*   *Date*

WORKSHOP 03

OBLONG – AIR FORMING/ SCRUNCH-DRYING

Many clients with naturally curly or permed hair texture want to wear a more controlled or stylized look that incorporates their curls. Creating waves that move off the face and scrunch-drying the remaining lengths will create the effect this client desires quickly and effectively.

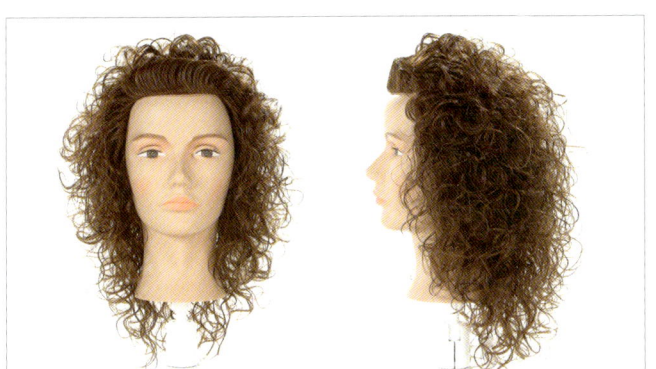

This highly activated, curly textured design is produced by a scrunching technique. Air formed waves at the center front move away from the face and blend well to the curly texture.

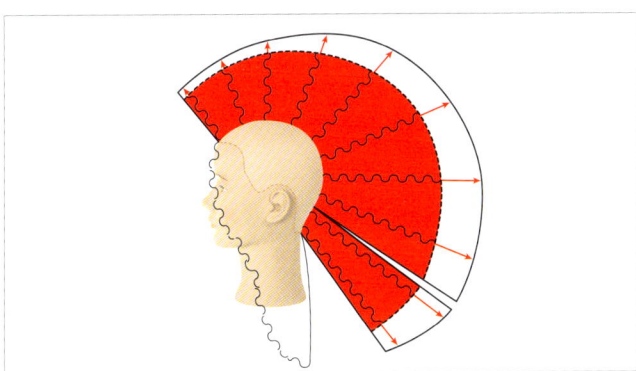

This exercise will be performed on a diagonal-forward increase-layered form.

01 Apply styling foam to freshly shampooed hair. Apply from the base through to the ends.

02 Comb the product through for even distribution.

03–05 Begin air forming an oblong by positioning the teeth of a 9-row brush at the front hairline at the concave end. Gently direct the hair in the first direction and then the second direction, pushing the hair slightly forward. Direct the airflow from the concave end toward the convex end. Work toward the convex end using the same technique. Repeat the movement as many times as necessary until the desired oblong movement is achieved. Note that this technique will automatically create the beginning of another oblong movement, blending into the curls at the back.

06–07 Attach the diffuser attachment to the blow dryer and move to the back. Tilt the head back and use your hand to gently lift and scrunch lengths. Begin at the center back nape lengths. With the blow dryer set on low heat and low speed, place it directly under the lengths. Work from center to one side.

08 Work from the center to the other side.

09 Work toward the top of the back, working systematically from the center to either side. Avoid over-manipulating the lengths.

10 Move to one side. Starting in interior, use your fingers to blend the oblong with the diffused lengths. Continue to gently lift and scrunch the lengths, placing the diffuser beneath the strands.

11 Work to the exterior. Be aware of the placement of the dryer next to the ear.

12 Move to the other side and repeat the same techniques. Be sure to blend the oblong with the diffused lengths.

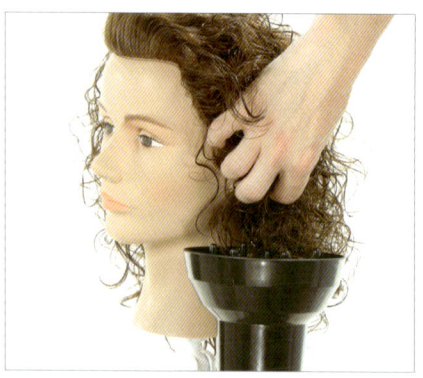

13 Continue to diffuse the lengths, paying close attention to the balance of the design.

14 Move to the top and lift the hair, blending the oblong with the curly lengths while creating more volume.

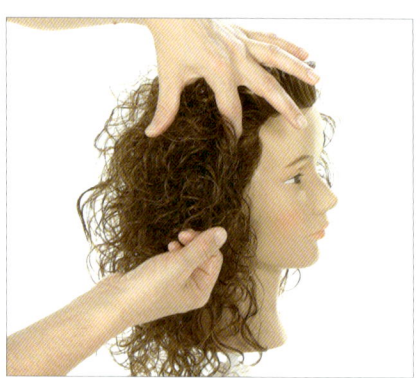

15 To complete the design, apply a shine product to the lengths. Detail, working through the design with your fingers as necessary.

16–17 The finish shows soft, natural-looking curls that are accentuated with beautiful waves moving away from the face.

DESIGN DECISIONS *WORKSHOP 03*

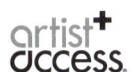

OBLONG – AIR FORMING/ SCRUNCH-DRYING

artist+ access.

Draw or fill in the boxes with the appropriate answers.

STRUCTURE

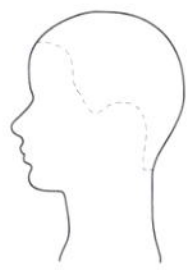

FORM/TEXTURE

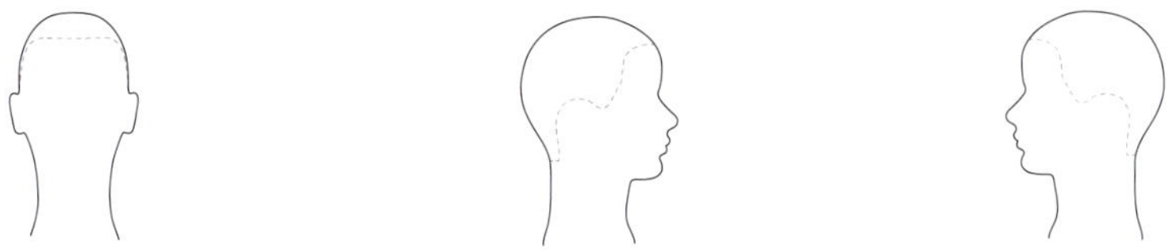

DIRECTION

AIR-FORMING PATTERN

COMB-OUT/FINISH

☐ RELAX ☐ DRY MOLD ☐ BACKCOMB/BACKBRUSH ☐ DEFINE THE FORM ☐ DETAIL

TOOLS/PRODUCT CHOICE

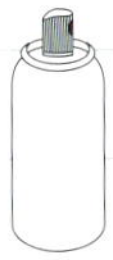

Educator Signature

Date

VARIATION 02
OBLONG – AIR FORMING/ SCRUNCH-DRYING

You may also set the hair on loose, flat pincurls for scrunch-drying to achieve a slightly more controlled texture and reduce the appearance of frizz, especially on drier, more unruly hair textures.

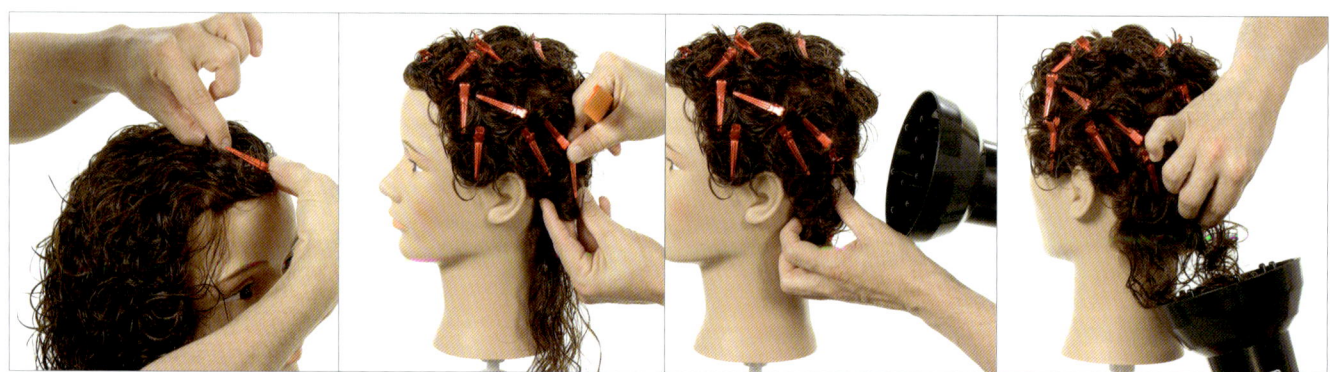

After applying styling lotion or foam to clean, damp hair, random sections are taken, starting at the front hairline. The fingers and the tail of the comb are used to manipulate the hair into loose, irregular, flat pincurls. Each pincurl is secured with a clip. As an option, some strands or the ends may be left out or not incorporated. The same technique is used throughout, working to the longest lengths at the back. The hair is then air formed using a diffuser until it is approximately 75% dry. Then the pincurls are released individually and diffused while gently lifting the lengths without disturbing the curl formation. Finishing products are applied to define the texture and to add shine.

HAIR DESIGN RUBRIC *WORKSHOP 03*

OBLONG – AIR FORMING/SCRUNCH-DRYING

This rubric is a performance assessment tool designed to measure your ability to create *Pivot Point hair designs.*

	LEVEL 1 *in progress*	LEVEL 2 *getting better*	LEVEL 3 *entry-level proficiency*
PREPARATION			
• Assemble hair design essentials	☐	☐	☐
CREATE			
• Shampoo, condition and apply suitable styling product	☐	☐	☐
• Air form oblong using 9-row brush positioned at front hairline at concave end	☐	☐	☐
• Gently direct hair in first direction, then second direction, and push slightly forward; work to convex end; repeat airflow from concave to convex end	☐	☐	☐
• Air form back starting at center nape; attach diffuser to blow dryer	☐	☐	☐
• Tilt head back; gently lift and scrunch lengths with fingers over blow dryer set at low heat and low speed	☐	☐	☐
• Air form using same technique from center to either side	☐	☐	☐
• Work toward top	☐	☐	☐
• Air form both sides starting in interior; use fingers to blend oblong with diffused lengths	☐	☐	☐
• Work toward exterior using same technique	☐	☐	☐
• Air form top by lifting hair to blend oblong with curly lengths	☐	☐	☐
• Apply shine product to length to complete design	☐	☐	☐
• Detail using fingers as necessary	☐	☐	☐

TOTAL POINTS = _____ + _____ + _____

TOTAL POINTS _____ ÷ HIGHEST POSSIBLE SCORE 39 X 100 = _____ %

Record your time in comparison with the suggested salon speed. _____

To improve my performance on this procedure, I need to: _____

_____   _____   _____
Student Signature   Educator Signature   Date

WORKSHOP 04
CURVATURE AND STRAIGHT VOLUME – ROLLERS/PINCURLS

The length of the uniformly layered form greatly influences the amount of expansion achieved. Longer lengths allow for greater expansion, while the same techniques applied to shorter lengths create a more contoured effect.

Alternating oblongs at the top set the pattern for this off-the-face design. Skipwaves at the sides create closeness, while volume pincurls at the back create a highly activated texture.

The finished set shows rollers set within three alternating volume oblongs in the interior, while alternating oblongs are molded and set in volume and indentation pincurls at the sides. The remaining back lengths are set in volume pincurls using a bricklay technique.

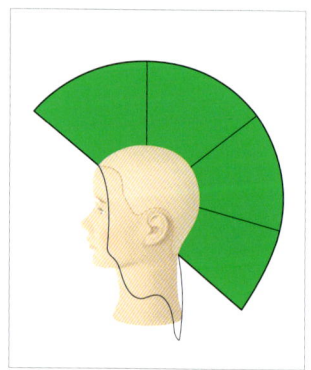

This exercise is performed on uniformly layered lengths.

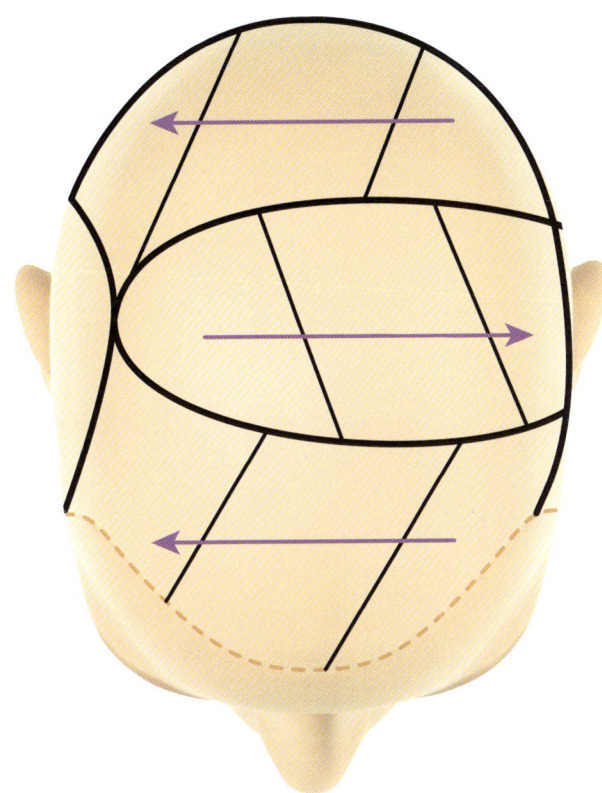
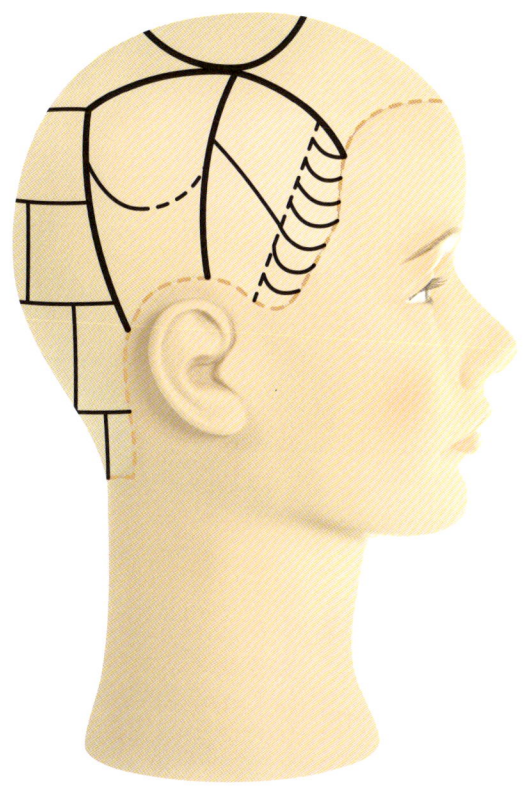

The art shows the molding directions and parting patterns used along the top, sides and back areas of this design. The top shows alternating oblongs that move back and away from the face set with rollers. The sides show alternating oblongs, which will be parted and applied in both volume and indentation pincurls, with the oblong at the hairline molded and not set. In the back, a bricklay pattern will be set with straight volume pincurls.

01 Begin at the front hairline and mold and scale a horizontal, counterclockwise oblong.

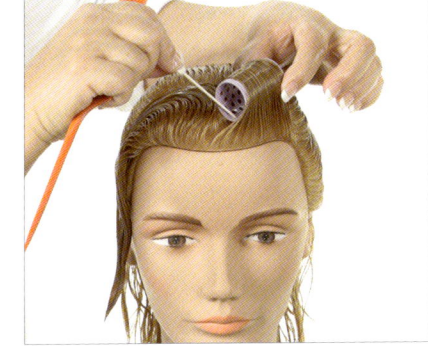

02–03 Part a one-diameter (1x) base at 45° in the first direction, starting at the convex end. Project the hair at 90° and roll downward with even tension. Position the roller half-off base and secure with a pick.

04 Part and apply the remainder of the shape using the same base control.

05 Mold and scale the second oblong in the opposite direction moving clockwise.

06 Start at the convex end. Continue parting at a 45° angle in the first direction and use 1x half-off base control.

07 Use the same technique to complete the second oblong.

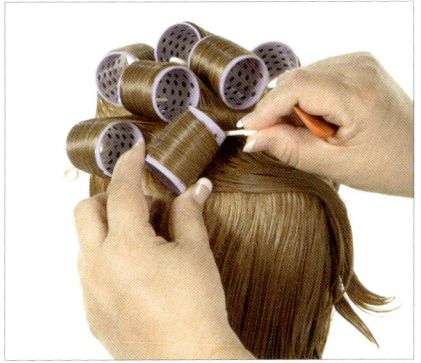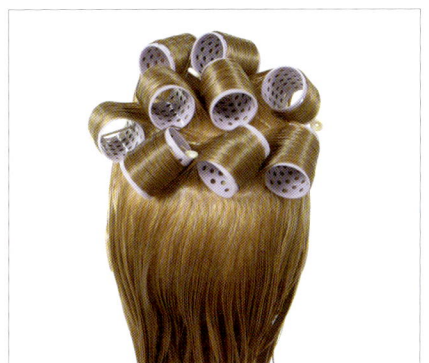

08–09 Mold and scale the last counterclockwise oblong in the top. Part and apply using 45° partings and half-off base control. Start at the convex end.

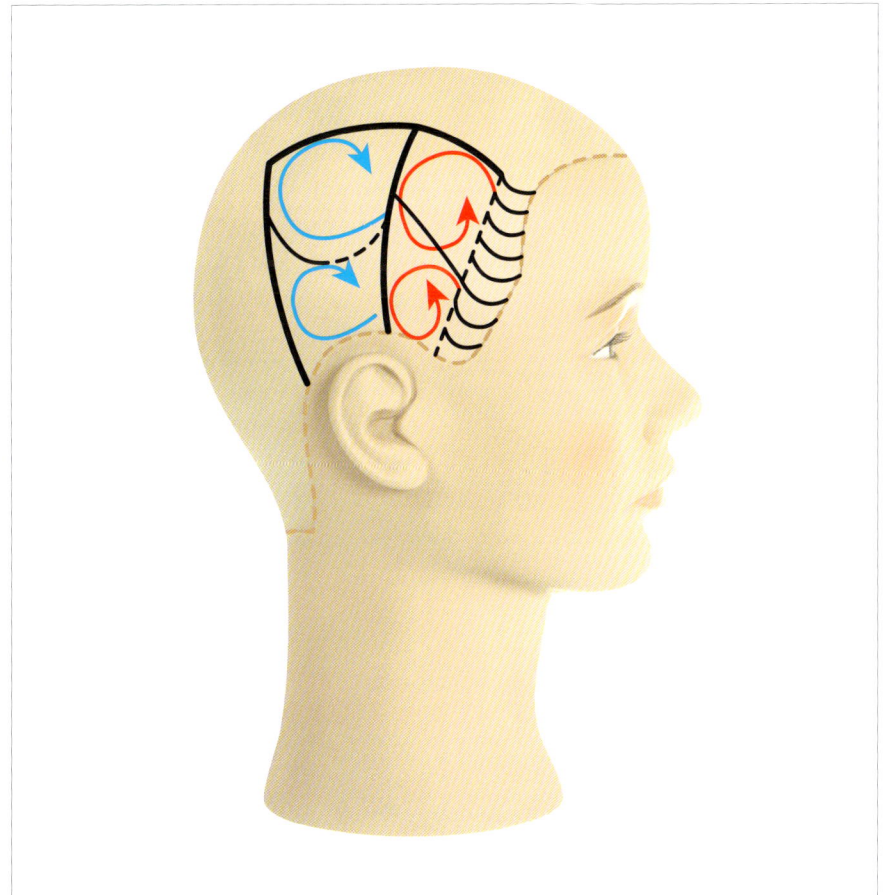

10 The art shows the alternating oblongs and parting pattern used at the sides.

11 Mold and scale the front two alternating oblongs. You may use clips to avoid disturbing the first oblong, which is left molded.

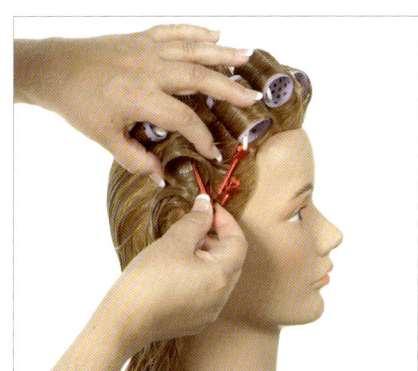

12 At the convex end of the volume oblong, part in a curved degree with the first direction. Reinforce the arc and form a volume pincurl. Position the pincurl half-off base, secure in the first direction and repeat with the next pincurl.

13–15 Mold and scale the next oblong in indentation. Begin setting at the concave end. Part and apply an indentation pincurl, positioning the circle in the upper portion of its base. Secure in the second direction. You may use long hairpins for control and to help support the pincurls. Use the same technique to complete this oblong.

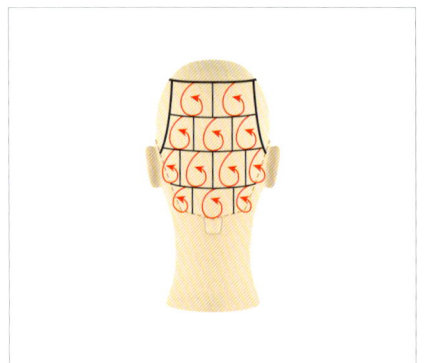 

16 The art shows the bricklay pattern that will be used to set volume pincurls in the back.

17–18 Distribute and mold the remaining lengths downward and set in volume pincurls. Use 1x half-off base control throughout, staggering the bases in a bricklay pattern.

19 Here we see the finished roller and pincurl set.

20 Relax the entire set with one or two cushion brushes.

21 Use a small cushion brush to dry mold the hair following the lines of the set.

22 Backbrush hair at the top in the direction in which it was set using a one-stroke technique.

23 Retrace the lines of the design in this area.

24 Move to the sides, then the back, backbrushing and blending into the top of the design.

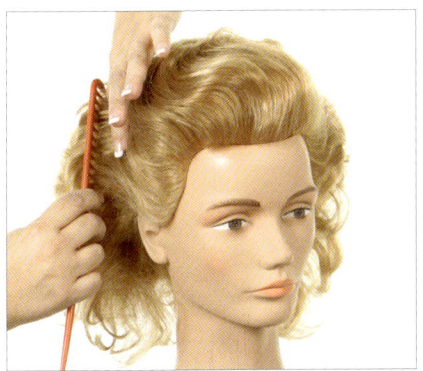

25 Retrace the lines of the shapes at the sides, then use a large-tooth comb to separate and detail the activated texture.

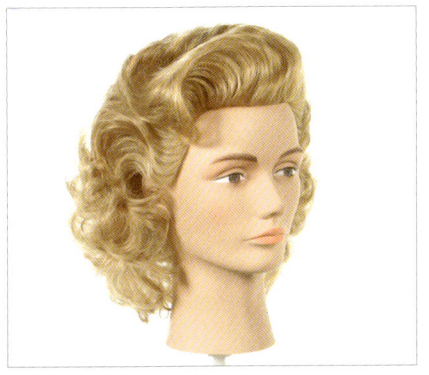

26–27 The finished design reveals alternating waves moving away from the face that lead into the expanded, activated texture at the back of the design.

CURVATURE AND STRAIGHT VOLUME – ROLLERS/PINCURLS

Draw or fill in the boxes with the appropriate answers.

STRUCTURE

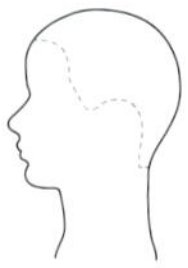

FORM/TEXTURE

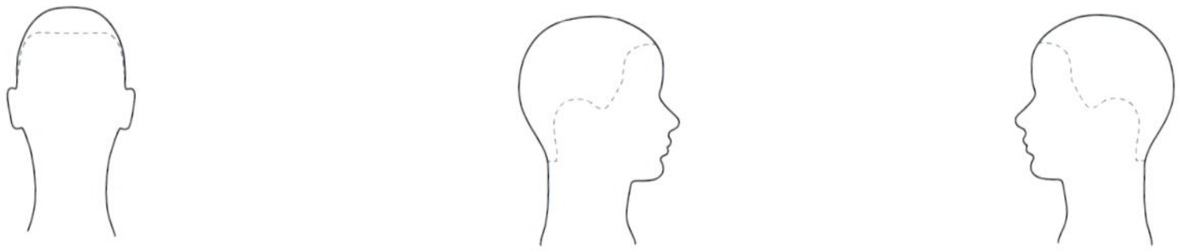

DIRECTION

MOLDING/SCALING

SETTING PATTERN

COMB-OUT/FINISH

- ☐ RELAX
- ☐ DRY MOLD
- ☐ BACKCOMB/BACKBRUSH
- ☐ DEFINE THE FORM
- ☐ DETAIL

TOOLS/PRODUCT CHOICE

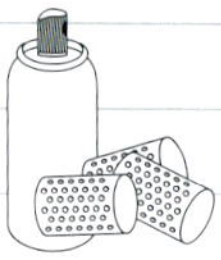

Educator Signature

Date

03

HAIR DESIGN RUBRIC *WORKSHOP 04*

CURVATURE AND STRAIGHT VOLUME – ROLLERS/PINCURLS

This rubric is a performance assessment tool designed to measure your ability to create *Pivot Point hair designs.*

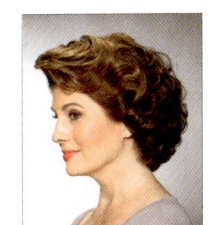

	LEVEL 1 *in progress*	LEVEL 2 *getting better*	LEVEL 3 *entry-level proficiency*
PREPARATION			
• Assemble hair design essentials	☐	☐	☐
CREATE			
• Shampoo, condition and apply suitable styling product	☐	☐	☐
• Mold and scale horizontal oblong counterclockwise at front hairline	☐	☐	☐
• Measure a 1x base and part at 45° in first direction, starting at convex end; project hair at 90° and position roller half-off base	☐	☐	☐
• Part and apply remainder of shape using same base size and tool position	☐	☐	☐
• Mold and scale second oblong in clockwise direction, and part at 45° in first direction; project at 90° and use half-off base control	☐	☐	☐
• Mold, scale, part and apply third counterclockwise oblong same as first oblong	☐	☐	☐
• Mold two vertical oblongs on one side; leave first oblong molded and scale second oblong	☐	☐	☐
• Set second oblong in volume pincurls, taking curved partings in first direction; position 2 pincurls half-off base without disturbing first molded oblong	☐	☐	☐
• Mold, scale, part and apply indentation pincurls in next side oblong; position circles in top half of base	☐	☐	☐
• Repeat same techniques on opposite side with one molded, one volume and one indentation oblong	☐	☐	☐
• Distribute and mold remaining lengths downward, then part and apply volume pincurls in bricklay pattern with 1x half-off base control	☐	☐	☐
• Relax and dry mold, blending bases following lines of the set	☐	☐	☐
• Backbrush hair in direction of set using a 1-stroke technique	☐	☐	☐
• Retrace lines of design	☐	☐	☐
• Detail and separate activated texture using a large-tooth comb	☐	☐	☐

TOTAL POINTS = _____ + _____ + _____

TOTAL POINTS _____ ÷ HIGHEST POSSIBLE SCORE 48 X 100 = _____ %

Record your time in comparison with the suggested salon speed.

To improve my performance on this procedure, I need to:

_____
Student Signature

_____
Educator Signature

_____
Date

DIRECTIONAL VOLUME – MOLDING/CURLING IRON SET

The purpose of this exercise is to provide practice in the techniques used to mold and curl short, relaxed hair. Molding the hair in the desired direction helps the style when hair has been relaxed, while using the curling iron gives the style the desired volume and texture.

This technique is a common salon service and can be a time-efficient method for styling short, relaxed hair.

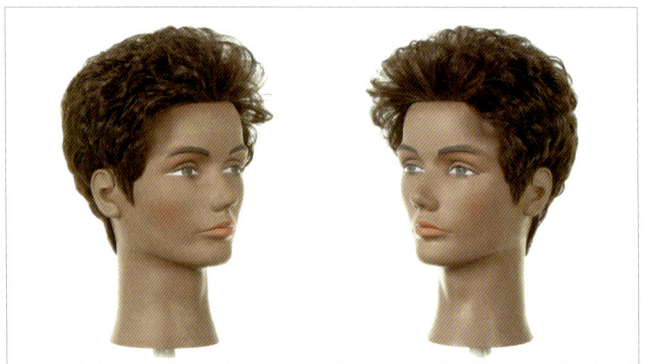

The finish shows an expanded interior that moves off the face. The molding technique in this design helps establish the foundation for the curling iron set and creates a close-fitting exterior.

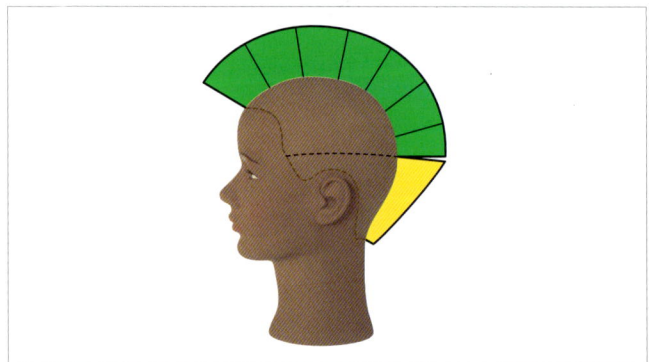

This exercise will be performed on a combination of short uniform lengths in the interior and short graduated lengths in the exterior.

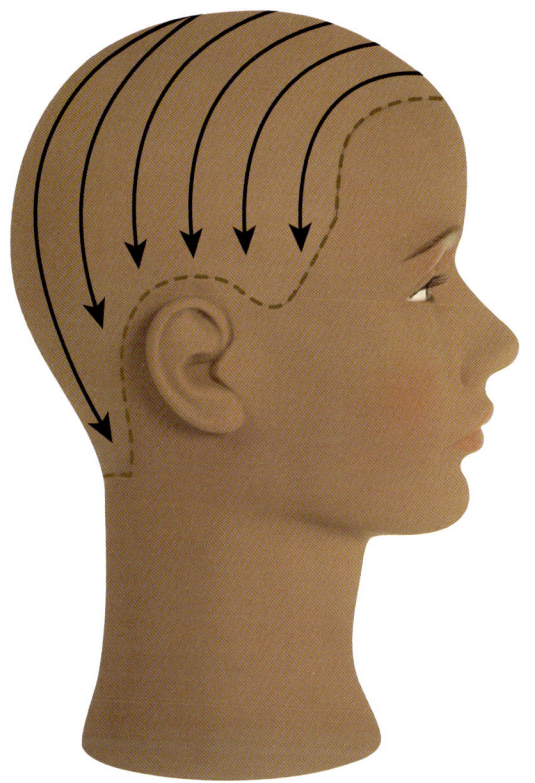
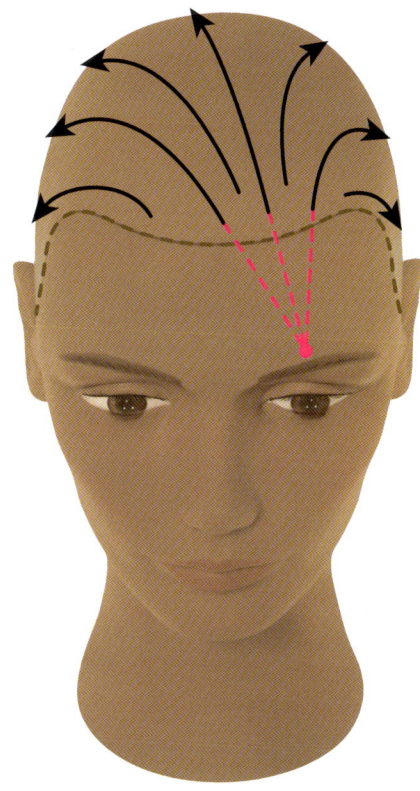

The art shows the directions used to mold the design. Even, parallel lines are molded back away from the face, curving around the sides in the interior, and blending vertically down toward the exterior nape. An imaginary point of origin over the left eye is used to establish the movement in the interior.

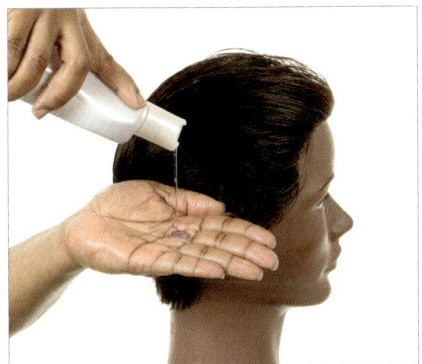
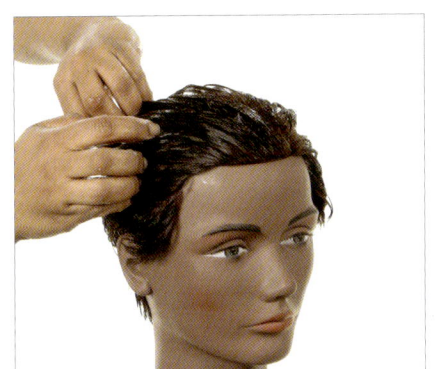

01–03 Dispense styling liquid or cream into your hands and apply evenly to the hair from base to ends. Use the comb to distribute the product thoroughly.

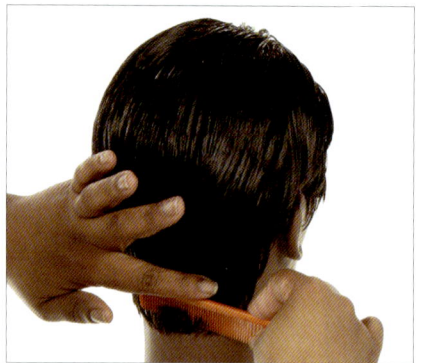

04 Begin molding the shortest lengths in the nape area. Use the fine teeth of the molding comb and mold vertically downward.

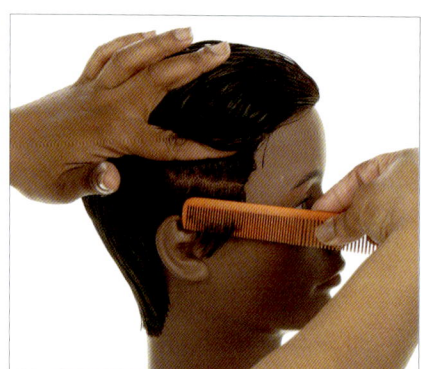
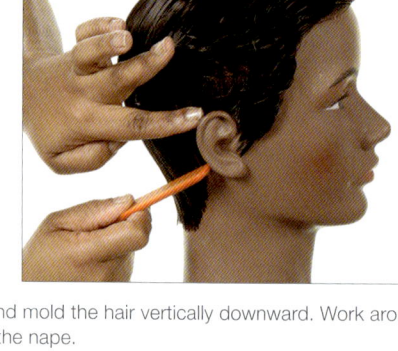

05–06 At the sides, take fine horizontal partings and mold the hair vertically downward. Work around the ear, blending into previously molded lengths in the nape.

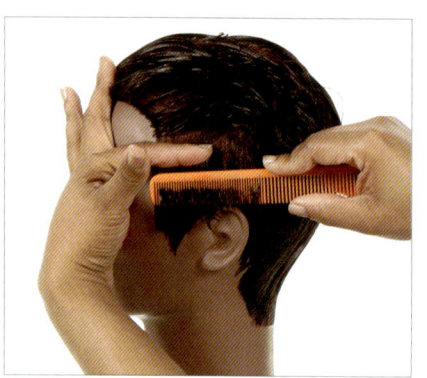
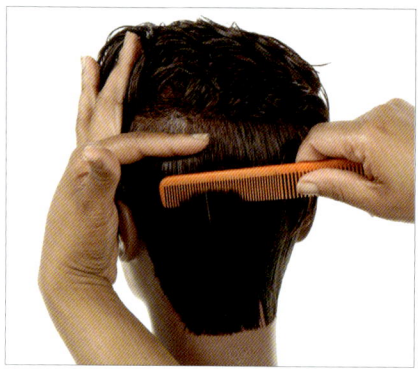

07–08 Continue working up to the crest area, beginning at the front hairline on one side. Mold the hair downward from thin horizontal partings. Work to the center back.

09 Move to the other side and use the same technique to mold the lengths.

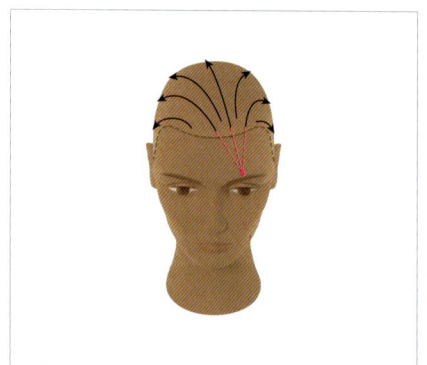

10 The art shows the directional movement used to mold the top interior, using an imaginary point of origin over the left eye.

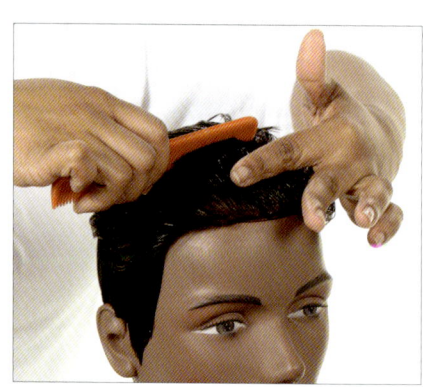

11 Begin at the front hairline and mold directionally back away from face. Use an imaginary point of origin over the left eye.

 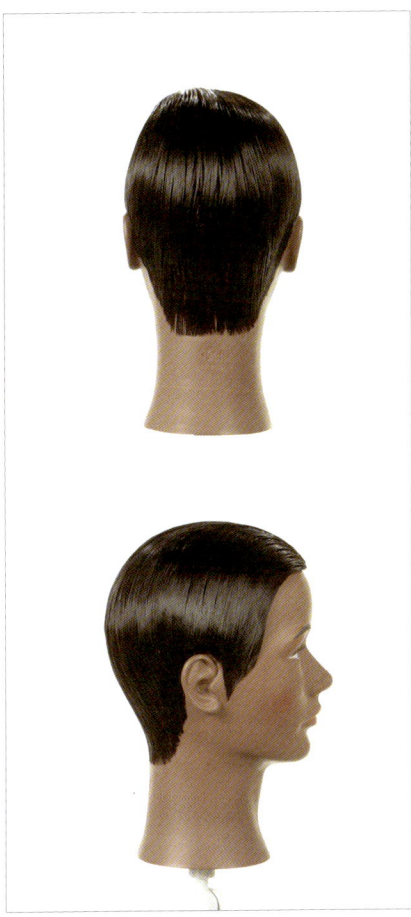

12–13 Blend into the sides and exterior using molded parallel, curved lines. Use your fingers to control the molding as you refine the lines. The molding forocasts the finish directions intended for the completed design. Dry the molded set under a heated dryer. Be sure the hair is completely dry and cool before proceeding.

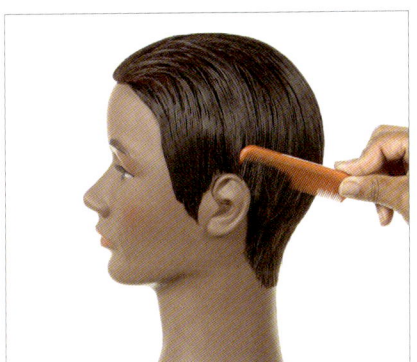 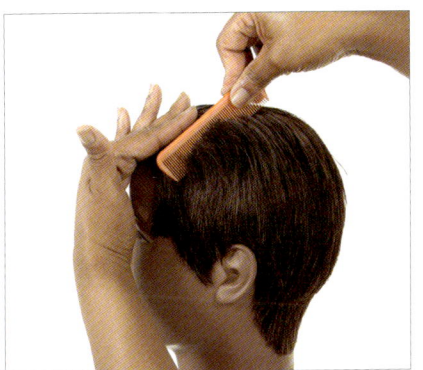 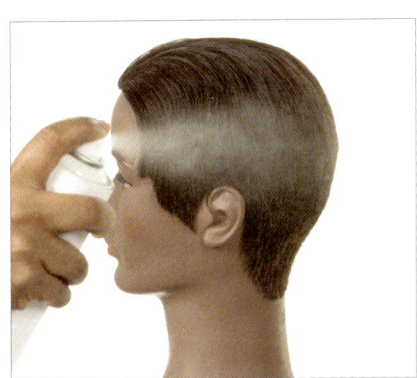

14–15 Next, gently comb the hair to loosen the molded set. Begin at the nape and work toward the sides. Then continue working toward the interior following the direction of the molded lines.

16 Apply a workable-hold hairspray to prepare the hair for thermal curling.

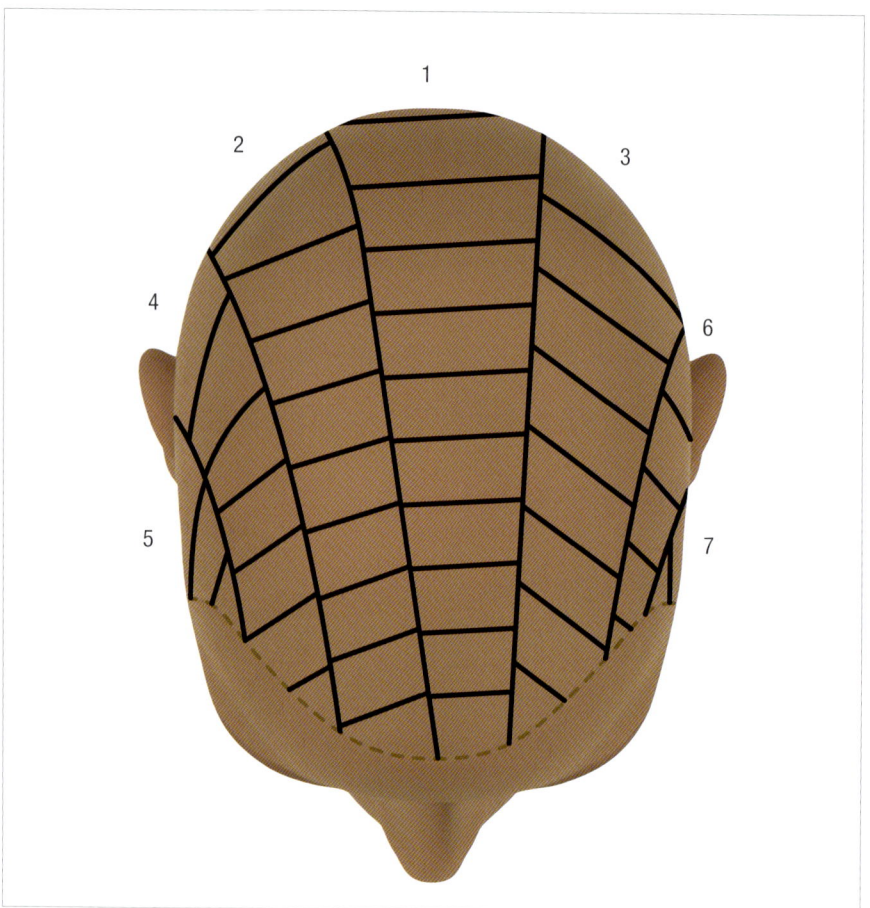

17 The art shows the approximate sectioning and parting pattern following the molding direction and beginning behind the imaginary point of origin. Seven sections will be used for the curling-iron technique.

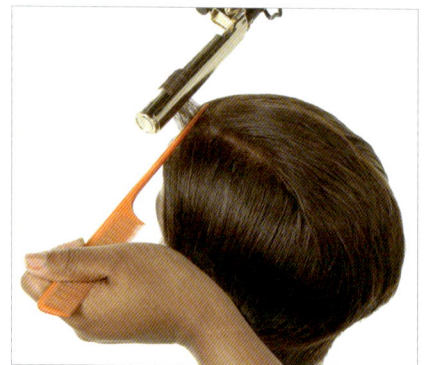

18–19 Begin behind the point of origin (1). Take approximately a one-diameter (1x) base measured with the medium-diameter curling iron. Project at 90° and support the base with the tail of the comb. Use a volume technique with half-off base control without curling all the way to the base. Work toward the back of the section, adapting the width of the partings to the width of the section.

20 Use the same technique working over the crown. Adapt the angle of the partings so that the position will be horizontal as you reach the exterior. If necessary, subdivide partings to accommodate the width of the section.

21 Use a smaller-diameter curling iron on the shorter, graduated lengths. Lower the projection angle as you work to blend into the exterior lengths.

22 Move to the adjacent section on one side (2). Adapt the angle of the partings to follow the directional distribution. Project each parting at 90°. Curl the ends with the volume technique, continuing to support the base of each parting with the tail of the comb.

23–24 Work to the back of the section. Be sure to adapt the angle of the partings to become horizontal as you reach the exterior. Use the smaller-diameter iron and use a lower projection angle as you reach shorter exterior lengths.

25 Move to the section on the opposite side of the first (3) and work from the front to the back. Adapt partings to follow the distribution and to become horizontal in the exterior.

  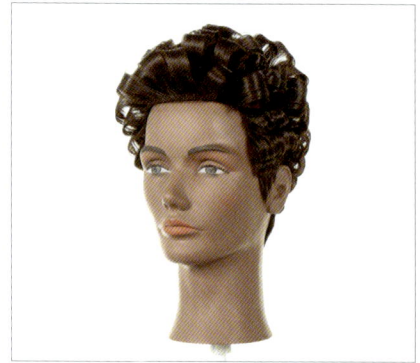

26-27 Repeat on the next section on the opposite side (4). Then move to the next adjacent section at the front hairline (5). Follow the molded distribution and adapt partings as needed. If lengths are too short, use the tip of the tail comb not only to part but also to pick up the lengths. Repeat the same techniques to curl the remaining sections on the opposite side (6, 7).

28 While the design is slightly asymmetric, strive for balance in the movement and placement of volume and texture.

29 Relax and detail the hair with a large-tooth comb. Begin at the nape and work toward the front hairline.

 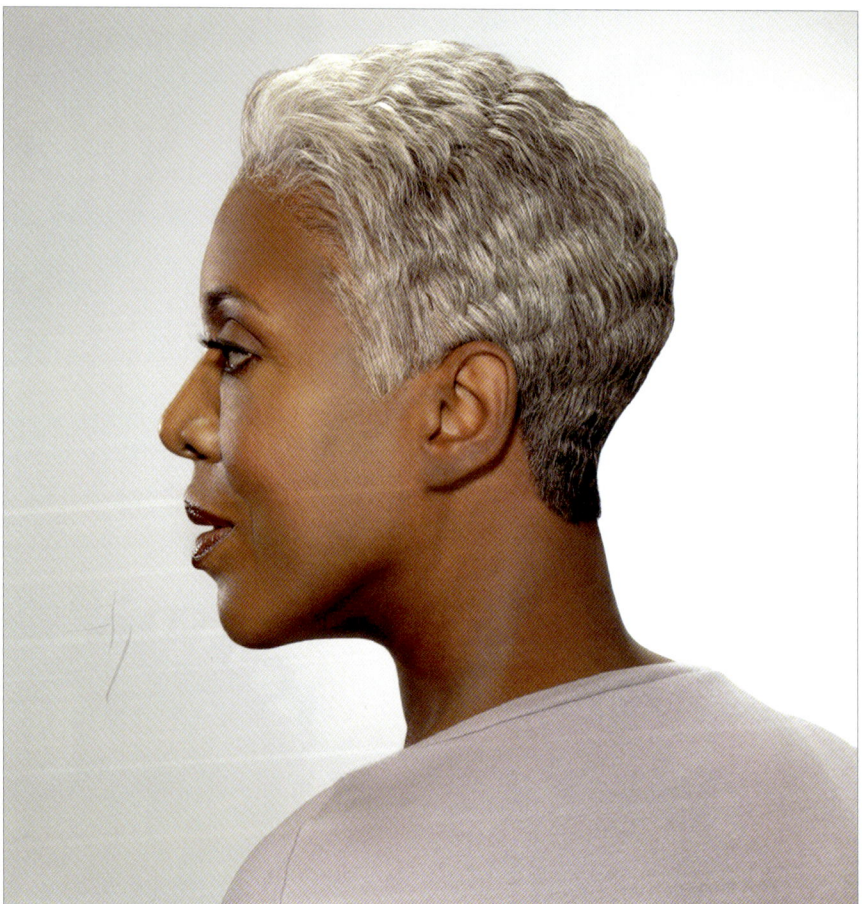

30–31 The finish shows a soft, textured look on short, relaxed hair that has initially been molded to help establish the directions of the design.

DIRECTIONAL VOLUME –
MOLDING/CURLING IRON SET

Draw or fill in the boxes with the appropriate answers.

artist⁺
access.

STRUCTURE

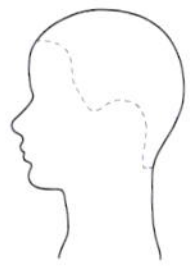

FORM/TEXTURE

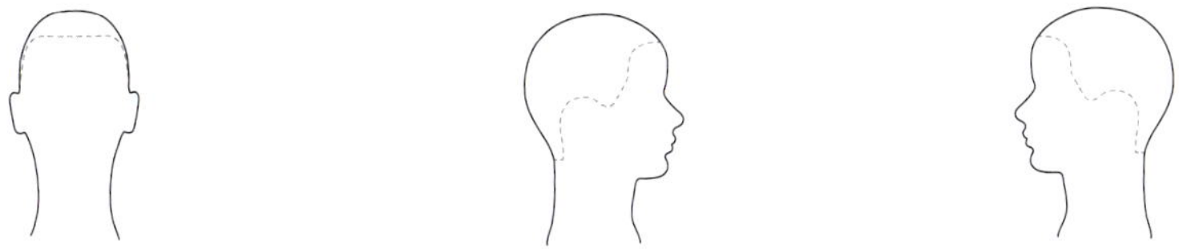

DIRECTION

CURLING PATTERN

COMB-OUT/FINISH

☐ RELAX ☐ DRY MOLD ☐ BACKCOMB/BACKBRUSH ☐ DEFINE THE FORM ☐ DETAIL

TOOLS/PRODUCT CHOICE

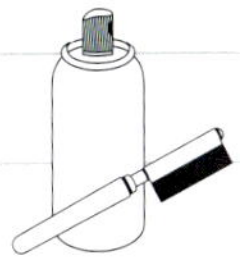

Educator Signature

Date

HAIR DESIGN RUBRIC *WORKSHOP 05*

DIRECTIONAL VOLUME – MOLDING/CURLING IRON SET

This rubric is a performance assessment tool designed to measure your ability to *create* Pivot Point hair designs.

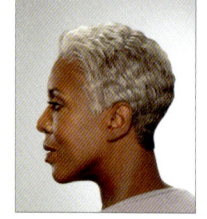

	LEVEL 1 *in progress*	LEVEL 2 *getting better*	LEVEL 3 *entry-level proficiency*
PREPARATION			
• Assemble hair design essentials	☐	☐	☐
CREATE			
• Shampoo, condition and towel-dry hair	☐	☐	☐
• Apply and distribute styling product evenly from base to ends	☐	☐	☐
• Mold exterior lengths, starting with shortest lengths in nape area, vertically downward; use fine teeth of molding comb	☐	☐	☐
• Mold perimeter and sides vertically downward using fine horizontal partings	☐	☐	☐
• Work around ear; blend into previously molded nape lengths; repeat on opposite side	☐	☐	☐
• Mold sides working up to crest area; begin at front hairline on one side working to center back; repeat on opposite side	☐	☐	☐
• Mold interior directionally back away from face using imaginary point of origin over left eye; blend into sides and exterior	☐	☐	☐
• Place under hood dryer, then comb hair to loosen molded set	☐	☐	☐
• Curl ends with medium-diameter iron, starting behind point of origin (1); use 1x horizontal partings and 90° projection; support base with tail of comb	☐	☐	☐
• Work toward back; adapt angle of partings to be horizontal at exterior; use smaller-diameter curling iron on shorter exterior lengths	☐	☐	☐
• Use same technique to curl adjacent section on one side (2); adapt angle of partings and follow directional distribution	☐	☐	☐
• Move to section on opposite side of first (3), and use same curling-iron techniques	☐	☐	☐
• Move to remaining sections on opposite side (4, 5), follow molded distribution and adapt partings as needed	☐	☐	☐
• Use same technique to curl remaining sections on opposite side (6, 7)	☐	☐	☐
• Detail and separate activated texture using a large-tooth comb	☐	☐	☐

TOTAL POINTS = _____ + _____ + _____

TOTAL POINTS _____ ÷ HIGHEST POSSIBLE SCORE 48 X 100 = _____ %

Record your time in comparison with the suggested salon speed.

To improve my performance on this procedure, I need to:

_____
Student Signature

_____
Educator Signature

_____
Date

WORKSHOP 06
CURVATURE VOLUME AND INDENTATION – AIR FORMING

Soft accents of texture combined with directional movements create a soft, stylized hair design. The use of varied finishing products can alter the design to appeal to a wide range of clients.

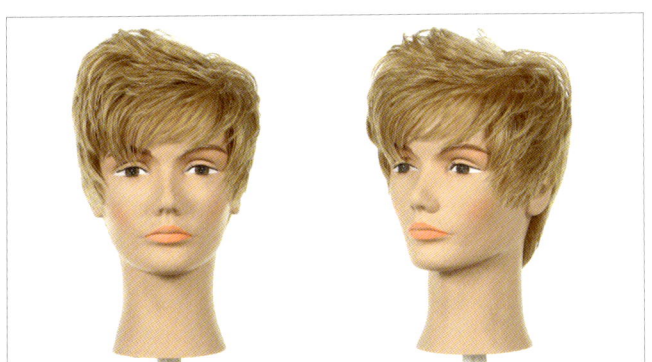

The finished exercise features curvature movements that are directed toward and away from the face. This is achieved using a 9-row brush to create volume and closeness and a small round brush to create volume and indentation.

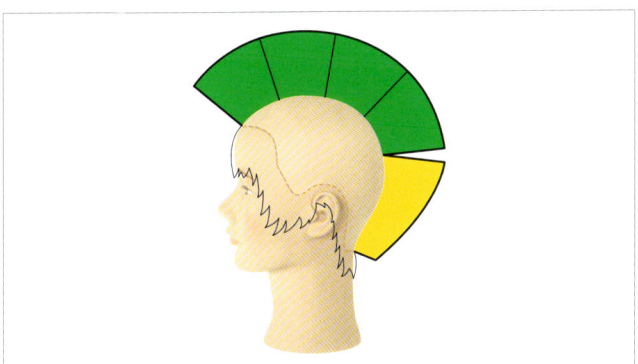

This exercise is performed on a combination of uniformly layered lengths in the interior with graduation in the exterior.

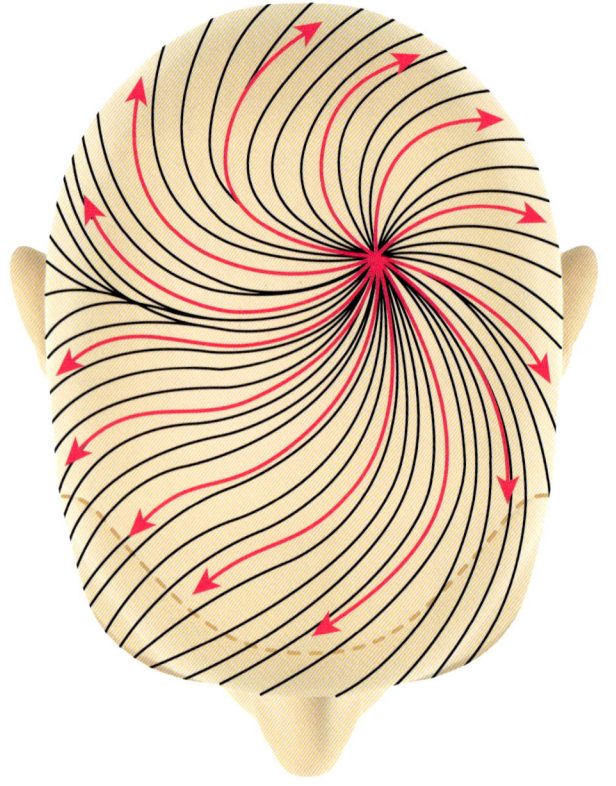

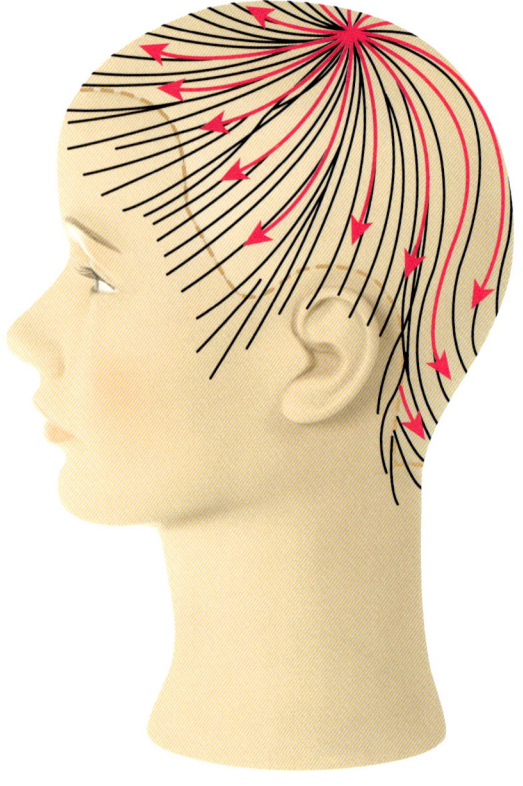

The art shows the radial and parallel distribution that will be used in the interior.

The art shows the curvature design directions for the sides and back.

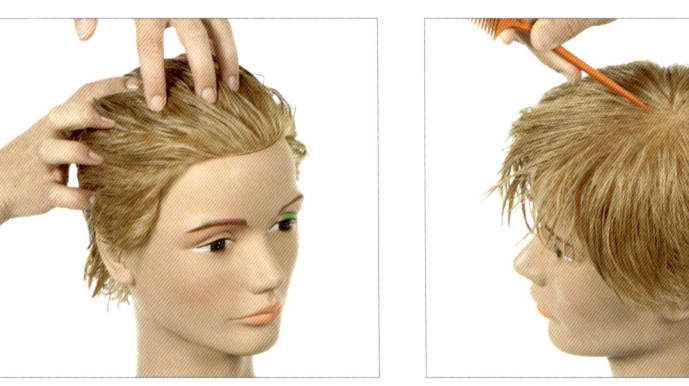

01–02 Apply a styling cream to your hands and use your fingers to distribute the product throughout the hair.

03 Use the tip of the comb to distribute radially from an off-center point of origin, near the crown.

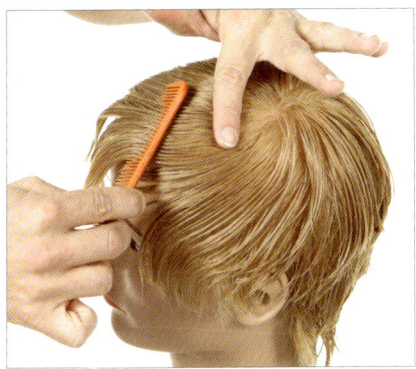

04 Mold curved lines in a clockwise direction using your finger to protect the point of origin.

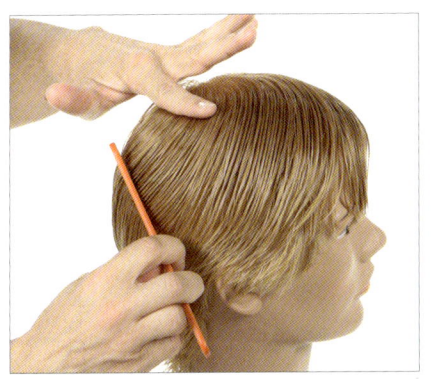

05 Continue to use curved lines as you mold the crown.

06 Once you have molded the interior, use a gentle curve to mold the hair below the crest in a counterclockwise direction.

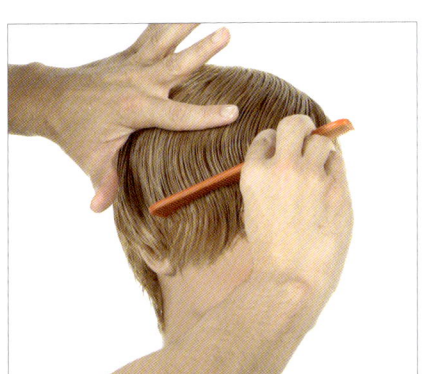

07 At the front hairline, distribute the lengths toward the face in a gentle curved movement.

08 Begin air forming at the nape. Position the 9-row brush on the surface and follow the lines of the molded pattern as you air form for closeness.

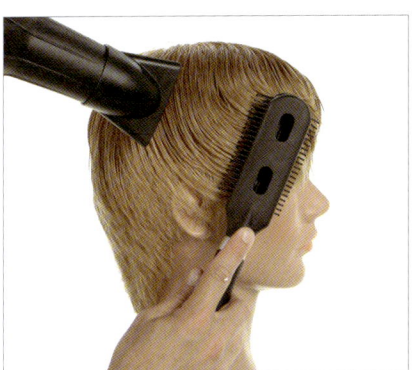

09 Move to one side and continue to use the 9-row brush on the surface as you follow the lines of the molded pattern. Continue to air form to create closeness and gentle curved movement.

10 Repeat the same air-forming technique on the opposite side, following the molded lines.

11–12 Move to the crown. Use the 9-row brush and lift the base of the hair to achieve base lift. Then smooth the ends of the hair to blend into the previously air-formed curved direction.

14 Then release the brush and direct the hair ends to blend into the exterior movements with minimal volume.

13 Work in a clockwise direction, continuing to lift the base and directing the ends to achieve curvature volume.

15 At the front hairline, continue to lift the base as you air form to achieve volume.

16 Then smooth the ends to create closeness in the intended curved direction.

17 Work through the top, taking diagonal-back partings. Use the 9 row brush to lift and dry the base for volume.

18 Then smooth the front hairline toward the face to follow the molded direction and create more closeness.

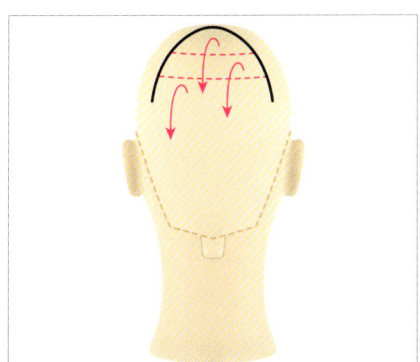

19 Maximum to diminishing volume is air formed within a triangular shape at the crown. This section will blend with the previously air-formed lengths in the nape.

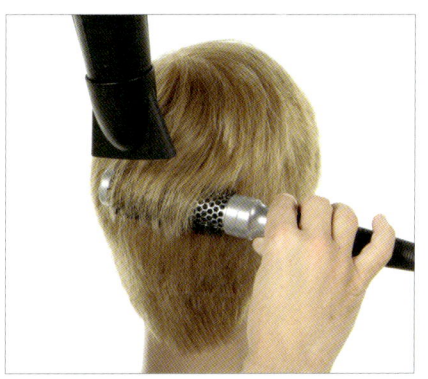

20 Return to the back and switch to a small-diameter round brush. Air form for volume from horizontal partings, positioning the round brush half-off base.

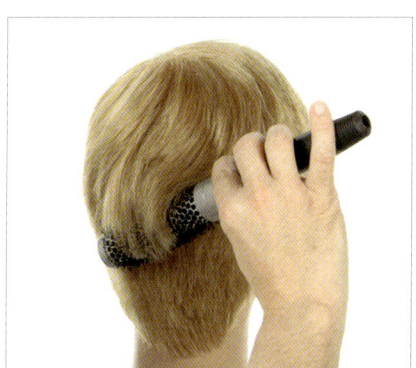

21 Then turn the brush into the intended direction as you remove it to support curved end texture. Work from the center to either side.

22 Take a horizontal parting in the crown and air form for volume using on-base control. You may choose to clip the remaining lengths out of the way.

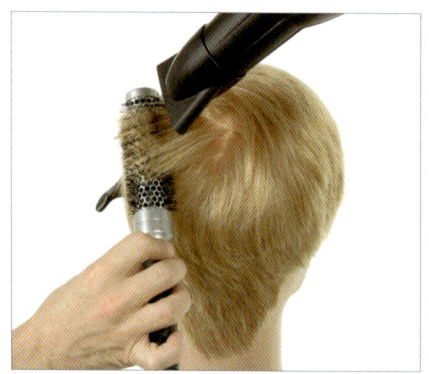

23 Continue to use on-base control through the crown. Turn the brush into the intended finish direction when removing it from the hair.

24 Repeat the same techniques to air form on the sides.

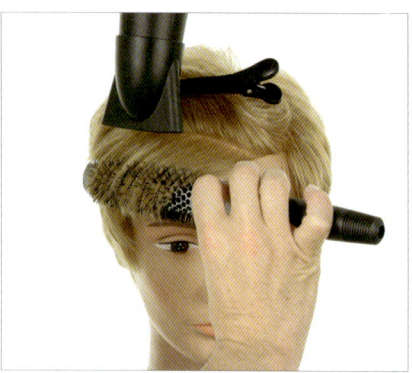

25 Release a diagonal parting at the front hairline. Air form for volume and direct the hair toward the face in the molded direction.

26 Then, release another diagonal-back parting. Air form the base first for volume.

27 Next, position the round brush on top of the hair above the left eye, and air form for indentation. Use the airflow to help direct the hair onto the round brush. Work to the crown.

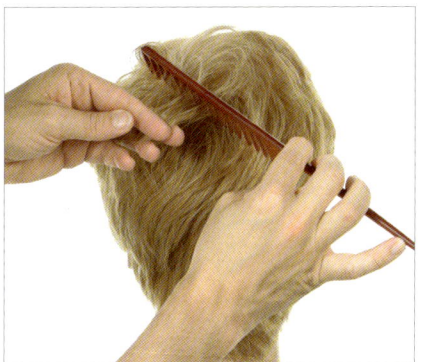

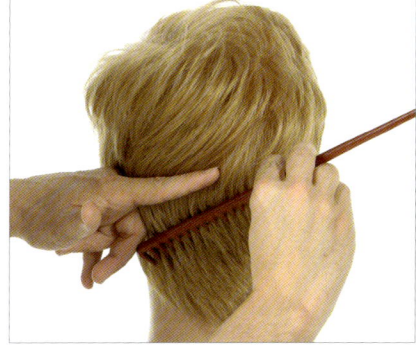

28 Then, run your fingers through the hair while air forming. This will help to blend the movements.

29–30 In the crown, use the large-tooth tail comb and gently backcomb on the surface to create additional volume. Then use the same comb to refine the surface and retrace the curved movement, blending to the movements in the nape.

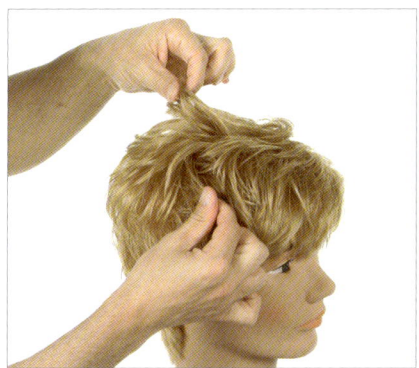

31 Define the curved movements at the top, sides and fringe area. For added shine, apply a small amount of gloss to your hands and work it through the hair.

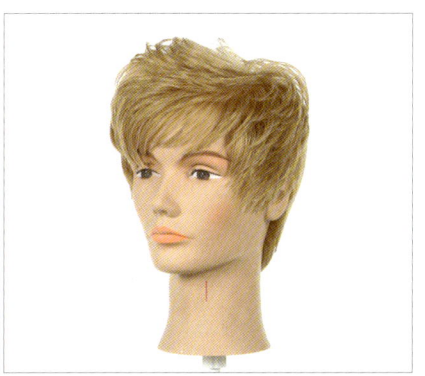

32–33 The finish shows directional curved movements that enhance the activated texture of the form.

DESIGN DECISIONS *WORKSHOP 06*

CURVATURE VOLUME AND INDENTATION – AIR FORMING

artist+ access.

Draw or fill in the boxes with the appropriate answers.

STRUCTURE

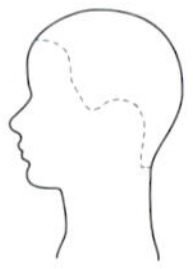

FORM/TEXTURE

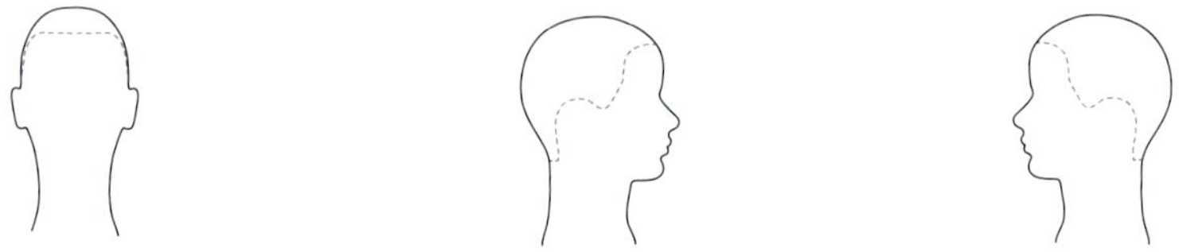

DIRECTION

MOLDING/SCALING

AIR-FORMING PATTERN

COMB-OUT/FINISH

- [ ] RELAX
- [ ] DRY MOLD
- [ ] BACKCOMB/BACKBRUSH
- [ ] DEFINE THE FORM
- [ ] DETAIL

TOOLS/PRODUCT CHOICE

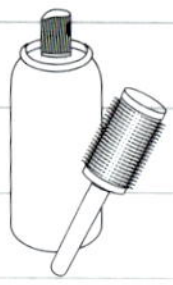

Educator Signature

Date

 HAIR DESIGN RUBRIC *WORKSHOP 06*

CURVATURE VOLUME AND INDENTATION – AIR FORMING

This rubric is a performance assessment tool designed to measure your ability to **create** *Pivot Point hair designs.*

	LEVEL 1 *in progress*	LEVEL 2 *getting better*	LEVEL 3 *entry-level proficiency*
PREPARATION			
Assemble hair design essentials	☐	☐	☐
CREATE			
Shampoo, condition and apply styling cream	☐	☐	☐
Use radial distribution from off-center point of origin	☐	☐	☐
Mold top and crown in curved lines in a clockwise direction	☐	☐	☐
Use gentle curve to mold hair below crest in a counterclockwise direction	☐	☐	☐
Distribute front hairline lengths toward face in gentle, curved movement	☐	☐	☐
Air form for closeness at nape, positioning 9-row brush on surface; follow lines of molded pattern; repeat at sides following molded lines	☐	☐	☐
Air form crown for curvature volume using 9-row brush to lift hair at base; smooth ends in molded direction	☐	☐	☐
Air form a triangle-shaped section in crown for maximum to diminished volume	☐	☐	☐
Air form for volume from horizontal partings using small round brush	☐	☐	☐
Turn brush into intended finish direction while removing it	☐	☐	☐
Air form for volume from diagonal parting at front hairline; direct hair toward face	☐	☐	☐
Air form ends in front interior for indentation, positioning round brush on top of hair	☐	☐	☐
Backcomb surface for volume then retrace curvature movements using large-tooth tail comb	☐	☐	☐
Define and separate ends and curvature movements from sides to fringe using a large-tooth tail comb	☐	☐	☐
Personalize form and apply pomade or gloss	☐	☐	☐

TOTAL POINTS = _____ + _____ + _____

TOTAL POINTS _____ ÷ HIGHEST POSSIBLE SCORE 48 X 100 = _____ %

Record your time in comparison with the suggested salon speed.

To improve my performance on this procedure, I need to:

Student Signature   Educator Signature   Date

❝ VOICES OF SUCCESS

"Thanks to our team's solid design skills and a repertoire that goes beyond the basic finishes, our salon is known for the excellent design work we do. During the holiday, prom and wedding seasons, our books are filled with appointments for formal hair designs."

THE SALON OWNER

IN OTHER WORDS

Taking an advanced approach to wet and thermal hair design incorporates design techniques and patterns that increase creative options and sharpen the competitive edge of talented hair designers.

"I used to wear my curly hair pulled back in a ponytail not knowing what to do with it. My stylist taught me how to make the most of my hair, and now I get compliments all the time. When my friend got married, my stylist designed my hair in an elegant, wavy fashion that pulled my whole look together, while I still felt like myself."

THE CLIENT

"It wasn't long after I graduated that I had the opportunity to work on a photo shoot. I'm really glad I listened to my educator at school, who kept working with me until I perfected fingerwaving. The shoot was very creative and I needed to do a fingerwave design on my model. It turned out great! Now I get more and more requests to do editorial work, and I love it! "

THE DESIGNER

LEARNING CHALLENGE

artist⁺ access.

Circle the letter corresponding to the correct answer.

1. Increase-layered/graduated combination forms offer greatest expansion possibilities:
   a. at the front
   b. at the perimeter
   c. at the top of the head
   d. where the two structures meet

2. Uniform/graduated combination forms show a rounded silhouette:
   a. overall
   b. in the interior
   c. in the exterior
   d. at the perimeter

3.	Freeform designs include both wet and thermal design compositions that:
	a.	are not predictable
	b.	cannot be duplicated
	c.	do not require a systematic step-by-step process
	d.	cannot be classified with specific geometric forms or design techniques

4.	The thermal design technique that utilizes a diffuser and the fingers to style the hair is referred to as:
	a.	blast-drying
	b.	scrunch-drying
	c.	freeform styling
	d.	volume air forming

5.	Setting for volume oblongs begins:
	a.	at the open end
	b.	at the convex end
	c.	at the concave end
	d.	in the front of the oblong shape

LESSONS LEARNED

- Advanced wet and thermal designs require a step-by-step process and incorporate the use of advanced techniques and patterns.
- When designing for combination forms, it is important to consider the form, texture and direction desired.
- Flat-ironing is a thermal technique that utilizes a flat iron to temporarily straighten the hair and achieve a shiny finish.
- Many clients are willing to explore advanced wet and thermal designs for special occasions.
- Hair that is set in alternating oblongs, whether with fingerwaves, rollers or pincurls will display wave patterns.

LONG HAIR DESIGN

CONFIDENCE AND
CREATIVITY THRIVE WHEN
PREDICTABLE LONG HAIR
DESIGN PROCEDURES ARE
COMBINED WITH LONG HAIR
DESIGN TECHNIQUES

FOLLOWING THIS LESSON
YOU WILL BE ABLE TO:

Explain how hair preparation affects long hair design

Relate wet and thermal design procedures and techniques to long hair design

Demonstrate the knowledge and ability to use the long hair design procedures to create predictable long hair design results

Create a variety of basic and advanced long hair designs using the six most common long hair techniques

Long hair design presents many unique opportunities to you as a designer. These include designing for runway shows, styling for editorial photo shoots and servicing bridal clients. Building a solid repertoire of long hair design techniques and procedures will position you to become a successful and creative long hair designer with more career opportunities and the confidence to pursue them.

Studying and practicing the procedures and techniques presented in *Chapter 4, Long Hair Design,* will help you unleash your creativity and create memorable designs of your own.

4.1 ESSENTIAL LONG HAIR DESIGN TECHNIQUES

Though long hair design trends change over time, the techniques used to create them are timeless. The six basic long hair design techniques combined with the predictable long hair design procedures will give you the tools and confidence to adapt to the changing trends as well as create trends of your own. The twist, knot, overlap, braid, loop and roll techniques have countless variations that can be designed in endless combinations, allowing you to create any design you can imagine.

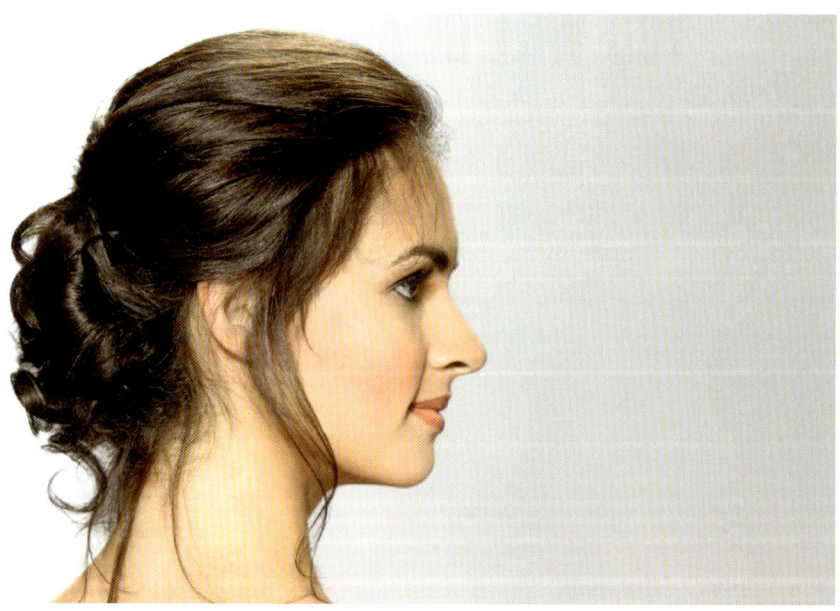

In this chapter, you will learn how to prepare the hair and apply the six basic long hair design techniques while following the long hair design procedures to achieve predictable results.

PREDICTABLE LONG HAIR RESULTS

Learning the basic long hair design techniques and procedures will give you predictable results that you and your clients can rely on.

As in previous hair design chapters, it is critical to choose and follow the proper steps to prepare the hair. These preparation steps then need to be followed by long hair design procedures, resulting in predictable long hair design results.

PREPARATION

Just as a professional wardrobe stylist meticulously prepares the garments by steaming, pressing or folding the fabric to drape or hang on the body in a particular fashion, a hair designer prepares the hair to move, bend or drape in the desired direction of the final design.

This preparation may seem like a timely expense, but experienced designers usually find that this step saves time later in the design, producing cleaner and more professional results. When deciding on how to prepare the hair for a long hair design, it is important to carefully choose the proper:

- Products
- Tools
- Setting techniques
- Patterns

PRODUCTS

Long hair is exposed to more natural stress (such as sunlight and water) as well as physical stress (such as the use of thermal tools or wearing ponytails too often or too tight). This stress may show in the form of dull, dry or unruly hair lengths. Using the right products at the right time can tame unruly hair and make it look healthier while adding support to the design. Knowing which products to use before, during and after the set as well as the design will help you achieve beautiful results.

The chart below gives you some general ideas about the products, which you may choose to use with different natural hair textures, and when to use them. Keep in mind that in long hair design tool selection is usually based more on the desired texture than the natural texture of the hair.

ALL HAIR TYPES	• Thermal protective spray—Before and during set
	• Working hairspray—Before and during set and design
	• Finishing hairspray—After design is complete
	• Shine spray—During and after design
FINE-MEDIUM	• Detangler—Before set
	• Mousse—Before set
	• Volumizing spray—Before and during set
	• Pomade—During and after design
MEDIUM-COARSE	• Leave-in conditioner—Before set
	• Gel—Before set
	• Silicone serum—Before and after set, during design
	• Wax—During and after design

TOOLS

Designers use many tools to prepare hair for long hair designs, some of which are familiar to you from studying wet and thermal design techniques.

Common tools designers use for hair preparation and during the design are: thermal rollers, cushion brushes, elastic hair bands, bobby pins, hairpins, long bobby pins and hairpins, synthetic hair fibers and hairnets.

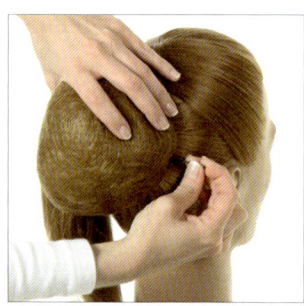

Designers often use thermal rollers to create volume and soft curvature shapes. These make the hair smoother and easier to bend into place when curved shapes are applied.

The cushion brush has dense bristles that can be made of natural fiber, synthetic fiber or a combination. Designers may use this brush to increase shine and to smooth the hair.

Elastic bands, bobby pins, and hairpins are used to support and secure long hair designs. They come in a wide variety of colors and sizes. Designers often choose bands and pins to match the hair color to help conceal them.

Synthetic hair fibers and hairnets have many uses. As you will see later in this chapter, synthetic fibers placed inside a hairnet can be used to create a filler. The filler provides shape and support in the design.

SETTING TECHNIQUES

Depending on the chosen long hair design, the hair may be set to achieve smooth and straight, tightly curled, wavy or combinations of different textures. The direction of the set should mimic the direction of the finished long hair design, both in the overall direction and within specific areas.

Long hair designers commonly use thermal design setting techniques that include the use of thermal rollers, curling irons, flat irons, scrunch-drying and round brushes.

To accommodate the placement and proportions of different textures and volume, designers may set the hair after it has been gathered into a ponytail.

LONG HAIR PREPARATION

Below are just some of the common wet and thermal design techniques and tools used to prepare long lengths for a long hair design.

THERMAL ROLLERS

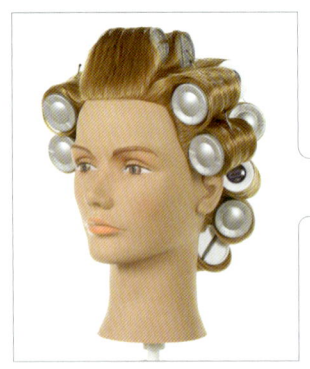   

CURLING IRON

AIR FORM

 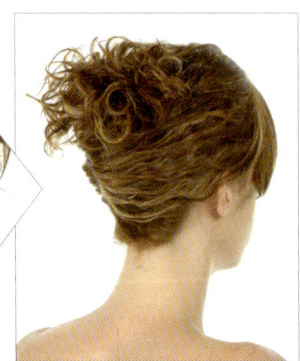  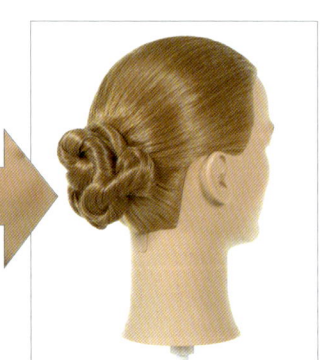

LONG HAIR DESIGN PROCEDURES

The five long hair design procedures can be used in any long hair design to provide an organized path leading to the desired design result. Several of these procedures are similar to the setting and finishing procedures from the previous hair design chapters.

FIVE-STEP LONG HAIR DESIGN PROCEDURE

DISTRIBUTE

SECTION

PART

APPLY

DETAIL

 **DISTRIBUTE**

The overall distribution of the hair determines the directions in which the eye will travel throughout the design. Distribution can lead the eye to a focal point at the crown, the nape, or asymmetrically on either side, just to name a few options.

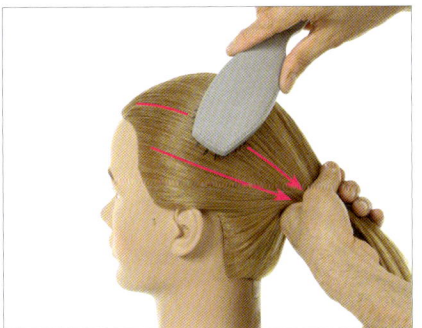

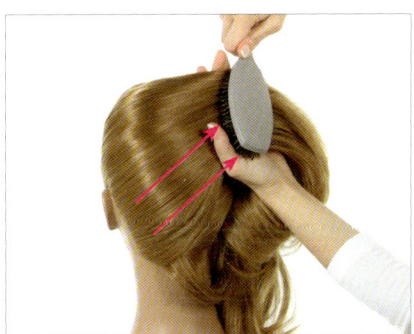

Designers use the distribution of individual strands or partings to create detail and movement that lead the eye through the design and create interest.

② SECTION

Designers use sectioning for several different purposes. Similar to sculpture, sectioning is used to separate areas of the design that will be treated with different techniques. Therefore, sectioning also influences the proportions within the design. Sectioning helps the designer stay organized and follow the plan. The initial sectioning of the hair often creates a base, such as a ponytail or a seam with interlocking bobby pins. Proper sectioning will ensure that the base is positioned in the most favorable spot, assuring that the overall direction and placement of the focal point are accurate before proceeding.

A designer may choose to section the front, back, hairline, fringe, nape or crown from the rest of the hair just to name a few options.

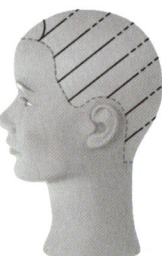 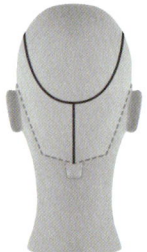 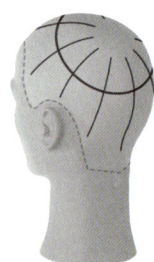

③ PART

Designers use partings to subdivide larger sections of hair for control. Specific techniques are usually applied to individual partings, which, when combined, create the surface texture of the design. More partings will usually result in more detail, textural interest and smaller individual shapes.

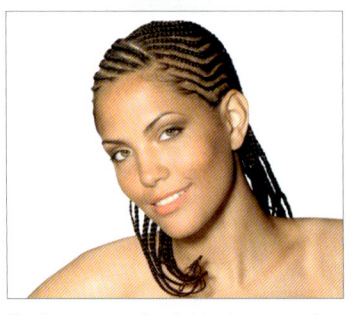

Partings may also be incorporated into one technique, as with on-the-scalp design.

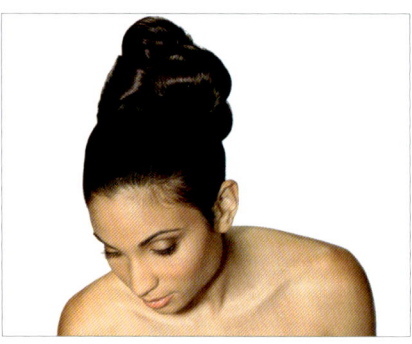

A single ponytail divided into 5 partings, creates a moderate amount of detail.

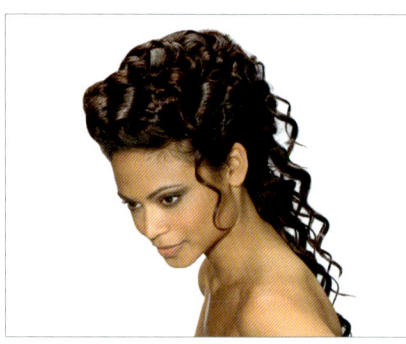

Many individual loops positioned throughtout the interior of a design create lots of interest and intricacy.

04

APPLY

In long hair design, the application procedure does not always require tools, such as rollers or brushes, as it did with much of wet and thermal hair design. Designers use their hands to apply the chosen long hair design technique. In order to give each of your long hair designs a balanced and polished look, it is critical to master the application of the six basic long hair techniques.

SIX BASIC LONG HAIR TECHNIQUES

 TWISTS

The twist technique often creates a rope-like appearance and may be applied on or off the scalp with one or two strands. When using two strands, the double-twist technique may be applied to achieve more distinction between them. The tension and direction of the twist—clockwise or counterclockwise—will affect the final result. Texture and intricacy can be increased in the design by applying the twist technique to more and smaller strands.

 KNOTS

The knot technique consists of the interlacing or tying together of one or two partings to create a knot. This knot technique may be applied on or off the scalp. Like the twist, the direction in which the single strand knot is tied—clockwise or counterclockwise—will change the effect. The knot technique can be applied to small individual partings for textural detail or to larger sections of hair, encompassing a larger area of the head.

OVERLAP

The overlap technique is the crossing of two strands of hair over one another creating a crisscross effect. Overlaps may be applied on or off the scalp, and the parting size will change the result of the design significantly. This technique is commonly combined with other techniques to add interest to the design.

BRAID

Weaving three or more partings together, on or off the scalp, creates a braid. The 3-strand braid may be created using either the overbraid or underbraid technique. The difference in result is most obvious when applied on the scalp. The overbraid has an inverted appearance and is created by crossing the strands over one another. The underbraid is created by crossing the strands under one another to create a visible or projected braid. Braids may also be applied using multiple strands, such as the 5-strand braid.

LOOP

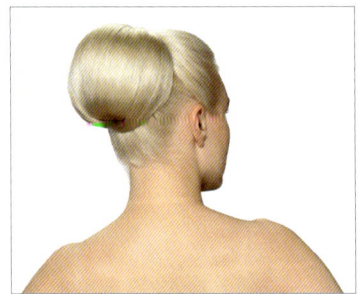

Folding or bending the hair in a circular shape and then securing it creates loops. When a designer uses the single-loop technique, one strand of hair is used to form one loop. Using one strand of hair to form two loops is called the double-loop technique. Small loops in larger quantities will usually create more movement and texture within the design, while a single large loop will give a smoother, less "busy" look. One large loop may also need a filler to support the shape.

ROLL

 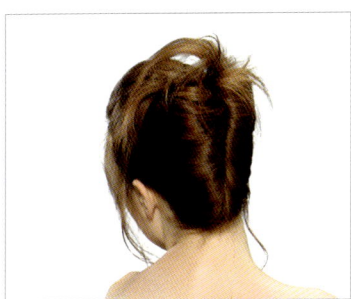

When using the roll technique, the designer is wrapping or winding the hair around itself. Rolls are typically the main feature in a design and sometimes incorporate all of the lengths. However, other techniques can be integrated to soften the look. Rolls are often achievable on shorter lengths and may give the illusion of longer hair. Fillers are sometimes used with the roll technique to give the appearance of more volume.

SECURING

The design's ability to last through the event for which it was created is essential. Not only must it have the endurance to last, it must also conceal its inner strength to be aesthetically pleasing. The design's strength, produced by bobby pins, hairpins and the base to which the lengths are secured, must be hidden. The design should appear weightless as if to defy gravity.

BOBBY PINS

In general, designers use bobby pins to secure large or heavy sections to other large areas. Usually the pin is opened slightly and then slid into the hair to be secured.

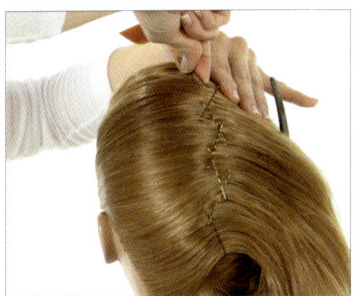

LOCKING

Designers use a bobby pin technique called "locking" to create extra security. Locking bobby pins means to cross them over one another. This is especially useful for creating lines of bobby pins, such as the vertical line of locked bobby pins used in a vertical roll design.

PONYTAIL

Designers usually prefer to use an elastic hair band with one or two bobby pins to secure a ponytail. This allows the hand that controls the hair to stay in one position tight against the head while securing. Not moving the hair while securing the ponytail helps to keep it smooth, tight and positioned correctly.

ONE-BOBBY-PIN TECHNIQUE

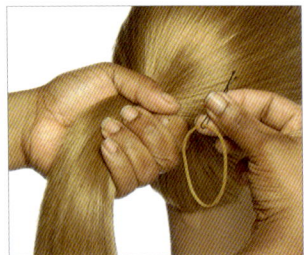

Prepare elastic hair band by sliding one bobby pin through it.

Gather hair with thumb up and hand close to head. Hook elastic band around your thumb.

Hold bobby pin while wrapping band around hair.

Continue to wrap the band around hair. Then insert the end of the band that is wrapped around thumb into the bobby pin.

Pull bobby pin up slightly, then turn it downward so that open end faces gathered hair and push under base of ponytail.

TWO-BOBBY-PIN TECHNIQUE

Prepare elastic hair band by sliding two bobby pins onto it.

Gather hair into position holding hand close to head. Insert one bobby pin at base of intended ponytail.

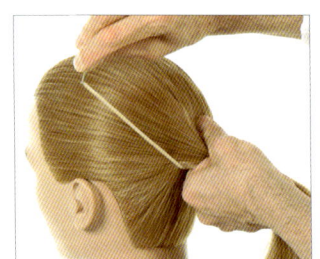

Push hand firmly against head to hold bobby pin in place while wrapping band around hair.

Push second pin into hair close to head so it will cross the first bobby pin in an "X" formation. Make sure pins are interlocked.

HAIRPINS

Hairpins are usually used to secure smaller and more delicate areas of the design. Hairpins are easier to conceal and are often placed closer to the surface of the design.

HAIRNETS AND FILLERS

Designers sometimes use a hairnet for extra support and security in areas that are especially heavy or long. Hairnets are also used to create fillers. Designers use fillers to create shape and support within the design. Fillers are often made from synthetic hair fibers that have been backcombed and placed into a hairnet. This method allows the designer to customize the filler in the shape and volume desired for the design. Manufactured fillers may also be used and come in a variety of different colors, shapes and materials.

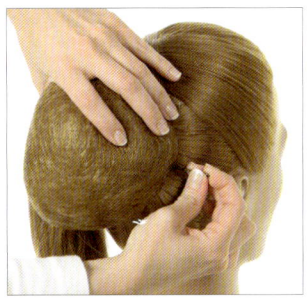 

⑤ DETAIL

The detailing that goes into the finish of the design is another element that can distinguish one designer from others. Detailing in long hair design includes refining, smoothing stray hairs into place, adding finishing spray and shine spray, and double-checking pins. For many special occasions it may also include adding decorative details or accessories.

The first step is to take a step back and analyze the design from all sides. Check for balance in the silhouette and in the proportions of the design. Look for pins that are showing or loose and make any adjustments as necessary.

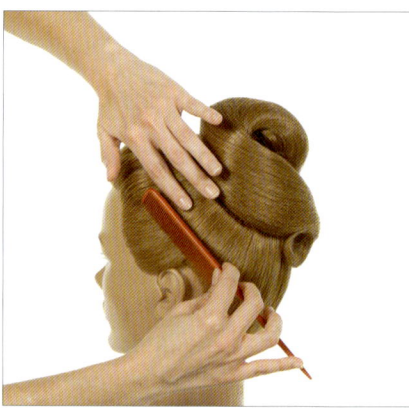

Then, using the tip of the tail comb, the teeth of the comb, a hairpin or your fingers, trace the lines and directions in the design to smooth stray hairs into place. Stay organized and work your way around the head. Then work into the design.

A firm hold finishing spray can be used to keep the hair in place and give the overall design more support. Afterward a shine spray may be used to give a healthy glow, add a touch of dimension and further calm stray hairs.

Some designs will end here while others will require the addition of hair accessories. Flowers, veils, decorated pins, headbands and tiaras are all common adornments designers may incorporate.

PRACTICE
MAKES PERFECT 01
SINGLE-STRAND TWIST

The focus of this exercise is to provide practice in techniques used to create a single-strand twist.

Practice this exercise to build rhythm, skill and accuracy using medium tension and alternation of hand position to create a single-strand twist.

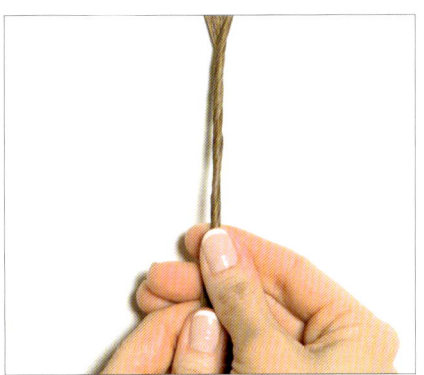

01–02 Begin the single-strand twist starting at the top. Using medium tension, twist the strand counterclockwise or to the left with your thumb, index and middle fingers.

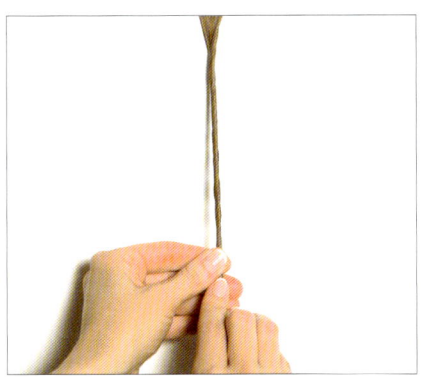

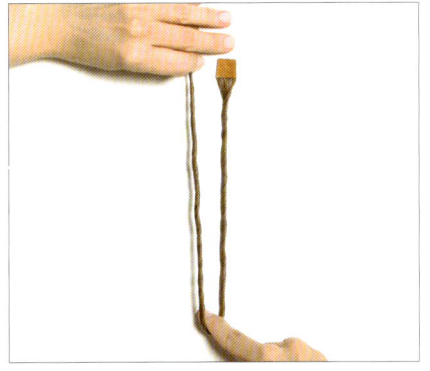

03-04 Alternate your hand position and use even tension as you work toward the ends. Place your index finger at the center of the strand and bring the ends toward the top. Remove your finger and watch as the double twisting occurs.

05 The finish shows a double-twist pattern created from a single twist.

COILED SINGLE-STRAND TWIST

The focus of this exercise is to provide practice in techniques used to create a coiled single-strand twist.

Practice this exercise to build rhythm, skill and accuracy using tight tension and a hand-over-hand technique to create a coiled single-strand twist.

01–02 Starting at the top, twist the strand in a counterclockwise direction using tight tension. Twist a small portion of the strand at a time.

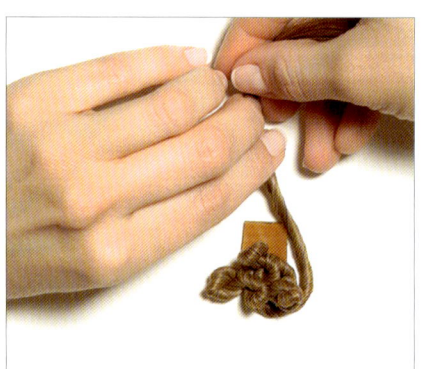

03-04 Push up slightly, then direct the strand upward and use a hand-over-hand technique to encourage the coiled effect near the base. Continue to use this technique until you reach the ends.

05 The finish shows a coiled twist effect.

PRACTICE
MAKES PERFECT 03
2-STRAND TWIST

The focus of this exercise is to provide practice in techniques used to create a 2-strand twist.

Practice this exercise to build rhythm, skill and accuracy using a palm-up, palm-down hand position to create a 2-strand twist.

01–02 Begin the 2-strand twist with your palm up and your index finger between the two strands. Next, turn your palm down to cross the two strands.

03-04 Control the left strand with your left hand before repositioning your right hand in the palm-up position. Continue to use the palm-up, palm-down technique as you work toward the ends. This technique automatically creates the twisted pattern.

05 The finish shows the subtle rope-like texture created with the 2-strand twist.

PRACTICE
MAKES PERFECT 04
2-STRAND DOUBLE TWIST

The focus of this exercise is to provide practice in techniques used to create a 2-strand double twist.

Practice this exercise to build rhythm, skill and accuracy using a palm-down, palm-up hand position to create a 2-strand double twist.

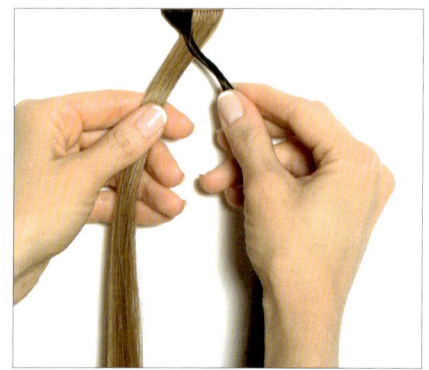

01–02 Start the 2-strand double twist with a palm-down hand position with your index finger between the two strands, then turn your palm up. Twist the right strand in a counterclockwise direction.

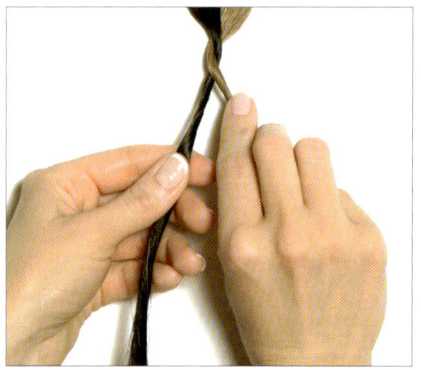
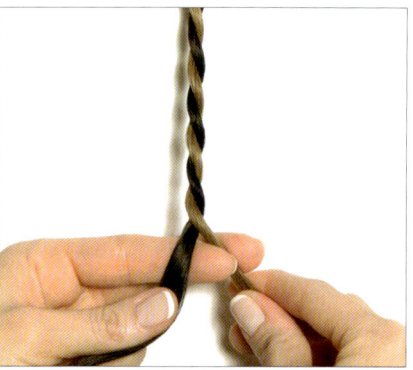

03-04 Use your left hand to control the hair and use the right hand to twist the strand that is now on the right side. Continue to use this technique as you work toward the ends.

05 The finish shows a pronounced rope-like appearance.

PRACTICE
MAKES PERFECT 05
SINGLE-STRAND KNOT

The focus of this exercise is to provide practice in techniques used to create a single-strand knot.

Practice this exercise to build rhythm, skill and accuracy using the appropriate tension and hand positions to create a single-strand knot.

01–02 Begin creating the first knot by directing the ends in a counterclockwise direction. Next, bring the ends through the center of the circle using your index and middle fingers.

03-04 Then, direct the strand in a clockwise direction. Use your index and middle fingers to bring the ends through the second knot. Note the overhand technique is used for both knots.

05 The finish shows two single-strand knots positioned on opposite sides of the strand.

PRACTICE
MAKES PERFECT 06
2-STRAND KNOT

The focus of this exercise is to provide practice in techniques used to create a 2-strand knot.

Practice this exercise to build rhythm, skill and accuracy using the appropriate tension and hand positions to create a 2-strand knot.

01–02 Begin creating the 2-strand knot by crossing the left strand over the right strand. Then, bring the left strand under the right strand and pull it through with your thumb.

03-04 Create the next knot using the same technique. Continue to cross the left strand over the right strand and gently pull the strand through with your thumb.

05 The finish shows multiple 2-strand knots, which create a chain effect.

PRACTICE MAKES PERFECT 07
2-STRAND OVERLAP

The focus of this exercise is to provide practice in techniques used to create a 2-strand overlap.

Practice this exercise to build rhythm, skill and accuracy using the appropriate hand positions and finger manipulations to create a 2-strand overlap.

   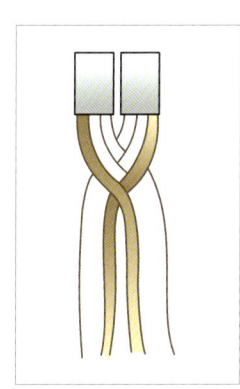

01–04 Begin with two small center strands and cross the left strand over the right strand. Then take another small portion on either side and repeat the same technique. Repeat the same technique to incorporate the remaining two strands.

 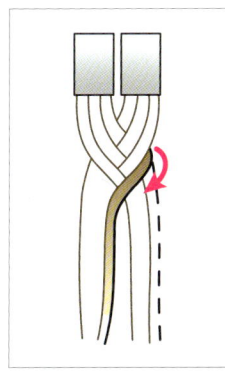  

05-08 Now pick up a small strand from the outside of each section. Cross these sections over to the opposite side, alternating from one side to the other. Continue to overlap using the same techniques as you work toward the ends.

09 The finish shows an overlap, which creates a crisscross effect.

PRACTICE MAKES PERFECT 08
3-STRAND UNDERBRAID

The focus of this exercise is to provide practice in techniques used to create a 3-strand underbraid.

Practice this exercise to build rhythm, skill and accuracy using the appropriate hand positions and finger manipulations to create a 3-strand underbraid.

01–02 Begin by crossing the left strand under the center strand. Next, cross the right strand under the center strand. Note how the thumb is used to lift the strand while the index and middle fingers are used to control the center strand.

03-04 Again, cross the left strand under the center strand and the right strand under the center. Continue to use the same technique as you work toward the ends, then secure with an elastic band.

05 The finish shows a 3-strand underbraid.

PRACTICE
MAKES PERFECT 09
3-STRAND OVERBRAID

The focus of this exercise is to provide practice in techniques used to create a 3-strand overbraid.

Practice this exercise to build rhythm, skill and accuracy using the appropriate hand positions and finger manipulations to create a 3-strand overbraid.

01 Begin by crossing the left strand over the center.

02-03 Next, cross the right strand over the center. Alternate hands as you continue to use the same technique working toward the ends.

04 The finish shows the woven texture of a 3-strand overbraid.

PRACTICE
MAKES PERFECT 10
5-STRAND BRAID

The focus of this exercise is to provide practice in techniques used to create a 5-strand braid.

Practice this exercise to build rhythm, skill and accuracy using the appropriate hand positions and finger manipulations to create a 5-strand braid.

01–02 First, begin with the three center strands. Cross the left strand over the center, then the right strand over the center. Next, pick up the fourth strand on the left and cross it under the strand next to it and over the center.

03-04 Then, pick up the fifth strand from the right side and cross it under the strand next to it and over the center. Continue to use the same technique. Always weave the outside strand under the one next to it and over the center strand. Work to the ends and secure.

05 The finish shows the completed 5-strand braid.

NOTE: *See video segment for an alternative method, which uses the index and middle fingers to cross the strands.*

SALON SAVVY

Many commonly practiced methods of the seasoned professional are often passed down from one designer to the next, and now to you. When put into practice these tips can have a big impact on a busy day in the salon, positioning you one more step ahead.

DIRTY UP

Designers often "dirty up the hair" before they begin their long hair design. Clean hair is often too soft and slippery to work with effectively. "Dirty up the hair" means to work product through the hair before the set or the design begins. This technique gives the hair more grip, making it easier to work with.

CHIN UP

The head will naturally tend to tilt forward when the designer is working in the back. If the head stays in this position, the nape will loosen, sag, or buckle when the head lifts. When creating a ponytail or any technique in the back or nape area, check that the client has her chin up.

STRONG AND QUICK

A strong set makes the designer's job easier. To achieve a strong set, allow it to cool in the desired shape. Thermal styling tools, such as a blow dryer when switched to the coolest setting, can be used to speed up the cooling time of a set. Allow the hair to cool completely in all areas, and then release the set.

TAIL SPIN

After a ponytail or other area is secured, the tip of the tail comb is used to smooth uneven areas. The tip of the tail comb is inserted about ½" (1.25 cm) from the hairline. The tail of the comb should be held parallel to and near the surface. The comb is gently pulled back toward the base of the ponytail. This technique is used in small sections around the ponytail where necessary.

HANDS IN

Designers understand the need to occasionally put down their comb or brush and get their hands in the hair. This is often the best remedy for unruly hair. Working your hands through the hair will sometimes tame and smooth it better than any man-made tool or product.

HAIRPIN HELP

Hairpins sometimes need help to achieve a stronger hold. This may be achieved in a couple of ways. First, you can make sure the hairpin penetrates the dense area of the strand being secured. Next, you can weave the hairpin in and out of the two areas to be adjoined, similar to a needle weaving in and out of two pieces of fabric.

SPRAY AND GLIDE

To smooth stray hairs, designers work in small areas. First, the section is given a light coat of hairspray. Then, in the same direction the hair is flowing, the surface is smoothed with the teeth of the comb on a 45° angle. Avoid allowing the teeth to penetrate the surface.

GUIDELINES FOR CLIENT-CENTERED LONG HAIR DESIGNS

A stunning long hair design makes a person wonder how it was achieved and how it stays in place. It is this thought-provoking mystery that helps to make the design memorable. Because long hair designs are often requested for special occasions, it is your job to ensure that the client remembers the event, not a headache from her long hair design.

PROCEDURAL GUIDELINES

The following chart will help you assure your client's comfort and safety during the long hair design service.

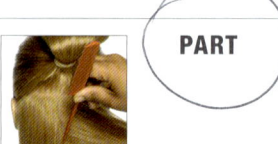	**DISTRIBUTE**	• Turn your client to the side and analyze her profile in the mirror while distributing the hair to different areas of the head to assess which will be most flattering. • When using a ponytail to establish a base for a long hair design, ask your client whether she feels any pulling or discomfort before proceeding. Loosen the ponytail slightly to relieve any discomfort.
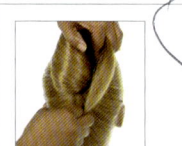	**SECTION**	• Section and clip areas of the hair as necessary to stay organized and keep the design balanced. • Be sure your sectioning pattern and distribution conceal sectioning lines as much as possible.
	**PART**	• Determine the number of partings to use based on how intricate or "busy" the design is intended to be. Balance this texture with the texture and intricacy of the clothing.
	APPLY	• Use a "working" hairspray while applying long hair techniques to individual partings. • Instruct your client to inform you if a pin causes discomfort and make adjustments to relieve the discomfort.
	DETAIL	• Use long hairpins to position and hold the hair in place while using spray. • Use finishing spray and shine spray after the application and detailing procedures to give the design a firm and polished finish.

COMMUNICATION GUIDELINES

The following chart will help you respond to some of the most common client cues in a way that encourages client trust and open communication.

CLIENT CUE	DESIGNER RESPONSE
"Updos always give me a headache."	*"I don't want your head to hurt during this important event. Let's do a trial-run, and take into consideration the tightness of the ponytail, individual pins hurting, and the overall weight and balance of the design. These are often unnecessary irritations that are easily prevented if we communicate about your comfort level during the design."*
"What do I need to do to prepare for the big day?"	*"Gather everything in one place that you need to bring to the salon the day before. When you shampoo your hair, apply conditioner only to the middle of the strands and through to the ends. This will keep more volume and shine in the hair where it is needed the most. Wear a shirt that does not have to be pulled over your head. This way, changing your clothes will not jeopardize the design."*
"I would like my hair to be styled half-up."	*"Okay. Sometimes clients have different ideas of how much hair should be up or down when they ask for their hair to be half-up. Let's look at some pictures of designs that are partially up and partially down so I can get a better idea of the proportions you have in mind."*
"I know my hair is much finer than the hair in this picture, but I really want this design."	*"You are right. Your hair is very different than the hair in this picture. You have several options to try to achieve a similar result. Show me what you like best about the design. The same techniques modified to work on your hair can be used to create a similar texture. The result will be a smaller design with less volume. If the silhouette or volume of the design is more appealing to you, different techniques can be used to create a similar look."*

4.2 BASIC LONG HAIR DESIGNS

Your fingers and hands are now more adept at the skills required to apply long hair design techniques to hair lengths. Next, we will learn to incorporate these techniques with the long hair design procedures to create predictable design results.

WORKSHOP 01
SINGLE-STRAND TWISTS

The single-strand twist technique is used to create a beautiful, textured, classic chignon. The low position and the cluster of twists create eye-catching interest.

The finish shows a single-strand twist wrapped around the base of a ponytail with two more single-strand twists that have been coiled and positioned individually.

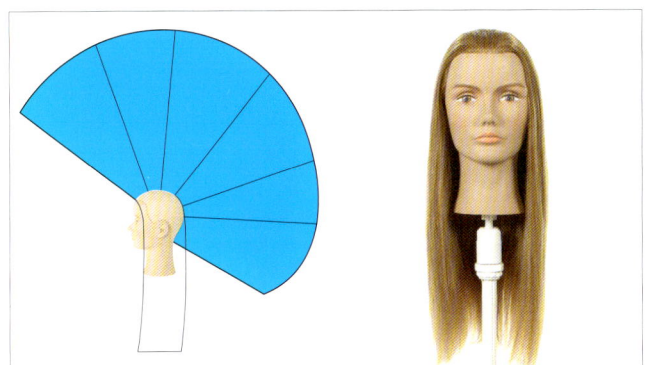

This exercise is performed on long solid lengths. The hair was prepared by air forming the lengths straight.

The art shows the distribution of the hair and position of the ponytail.

01 Begin by positioning your palm at the location of the ponytail and distribute the hair into your palm using a large cushion brush.

02 Secure the ponytail using the one-bobby pin technique.

03–04 Divide the ponytail into three equal strands and clip the two right strands. Use medium tension and twist the left strand beginning at the base clockwise, or to the right, until you reach the ends. Direct this strand upward and wrap it to the right around the base of the ponytail while maintaining tension and securely holding the ends of the hair.

LONG HAIR DESIGN

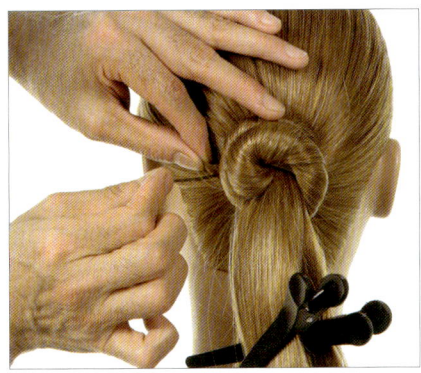

05 Continue to wrap the twisted strand around the ponytail and secure at the base with bobby pins.

06 Twist the center strand in the opposite, counterclockwise (left) direction until you reach the ends.

07 Direct the twist upward and to the right, then downward toward the left of the ponytail, using your opposite hand to help direct the hair.

08 Use your hand to encourage the coiled effect and position the twist.

09 Use bobby pins to secure the twist while positioning it in the desired area. You may also use hairpins to secure the coiled twist.

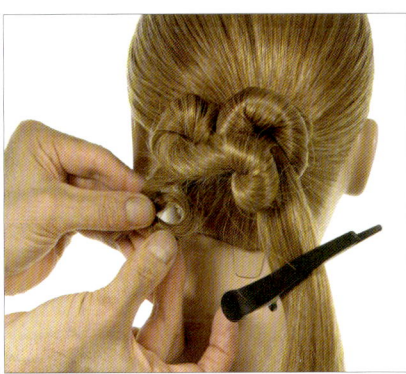

10 Form a flat loop with the ends and tuck it under the coil.

11 Secure the loop with bobby pins. Use additional bobby pins or hairpins to secure the twist if needed.

12 Twist the third strand in the opposite, clockwise direction. Use the same amount of tension on all three strands.

13 Then, with your left hand, direct the strand up to the left and down to the right. Use your index finger to position the coil.

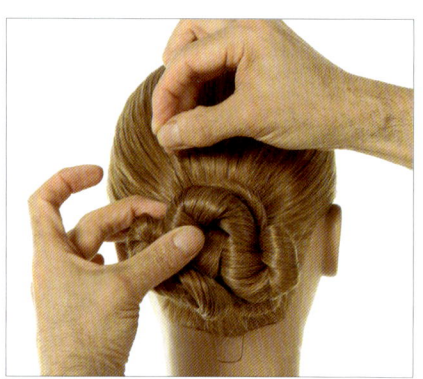

14 Continue to twist the strand and use bobby pins or hairpins to secure.

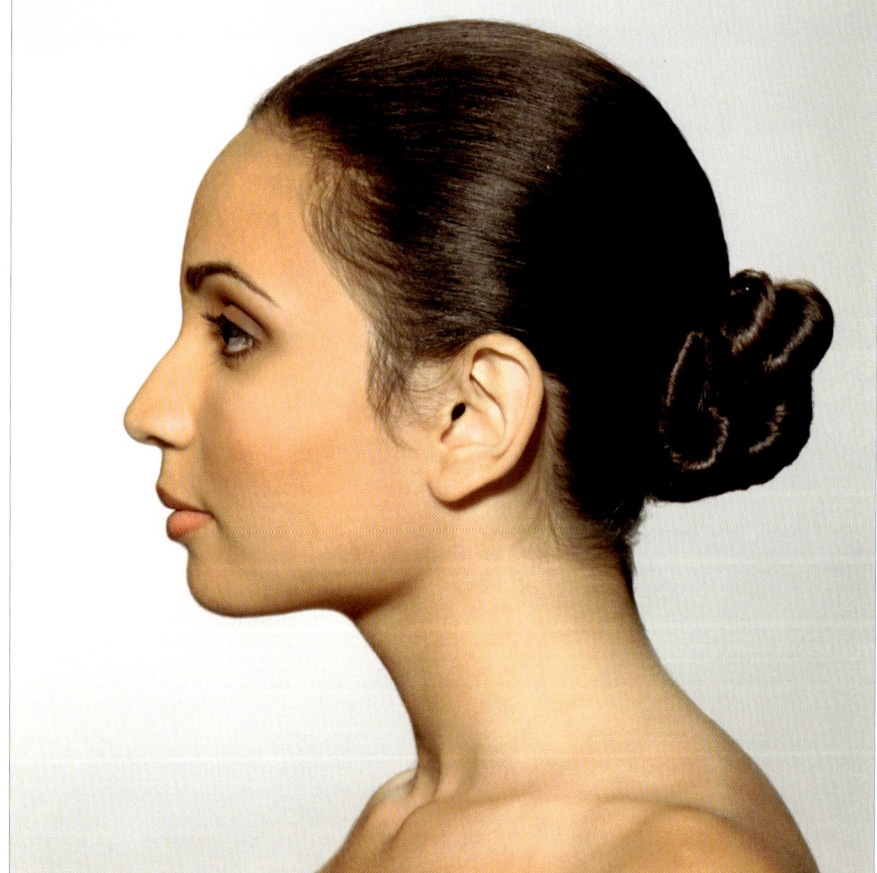

15–16 The single-strand twist design displays a cluster of twists that creates an intricate chignon effect.

DESIGN DECISIONS *WORKSHOP 01*
SINGLE-STRAND TWISTS

Draw or fill in the boxes with the appropriate answers.

artist**access**

STRUCTURE

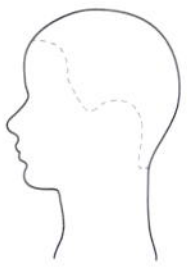

FORM/SHAPE

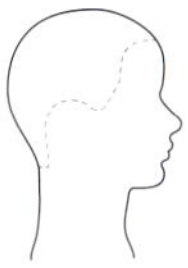

DIRECTION OF FORM

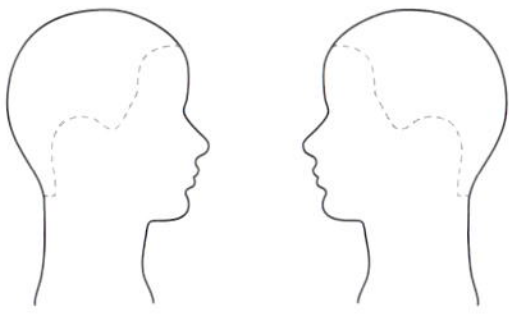

TECHNIQUE

☐ ☐ ☐ ☐ ☐ ☐

DESIGN PRINCIPLES

☐ REPETITION
☐ ALTERNATION
☐ PROGRESSION
☐ CONTRAST

DISTRIBUTION

SECTIONING/PARTING

PREPARATION

☐ CURLING IRON
☐ FLAT IRON
☐ THERMAL ROLLERS
☐ ROLLER SET
☐ AIR FORM

TOOLS/PRODUCT CHOICE

Educator Signature

Date

2-STRAND TWISTS

This 2-strand twist is performed using light tension on the strands, creating the illusion of loops. The result displays a twisted design with a strong commercial look.

All the hair is distributed into a center back ponytail even with the top of the ears. A small section of hair is wrapped around the base of the ponytail, covering the elastic band. The ponytail is then separated into two sections with the palm up and the index finger separating the two strands. Then the hand is turned to the left to face the palm down. The hair is controlled with the left hand and repositioned with the right hand. This procedure is repeated to the ends. The twisted strand is then wrapped around the base in a counterclockwise direction using very light tension and secured with bobby pins. The form is expanded using long hairpins, checking for balance while working. Hairspray is used for control, then the pins are removed. Note that a more classic effect can be achieved by incorporating less expansion into the design.

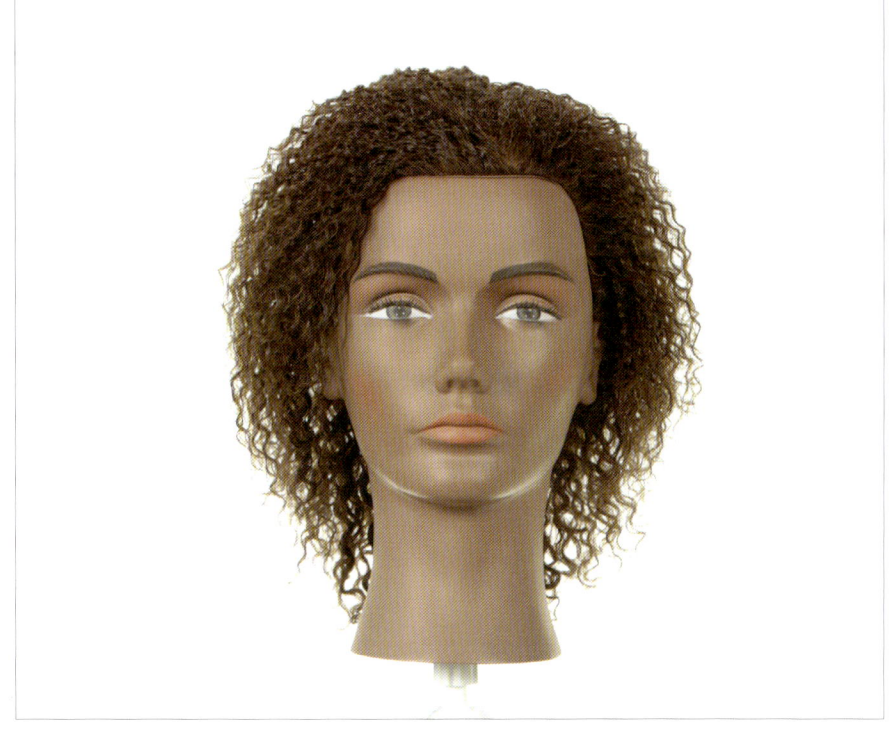

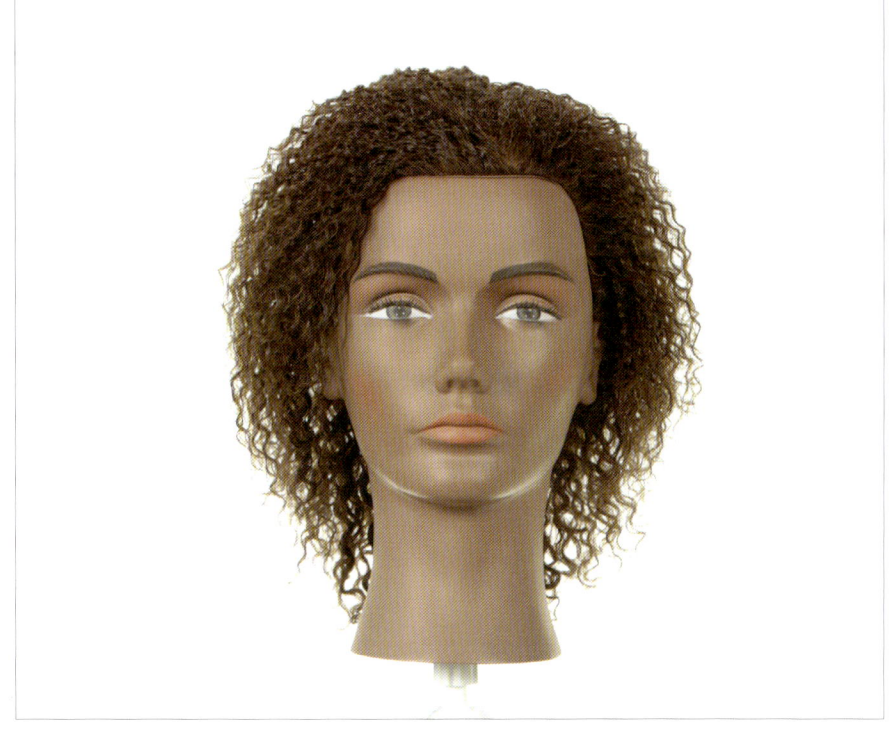

VARIATION 02
2-STRAND TWISTS

In this design variation, 2-strand on-the-scalp twists are combined with 2-strand off-the-scalp double twists to give tightly curled textured hair a more defined curl pattern. This design can also be worn without releasing the twists.

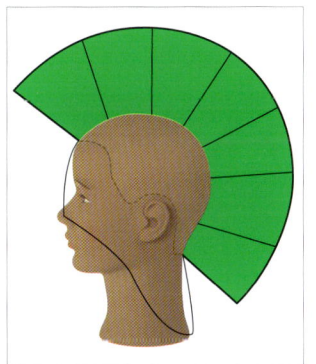

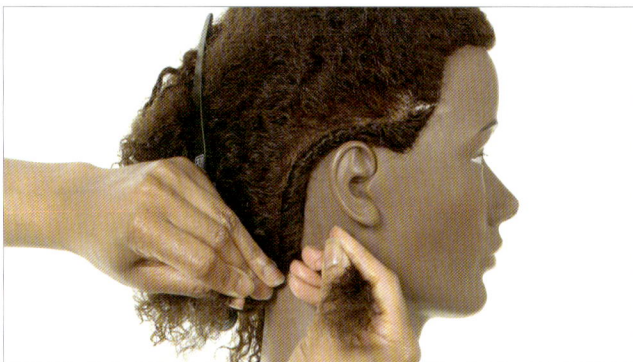

Tightly curled uniform lengths are shampooed and conditioned prior to the service. To establish subtle asymmetry, initial partings on either side are extended to different points on the front hairline. Alternating from one side to the other and working to the interior, partings eventually meet at an off-center point of the front hairline. A slight diagonal part is taken from this point and diagonal partings are twisted, working off the part. Setting lotion and pomade are applied to each section before twisting. In each parting, two strands are twisted off the scalp to begin the twisted pattern. Then, the strands are joined with the hair on the scalp using the thumb and index finger to pick up strands while continuing to twist along the hairline parting.

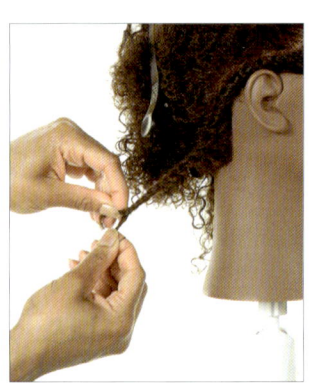 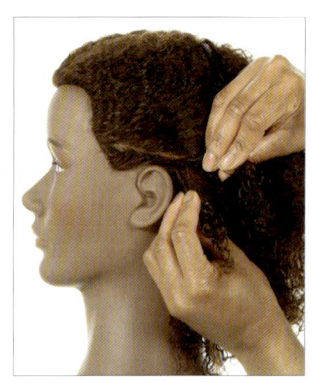 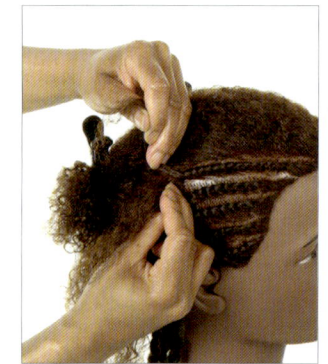 

  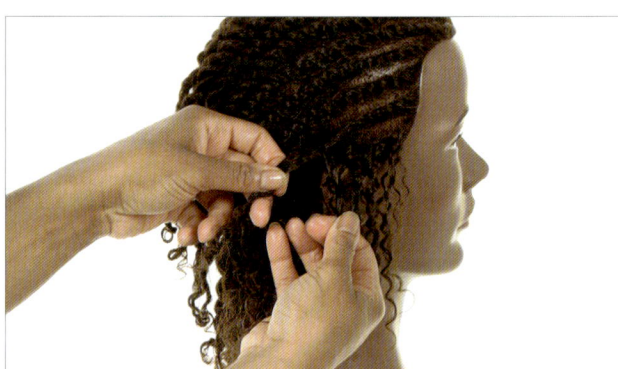

A 2-strand double-twist technique is then used to twist the hair off the scalp. The ends are coiled around the finger to encourage natural curl. Partings are worked to the nape hairline, eventually meeting near the center back. Subsequent partings are also taken and twisted to meet near the center back, then worked off the scalp using a 2-strand double-twist technique. After drying the hair completely under a hood dryer, the twists are released, alternating from one side to the other, starting at the perimeter sides and working toward the interior. As each twist is released, the strands are separated farther to create volume and fullness.

HAIR DESIGN RUBRIC *WORKSHOP 01*

SINGLE-STRAND TWISTS

This rubric is a performance assessment tool designed to measure your ability to **create** *Pivot Point hair designs.*

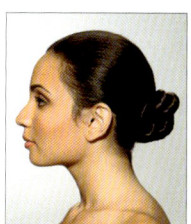

	LEVEL 1 *in progress*	LEVEL 2 *getting better*	LEVEL 3 *entry-level proficiency*
PREPARATION			
• Assemble long hair design essentials	☐	☐	☐
CREATE			
• Distribute hair into palm of hand at location of ponytail	☐	☐	☐
• Secure ponytail by wrapping elastic band around base and using the one-bobby pin technique	☐	☐	☐
• Divide ponytail into three equal strands, using clips for control	☐	☐	☐
• Twist left strand in clockwise direction (right) using medium tension	☐	☐	☐
• Direct twisted strand upward and wrap to right, around base; secure with bobby pins	☐	☐	☐
• Twist center strand in counterclockwise (left) direction using medium tension	☐	☐	☐
• Direct center strand up to right then down to left and use other hand to position twist; secure with bobby pins	☐	☐	☐
• Twist last strand clockwise (right) using medium tension	☐	☐	☐
• Direct last strand up to left and down to right; wrap around index finger to position coil	☐	☐	☐
• Position twisted strand, then secure	☐	☐	☐

TOTAL POINTS = _____ + _____ + _____

TOTAL POINTS _____ ÷ HIGHEST POSSIBLE SCORE 33 X 100 = _____ %

Record your time in comparison with the suggested salon speed.

To improve my performance on this procedure, I need to:

Student Signature   Educator Signature   Date

SINGLE-STRAND KNOTS

Perimeter knots from an asymmetrical parting that lead to a cluster of knots at the nape give this design a unique, progressive look.

The finish shows smoothly formed knots that move diagonally from the front hairline and gather into a cluster of knots at the nape.

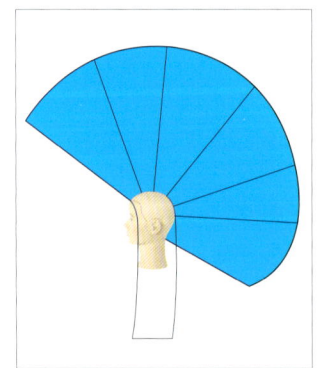

This design is easiest to perform on long solid lengths.

The hair was prepared using a large-diameter curling iron from midstrand to ends to achieve movement within hair lengths.

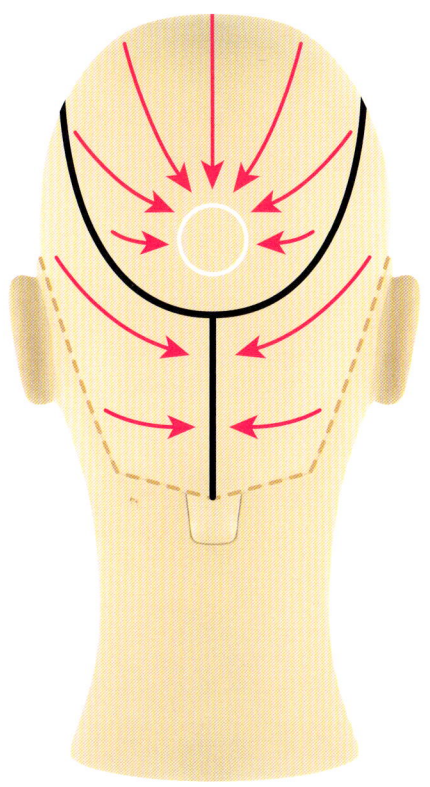

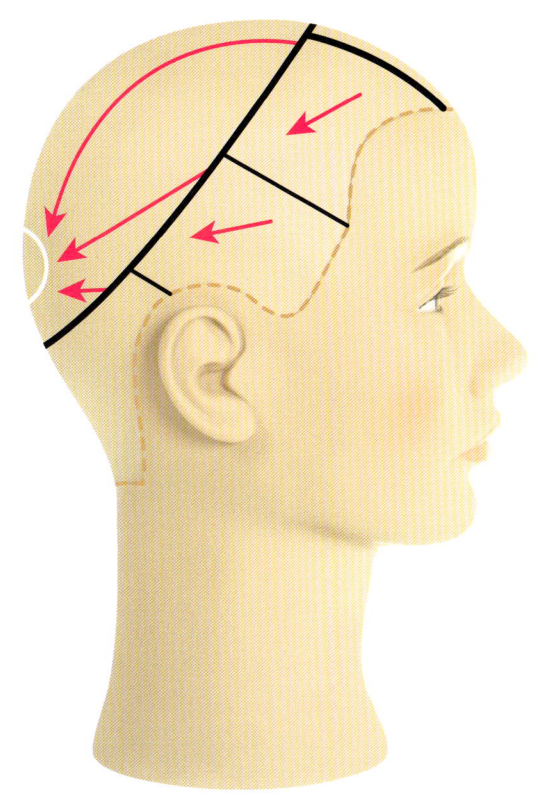

A large rounded section from the apex to the nape is secured above the occipital. A right side parting is used with the remaining lengths.

01 Distribute and position a ponytail above the occipital bone. Secure with an elastic band.

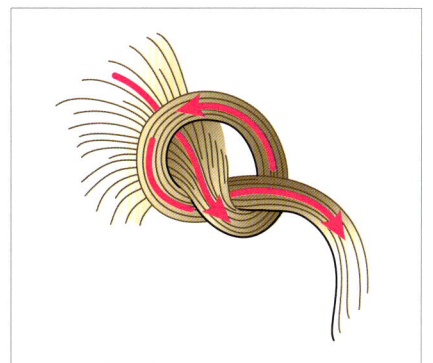

02 The art shows the path the hair will follow to form a counterclockwise knot.

03 Take a diagonal parting on the left side. Distribute the front lengths and direct them up to the left.

04–06 Create a counterclockwise knot. Use your index and middle fingers to pull the strand through the center of the circle. Place the knot into position covering the circular sectioning line. Use your free hand to support the knot and secure with bobby pins.

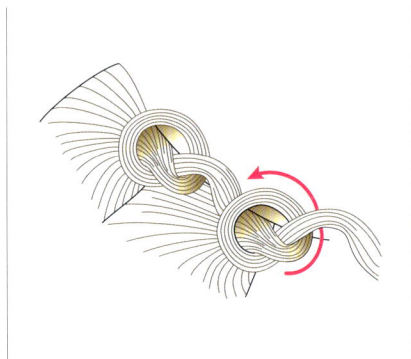

07 The art shows the ends of the first strand joining with the next section and creating a counterclockwise knot.

08 Take the next diagonal parting and join this section with the ends of the previous strand.

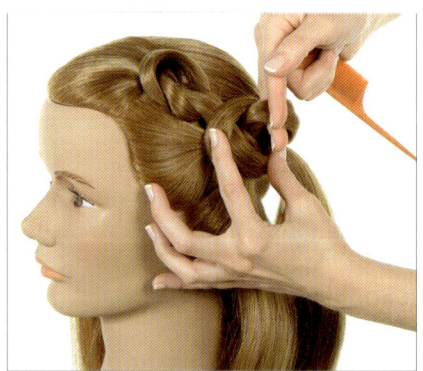

09 Direct the lengths to create a counterclockwise knot. Use your index finger to pull the strand through the center of the circle.

10 Secure the knot with bobby pins. The remainder of the strand will be incorporated into the design later.

11 On the right side, take a diagonal parting and create a clockwise knot.

12 Pull the ends through and secure the knot.

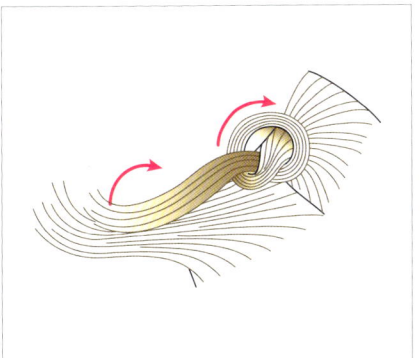

13 The art shows the ends of this section joined with the next and distributed in a clockwise direction.

14 Join this strand with the next section and create another clockwise knot. Again, use your index and middle fingers to pull the strand through the circle.

15 Secure the knot with bobby pins and allow the remainder of the strand to hang free. This will be incorporated into the design later.

16 The art indicates the knotting direction and position of each knot in the back of the design.

17 Subdivide the ponytail into three equal strands.

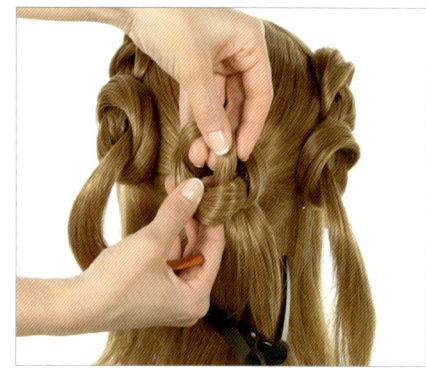

18 Create a clockwise knot with the center strand. Position the knot above the base of the ponytail and secure where necessary.

19–21 Create a counterclockwise knot with the left strand and secure it, leaving the ends out. Then create a clockwise knot with the right strand. Secure the knot and leave the ends out.

22–24 Join the previous strands that have been left out with the final two knots in the nape. Form a clockwise knot on the left side and secure. Then form a counterclockwise knot on the right side and secure.

25 Tuck in and secure the ends of these knots to complete the design.

26–27 Careful consideration of the direction of each knot ensures a well-balanced design.

DESIGN DECISIONS *WORKSHOP 02*

SINGLE-STRAND KNOTS

artist+ access

Draw or fill in the boxes with the appropriate answers.

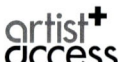

STRUCTURE

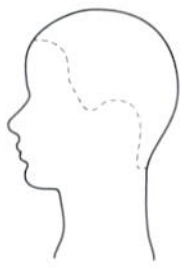

FORM/SHAPE

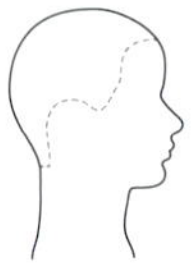

DIRECTION OF FORM

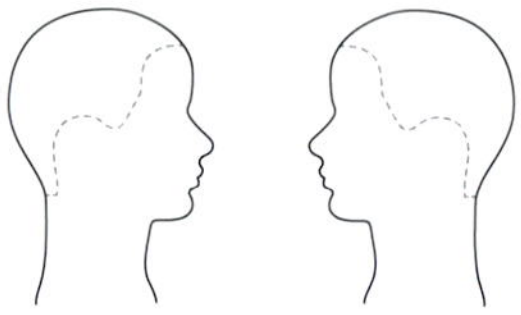

TECHNIQUE

☐ ☐ ☐ ☐ ☐ ☐

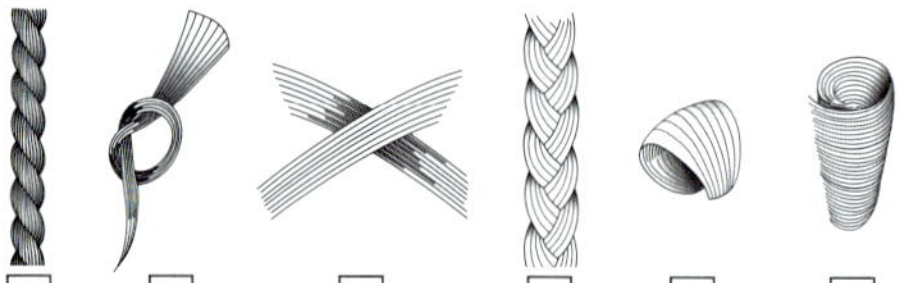

DESIGN PRINCIPLES

- ☐ REPETITION
- ☐ ALTERNATION
- ☐ PROGRESSION
- ☐ CONTRAST

DISTRIBUTION

SECTIONING/PARTING

PREPARATION

- ☐ CURLING IRON
- ☐ FLAT IRON
- ☐ THERMAL ROLLERS
- ☐ ROLLER SET
- ☐ AIR FORM

TOOLS/PRODUCT CHOICE

____

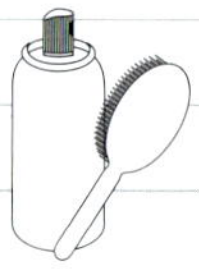

Educator Signature

____

Date

VARIATION 03
2-STRAND KNOTS

Knotting the ends of two ponytails on long solid lengths creates a harmonious blend of alternating directions. In this design, a modern, asymmetrical feel has been achieved by placing ponytails diagonally. The design features an expanded shape at the back that contours the curve of the head from the crown to the nape.

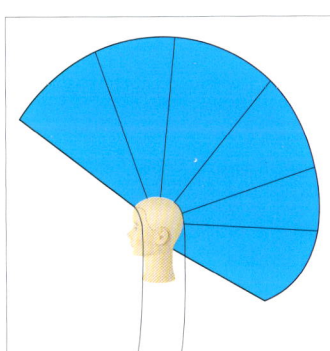
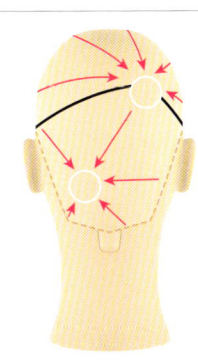

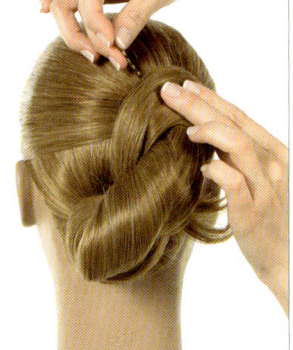

The hair is sectioned diagonally from ear to ear, then distributed and positioned with a top ponytail to the right of the lower crown and a bottom ponytail to the left of the occipital. The ponytails are then crossed over each other. The bottom ponytail is directed upward and crossed over the top ponytail. The lengths of the lower ponytail are pulled through and the ends are wrapped around the base of the crown ponytail and secured with bobby pins. Then the ends of the crown ponytail are directed under the bottom ponytail, pulled through, brought around the top and secured. The shape is expanded for asymmetrical balance. Long hairpins may be used to hold the shape.

HAIR DESIGN RUBRIC *WORKSHOP 02*
SINGLE-STRAND KNOTS

This rubric is a performance assessment tool designed to measure your ability to ***create*** *Pivot Point hair designs.*

	LEVEL 1 *in progress*	LEVEL 2 *getting better*	LEVEL 3 *entry-level proficiency*
PREPARATION			
• Assemble hair design essentials	☐	☐	☐
• Prepare hair using large-diameter curling iron from midstrand to ends	☐	☐	☐
CREATE			
• Distribute and create rounded section from apex to nape; position ponytail above the occipital bone; secure with elastic band	☐	☐	☐
• Take diagonal parting on left side and create counterclockwise knot; secure	☐	☐	☐
• Take next diagonal parting; join section with ends of previous strand	☐	☐	☐
• Create second counterclockwise knot and secure with bobby pins	☐	☐	☐
• Take diagonal part on right side and create clockwise knot; secure	☐	☐	☐
• Join first section with next section and create second clockwise knot; secure	☐	☐	☐
• Subdivide ponytail into three equal strands	☐	☐	☐
• Create clockwise knot with center strand; secure	☐	☐	☐
• Create counterclockwise knot with left strand; secure and leave ends out	☐	☐	☐
• Create clockwise knot with right strand; secure and leave ends out	☐	☐	☐
• Join previous strands that have been left with ends of final two knots in nape	☐	☐	☐
• Form clockwise knot on left side and secure	☐	☐	☐
• Form counterclockwise knot on right side and secure	☐	☐	☐
• Tuck in ends of knots and secure	☐	☐	☐

TOTAL POINTS – _____ | _____ + _____

TOTAL POINTS _____ ÷ HIGHEST POSSIBLE SCORE 48 X 100 = _____ %

Record your time in comparison with the suggested salon speed.

To improve my performance on this procedure, I need to:

_____

Student Signature

_____

Educator Signature

_____

Date

LONG HAIR DESIGN

WORKSHOP 03
OVERLAP

The 2-strand overlap is a design that presents great versatility for the designer. Overlaps can be worn loose and draped for an elegant feel or tight and form-fitting for a more structured, dramatic look.

This finish shows an elongated shape that leads the eye upward. The overlapped pattern can be altered by the width of the partings used.

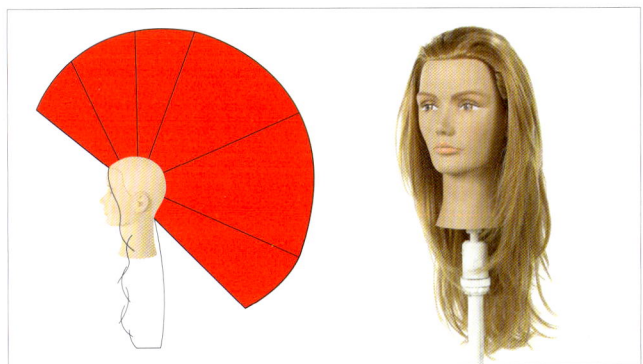

This exercise is performed on increase-layered lengths, which were air formed straight with slight end texture.

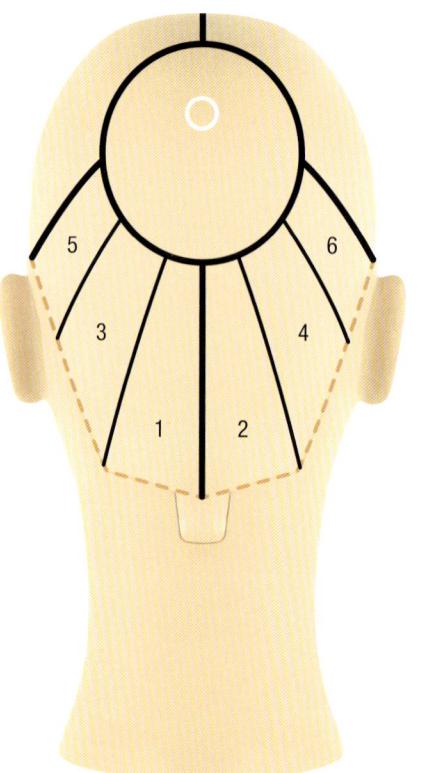
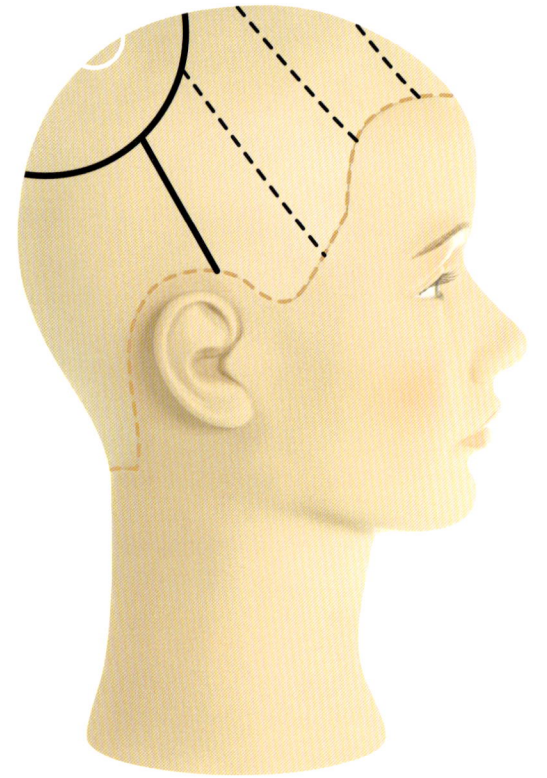

The art shows the sectioning and approximate parting pattern that will be used to create this design. A ponytail is positioned in the upper portion of a circular section in the crown area. The front is sectioned from the back with diagonal-forward partings from the front of the ear to the base of the ponytail. The front and back are each divided in half at the center.

01–02 Begin by backcombing underneath the ponytail using a large comb to create support. Then, lightly smooth the surface on top and underneath the ponytail using a small cushion brush. Spray the surface with a light holding spray and smooth the strand using your fingers.

03 Next, gently wrap the lengths counterclockwise around the base of the ponytail.

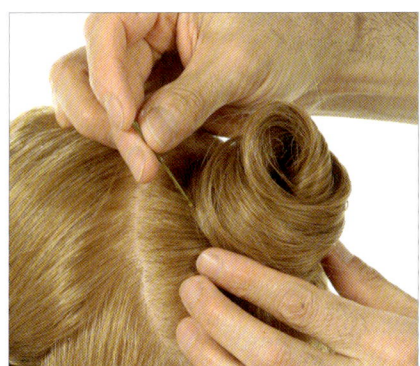

04 Secure the lengths using bobby pins or hairpins as you continue to wrap, then secure the ends.

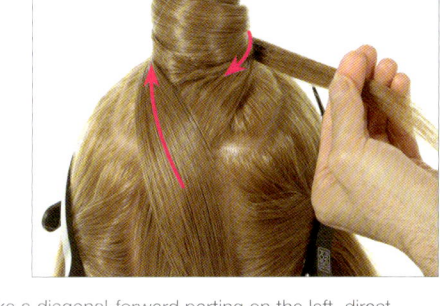

05–06 Divide the back vertically at the center. Take a diagonal-forward parting on the left, direct lengths upward to the right side, then wrap the ends smoothly around the base. Secure using bobby pins or hairpins. Note you may lightly spray each strand for control before securing. Then take a diagonal parting on the right and use the same technique, directing the lengths to the left. Wrap the ends around the base.

07 Hold the strand firmly in place, then secure.

08 Continue to work from side to side using the overlap technique. Adapt the angle of diagonal partings as you work toward the sectioning line at the ear.

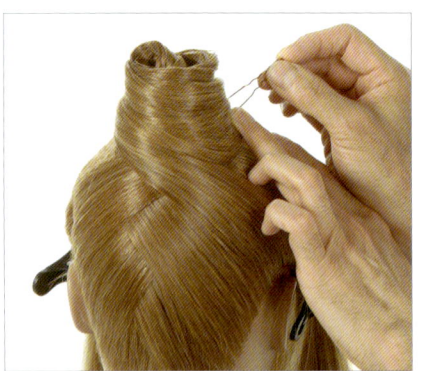

09 Carefully smooth the ends of each section and secure.

10–11 Next, release a triangular section at the center front hairline and direct it back. Move the strand slightly forward to create volume at the hairline. Secure on the right side of the crown. Then, wrap the remaining lengths around the shape and secure.

12 Next, take a diagonal parting on the right side adjacent to the center. Direct the section back and to the left side, slightly twisting the hair for a curved movement.

13 Secure the strand on the left side at the base, then wrap and secure the remaining lengths.

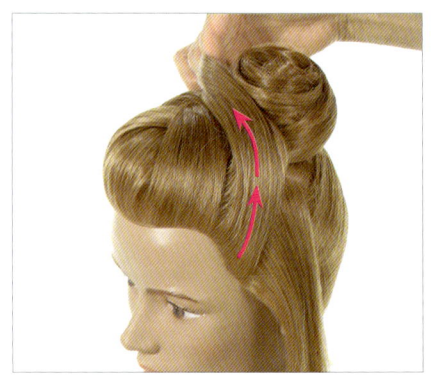

14 Alternate sides and continue to use the same technique. Carefully place the hair to blend with the previous sections.

The art shows a crescent-shaped section at the front hairline. Partings that conform to the curve of the head are taken toward the center for the remainder of the exercise.

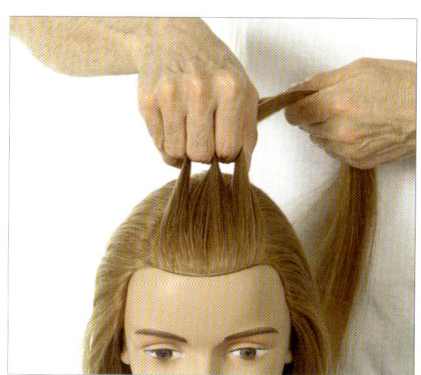

01 Start by dividing the crescent-shaped section into three equal strands.

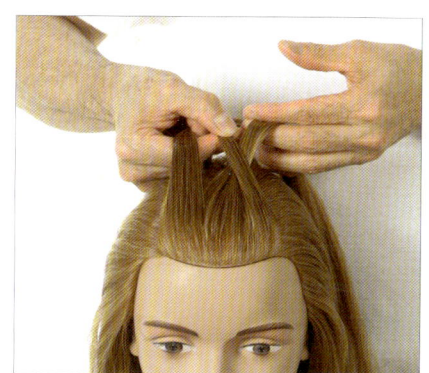

02 With a palm-up position, cross the left strand over the center.

03 Next, cross the right strand over the center. You have now completed the three-strand sequence.

04–05 Cross the left strand over the center again. Then, take a diagonal parting on the left side and join this section to the center strand.

06 Switch hands and repeat the same procedure on the right side. Remember to always hold the strands that were last crossed.

07 Pick up consistent partings as you work from side to side. These partings should conform to the curve of the head.

08 As you work toward the nape, tilt the head slightly forward. This will allow you to maintain tension and work along the curve of the head.

09 Off the scalp, continue to cross the left strand over the center and the right strand over the center as you work toward the ends. Finally, secure the ends with an elastic band.

10–11 The finish shows a contoured overbraid with an elongated form.

DESIGN DECISIONS *WORKSHOP 04*

3-STRAND OVERBRAID

Draw or fill in the boxes with the appropriate answers.

STRUCTURE

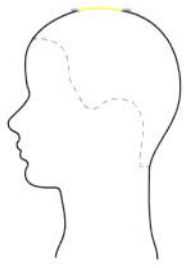

FORM/SHAPE

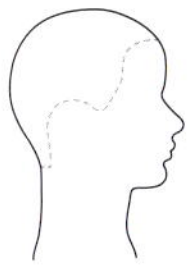

DIRECTION OF FORM

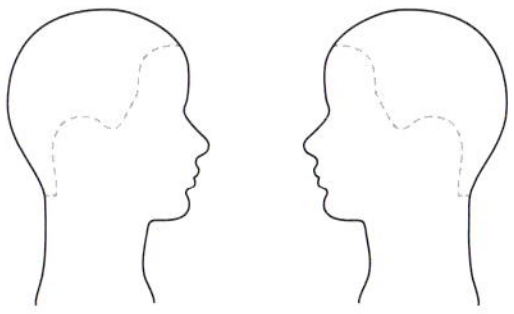

TECHNIQUE

- [ ]
- [ ]
- [ ]
- [ ]
- [ ]
- [ ]

DESIGN PRINCIPLES

- [ ] REPETITION
- [ ] ALTERNATION
- [ ] PROGRESSION
- [ ] CONTRAST

DISTRIBUTION

SECTIONING/PARTING

PREPARATION

- [ ] CURLING IRON
- [ ] FLAT IRON
- [ ] THERMAL ROLLERS
- [ ] ROLLER SET
- [ ] AIR FORM

TOOLS/PRODUCT CHOICE

_____
Educator Signature

_____
Date

3-STRAND UNDERBRAID

This 3-strand underbraid is performed on the scalp using firm tension. Alternately crossing the outside strands under the center strand positions the braid on the surface, which many clients find more interesting than the 3-strand overbraid. The result will be a projected braid appearance.

A crescent-shaped section at the center front hairline is divided into three strands. The right strand is crossed under the center strand, then the left strand is crossed under the center. Then, a diagonal parting is taken on the right side and joined with the center strand. After switching hands, the same technique is used on the left side. The exercise is completed by alternately adding to and crossing the outside strands under the center strand, working to the ends. The ends are secured with an elastic band. Note that the head may be positioned forward while working in the nape to ensure closeness.

HAIR DESIGN RUBRIC *WORKSHOP 04*

3-STRAND OVERBRAID

This rubric is a performance assessment tool designed to measure your ability to **create** *Pivot Point hair designs.*

	LEVEL 1 *in progress*	LEVEL 2 *getting better*	LEVEL 3 *entry-level proficiency*
PREPARATION			
• Assemble long hair design essentials	☐	☐	☐
CREATE			
• Create crescent-shaped section at front hairline	☐	☐	☐
• Part crescent-shaped section into three equal strands	☐	☐	☐
• Cross left strand over center strand	☐	☐	☐
• Cross right strand over center strand	☐	☐	☐
• Cross left strand over center strand again	☐	☐	☐
• Part diagonally on left side and join this section with center strand	☐	☐	☐
• Switch hands and repeat same procedure on right side, holding strands that were last crossed	☐	☐	☐
• Alternate from side to side, picking up consistent partings that conform to the curve of the head	☐	☐	☐
• Tilt head slightly forward to work toward nape, keeping hands close to head	☐	☐	☐
• Continue the 3-strand braid to ends	☐	☐	☐
• Secure ends with elastic band	☐	☐	☐

TOTAL POINTS = _____ + _____ + _____

TOTAL POINTS _____ ÷ HIGHEST POSSIBLE SCORE 36 X 100 = _____ %

Record your time in comparison with the suggested salon speed.

To improve my performance on this procedure, I need to:

_____   _____   _____
Student Signature   *Educator Signature*   *Date*

ON-THE-SCALP 3-STRAND BRAIDS

Three-strand on-the-scalp braids are most often worn by clients with curly to tightly curled textures, but can also be enjoyed by clients with chemically relaxed hair. This technique or style is often referred to as "cornrowing".

Clients love the infinite number of design possibilities a designer can create, as well as the easy maintenance of the design.

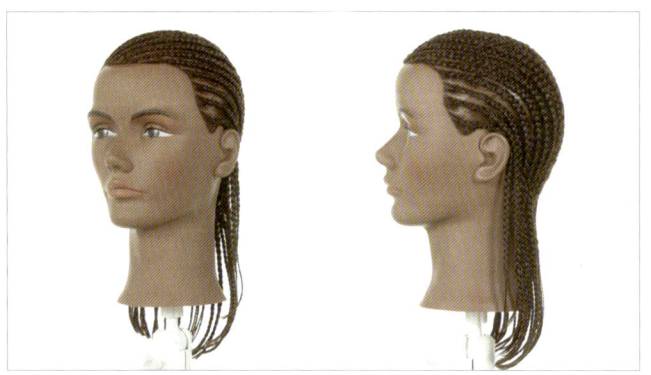

The finish shows an asymmetrical on-the-scalp braid design adapted to the contours of the head with hanging lengths at the nape.

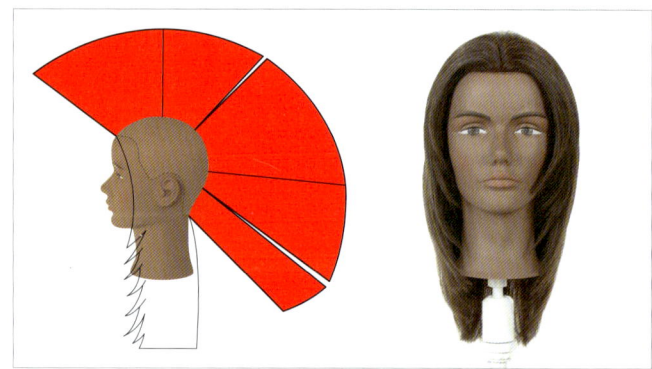

This exercise is performed on increase-layered lengths. The hair was air formed straight in preparation for the design.

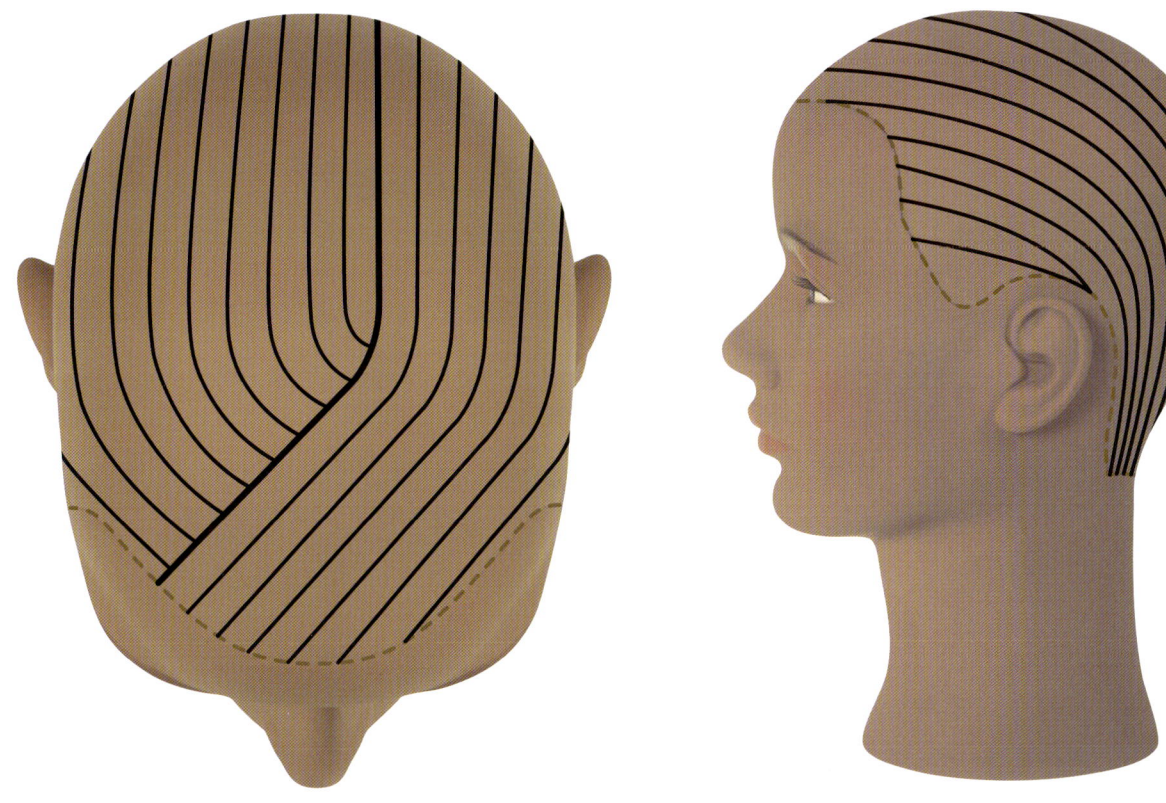

The art shows the sectioning and approximate parting pattern that will be used to create this design. The hair is sectioned with a diagonal part from over the right eye to slightly left of the apex. This part is then extended to the center nape. Partings on the heavier side first follow the sectioning line, then are adapted to the contour and size of the head. Modified diagonal partings are used on the lighter side. All partings are adapted to become vertical and slightly narrower at the back.

01–02 Release a parting parallel to the sectioning line from the front hairline to the nape.

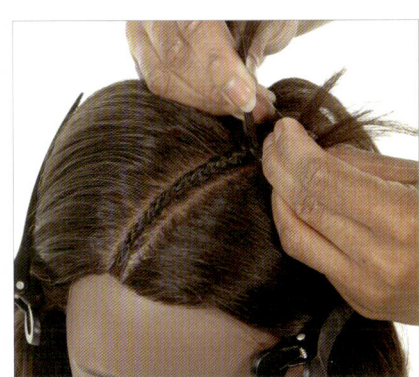

03 Perform a 3-strand, on-the-scalp underbraid starting at the front hairline. Use the index finger and thumb to pick up and cross the outside strands under the center strand.

04–05 Continue to work within the parting using firm and even tension. While working in the nape, the head may be tilted forward for comfort and ease. When you reach the hairline, continue to braid off the scalp, working to the ends.

06 Work toward the left, using the same partings and the same braiding technique.

07 Maintain the tension and hand position close to the scalp while working over the curves of the head.

08 As you reach the nape, be sure that the braids become narrower.

09 On the side adapt the partings to follow the contours of the head.

10 Further adapt the partings to conform to the hairline. Note that braids near the ear will not extend to the back.

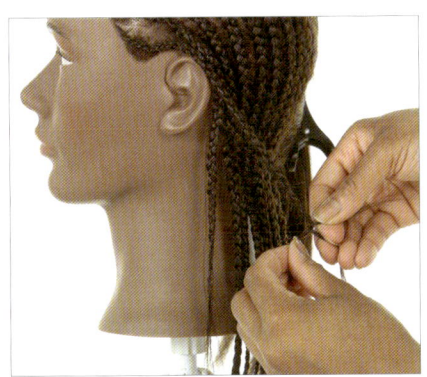

11 Braid off the scalp to complete these braids, which will hang freely. Braid to the ends to complete this side.

12 Move to the right side. Starting at the temple area, release a parting that extends to the back of the ear and braid following the hairline.

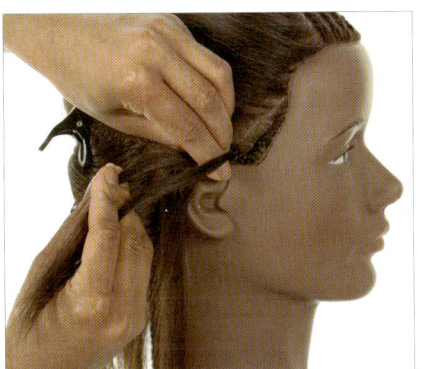

13 Continue to follow the hairline working toward the back and braiding off the scalp behind the ear.

14 Take subsequent partings working farther up the hairline with each one.

15 Continue to adapt the partings to the contours of the head as you work.

16 The art shows that diagonal partings are taken from the sectioning line, curving to conform to previous partings and to become vertical at the back.

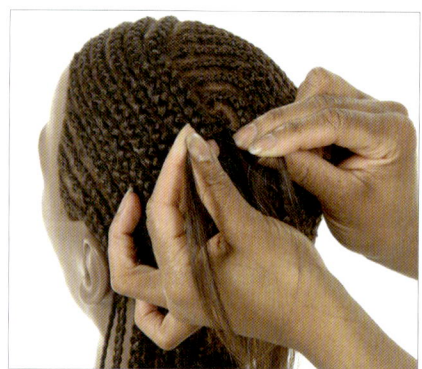

17 Maintain even tension as you work through the curved partings.

18 Continue braiding off the scalp to complete each braid.

19 Braid the remaining section at the crown using the same techniques.

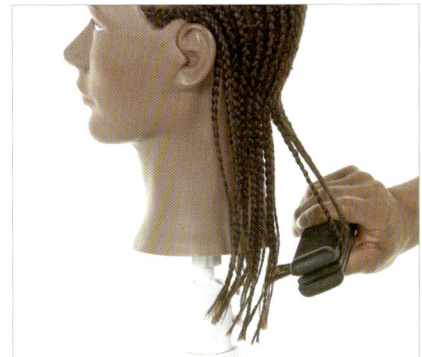

20–21 Remember that the position of the braids will be determined by the partings. You may need to adjust partings as you work.

22 Trim the ends if necessary and use a flat iron to create a slight underbevel to complete the design.

23–24 The finish shows a beautiful, yet functional, braided design that creates textural interest.

ON-THE-SCALP 3-STRAND BRAIDS

Draw or fill in the boxes with the appropriate answers.

STRUCTURE

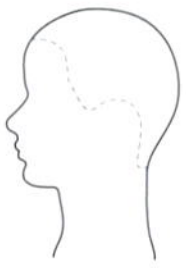

FORM/SHAPE

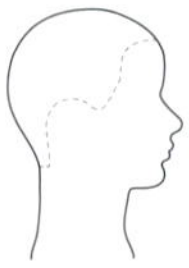

DIRECTION OF FORM

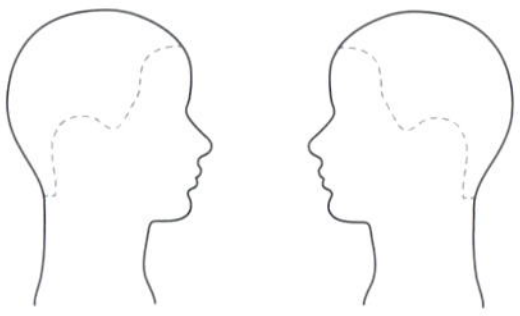

TECHNIQUE

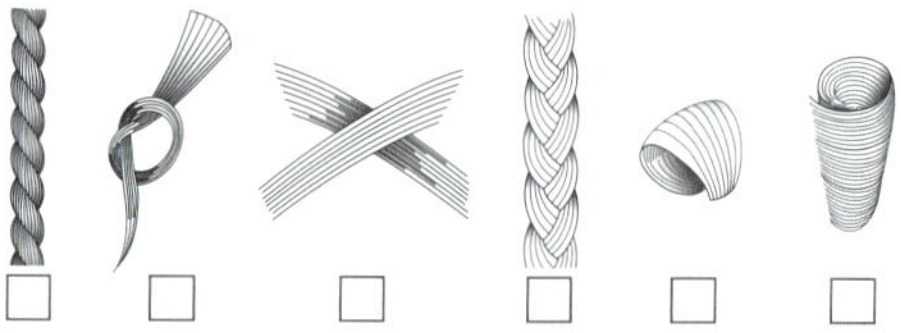

☐ ☐ ☐ ☐ ☐ ☐

DESIGN PRINCIPLES

☐ REPETITION

☐ ALTERNATION

☐ PROGRESSION

☐ CONTRAST

DISTRIBUTION

SECTIONING/PARTING

PREPARATION

☐ CURLING IRON

☐ FLAT IRON

☐ THERMAL ROLLERS

☐ ROLLER SET

☐ AIR FORM

TOOLS/PRODUCT CHOICE

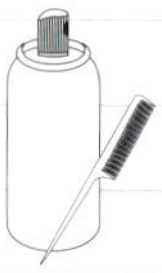

Educator Signature

Date

VARIATION 05
ON-THE-SCALP 3-STRAND BRAIDS

On-the-scalp braid designs offer limitless possibilities. The designer can express great creativity when performing this service on women and men alike. In this on-the-scalp underbraid variation, you will create a braided design featuring alternating directions and curved lines to produce a graphic pattern.

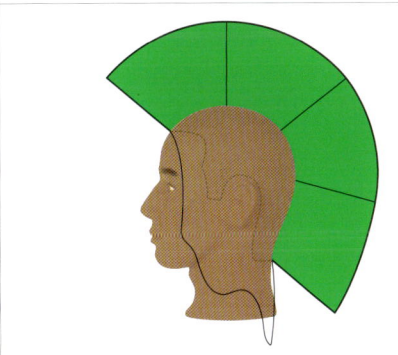

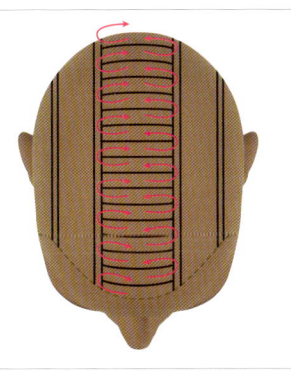

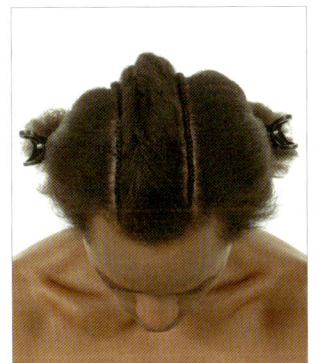

This on-the-scalp braid exercise is performed on uniform, tightly curled lengths. Between partings that extend from the front hairline to the back, a single braid is created using horizontal partings and alternating directions, which are connected by sharp curves in the braid. A center section is established from the front hairline to the nape, narrowing slightly at the nape. A narrow on-the-scalp underbraid is braided on either side of the center section. Within the center section, a horizontal underbraid is started at the front hairline, working from left to right. The hair is braided to slightly beyond the end of the parting to hold it.

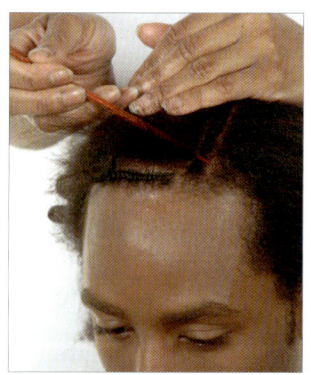
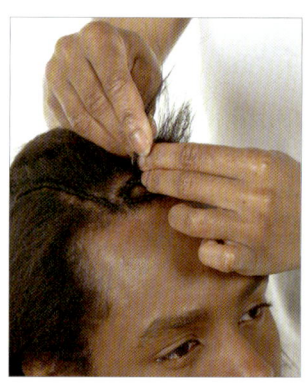

Then, another horizontal parting is taken the same width as in the previous parting. After undoing the crossed portion of the braid, the hair is braided in a curved movement to connect with the new parting. This technique is repeated, alternating directions to complete the center section. The remaining ends are braided off the scalp. Another braid extending from the front hairline to the back is used to establish each subsequent section. The same underbraiding technique is then used to create the alternation of direction within each section. The same technique is used to complete the entire design. Alternating sections from one side to the other helps maintain balance. The sides are finished with a single braid along the perimeter hairline. Shears are used along the surface to remove any stray hair. To complete the design, the front hairline is outlined using trimmers.

HAIR DESIGN RUBRIC *WORKSHOP 05*
ON-THE-SCALP 3-STRAND BRAIDS

This rubric is a performance assessment tool designed to measure your ability to create Pivot Point hair designs.

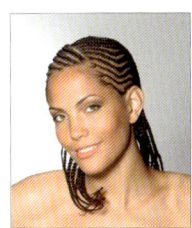

	LEVEL 1 *in progress*	LEVEL 2 *getting better*	LEVEL 3 *entry-level proficiency*
PREPARATION			
• Assemble long hair design essentials	☐	☐	☐
• Air form hair straight	☐	☐	☐
CREATE			
• Section with diagonal part from above right eye to slightly left of apex	☐	☐	☐
• Release parting parallel to sectioning line from front hairline to nape	☐	☐	☐
• Perform 3-strand on-the-scalp underbraid starting at front hairline using index finger and thumb to pick up and cross outside strands under center strand; use firm, even tension within parting	☐	☐	☐
• Braid off scalp at nape hairline toward ends	☐	☐	☐
• Work toward left using same partings and braiding technique	☐	☐	☐
• Maintain tension and hand position close to head; adapt partings to follow contours of head and hairline using same techniques	☐	☐	☐
• Release parting at temple area on right side extending to back of ear; braid following hairline as you work up to sectioning line	☐	☐	☐
• Continue taking diagonal partings from sectioning line and curve to conform to previous partings	☐	☐	☐
• Trim ends of braids (if necessary) and flat iron with a slight underbevel	☐	☐	☐

TOTAL POINTS = _____ + _____ + _____

TOTAL POINTS _____ ÷ HIGHEST POSSIBLE SCORE 33 X 100 = _____ %

Record your time in comparison with the suggested salon speed.

3

To improve my performance on this procedure, I need to:

_____   _____   _____
Student Signature   Educator Signature   Date

WORKSHOP 06
5-STRAND LOOPS

The 5-strand loop is a beautiful design with timeless and classic appeal. It can be altered in position and height to complement many different facial features and is a favorite of many bridal clients.

Although the size, number and position of single loops in a design may vary, the basic loop technique remains the same. Keep in mind that pre-planning the position, direction and balance is very important.

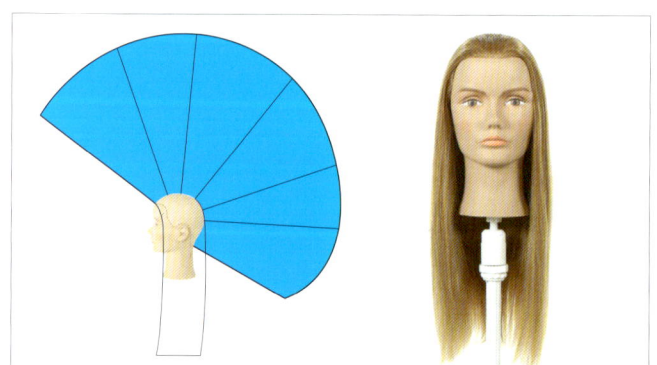

This exercise is performed on long solid lengths. The hair was prepared by air forming the lengths straight.

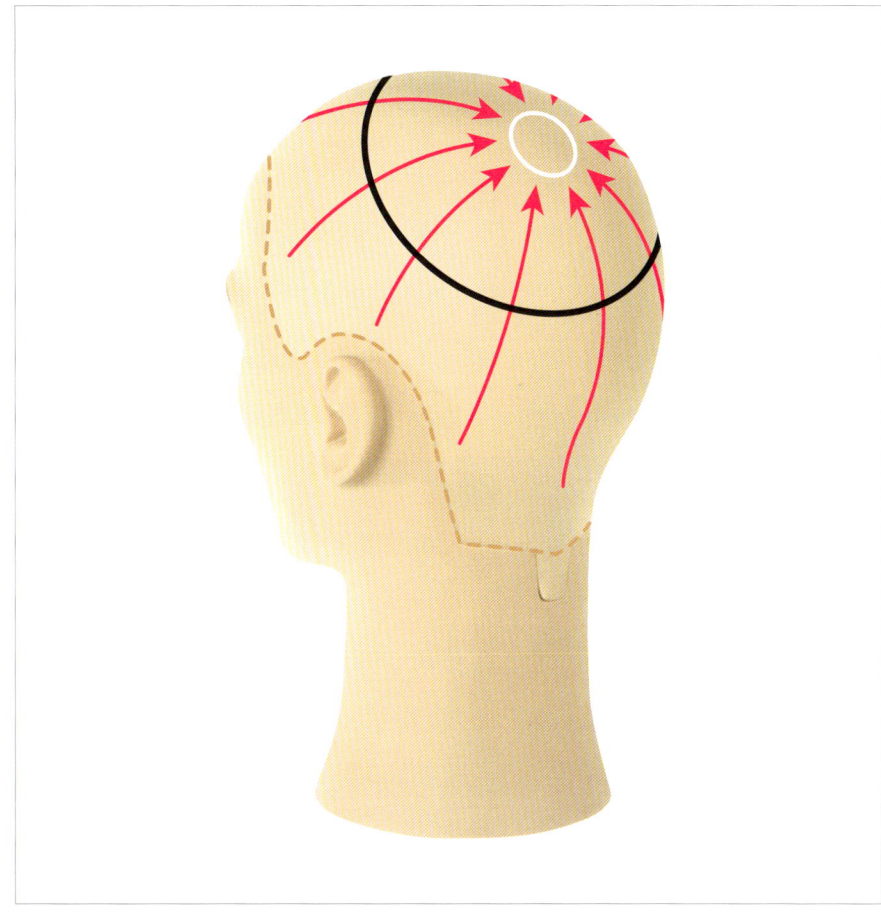

The art shows the distribution and position of a ponytail at the upper crown.

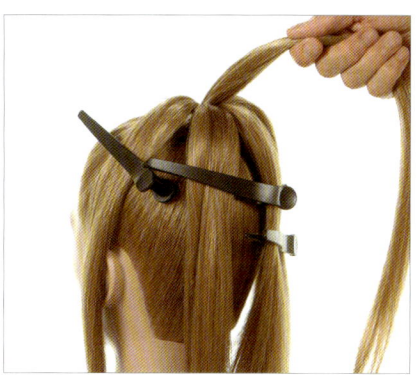

01 Distribute the hair toward the upper crown and position a ponytail. Subdivide the ponytail into five equal strands with the fifth strand at the center of the ponytail.

02 Begin by backcombing underneath the first strand for support.

03 Next, smooth the top surface of the strand and use hairspray for control.

04–05 Use your index and middle fingers and fold toward the right as you direct the ends to the left. While folding, the position of your fingers along the strand will determine the size of the loop. Position the loop diagonally and secure with bobby pins. Wrap the remaining ends around your finger and tuck them inside the loop.

06 Use bobby pins to secure the ends.

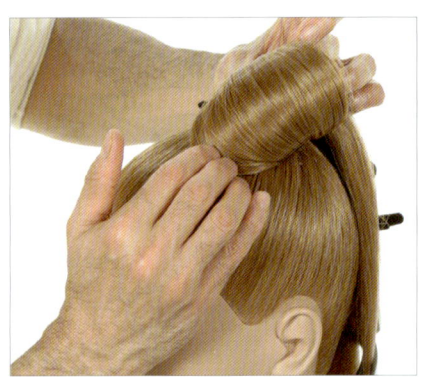

07 Expand the loop and close one end. Use hairspray as needed for control. You may also use long hairpins to control the shape as you work.

08 Use the same technique to create the next loop. Backcomb, smooth and then position the loop diagonally and secure with bobby pins. Again, tuck the remaining ends inside and secure. Then expand the shape and close one end.

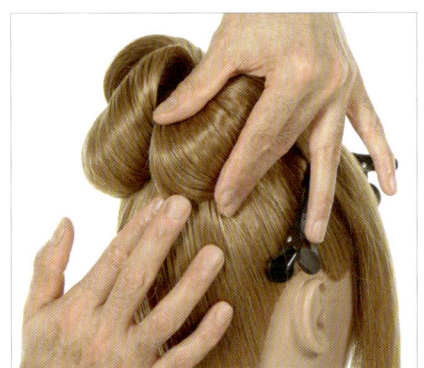

09 Repeat the same technique with the third loop. Strive to create consistent-sized loops for a well-balanced design.

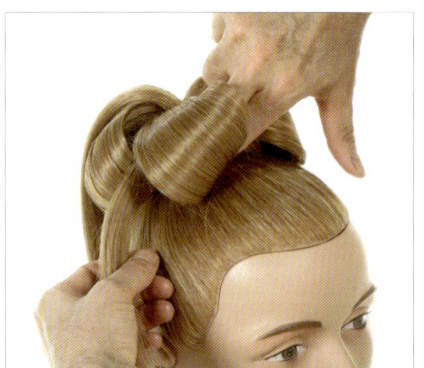

10–11 Fold the fourth loop to the right and position it diagonally. Carefully tuck the ends inside and secure with bobby pins. Continue to use long hairpins as needed to maintain the shape of the loops.

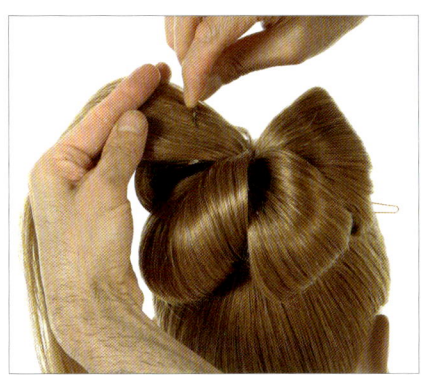

12 Direct the fifth strand toward the left and secure the base to the first loop. This will give the last loop more support and stability.

13 Direct the strand toward the right and position it diagonally on top of the other four loops at the center. Secure with bobby pins or hairpins.

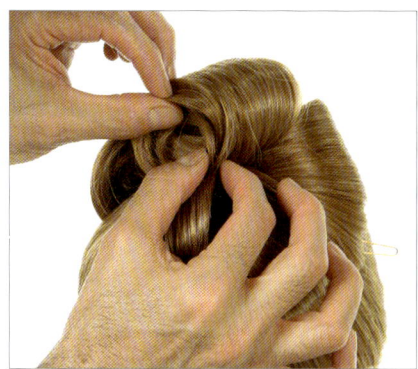

14 Tuck in the ends and close the loop at the back. Use hairspray for control and check the form for balance.

15–16 The length of the hair will influence the size of the loops for this design. Strive to create a consistent loop design.

5-STRAND LOOPS

Draw or fill in the boxes with the appropriate answers.

STRUCTURE

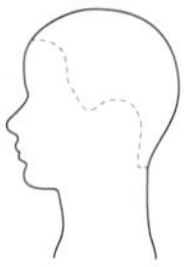

FORM/SHAPE

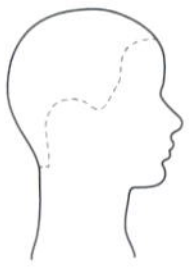

DIRECTION OF FORM

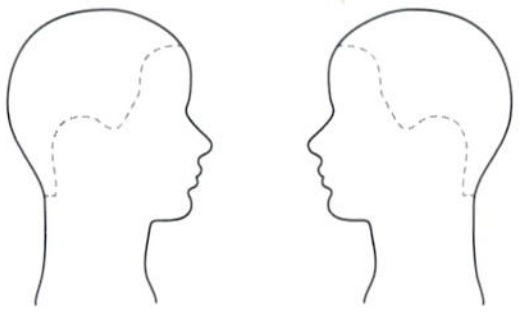

TECHNIQUE

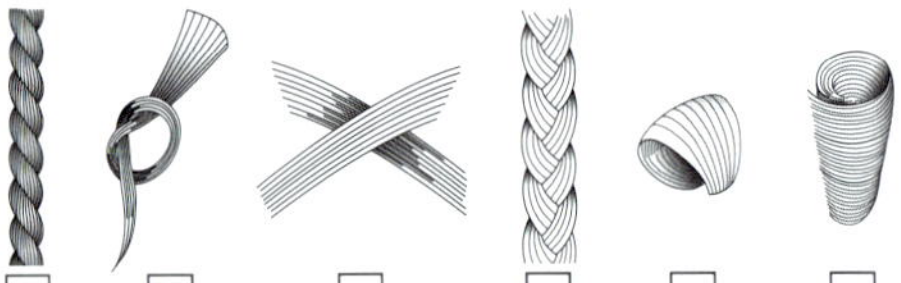

DESIGN PRINCIPLES

- [ ] REPETITION
- [ ] ALTERNATION
- [ ] PROGRESSION
- [ ] CONTRAST

- [ ]
- [ ]
- [ ]
- [ ]
- [ ]
- [ ]

DISTRIBUTION

SECTIONING/PARTING

PREPARATION

- [ ] CURLING IRON
- [ ] FLAT IRON
- [ ] THERMAL ROLLERS
- [ ] ROLLER SET
- [ ] AIR FORM

TOOLS/PRODUCT CHOICE

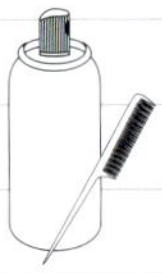

Educator Signature

Date

04

HAIR DESIGN RUBRIC *WORKSHOP 06*

5-STRAND LOOPS

This rubric is a performance assessment tool designed to measure your ability to **create** *Pivot Point hair designs.*

	LEVEL 1 *in progress*	LEVEL 2 *getting better*	LEVEL 3 *entry-level proficiency*
PREPARATION			
• Assemble long hair design essentials	☐	☐	☐
CREATE			
• Distribute all lengths to upper crown	☐	☐	☐
• Position and secure a ponytail in the upper crown	☐	☐	☐
• Divide ponytail into five equal strands with fifth strand at center	☐	☐	☐
• Backcomb and smooth top surface of first strand using hairspray for control	☐	☐	☐
• Fold strand toward right with index and middle fingers, directing ends toward left	☐	☐	☐
• Position first loop diagonally and secure with bobby pins; wrap and tuck ends and secure	☐	☐	☐
• Expand shape and use hairspray for control	☐	☐	☐
• Repeat same techniques on second, third and fourth loops; backcomb and smooth each section before positioning each loop diagonally; use long hairpins as needed to support loops	☐	☐	☐
• Secure fifth strand to base of first loop	☐	☐	☐
• Direct fifth strand toward right, then tuck in ends and secure	☐	☐	☐
• Check form for balance and remove long hairpins	☐	☐	☐

TOTAL POINTS = _____ + _____ + _____

TOTAL POINTS _____ ÷ HIGHEST POSSIBLE SCORE 36 X 100 = _____ %

Record your time in comparison with the suggested salon speed.

To improve my performance on this procedure, I need to:

Student Signature   Educator Signature   Date

WORKSHOP 07
VERTICAL ROLL

The vertical roll is a great staple for many formal hair designs. It can be used alone to create a classic look with a timeless appeal or it can be used in conjunction with many other long hair design techniques.

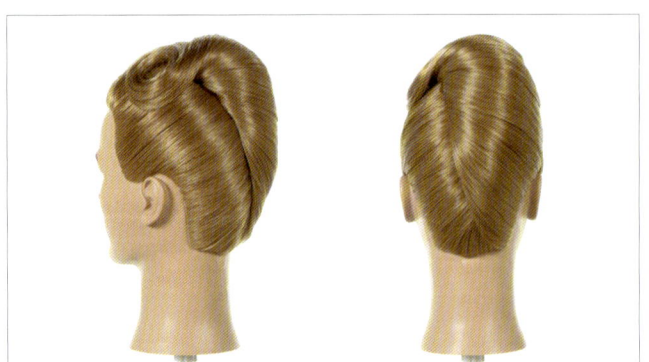

The finish shows an elongated look that can be adapted to medium lengths and a variety of textures.

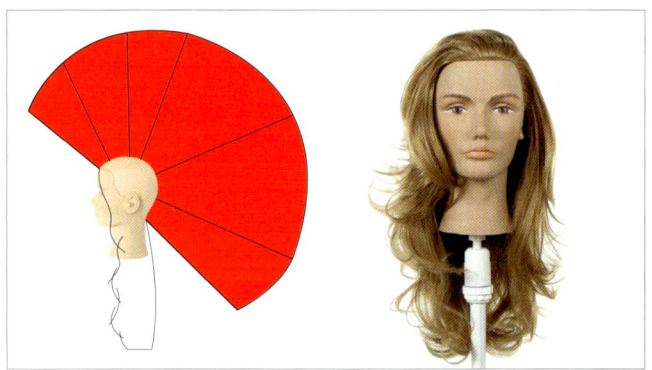

This exercise is performed on long increase-layered lengths. The hair was prepared by setting on thermal rollers.

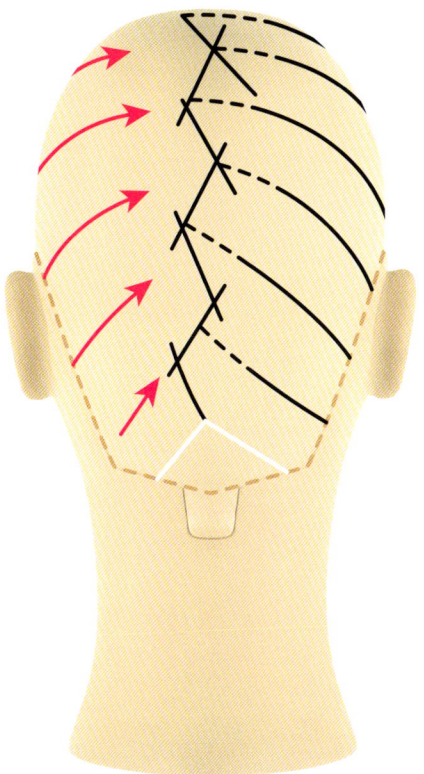

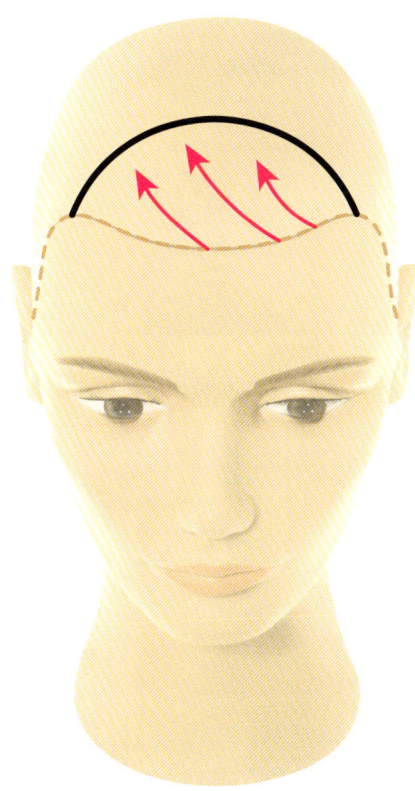

The art shows that the hair on the left side is distributed toward the right and pinned slightly off center. Diagonal partings are used to subdivide the sections on the right side. A crescent-shaped parting is isolated at the front hairline and worked into the last part of the roll.

01 After sectioning the fringe, isolate a small, slightly off-center triangle at the base of the nape.

02 Distribute the hair from the left over to the right side.

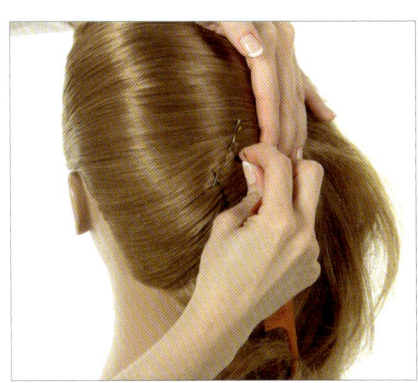

03 Next, interlock a slightly off-center row of bobby pins vertically to establish the position of the roll. Position the pins with the open end facing upward.

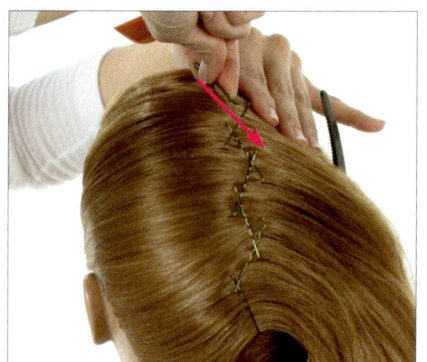

04 Secure the last bobby pin in a downward direction.

05 Backcomb the base of the triangle section at the nape. Then smooth the surface upward.

06 Use your right hand to fold this section over the bobby pins while using your left hand to control the ends.

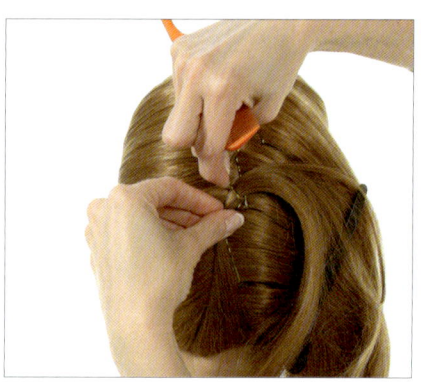

07 Secure the inside of the roll with bobby pins or hairpins.

08 Then, wrap the remaining lengths around your finger and pin just in front of the roll. This will act as a filler for the next section.

09 Take the next diagonal parting, distribute the lengths upward and fold this section over the filler.

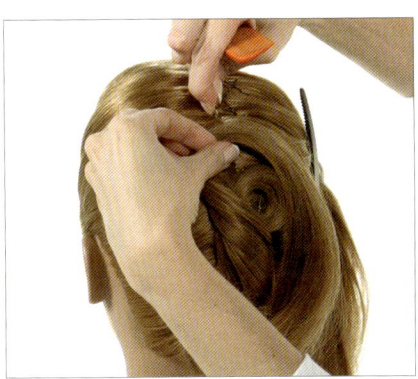

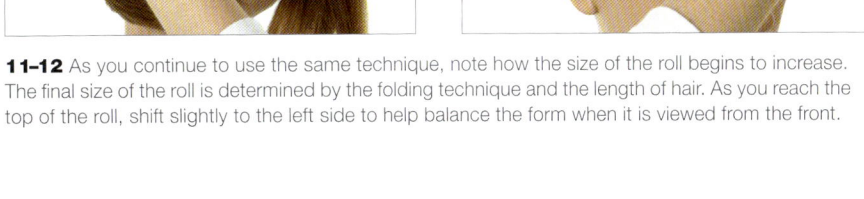

10 Then, secure the inside of the roll and again create a filler for the next section. Be sure to blend each section into the previous one to avoid splits. Secure the inside of the roll.

11–12 As you continue to use the same technique, note how the size of the roll begins to increase. The final size of the roll is determined by the folding technique and the length of hair. As you reach the top of the roll, shift slightly to the left side to help balance the form when it is viewed from the front.

13 Direct the fringe lengths back toward the roll. Distribute the lengths in a curvature movement to close the roll. Use the ends to create a flat loop on the left and secure with hairpins.

14–15 The finish shows a classic roll with timeless appeal.

DESIGN DECISIONS *WORKSHOP 07*

VERTICAL ROLL

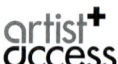

Draw or fill in the boxes with the appropriate answers.

artist+ access.

STRUCTURE

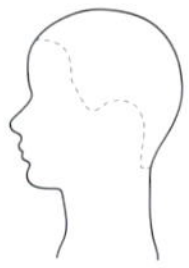

FORM/SHAPE

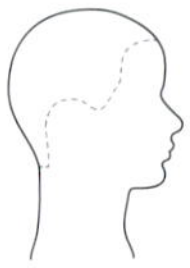

DIRECTION OF FORM

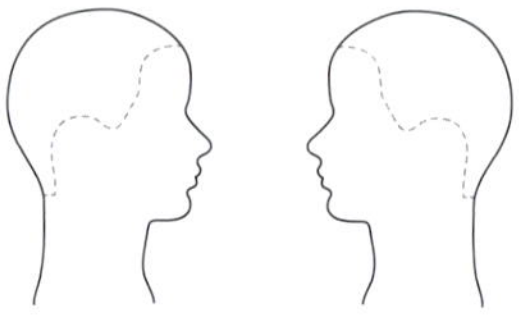

TECHNIQUE

☐ ☐ ☐ ☐ ☐ ☐

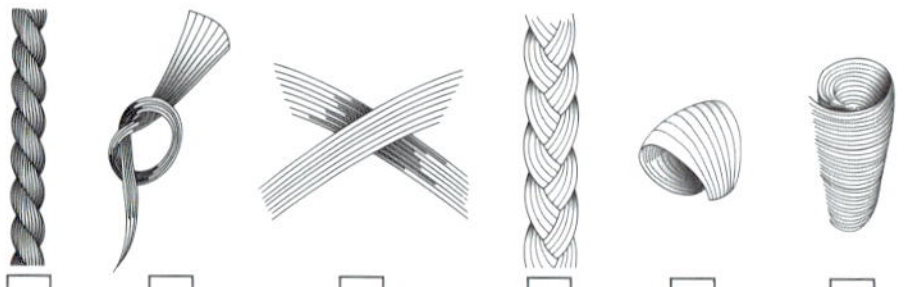

DESIGN PRINCIPLES

- ☐ REPETITION
- ☐ ALTERNATION
- ☐ PROGRESSION
- ☐ CONTRAST

DISTRIBUTION

SECTIONING/PARTING

PREPARATION

- ☐ CURLING IRON
- ☐ FLAT IRON
- ☐ THERMAL ROLLERS
- ☐ ROLLER SET
- ☐ AIR FORM

TOOLS/PRODUCT CHOICE

____

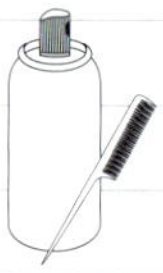

Educator Signature

____

Date

very easy & very pretty ☺

VARIATION 06
VERTICAL ROLL

This twisted roll variation is performed using the end of a large tail comb, which requires less pinning than the traditional vertical roll. This technique is recommended for extra long, solid lengths. The result will be a smooth, close-fitting twisted roll.

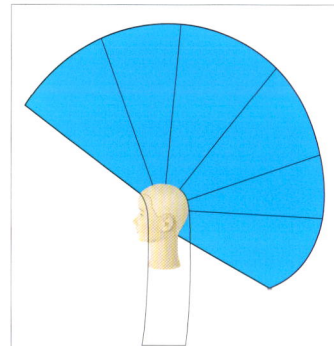
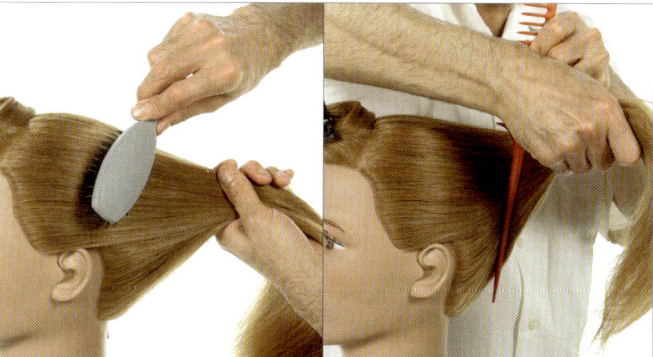

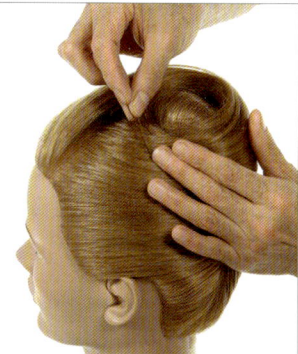

After isolating a curved section at the center front hairline, the remaining lengths are distributed toward the center back into the palm. Then, a large tail comb is positioned vertically and the hair is wrapped around the tail with tension. The other hand is used to continue wrapping the hair around the comb while moving the comb upward. After removing the comb, the hair is twisted to the ends, then twisted around itself and secured with bobby pins. The isolated section is then lightly backbrushed from underneath for support. This section is directed toward the right and the ends are arranged to blend with the roll, leaving the twisted shape at the crown visible. Hairpins are used to secure and complete the design.

HAIR DESIGN RUBRIC *WORKSHOP 07*

VERTICAL ROLL

This rubric is a performance assessment tool designed to measure your ability to
create Pivot Point hair designs.

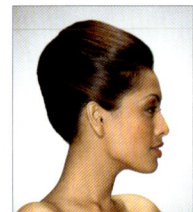

	LEVEL 1 *in progress*	LEVEL 2 *getting better*	LEVEL 3 *entry-level proficiency*
PREPARATION			
• Assemble long hair design essentials	☐	☐	☐
• Prepare hair by setting on thermal rollers	☐	☐	☐
CREATE			
• Isolate crescent-shaped fringe and small, slightly off-center triangle at nape	☐	☐	☐
• Brush hair to right side and secure off-center row of interlocking bobby pins	☐	☐	☐
• Backcomb, smooth and fold off-center triangle over row of bobby pins	☐	☐	☐
• Secure inside of roll at fold; wrap remaining lengths and secure to create filler for next section	☐	☐	☐
• Fold next diagonal parting over filler and secure inside roll; create filler for next section with remaining lengths	☐	☐	☐
• Continue folding each subsequent section over filler and securing inside roll	☐	☐	☐
• Shift top lengths slightly to the left to balance form	☐	☐	☐
• Direct fringe lengths back to roll to close and create flat loop	☐	☐	☐

TOTAL POINTS = _____ + _____ + _____

TOTAL POINTS _____ ÷ HIGHEST POSSIBLE SCORE 30 X 100 = _____ %

Record your time in comparison with the suggested salon speed. _____

To improve my performance on this procedure, I need to: _____

_____ _____ _____
Student Signature *Educator Signature* *Date*

4.3 ADVANCED LONG HAIR DESIGNS

Once you have mastered the basic long hair design techniques, you will easily be able to take your craft to the next level of complexity and creativity. Combining different techniques into a single design or using variations of techniques that require more patience and skill will enable you to go above and beyond basic long hair design. Your creativity will blossom and set you apart from your competition.

5-STRAND BRAID

The 5-strand braid is considered more advanced than the 3-strand, requiring more skill and dexterity. Many clients are unfamiliar with braiding possibilities but are fascinated by the eye-catching results of the 5-strand braid.

The finish displays an elegant 5-strand braid that projects slightly from the head with a wider pattern than the 3-strand braid. The braid is positioned vertically down the center.

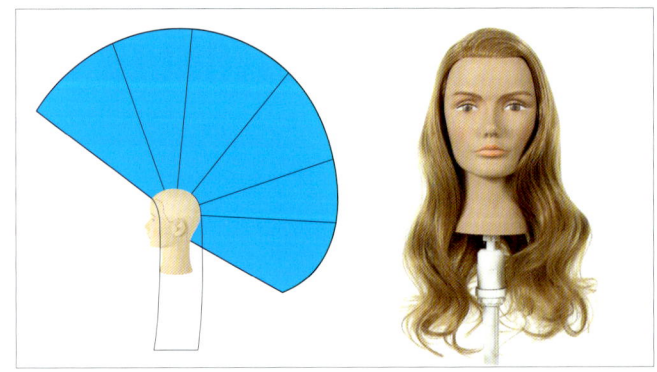

This design is performed on long solid lengths. The hair was prepared by applying thermal rollers prior to starting the exercise. This design may also be performed on straight lengths.

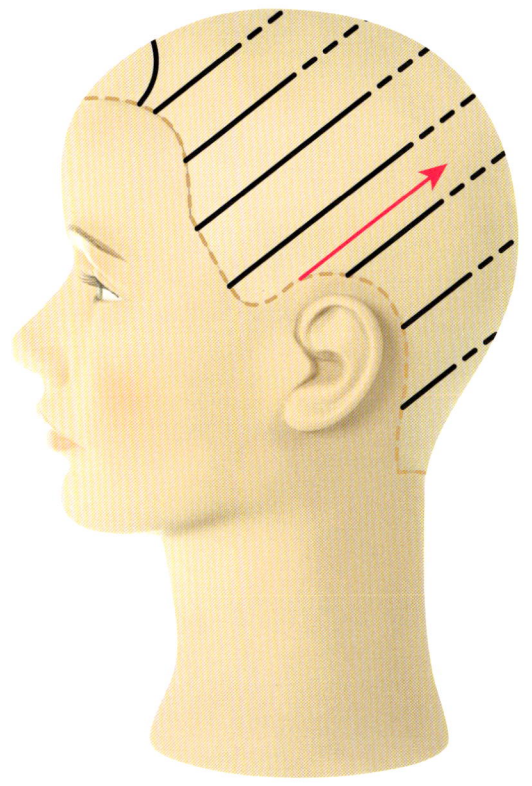

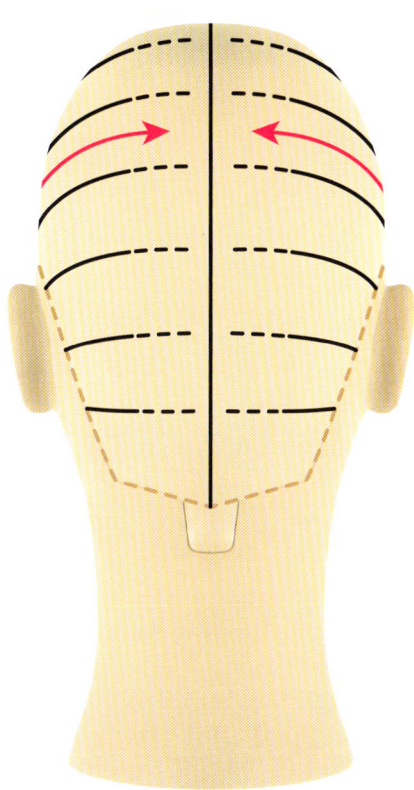

The art shows a crescent-shaped fringe section that is used to begin this exercise. Partings used for the remainder of the exercise contour the curves of the head.

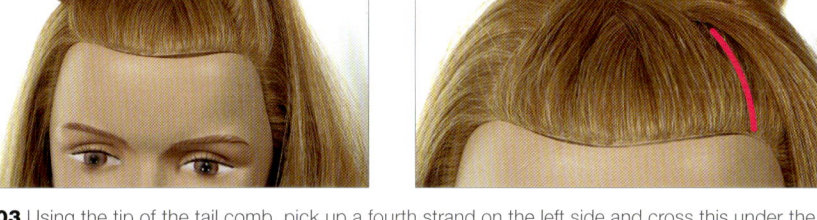

01 Start by creating the basic 3-strand braid by crossing the left strand over the center, and then the right strand over the center.

02–03 Using the tip of the tail comb, pick up a fourth strand on the left side and cross this under the outside strand and over the center strand.

05 Now add hair to the outside strands. Take a new parting on the left side and join this to the outside strand. Weave this under the next strand and over the center strand.

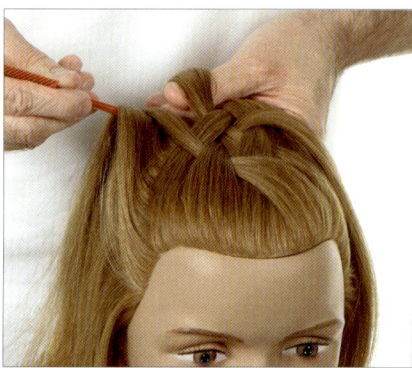

06 Pick up the next parting on the right side using the tail of the comb. Incorporate it into the outside strand, then weave under the next strand and over the center.

04 Switch hands and use the tail of the comb to pick up the fifth strand on the right side. Weave it under the strand next to it and over the center strand. There are now five strands. Control the center strand with your index and middle fingers.

07 Work toward the crown, alternating sides. Keep the width of the partings consistent on either side.

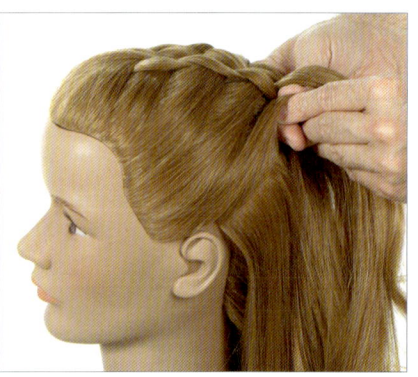

08–09 Maintain even tension by positioning your hand against the curve of the head. Continue to use consistent partings and smooth the hair as you join each new parting to the outside strand. Weave under the next strand, then over the center strand.

10–11 Continue working toward the nape while incorporating new partings from either side.

12 Tilt the head forward as you work toward the nape. This allows you to work close to the head to avoid projecting the hair.

13 Continue braiding until you reach the ends of the hair, weaving the outside strands with the same technique. Use an elastic band to secure the ends.

14–15 The results display a 5-strand on-the-scalp braid with a combination of smooth and woven texture patterns.

DESIGN DECISIONS *WORKSHOP 08*

5-STRAND BRAID

artist+ access

Draw or fill in the boxes with the appropriate answers.

STRUCTURE

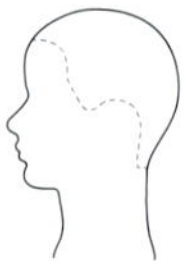

FORM/SHAPE

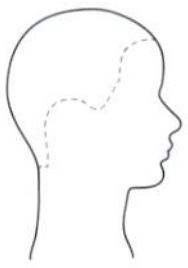

DIRECTION OF FORM

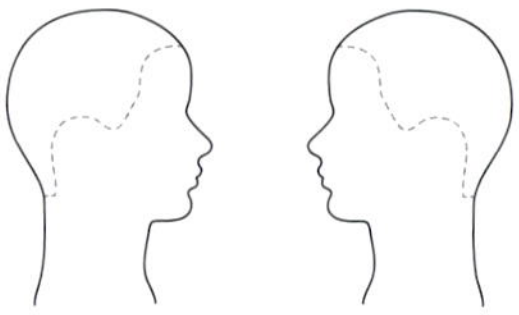

TECHNIQUE

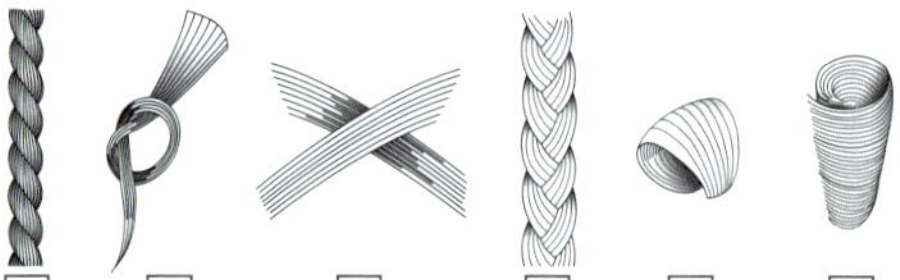

DESIGN PRINCIPLES

- ☐ REPETITION
- ☐ ALTERNATION
- ☐ PROGRESSION
- ☐ CONTRAST

DISTRIBUTION

SECTIONING/PARTING

PREPARATION

- ☐ CURLING IRON
- ☐ FLAT IRON
- ☐ THERMAL ROLLERS
- ☐ ROLLER SET
- ☐ AIR FORM

TOOLS/PRODUCT CHOICE

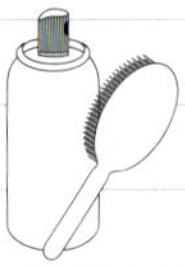

Educator Signature

Date

HAIR DESIGN RUBRIC *WORKSHOP 08*

5-STRAND BRAID

This rubric is a performance assessment tool designed to measure your ability to
create Pivot Point hair designs.

	LEVEL 1 *in progress*	LEVEL 2 *getting better*	LEVEL 3 *entry-level proficiency*
PREPARATION			
• Assemble long hair design essentials	☐	☐	☐
• Prepare hair by applying thermal rollers	☐	☐	☐
CREATE			
• Section crescent shape at front hairline and subdivide into three equal strands	☐	☐	☐
• Cross left strand over center then right strand over center; use index and middle fingers to control center strand and thumb to control outside strand	☐	☐	☐
• Incorporate fourth strand on left side by taking a diagonal parting and weaving it under strand next to it and over center strand	☐	☐	☐
• Incorporate fifth strand on right side by taking a diagonal parting and weaving it under strand next to it and over center strand	☐	☐	☐
• Pick up another diagonal section on left side and join it to outside left strand; cross it under strand next to it, then over center strand	☐	☐	☐
• Repeat on right side ensuring consistent-sized partings	☐	☐	☐
• Alternate picking up diagonal partings on either side; continue to cross outside strands under strand next to them and over center, keeping partings consistent	☐	☐	☐
• Position each hand close to head, maintaining tension while braiding toward nape	☐	☐	☐
• Tilt head slightly forward when braiding in nape and avoid projecting hair	☐	☐	☐
• Weave outside strands with same technique when braiding off the scalp	☐	☐	☐
• Continue to use same technique until you reach ends and secure them with elastic band	☐	☐	☐

TOTAL POINTS = _____ + _____ + _____

TOTAL POINTS _____ ÷ HIGHEST POSSIBLE SCORE 39 X 100 = _____ %

Record your time in comparison with the suggested salon speed.

To improve my performance on this procedure, I need to:

Student Signature   *Educator Signature*   *Date*

3-STRAND OVERBRAID/LOOPS

This design features a combination of a very loose on-the-scalp overbraid and vertical loops, placing emphasis at the back of the design. Soft tendrils and varied curvature movements create a dreamy "old-world" feeling.

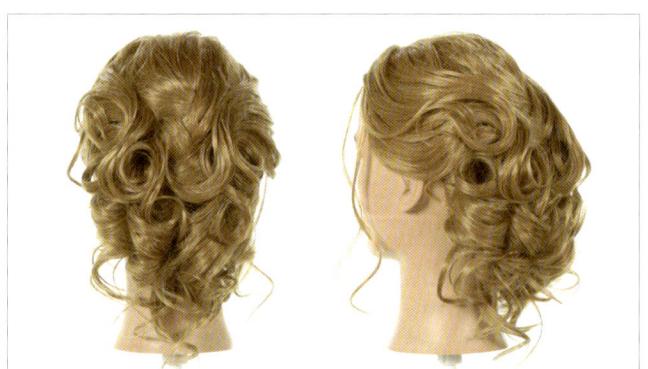

This finish shows a tousle of curls with loops positioned in the back for volume.

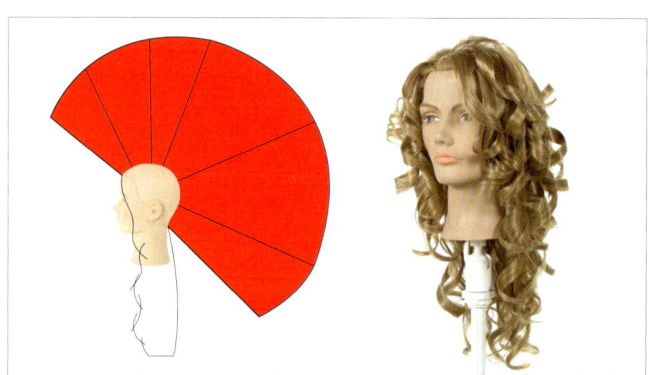

This exercise is performed on long increase-layered lengths, which were spiral-curled using a thermal iron to create a slightly uneven texture.

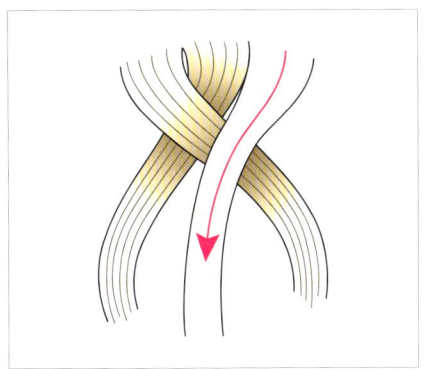

The art shows a 3-strand braid. In this design, the work will not be done for a clean, tight effect, but rather a loose, undone look.

01 Begin by working a lightweight pomade through the hair using your fingers. Start at the front hairline and work toward the nape.

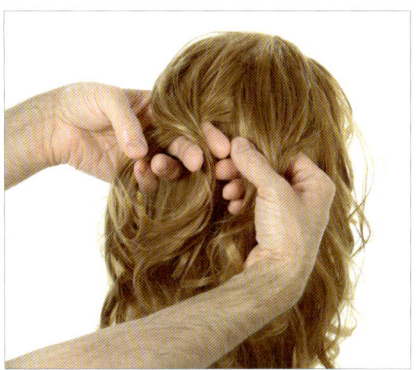

02 Direct front lengths back, leaving the hairline loose. Starting at the crown, loosely form a 3-strand overbraid, crossing the left strand over the center strand.

03 Next, cross the right strand over the center strand.

04–05 Continue to use the same braiding technique, adding to the outside sections, until you reach the occipital area. Note that loose ends may be released as you work.

06 Then, secure the braid using bobby pins.

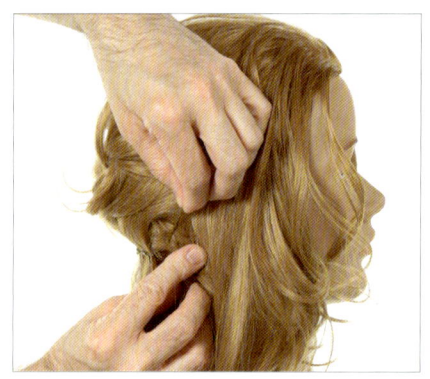

07 Continue securing the braid as needed. Be sure that the lengths are secure since this area will act as a base for the remainder of the design.

08 The art shows the directions in which vertical loops will be formed, working from the center nape toward either side. Note that the loops at the sides of the nape are positioned slightly higher than those at the center.

09–10 Release a section adjacent to the center on the right side. Lightly backcomb the inside of the section for support using a wide-tooth tail comb. Then smooth the surface using the tail of the comb. Avoid smoothing too much.

11 Next, wrap the lengths around your fingers toward the right, leaving the ends loose.

 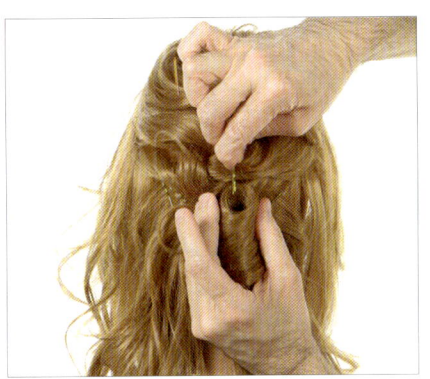 

12–14 Position the loop vertically at the nape. Hold the loop gently in place and secure it as needed using bobby pins and hairpins.

15 Move to the left side adjacent to the center, and repeat the same techniques. Wrap the hair toward the left.

16 Position the loop vertically and secure it with bobby pins and hairpins as needed.

17 Next, use a hairpin to secure the two center loops together for added stability.

18 Return to the right side and create another vertical loop that is positioned slightly higher. After securing the loop, secure it to the adjacent loop using a hairpin. Repeat on the left side.

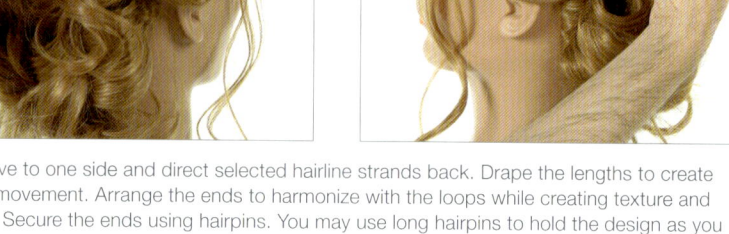

19–20 Move to one side and direct selected hairline strands back. Drape the lengths to create directional movement. Arrange the ends to harmonize with the loops while creating texture and movement. Secure the ends using hairpins. You may use long hairpins to hold the design as you work. Repeat on the other side.

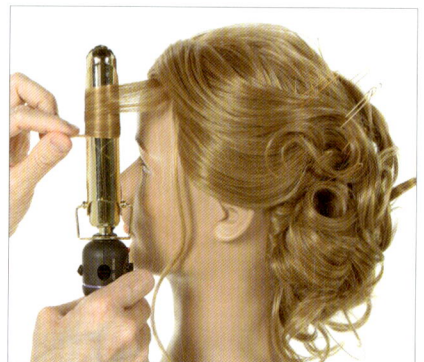

21 If necessary or desired, reinforce the spiraled texture of the remaining loose lengths using a thermal iron.

22–23 The finish shows a combination of braided texture and loops accented by a tousle of curls for a soft, romantic look.

DESIGN DECISIONS *WORKSHOP 09*
3-STRAND OVERBRAID/LOOPS
Draw or fill in the boxes with the appropriate answers.

STRUCTURE

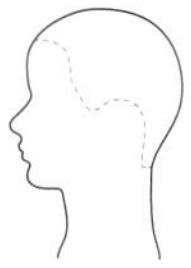

FORM/SHAPE

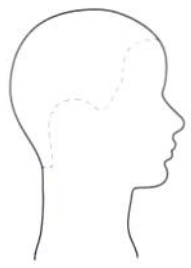

DIRECTION OF FORM

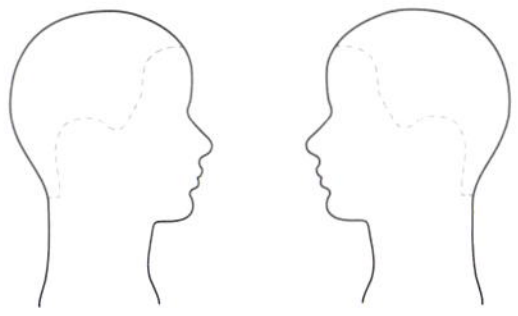

TECHNIQUE

- [ ]
- [ ]
- [ ]
- [ ]
- [ ]
- [ ]

DESIGN PRINCIPLES

- [ ] REPETITION
- [ ] ALTERNATION
- [ ] PROGRESSION
- [ ] CONTRAST

DISTRIBUTION

SECTIONING/PARTING

PREPARATION

- [ ] CURLING IRON
- [ ] FLAT IRON
- [ ] THERMAL ROLLERS
- [ ] ROLLER SET
- [ ] AIR FORM

TOOLS/PRODUCT CHOICE

_____
Educator Signature

_____
Date

HAIR DESIGN RUBRIC *WORKSHOP 09*

3-STRAND OVERBRAID/LOOPS

This rubric is a performance assessment tool designed to measure your ability to **create** *Pivot Point hair designs.*

	LEVEL 1 *in progress*	LEVEL 2 *getting better*	LEVEL 3 *entry-level proficiency*
PREPARATION			
• Assemble long hair design essentials	☐	☐	☐
• Spiral-curl hair with thermal iron	☐	☐	☐
CREATE			
• Apply lightweight pomade using fingers	☐	☐	☐
• Direct lengths back leaving hairline loose	☐	☐	☐
• Form a 3-strand overbraid starting at crown, crossing left strand over center strand	☐	☐	☐
• Cross right strand over center strand	☐	☐	☐
• Continue braiding technique, adding to outside sections up to occipital area	☐	☐	☐
• Secure braid with bobby pins	☐	☐	☐
• Release right section adjacent to center	☐	☐	☐
• Backcomb lightly inside section with wide-tooth tail comb; smooth surface using tail of comb	☐	☐	☐
• Wrap lengths around fingers toward right, leaving ends loose	☐	☐	☐
• Position loop vertically at nape; gently hold in place and secure with bobby pins	☐	☐	☐
• Release left section adjacent to center	☐	☐	☐
• Wrap lengths around fingers toward left, leaving ends loose	☐	☐	☐
• Position loop vertically at nape; gently hold in place and secure with bobby pins	☐	☐	☐
• Secure two center loops together with bobby pins	☐	☐	☐
• Create another vertical loop on right side; position it slightly higher and secure it to adjacent loop; repeat on left side	☐	☐	☐
• Direct selected hairline strands back, drape lengths and arrange ends; secure with bobby pins	☐	☐	☐

TOTAL POINTS = _____ + _____ + _____

TOTAL POINTS _____ ÷ HIGHEST POSSIBLE SCORE 54 X 100 = _____ %

Record your time in comparison with the suggested salon speed.

To improve my performance on this procedure, I need to:

_____   _____   _____

Student Signature   *Educator Signature*   *Date*

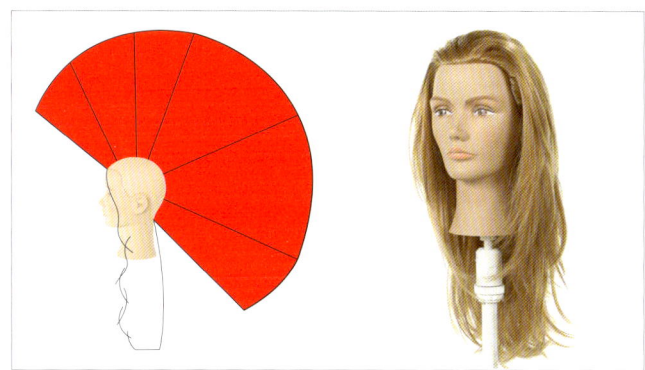

WORKSHOP 10
FREEFORM LOOPS

This design makes a rich textural statement and features asymmetric balance and lengths that cascade down the back. A buildup of product is essential to the success of this design.

The finish shows an elongated look created by positioning loops at the base throughout most of the interior, creating volume with well-defined, spiral-curled texture.

This exercise is performed on long increase-layered lengths. The hair was initially prepared by air forming the lengths straight with a slight end texture.

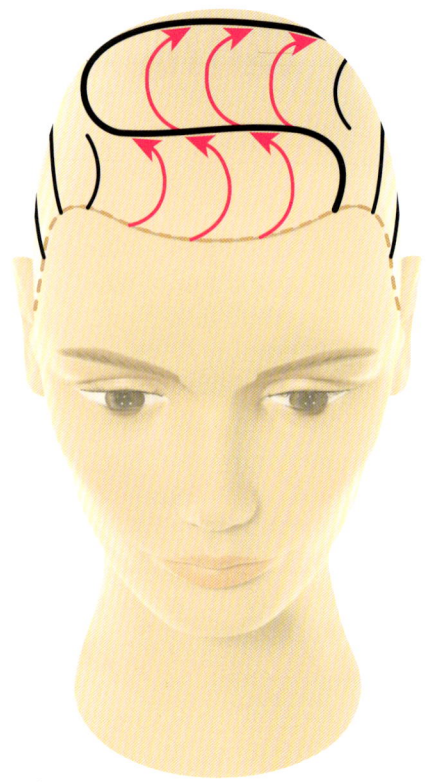

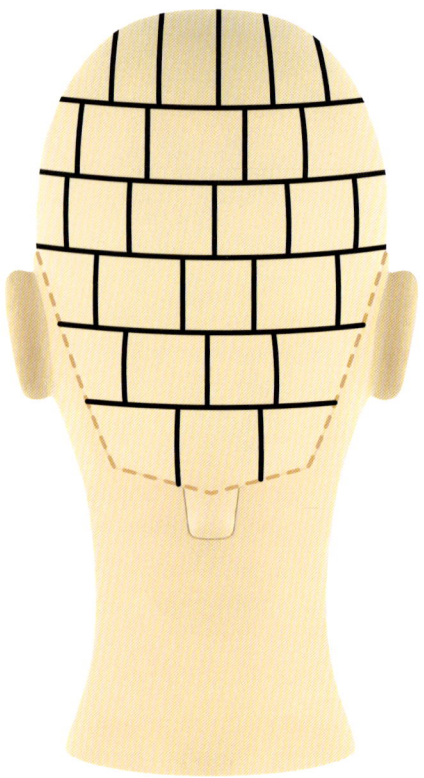

The art shows the partings that will be used to create the desired curled texture for this design. Alternating oblongs are used in the interior, with diagonal-forward partings at the sides and an irregular bricklay pattern throughout the back.

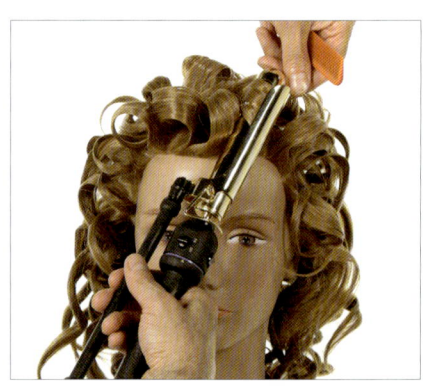

01–02 In the back use small rectangular sections working from the nape to the top. Spray each section with hairspray and wrap the hair around the barrel of the curling iron without releasing the strands, causing the hair to twist as it is wrapped. At the sides, use diagonal-forward partings and the same technique. Direct the lengths upward toward the back of the partings.

03 In the interior, set alternating oblongs, creating an alternation in the base direction. Continue wrapping to direct the ends away from the face.

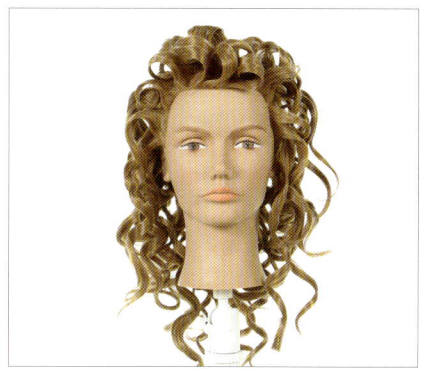

04 The finished curling iron set shows irregular twisted curls that are positioned to move away from the face.

05 Next, apply a silicone-based product to both sides of your hands and separate individual curls. Twist or twirl the lengths back into the spiral formation.

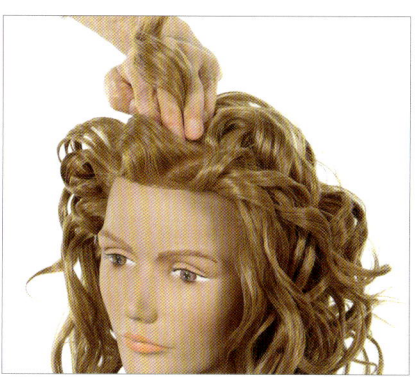

06 Take a section to the right of the center front hairline. Form a loop or a barrel curl at the base. Note that the section is somewhat random and blends the bases of the thermal set.

07 Secure the loop with bobby pins, temporarily leaving the ends loose.

08 Work toward the right side, using the same technique on the next base. Use a bobby pin and secure the loops together.

09 Then join the ends of the two sections and form a loop behind these sections. Do not comb through the ends, but allow the curl pattern to remain crisp and obvious. Secure with bobby pins.

10 Move to the next oblong and take a random section behind the first two loops. Form a loop in the opposite direction. Pin to secure.

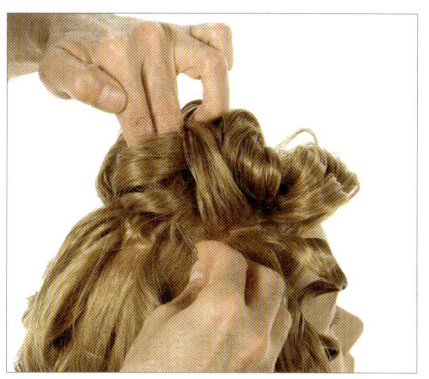

11 Use the same technique to form more loops. Position these loops to build volume in this area. Then join the ends to form more loops, creating additional volume.

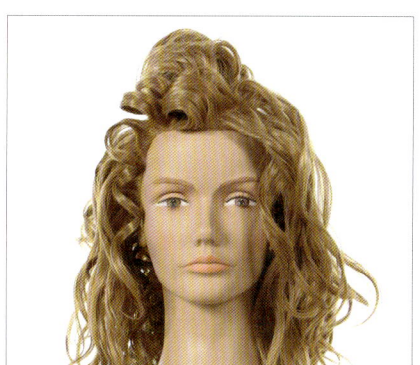

12 Note that the volume is being placed asymmetrically in this design.

13–14 Direct the remainder of the fringe lengths slightly back and toward the right side, using the same techniques to form loops and secure with bobby pins.

15 Move to the crown and take a random section. Use the same technique to form a loop at the base, leaving the ends free.

16 Create more loops on either side of the previous one. Then join the ends of these sections to form additional loops to increase volume in this area. Secure with bobby pins.

17 At the sides take random diagonal-forward sections. Direct the sections toward the crown while forming loops at the base. Pin to secure, leaving the ends free. Work to the perimeter and then repeat on the opposite side.

18 The art shows a large irregular triangle-shaped section used in the center back.

19 Temporarily secure the ends from the sides up and out of the way. Then take a large irregular triangle section near the occipital. Push the base upward and secure.

20 Loosely direct the side nape lengths slightly upward and toward the center back triangular section. Pin to secure.

21 Repeat at the center nape, allowing lengths to blend more harmoniously.

22 Finish the design by arranging any loose ends to balance the texture and shape of the design. Pin and spray as needed.

23–24 The finish shows a romantic style created with loops at the base in the interior and slightly twisted curls throughout.

FREEFORM LOOPS

Draw or fill in the boxes with the appropriate answers.

STRUCTURE

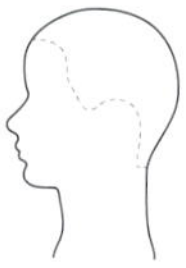

FORM/SHAPE

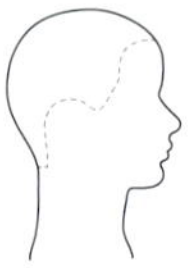

DIRECTION OF FORM

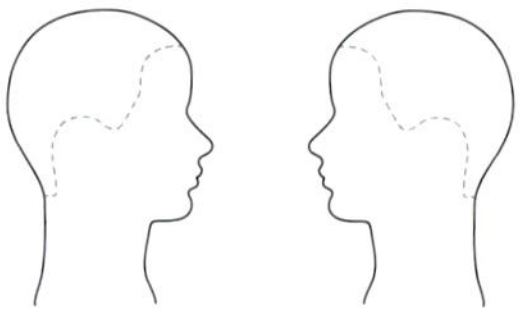

TECHNIQUE

☐   ☐   ☐   ☐   ☐   ☐

DESIGN PRINCIPLES

☐ REPETITION

☐ ALTERNATION

☐ PROGRESSION

☐ CONTRAST

DISTRIBUTION

SECTIONING/PARTING

PREPARATION

☐ CURLING IRON

☐ FLAT IRON

☐ THERMAL ROLLERS

☐ ROLLER SET

☐ AIR FORM

TOOLS/PRODUCT CHOICE

Educator Signature

Date

LONG HAIR DESIGN

HAIR DESIGN RUBRIC *WORKSHOP 10*

FREEFORM LOOPS

This rubric is a performance assessment tool designed to measure your ability to **create** *Pivot Point hair designs.*

	LEVEL 1 *in progress*	LEVEL 2 *getting better*	LEVEL 3 *entry-level proficiency*
PREPARATION			
• Assemble long hair design essentials	☐	☐	☐
CREATE			
• Wrap hair around barrel of curling iron without releasing strands, causing hair to twist around iron	☐	☐	☐
• Use diagonal-forward partings at sides and use same technique	☐	☐	☐
• Set alternating oblongs in front interior to create alternation in base direction; wrap ends away from face	☐	☐	☐
• Apply silicone product to hands and separate curls; twist or twirl lengths into spiral formation	☐	☐	☐
• Form a loop or barrel curl to right of center front hairline; secure loop with bobby pins and leave ends loose	☐	☐	☐
• Use same technique working toward right side; secure the loops together	☐	☐	☐
• Join ends and form loop behind previous two sections; do not comb through ends; secure with bobby pins	☐	☐	☐
• Form loops in opposite direction in next oblong; pin to secure	☐	☐	☐
• Build volume with loops working toward crown; join ends and form more loops	☐	☐	☐
• Form loops in crown using same techniques, leaving ends free	☐	☐	☐
• Direct diagonal-forward sections at sides toward crown while forming loops at base; pin to secure, leaving ends free	☐	☐	☐
• Work to perimeter, then repeat on opposite side	☐	☐	☐
• Take large irregular triangle section near occipital; push base upward and secure with bobby pins	☐	☐	☐
• Direct side lengths upward and toward center back triangle section; pin to secure	☐	☐	☐
• Finish design, arranging loose ends to balance; pin and spray as needed	☐	☐	☐

TOTAL POINTS = _____ + _____ + _____

TOTAL POINTS _____ ÷ HIGHEST POSSIBLE SCORE 48 X 100 = _____ %

Record your time in comparison with the suggested salon speed.

To improve my performance on this procedure, I need to:

Student Signature

Educator Signature

Date

DOUBLE ROLL

The double vertical roll technique is used to create a style that is youthful and feminine, without appearing uncontrolled or messy. This design can strike a perfect balance between "done" and "undone."

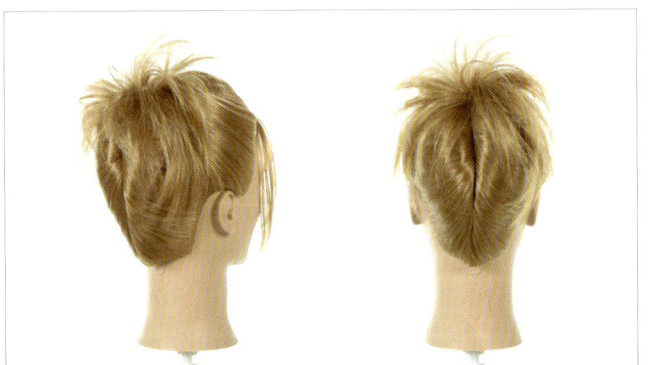

This finish features two vertical rolls positioned next to one another in the back of the design with loose ends extending from the rolls. The front lengths are directed to the crown, while creating subtle volume in the interior. Loose ends are arranged for a softer finish.

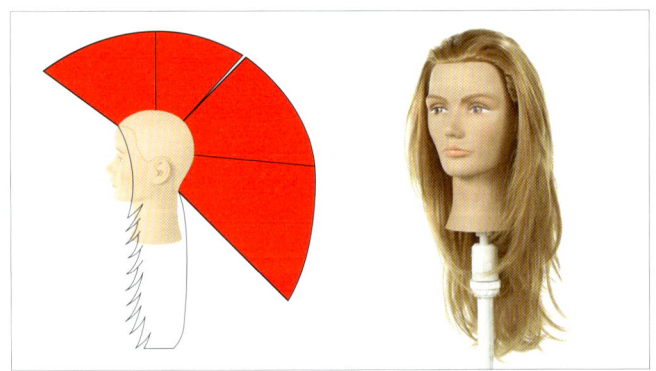

This exercise is performed on long, planar increase-layered lengths. The hair was prepared by air forming the lengths straight with a slight end texture.

The art shows the hair will be sectioned diagonally from ear to ear across the upper crown. The back is divided in half with a vertical center part. The front is then sectioned from the outside of each eyebrow back to the diagonal sectioning line.

01 Starting on the right side of the back, direct the lengths toward the center back. Smooth the surface of the section. Use a light hairspray as needed while working.

02 Wrap the ends around your left index and middle fingers. Turn your hand in and upward to position the vertical roll parallel to the center parting.

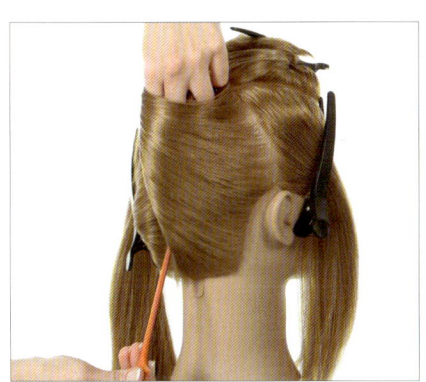

03 With your left hand controlling the position of the roll, use the tail of the comb to tuck the ends into it.

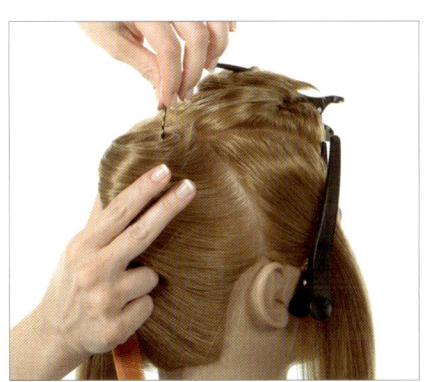

04 Hold the roll in place and use bobby pins to secure the roll from the inside.

05 Continue to secure the roll from the outside using bobby pins.

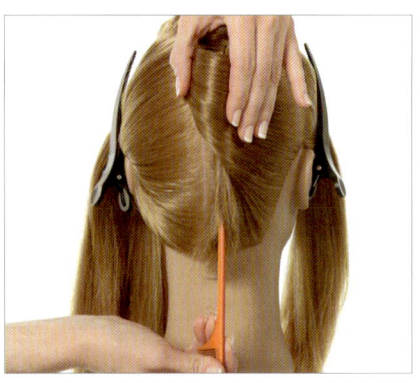

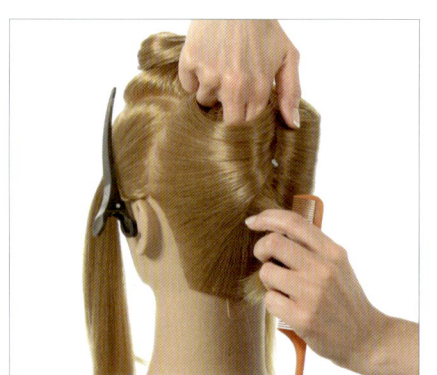

06 Use the tip of the tail comb to smooth and define the roll. Continue to use the tip of the tail comb to direct the ends into the roll.

07–08 Repeat the same procedure on the left side. Use the tail of the comb to tuck the ends into the roll as needed. Secure the second roll, inside and out, by using bobby pins and hairpins.

09 To ensure symmetry and stability, use a hairpin to secure the rolls to each other.

10 Move to the left side. Subdivide diagonally for control, direct the lengths toward the crown and backcomb lightly on top of the strands.

11 Next, smooth the surface in the same direction. Leave some of the hairline out to incorporate into the design later.

12 Lay the section across the crown, directing the ends to the right side.

13 Pin to secure at the center leaving the ends loose.

14 Repeat the same techniques on the right side.

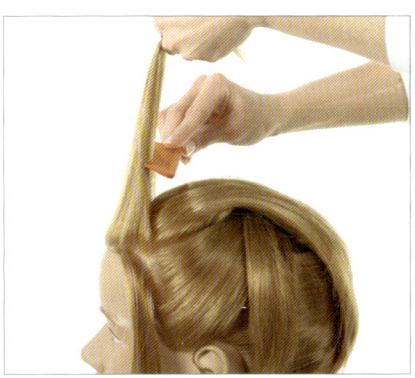

15 Now, move to the fringe. Subdivide for control, then project and backcomb the lengths for support starting at the front.

16–17 Join the sections and continue backcombing, making sure the sections are blended. Lower the projection angle while working toward the back to create less volume. Then smooth the section. Use hairspray as needed for additional control while working.

18 Twist the section approximately 2" (5 cm) from the base of the section.

19 Push the twist forward and position the hair so that the ends are directed upward.

20 Secure the twisted section with bobby pins or hairpins.

21 Take some of the loose ends from the side sections and incorporate them into the top of the rolls. Secure as needed, leaving the remaining ends loose.

22 If necessary, direct some of the hairline lengths back and secure. Then arrange the loose ends with your fingers.

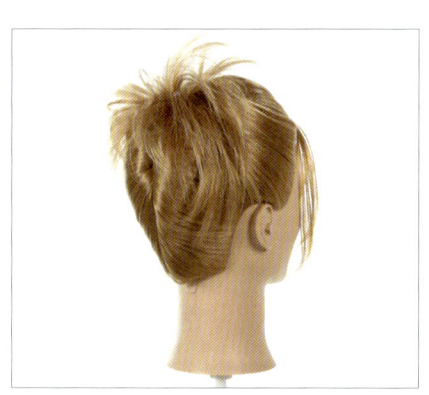

23–24 The finish shows two vertical rolls positioned next to one another with loose ends for a soft, romantic feeling.

DESIGN DECISIONS *WORKSHOP 11*
DOUBLE ROLL
Draw or fill in the boxes with the appropriate answers.

STRUCTURE

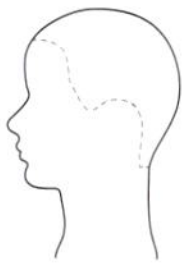

FORM/SHAPE

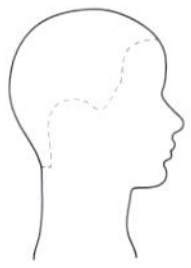

DIRECTION OF FORM

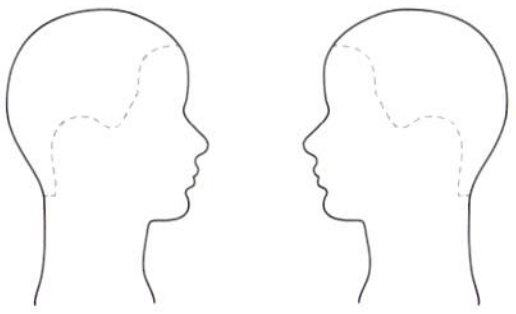

TECHNIQUE

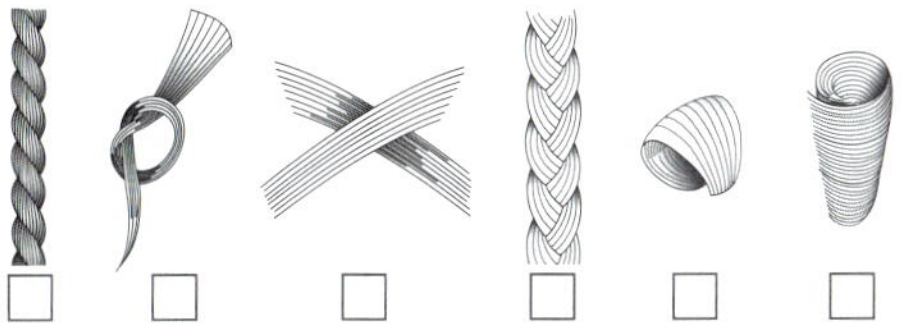

- [ ]
- [ ]
- [ ]
- [ ]
- [ ]
- [ ]

DESIGN PRINCIPLES

- [ ] REPETITION
- [ ] ALTERNATION
- [ ] PROGRESSION
- [ ] CONTRAST

DISTRIBUTION

SECTIONING/PARTING

PREPARATION

- [ ] CURLING IRON
- [ ] FLAT IRON
- [ ] THERMAL ROLLERS
- [ ] ROLLER SET
- [ ] AIR FORM

TOOLS/PRODUCT CHOICE

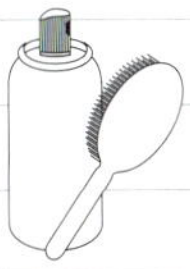

Educator Signature

Date

HAIR DESIGN RUBRIC *WORKSHOP 11*

DOUBLE ROLL

This rubric is a performance assessment tool designed to measure your ability to **create** *Pivot Point hair designs.*

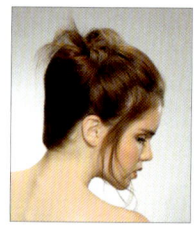

	LEVEL 1 *in progress*	LEVEL 2 *getting better*	LEVEL 3 *entry-level proficiency*
PREPARATION			
• Assemble long hair design essentials	☐	☐	☐
CREATE			
• Section diagonally from ear to ear across upper crown; section back with vertical center part; section front from outside of each eyebrow	☐	☐	☐
• Direct lengths of right back section toward center back	☐	☐	☐
• Lightly backcomb and smooth surface; use light hairspray while working	☐	☐	☐
• Wrap ends around index and middle finger; turn hand in and upward to position roll parallel to center parting	☐	☐	☐
• Position roll with left hand; use tail comb to tuck ends into roll	☐	☐	☐
• Secure from inside and outside of roll using bobby pins	☐	☐	☐
• Continue to use tip of tail comb to smooth and define roll; direct ends into roll	☐	☐	☐
• Repeat same procedure on left side	☐	☐	☐
• Secure rolls together using hairpin	☐	☐	☐
• Subdivide left side, direct lengths toward crown, backcomb and smooth on top of strands	☐	☐	☐
• Lay section across crown directing ends toward right side; pin to secure, leaving ends loose	☐	☐	☐
• Repeat same techniques on right side	☐	☐	☐
• Project and backcomb fringe lengths; use lower projection toward back	☐	☐	☐
• Smooth section and use hairspray for control	☐	☐	☐
• Twist and push forward; position ends upward and secure with bobby pins	☐	☐	☐
• Incorporate some ends from side sections into top of rolls	☐	☐	☐
• Finish design, arranging loose ends to balance; pin and spray as needed	☐	☐	☐

TOTAL POINTS = _____ + _____ + _____

TOTAL POINTS _____ ÷ HIGHEST POSSIBLE SCORE 54 X 100 = _____ %

Record your time in comparison with the suggested salon speed.

To improve my performance on this procedure, I need to:

_____ _____ _____
Student Signature   Educator Signature   Date

WORKSHOP 12
SINGLE-STRAND TWISTS AND LOOPS

This beautiful design, which combines on-the-scalp twists with loops, is a great option for clients who desire a look that can be worn for a formal occasion as well as for an everyday style.

Many clients with relaxed hair can benefit from this design. Depending on the client's lifestyle and at home daily maintenance, this design can last up to one week.

This finish shows on-the-scalp twists leading the eye to smooth, refined loops at the crown.

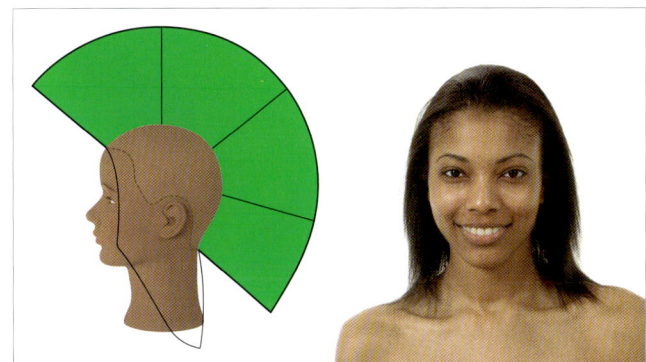

This exercise is performed on long uniformly layered lengths. A flat iron was used to prepare the hair for this service.

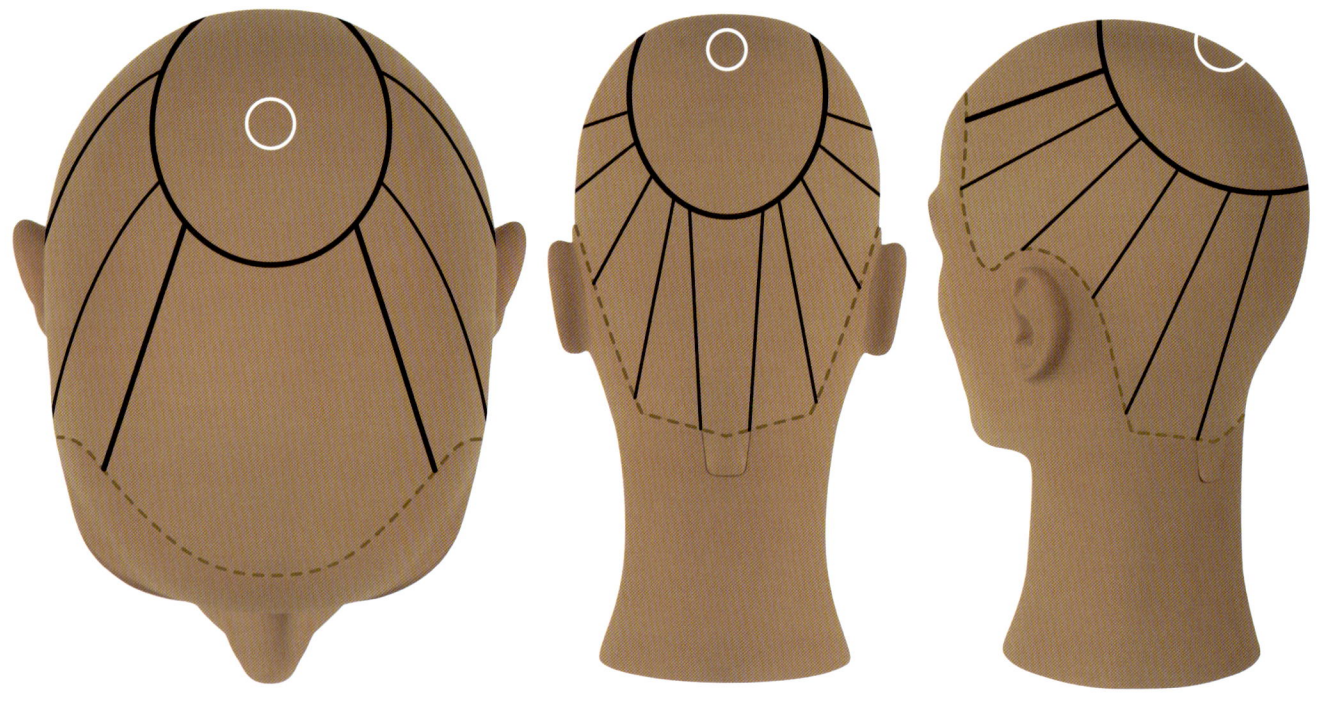

The art shows the sectioning and approximate parting pattern that will be used to create this design. A ponytail is positioned in the upper portion of a circular section in the crown and a center front section is isolated diagonally from either recession area to the circular section. Diagonal partings will be used around the remaining perimeter. Note that only the center back section is wider near the circle and narrower at the hairline.

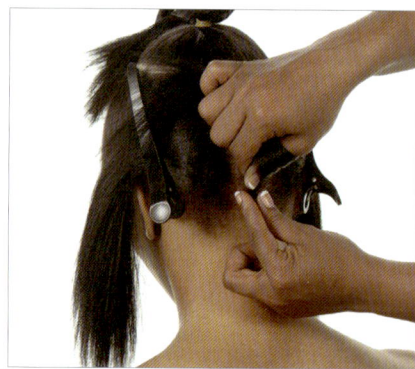

01–02 Begin by taking a section at the center back that is narrower at the hairline. Distribute lengths straight out from the base using a tail comb, and spray the section with holding spray.

03 Starting at the nape hairline, firmly twist the hair to the left using the right hand. Use the index finger and thumb of the left hand to maintain tension.

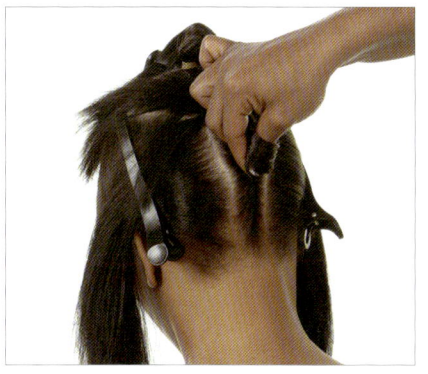  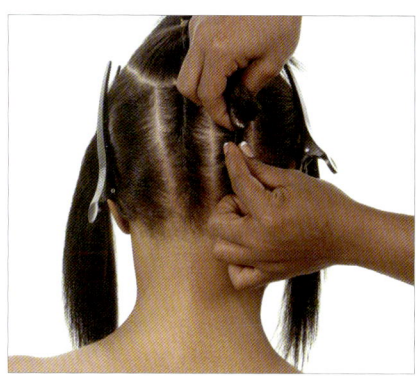

04–05 Continue to twist working upward, keeping the twist centered within the section. Twist off the scalp toward the ponytail. Then secure the twist using a bobby pin directed toward the ponytail.

06 Move to the adjacent section to the right and use the same technique. Note that this and subsequent sections are wider at the hairline.

07 Maintain even tension while working toward the ends.

08 Again, continue twisting toward the ponytail and secure the lengths next to the previous section.

09 Use the same technique on the section to the left of the center and secure. Note that each of the twists is secured with the bobby pins directed toward the ponytail.

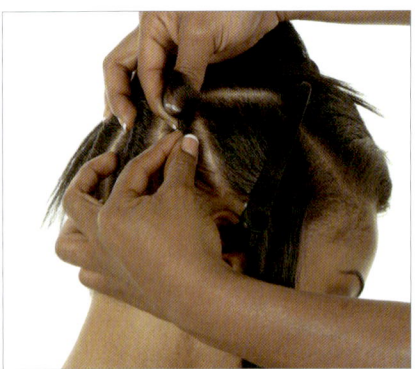

10–11 Return to the right side and take a diagonal-forward parting and use the same technique. Then, repeat the same technique on the left side. Secure the twist next to the previous section. Alternating from one side to the other will help maintain balance in sectioning.

12 Continue to alternate from side to side as you work toward the front. Be sure to alter the angle of the partings as you work.

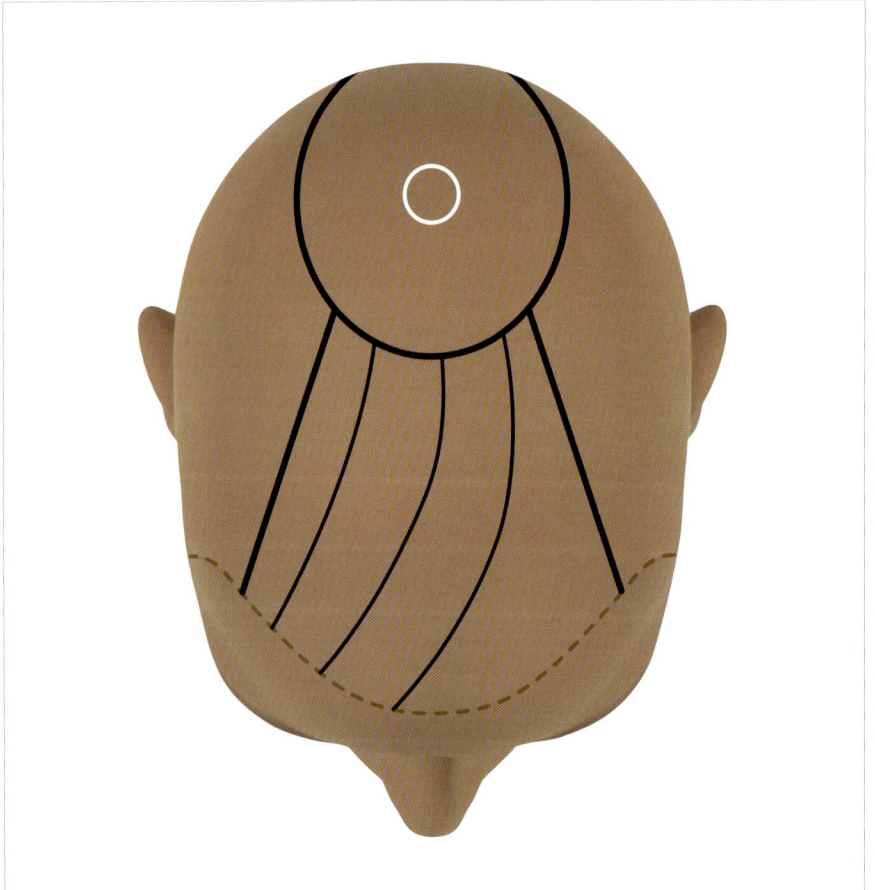

13 The art shows that curved partings will be taken within the center front section to add interest and create subtle asymmetry.

14 Move to the fringe section and take the first curved parting at the right. Following the curve, twist and secure using the same techniques.

15 Working across the fringe section, secure the twists next to one another.

16 Next, section and curl the ends of the twists and ponytail lengths using a large-diameter thermal iron.

17 Isolate the center of the ponytail, then work through the lengths in sections. Backcomb and smooth each section and form an open loop.

18 Secure the loops with hairpins. Continue to use the same technique on the remaining lengths, including the isolated portion. Arrange the ends for a harmonious effect.

19 Refine the perimeter of the design using a small amount of pomade if necessary.

20 Use the tail of the comb to refine the twists to complete the design.

21 The finish shows a polished-looking design with a great deal of control that can be worn for a special occasion or for an everyday, chic style. This technique can be adapted to create a wide variety of styles.

DESIGN DECISIONS *WORKSHOP 12*

SINGLE-STRAND TWISTS AND LOOPS

artist+ access

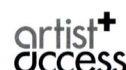

Draw or fill in the boxes with the appropriate answers.

STRUCTURE

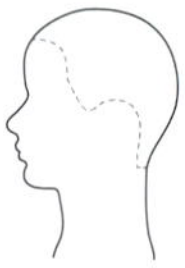

FORM/SHAPE

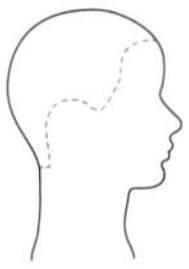

DIRECTION OF FORM

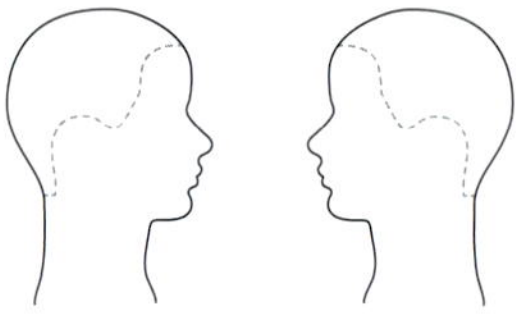

TECHNIQUE

☐ ☐ ☐ ☐ ☐ ☐

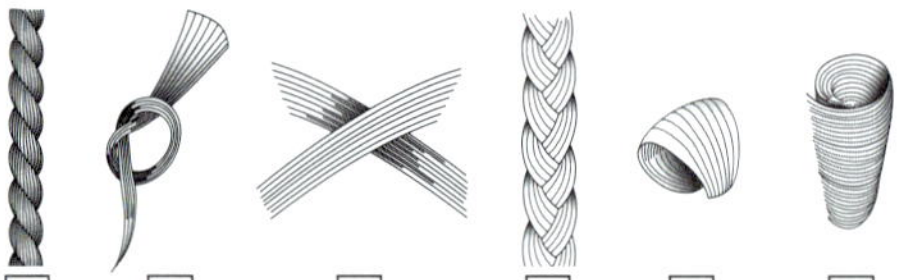

DESIGN PRINCIPLES

- ☐ REPETITION
- ☐ ALTERNATION
- ☐ PROGRESSION
- ☐ CONTRAST

DISTRIBUTION

SECTIONING/PARTING

PREPARATION

- ☐ CURLING IRON
- ☐ FLAT IRON
- ☐ THERMAL ROLLERS
- ☐ ROLLER SET
- ☐ AIR FORM

TOOLS/PRODUCT CHOICE

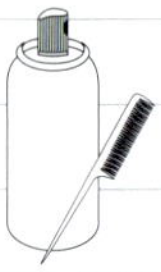

Educator Signature

Date

HAIR DESIGN RUBRIC *WORKSHOP 12*

SINGLE-STRAND TWISTS AND LOOPS

This rubric is a performance assessment tool designed to measure your ability to **create** *Pivot Point hair designs.*

	LEVEL 1 *in progress*	LEVEL 2 *getting better*	LEVEL 3 *entry-level proficiency*
PREPARATION			
• Assemble long hair design essentials	☐	☐	☐
• Flat iron hair	☐	☐	☐
CREATE			
• Section circular shape in crown and position ponytail in upper portion	☐	☐	☐
• Isolate center front with diagonal partings from front recession area on both sides to circular section	☐	☐	☐
• Take parting at center back, distribute lengths straight out with tail comb and spray with holding spray	☐	☐	☐
• Twist hair to left, beginning in nape and working upward using right hand; maintain tension with index finger and thumb of left hand keeping twist centered within section	☐	☐	☐
• Twist off the scalp toward ponytail and secure with bobby pins directed toward ponytail	☐	☐	☐
• Repeat same techniques on adjacent section on right	☐	☐	☐
• Repeat same techniques on section to left of center	☐	☐	☐
• Take diagonal-forward parting on right side; twist using same technique and secure with bobby pins next to previous section	☐	☐	☐
• Alternate from left to right side, working toward front using same techniques	☐	☐	☐
• Take curved parting within center-front section and twist following curve using same techniques	☐	☐	☐
• Work across fringe section using same technique	☐	☐	☐
• Section and curl ends of twists with large-diameter thermal iron	☐	☐	☐
• Isolate center of ponytail and curl lengths in sections	☐	☐	☐
• Backcomb and smooth each section, then form an open loop; secure with hairpins	☐	☐	☐
• Finish design, arranging loose ends to balance; pin and spray as needed	☐	☐	☐

TOTAL POINTS = _____ + _____ + _____

TOTAL POINTS _____ ÷ HIGHEST POSSIBLE SCORE 51 X 100 = _____ %

Record your time in comparison with the suggested salon speed. _____

To improve my performance on this procedure, I need to: _____

_____ _____ _____
Student Signature   Educator Signature   Date

WORKSHOP 13
CHIGNON

Long hair designs that feature a
single large loop, which incorporates
the majority of the hair are commonly
referred to as Chignons. Chignons
are used to create timeless and classic
long hair designs. The sleekness
created in this design is appealing
to many clients. Placing the chignon
slightly higher can create a more
youthful, retro feel.

The finish shows a sleek chignon positioned in the crown with overlapping
front lengths to create interest in the design. A filler is used to help create
the shape and size of the chignon.

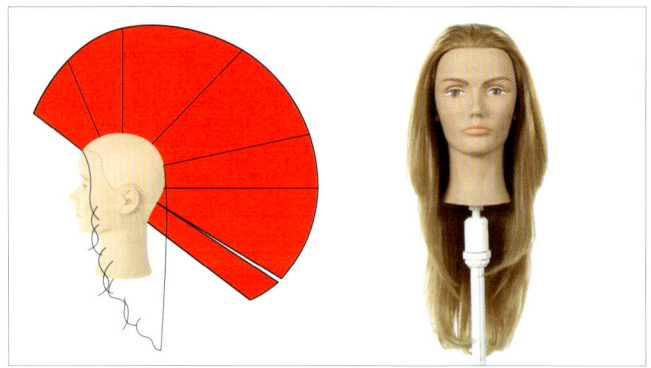

This exercise is performed on long increase-layered lengths. The hair was
prepped by flat ironing the hair and then beveling the hair under.

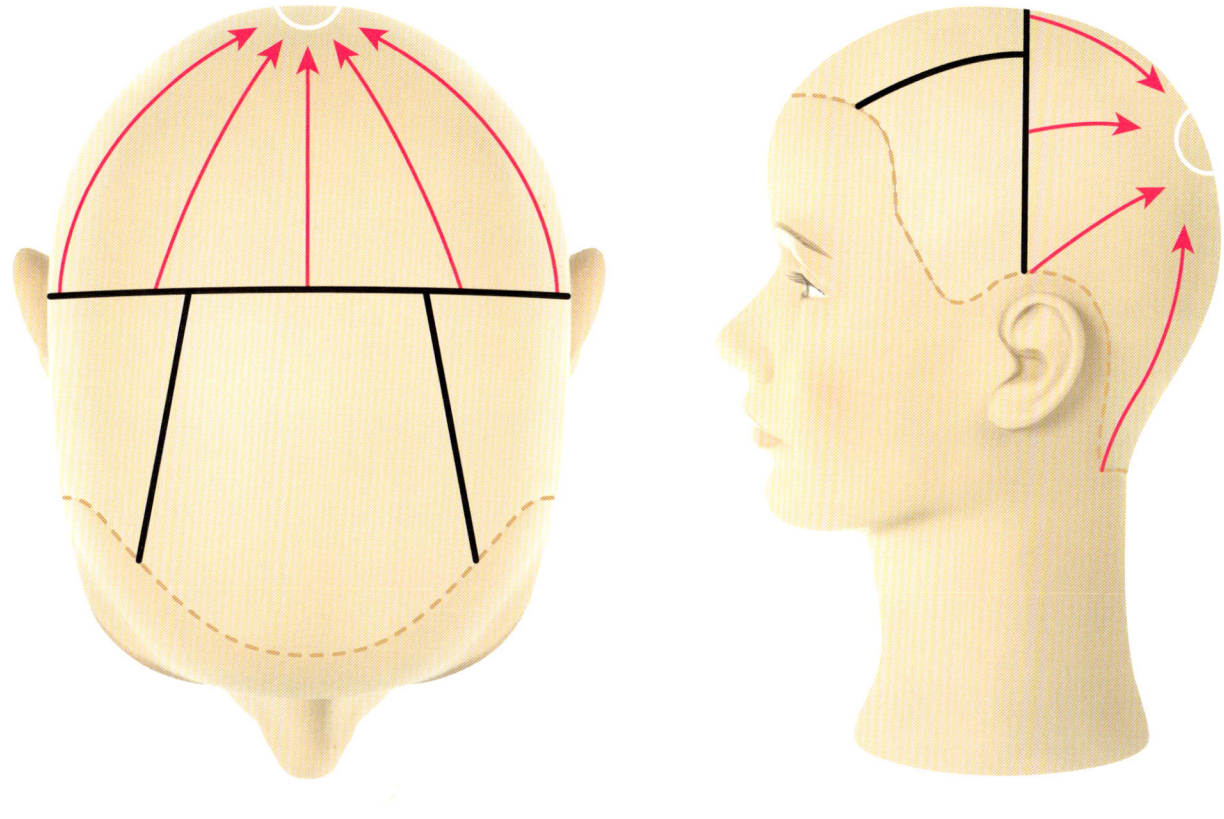

The art shows the sectioning used for the top and sides, and a ponytail positioned at the lower crown.

01–02 After sectioning and positioning the ponytail, take horizontal sections in the fringe and lightly backcomb from underneath the strand. Lower the projection angle as you work toward the back of the section.

03 Then use a cushion brush to smooth and direct the lengths toward the back.

04–05 Secure the section just above the ponytail with bobby pins. Crisscross the bobby pins for more support. Then direct the ends around one side of the elastic band and secure below the ponytail with bobby pins.

06 Use a cushion brush to direct the ponytail lengths up and toward the face. Then, use one hand to hold the ponytail out of the way.

07 Place an elastic band on the end of a large bobby pin. Insert the closed end of the bobby pin above the ponytail on one side of the secured fringe lengths.

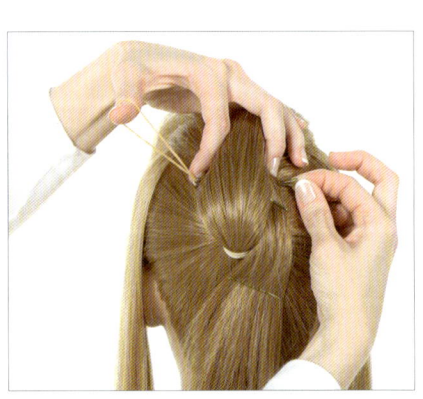

08 Slide the large bobby pin along the scalp to the other side of the secured fringe lengths. Hook the elastic band on the thumb of the hand holding the ponytail, forming a loop.

09 Pull the large bobby pin in the opposite direction out of the hair.

10 Push the bobby pin completely through the loop on your thumb.

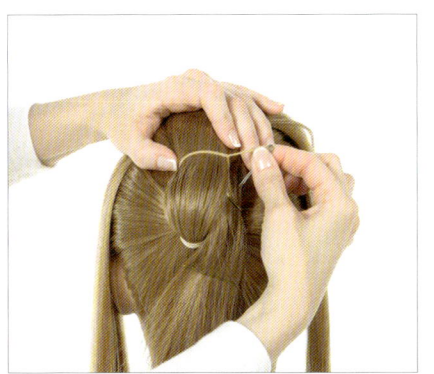

11 Turn the bobby pin and insert into the hair to secure this portion of the ponytail in this position.

12 Subsection each side with a diagonal-forward parting. Subsection both sides at the same time to ensure symmetry. Lightly backcomb and smooth the bottom right subsection up toward the crown.

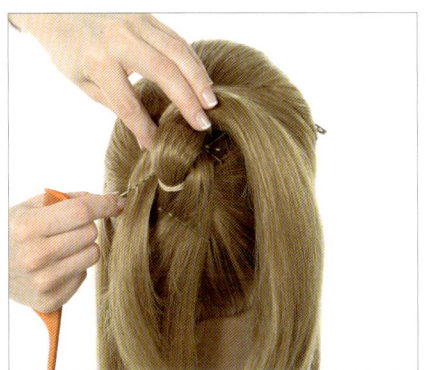

13 Move the ponytail lengths toward the right if necessary. Direct the side lengths to the opposite side of the ponytail and secure with bobby pins.

14 Repeat the same technique with the bottom subsection on the other side.

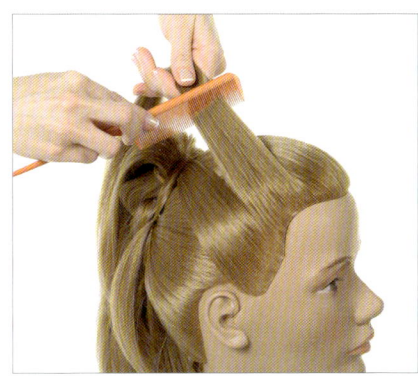

15 Then backcomb and smooth the top right subsection. Overlap the hair, directing it to the left side of the ponytail. Pin to secure. Repeat on the top left subsection.

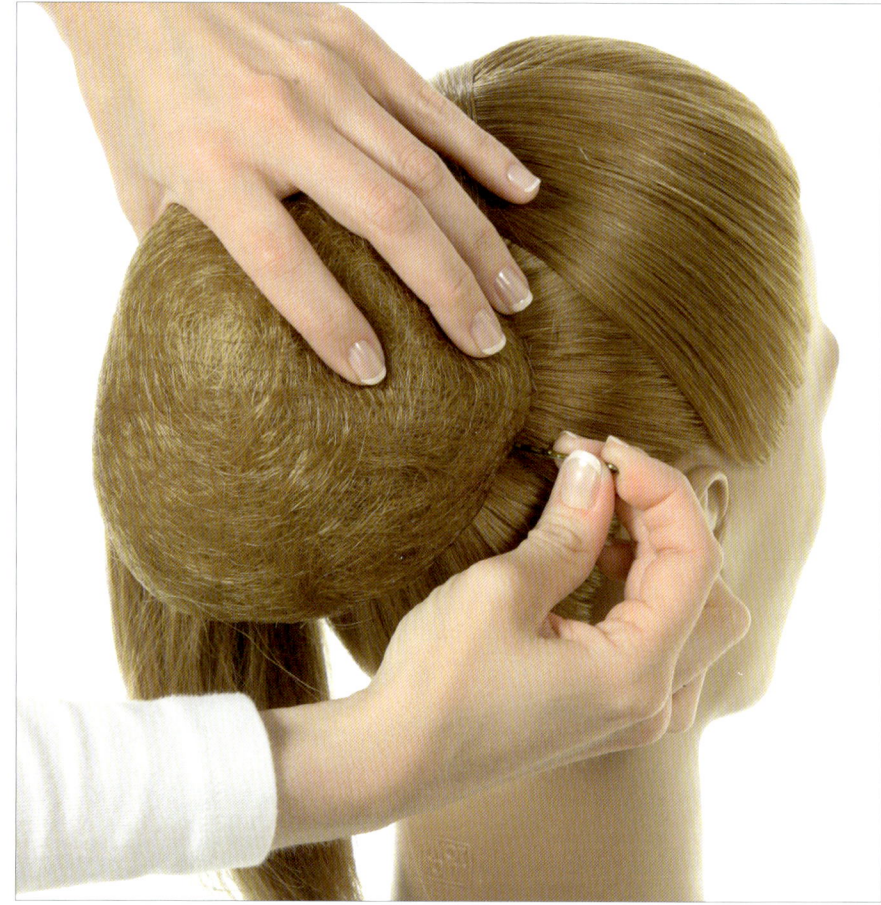

16 Fold the ends into a large flat loop and secure beneath the ponytail. Note that the placement of the chignon will cover these ends.

17 Position the filler directly underneath the base of the ponytail. Using bobby pins, secure the filler to the hair. Note that the size and shape of the filler will directly affect the size and shape of the chignon.

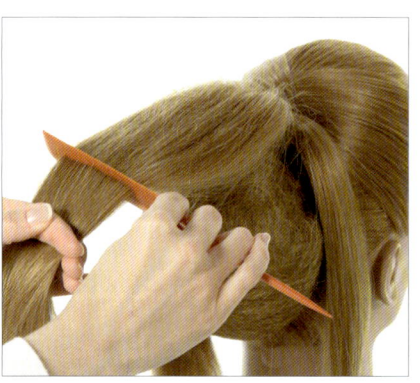

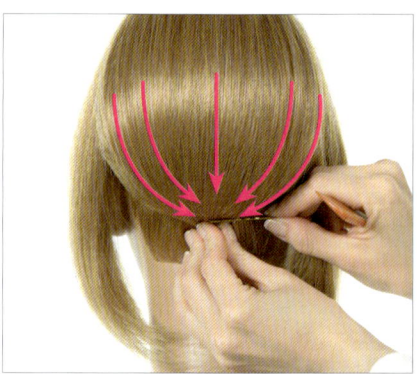

18 Next, subdivide the ponytail into three equal sections. Backcomb the center section from beneath the strand.

19 Smooth and spread the lengths with the comb.

20 Direct the lengths to the bottom, narrowing the section to contour the shape of the filler. Secure with bobby pins.

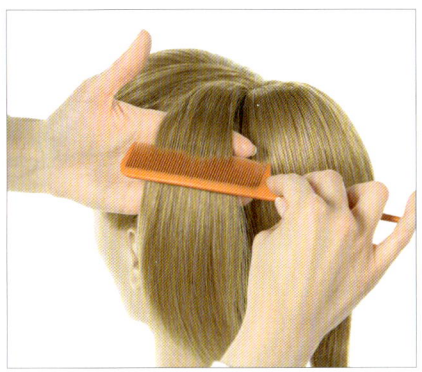

21 Move to the left section. Backcomb and smooth the second section using the same techniques.

22–23 Direct the lengths across the bottom to the opposite side. Pin to secure. Long hairpins can be used to hold lengths in place while working. Move to the right section and use the same techniques. Direct the ends to the left side and secure with bobby pins.

24 Subdivide the ends of the center section in half. Overlap the ends toward opposite sides and secure with bobby pins or hairpins.

25–26 The finish shows a sleek chignon with volume, accentuated by the use of an overlap technique.

DESIGN DECISIONS *WORKSHOP 13*

CHIGNON

artist+ access

Draw or fill in the boxes with the appropriate answers.

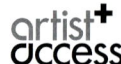

STRUCTURE

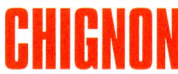

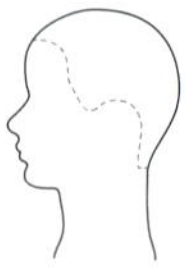

FORM/SHAPE

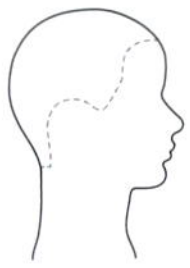

DIRECTION OF FORM

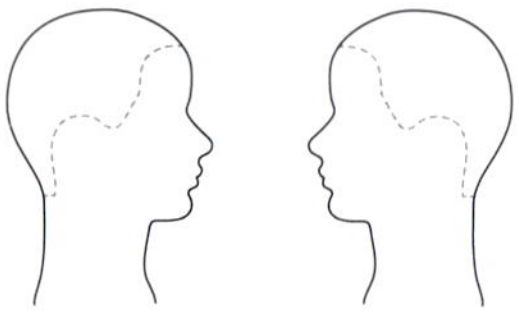

TECHNIQUE

☐ ☐ ☐ ☐ ☐ ☐

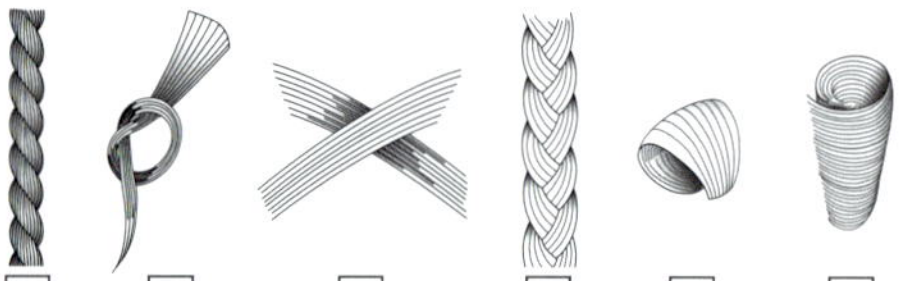

DESIGN PRINCIPLES

- ☐ REPETITION
- ☐ ALTERNATION
- ☐ PROGRESSION
- ☐ CONTRAST

DISTRIBUTION

SECTIONING/PARTING

PREPARATION

- ☐ CURLING IRON
- ☐ FLAT IRON
- ☐ THERMAL ROLLERS
- ☐ ROLLER SET
- ☐ AIR FORM

TOOLS/PRODUCT CHOICE

Educator Signature

Date

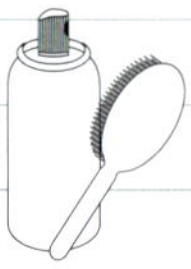

HAIR DESIGN RUBRIC *WORKSHOP 13*

CHIGNON

This rubric is a performance assessment tool designed to measure your ability to create *Pivot Point hair designs.*

	LEVEL 1 *in progress*	LEVEL 2 *getting better*	LEVEL 3 *entry-level proficiency*
PREPARATION			
• Assemble long hair design essentials	☐	☐	☐
CREATE			
• Section hair and position ponytail at lower crown	☐	☐	☐
• Backcomb horizontal sections in fringe underneath strand; lower projection angle working toward back; smooth and direct lengths toward back	☐	☐	☐
• Secure with bobby pins above ponytail; direct ends around elastic band and secure below ponytail	☐	☐	☐
• Direct ponytail lengths up; place elastic band on large bobby pin and direct bobby pin along scalp to other side of secured fringe lengths	☐	☐	☐
• Hook elastic band on thumb, pull bobby pin in opposite direction, push bobby pin through loop, turn and insert in hair	☐	☐	☐
• Subsection diagonal-forward partings on sides; alternate sides and backcomb and smooth each subsection up toward crown starting with bottom right	☐	☐	☐
• Overlap hair, directing lengths to opposite sides of ponytail	☐	☐	☐
• Fold lengths in large flat loop below ponytail; secure with bobby pins	☐	☐	☐
• Position filler underneath ponytail and secure with bobby pins	☐	☐	☐
• Subdivide ponytail into three equal sections; backcomb, smooth and spread center lengths; contour to shape of filler, secure with bobby pins	☐	☐	☐
• Backcomb and smooth side sections; direct lengths across bottom to opposite sides; pin to secure	☐	☐	☐
• Hold lengths in place using long hairpins	☐	☐	☐
• Subdivide center ends in half, overlap ends toward opposite sides and secure with bobby pins	☐	☐	☐

TOTAL POINTS = _____ + _____ + _____

TOTAL POINTS _____ ÷ HIGHEST POSSIBLE SCORE 42 X 100 = _____ %

Record your time in comparison with the suggested salon speed. _____

To improve my performance on this procedure, I need to: _____

_____
Student Signature

_____
Educator Signature

_____
Date

VOICES OF SUCCESS

"Long hair designs used to intimidate me. I kept working at them and now I am the most-requested designer in my salon for this service. It is a great outlet for my creativity and gives me more confidence with clients."

THE DESIGNER

IN OTHER WORDS

Long hair design techniques and procedures will give you the tools to become more creative and confident. Adding advanced long hair design skills to your repertoire will provide more career opportunities and help you build a clientele quickly.

"I used to dread having my hair styled for special events. It either gave me a headache, did not look polished or started falling apart before the event was over. Now, I always go to one particular designer who creates beautiful, pain-free results that last all day and night."

THE CLIENT

"We often get an entire bridal party in the salon for manicures and pedicures the day before as well as long hair designs and makeup the morning of the wedding. The salon would be missing out on a huge market if we were not able to cater to the needs of the bride and bridal party. Often members of the party have such a great experience they become regulars at the salon."

THE SALON OWNER

LEARNING CHALLENGE

Circle the letter corresponding to the correct answer.

1. Hair preparation requires the proper choice of products, tools, setting techniques and:
   a. patterns
   b. detailing
   c. distribution
   d. thermal rollers

2. In long hair design, a filler:
   a. is used to cover pins
   b. provides support and shape
   c. provides strength and texture
   d. fills an empty spot in the design

3. An on-the-scalp overbraid creates a/an:
   a. visible effect
   b. projected effect
   c. crisscross effect
   d. inverted appearance

4. Hairpins are usually used to secure:
   a. ponytails
   b. large areas
   c. heavy areas
   d. delicate areas

5. If the chin is tilted down while securing a ponytail, the nape area will:
   a. be tight
   b. be even
   c. be smooth
   d. sag or buckle

LESSONS LEARNED

- Long hair designs require planning, preparation and procedures along with technical skills to execute them proficiently with predictable results.

- Building a strong foundation of long hair design skills and techniques enables designers to create a large variety of long hair designs for years to come, however trends may change.

- Preparing long hair with the right tools, setting techniques and products prior to the actual long hair design will set you up for successful outcomes.

- Following client-centered guidelines when performing long hair design services ensures client satisfaction and helps build a more loyal clientele.

ADAPT AS A DESIGNER

Your new hair design skills allow you to finish the overall design composition by temporarily transforming the form, texture and direction of the hair to meet each client's individual needs. Taking into consideration the lifestyle and physical features of your clients is what helps set you apart from other designers.

Adapting hair design has two components: composing and personalizing. Composing involves integrating all of your knowledge and skills into a finished hair design. When you compose a hair design, you show that you understand how your design decisions and techniques yield the results you envision. Personalizing the design you compose helps ensure that it is appropriate and flattering either as the completion of another service, as a weekly or biweekly service, or as a design for a special occasion.

Within the pages of Pivot Point's *Meta*™ collections examples of dynamic hair designs created by adapting as a designer may also serve as inspiration. As you look through *Meta*, you will recognize that almost anything you visualize can be realized through adapting. Elevating your work from "satisfactory" to "breathtaking" is why adapting as a designer reflects the ultimate in professional hair design.

Now you are ready to develop your ability to adapt hair designs as a designer. Creating a personal portfolio to store "before and after" photographs of clients can be helpful in tracking your success. Keep notes describing your thought process for adapting hair designs for each client. Note the techniques used, what worked well, what didn't work well, and what you might have done differently. Your portfolio provides the chance for you to monitor your growth as a designer and your proficiency at adapting.

TERMS

Alternating Oblong – Two or more oblongs moving in opposite directions to create a wave pattern.

Analysis – The process of separating any whole into parts.

Arc – The area of the pincurl between the base and the circle; also referred to as the stem.

Arc Direction – The course of motion created in the base area.

Asymmetrical – Off-center balance; a hairstyle that has unequal proportions.

Axis – An imaginary straight line around which an object rotates.

Balance – Equilibrium of design elements; harmonious arrangement of parts in a design; emphasizes dissimilar or opposing parts that offset each other to make a harmonious whole.

Base – The area between partings.

BASE CONTROL

The size of the base in relation to the diameter of the tool, and the position of the tool in relation to the base.

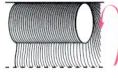 **Overdirected –** Exaggerated direction and volume, reduced base strength.

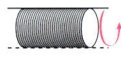 **On Base –** Maximum volume, maximum base strength.

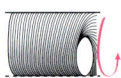 **Underdirected –** Reduced volume and base strength.

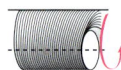 **Half-Off Base –** Less volume, less base strength.

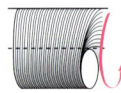 **Off Base –** Least volume, least base strength.

 Braid – The crossing or weaving together of three or more strands of hair.

Bricklay Pattern – A staggered, alternating pattern of base divisions within a shape that helps avoid splits in the finished design.

Chignon – A roll or loop of hair usually worn at the back of the head; any configuration of elements gathered or occurring closely together.

Coil – A series of connecting spirals or concentric rings formed by gathering and twisting the hair.

Combination Form Designing – Creating a design on hair that has been sculpted with more than one form.

Component – A simple part, relative to a larger system.

Composition – The arrangement of artistic parts so as to form a unified whole.

 **Concave –** Curving inward like the inside of a sphere.

CONNECTING LINES

The joining of two or more clockwise and counterclockwise shapes or forces; referred to as blending, converging and dividing.

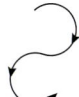 **Blending –** One force moves toward and the other force moves away from a common point or line.

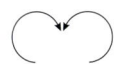 **Converging –** Both forces move toward a common point or line.

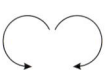 **Dividing –** Both forces move away from a common point or line.

 **Convex –** Curving outward like the surface of a sphere.

Curvature Shape – Includes circles, ovals and oblongs; implies movement or motion in hair in a clockwise or counterclockwise direction. The results will be curved lines or waves.

Curvilinear – Characterized by curved lines.

Degree – A small or progressional step.

Design Decision – The determination made through proper consultation with the client in regard to the end result of the hair design.

DESIGN ELEMENT

A major component or a part of the artistic whole; a basic part of the design.

Form – The outline or contour of the design; the three-dimensional shape of a design.

Texture – The visual appearance or feel of a surface.

Color – The visual perception of the reflection of light.

DESIGN PRINCIPLES

Arrangement patterns for design elements to follow; rules or standards that create an artistic whole.

Repetition – When all units are identical, except position.

Alternation – Sequential repetition where two or more units occur in a repeating pattern.

Progression – All units are similar, yet gradually change proportionately on an ascending or descending scale.

Contrast – A desirable relationship of opposites; creates variety and stimulates interest in a design.

Expansion – The width and/or height of a hair design.

Filler – Loose fiber used to expand a design or create certain specific forms.

Fingerwaving – Molding alternating oblongs using your fingers and a comb.

Finger Styling – The process of finishing a design by manipulating the hair with the hands and fingers.

FINISHING PROCEDURES

The steps used to finish a design.

Relax – After the hair is completely dry, relaxing is used to break up the set directions.

Dry Mold – Used to guide the hair into the desired final direction to assess where in the design additional support may be needed.

Backcomb/Backbrush – A technique used to increase height and control the form in a hair design.

Define the Form – The process of looking at the client's hair from a distance and from various angles to ensure that the finishing techniques have produced a well-balanced form. Various combs, brushes and fingers can be used to define the form.

Detail – Applying the finishing touches or finishing products to complete the hair design.

Flat-Ironing – The process of straightening the hair by using a flat iron.

Force – Energy or an action that causes motion, changes in motion or prevents motion.

GEOMETRIC SHAPES

A straight or curved enclosed outline.

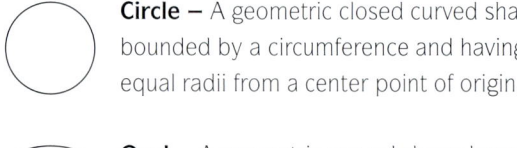 **Circle –** A geometric closed curved shape bounded by a circumference and having equal radii from a center point of origin.

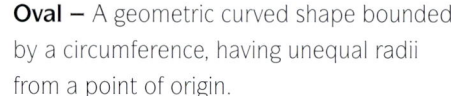 **Oval –** A geometric curved shape bounded by a circumference, having unequal radii from a point of origin.

 **Oblong –** An elongated curvature shape with parallel "C"-shaped lines, a convex end and a concave end.

 Square – A geometric shape with four right angles and four equal sides.

 Rectangle – A four-sided geometric shape with two sets of parallel sides.

Trapezoid – A geometric shape with two unequal, parallel sides and two equal, nonparallel sides.

Triangle – A three-sided shape; pie-shaped.

Diamond – Two equal triangles.

Hairpiece – A covering of human or artificial hair used to add length, color or shape to a design.

Hair Preparation – Carefully choosing the proper products, tools and setting techniques and patterns before the actual hair design begins.

Indentation – A hollow area or space.

Indentation Oblong – Setting begins at the concave end with the tool rolled up and away from the designer, creating depth and flare.

Indirect Technique – A setting technique used for expanding an oval.

Inner and Outer Circle – A setting technique used for expanding a circle.

Knot – The interlacing or tying together of a strand or strands of hair.

Line – An extended point.

Long Hair Design – A hair design created on long hair, generally for a special occasion.

Loop – The folding, bending or encircling of hair strands, which are then secured in curvature shapes.

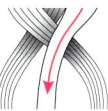

Overbraid – Braid achieved by alternately crossing the outside strands over the center strands.

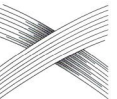

Overlap – A technique that uses two strands that are alternately crossed to the opposite side to create a crisscross effect.

Perimeter – The circumference, border or outer boundary.

Point – A dot or mark.

Point of Origin – The place where motion begins; the beginning of a design.

Proportional Relationship – A harmonious relationship or balance between shapes.

Radius (plural is radii) – A straight line extending from the center of a circle or sphere to the circumference.

Rectilinear – Characterized by straight lines.

Roll – Hair that is wrapped or wound within itself.

Scrunch-Drying – A finishing technique in which the hair lengths are gently squeezed as the hair is dried with a diffuser.

SETTING PROCEDURES

The procedures used to set the hair.

Distribute – The direction the hair is combed or dispersed over the curve of the head.

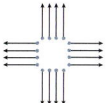

Parallel Distribution – Distributing the hair from multiple points of origin.

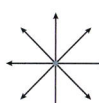

Radial Distribution – Distributing the hair from a single point of origin.

Mold – Designing curved or straight lines in hair to create a pattern.

Scale – Carving of shapes in the proper, predetermined size and proportion.

Part – Creating individual bases, or partings, to which the hair design tool and technique will be applied.

Apply – Refers to how the design tool, whether it be a brush, roller, thermal iron or pincurl, is used.

Shape – A two-dimensional outline of form as seen in its silhouette or outer boundary; the contour of an object.

Skipwave – Two alternating oblongs in which one oblong remains molded and the other oblong is set.

Straight Shape – Includes rectangles, squares, triangles and trapezoids. Hair within a straight shape moves in one direction without curves.

Strand – A tress of hair that can vary in width, length and density.

Symmetrical – A balance or harmonious arrangement.

Technique – The method or procedure by which a skill is performed from beginning to end; produces a predictable result.

Thermal Design – A hair design created using tools that require heat to design the hair, i.e., curling irons, hot rollers.

Thermal Roller – A roller that is heated electrically and applied to dry hair.

Three-Dimensional – Having length, width and depth.

 Twist – One, two or three strands of hair intertwined and/or rotated to form a rope-like appearance.

Two-Dimensional – Having length and width; flat.

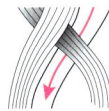 **Underbraid –** Braid achieved by alternately crossing the outside strands under the middle strand.

Variation – A design or technique that is slightly different from another of the same type.

Volume – Mass or fullness in a design.

Volume Oblong – Setting begins at the convex end with partings made at a 45° angle in the first direction with a tool rolled under to lift the base.

Wave – Two connecting oblong shapes that alternate in direction, creating an "S"-shaped pattern.

Wet Design – A hair design created using tools to form the hair while the hair is wet, i.e., roller setting.

INDEX

O

overbraid, 262
overlap, 262

P

perimeter, 10, 69, 86, 179
point, 32
point of origin, 32

R

radius, 63
roll, 263

S

scrunch-drying, 187
setting procedures, 31
    apply, 33
    distribute, 32
        parallel distribution, 32
        radial distribution, 32
    mold, 32
    part, 33
    scale, 32
shape, 8, 13-14, 22
skipwave, 224
straight shape, 12
strand, 261-262

T

technique, 3, 30, 178, 182
thermal design, 4, 10, 11, 30, 31, 198
thermal roller, 256
twist, 261

U

underbraid, 262

V

variation, 254, 335
volume, 8, 11, 18
volume oblong, 189

W

wave, 188
wet design, 4, 10, 11, 30, 31, 198